AF477542

RELATIONAL OBJECTS
MACBA Collection 2002–07

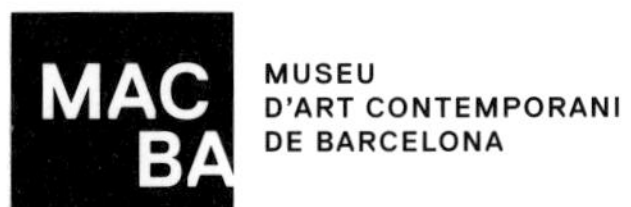

Leopoldo Rodés
President of the Fundació Museu d'Art Contemporani de Barcelona

The Fundació Museu d'Art Contemporani de Barcelona was founded in 1987 for the express purpose of contributing to the creation and development of the Museu d'Art Contemporani de Barcelona (MACBA). Since then, it has continuously acquired works of art that now constitute a sound and unique collection available to the Museum.

Building a collection is no easy task. Nonetheless, the Fundació's selection criteria have been steadfast since the very beginning. The collection is not focused on the past or on acquiring works by historical artists, nor does it attempt to repeat an existing model used by other institutions. We believed Barcelona deserved something more, and so the Fundació, in collaboration with the Museu d'Art Contemporani de Barcelona Consortium, decided to begin the Collection with works produced in the second half of the twentieth century. Henceforth, it would centre on a bold dialogue with the future by taking risks and innovating in order to strengthen the Collection in the hope of making it an important point of reference on the international art circuit.

The passage of time has confirmed the soundness of our initial choices. It is with great satisfaction that I can state that MACBA, with its considerable Collection, is among the most important contemporary art institutions in the world.

An art collection is, to a large extent, a reflection of the times, of the way a given society thinks and of its memory. MACBA, through the invaluable effort and experience of its directors and their teams, investigates and expands new artistic tendencies in synergy with established artists.

Determined to strengthen the artistic patrimony of Barcelona and Spain, the Fundació MACBA backs this project by contributing to the Collection.

The creation of this major Collection has been possible thanks to the effort and generosity of many individuals and companies, which, over the years, have unconditionally supported the work of the Fundació MACBA.

This publication features the works acquired between 2002 and 2007 thanks to the optimism and support of a civil society that believes in the patronage of culture.

Bartomeu Marí
Director of the Museu d'Art Contemporani de Barcelona

Ideas, images and objects do not belong to a single category of objects, except in the practice and reception of art. Art makes them equal, complementary and in many cases, interchangeable. Over the years, the MACBA Collection has become a testimony to the ideas that have been prevalent in the recent past, ideas that make up the present. This publication documents the patrimony of art in our time, albeit partially, and presents it as a narrative of the evolution of the Museum itself.
The Museu d'Art Contemporani de Barcelona (MACBA) does not attempt to constitute an encyclopaedic collection in which all objects occupy the same place: it has an opinion and heeds the present while relating it to the past. The museum is not a static temple; it is a tool that communicates traditions to make innovations visible.

The vital cycle of art makes it an almost perfect act of exchange. Art works convey that which makes the world change by transforming those who receive it, the public, the readers. This exchange does not only occur when the works are perceived or in the physical encounter with artefacts so loaded with intentions that we call works of art. They persist in memory and are capable of mutating; where there appeared to be only information, emotions arise: desire, anger, affection, repulsion – lasting emotions. In our time, art is an instrument for knowledge, since it now has little to do with the predominant conventions of beauty. Museums cannot be considered treasure chests, machines for envisioning or sanctuaries immune to the passage of time and the vicissitudes that life presents. The museum accompanies the world as it turns, but we also hope that it makes the world turn.

The main building of the MACBA opened on 28 November 1995 as a consortium that brought together the Generalitat de Catalunya, the Ajuntament de Barcelona and the Fundació Museu d'Art Contemporani de Barcelona. In 2007, the Ministry of Culture joined the consortium and made a financial contribution that, over time, matched the funding of the initial Catalan institutions. Since its founding in 1987, the Fundació MACBA, which includes important figures and corporations that are part of our cultural and economic surroundings, has been entrusted with obtaining funding to acquire artworks for the Museum's Collection. Patronage is a disinterested form of participation in a cultural project; the patrons' compensation is simply their participation in this project, without the benefits of advertising or similar advantages.

At its founding, the MACBA received the contemporary artworks that the two aforementioned Catalan institutions had collected since the return to democracy. These are heterogeneous collections, broadly representative testimonies of local artistic production. Since the very beginning, my predecessors at the museum have helped the Collection grow with the support of the Fundació MACBA.

Numerous donations by artists, individuals and corporations that are close to the institution have expanded this Collection over the years. At the same time, thanks to works lent by private collectors, the MACBA has had the opportunity to exhibit exceptional pieces that we hope will one day be an integral part of our Collection.

Nonetheless, the Museum has not been overly forthcoming when it comes to explaining what it is and what its ever-growing Collection is trying to say. A selection from the Collection is on permanent exhibit in the galleries on the building's ground floor. Every two years, MACBA exhibits its recent acquisitions in an exhibition that occupies the entire museum. In 2002, *MACBA Collection. Itinerary* was published, the first and only catalogue of the Collection until the publication of the volume you are now holding. In addition to presenting the works that make up the MACBA

Collection, this current catalogue provides information about how those works have come to form part of the Collection and their significance, both individually and as a whole. Indeed, this is one of the main purposes of this book, which covers a very specific period in the short history of the Museum, mainly from the publication of *Itinerary* until the change in the Museum's director. The Collection represented in the following pages was formed by Manuel J. Borja-Villel, director of MACBA from 1998 to 2007.

Museums are slow-growing organisms. They cannot be grasped hastily, but must be observed prudently. Though art may be quick, museums must be unhurried while remaining dynamic. For that reason, a museum is often identified with its collection, with what stays on permanently, as opposed to what is passing, that is, the temporary exhibitions or the activities offered to its users. One of the ways in which the MACBA has tried to distinguish itself is by attempting to balance the permanent with the transient: not only have certain temporary exhibitions played a key role in its identity, but the Museum's Collection is on display intermittently. Another key trait is all the activities encompassed in its extensive programmes. These programmes were crucial to the origin of what has subsequently become the notion of the museum as academy: the idea that the value of a museum resides mainly in the multiple forms of training and education that exist at the periphery of the normative rituals of learning.

We can no longer mistake the Museum for the building that houses it. Mostly because, slowly but surely, the MACBA has come to branch out to other activities and spaces. In 2006, it came to include the Capella dels Àngels as an exhibition space, and in 2007 it opened the Study Center, where another sort of Collection grows – one that includes documents and archives of artists, critics, historians, and spaces and institutions that have been witness to and players in the late-twentieth century avant-gardes.

The MACBA Independent Studies Program (PEI) brings together a library, a space dedicated to research and an exhibition hall open to the public in order to offer excellent training in the new field of creation and criticism. In contemporary art practices, the user determines the status of the work of art, whether it is exhibition object or document: it is not possible to understand the art of our times if we do not also consult archives and documents hitherto ignored by museums.

The museum of the twenty-first century will not be a safe containing treasures pillaged around the world and preserved at a certain site. It will, rather, be a platform from which to change the world on the basis of knowledge and feeling. Emotion, which for so many centuries was removed from reason by scientific methodology, will find in the museum its natural environment. The contemporary art museum is not a sanctuary of elites, a battlefield for dominant tastes at a given moment, or the tower of a castle in whose banners wave from the battlements. The museum is, rather, a place of exchange and relation between ideas and experiences.

Manuel J. Borja-Villel
Director of the Museo Nacional Centro de Arte Reina Sofía in Madrid,
director of the Museu d'Art Contemporani de Barcelona from 1998 to 2007

Museums, like biennials and other cultural events, have become the
privileged places for social consensus and reproduction, in which any type
of criticism is co-opted right from the beginning. In this context, it was
essential to redefine the raison d'être of the Museum and its nature as
a public institution. Though it is the apparently progressive sectors that have
made the argument for Museums as public institutions, it is an argument
that has become difficult to sustain, because the dichotomy between 'the
public' and 'the private' that had structured social organisation for over
a century and a half is no longer operative. Creativity lies in both the private
and the public, and the difference between the two is arbitrary. Even when
the management of creativity is in public hands, this is no guarantee that
it will not be expropriated for profit. In these times, 'the public' designates
a management regime based on property; its assets are thus inalienable,
although broad segments of the population may access these assets
to varying degrees and these assets may be managed by the state. It is
necessary to rethink the institution from the perspective of the communal,
which emerges from a multiplicity of singularities that do not construct
a state-based public sphere or a private sphere; instead, they create a space
that lies on the borders of both. For this purpose, it was critical to interrupt
the dynamics of 'franchises' that have become so popular of late and
imagine instead a sort of universal archive, a confederation of institutions
that shares the works housed in their centres, and – most especially – the
experiences and stories that arise in their surroundings. In this way, we can
say that our use of 'we' instead of 'I' depends on how involved we are with

others and not on our access to them. It is in that place between the 'I'
and the 'other' that the sphere of the communal lies; this is different,
however, from the public sphere. Deep down, the public does not belong
to us. The public – what the state provides for us – resides solely in
economic management, which is delegated by a collective whole to the
political class. The communal is not a broader expansion of the individual;
it is, rather, something that is never fully complete. It is only developed
through the other and by the other, at the communal headquarters, in the
shared being, to use Blanchot's term.

In the decade from 1998–2007, the Museu d'Art Contemporani de
Barcelona (MACBA) has been characterised by its political stance and its
determination to question the institutional mechanisms of discourse.
This is the aim that has inspired our work. It has been an enormous task,
one done by an exceptional group of individuals that includes, not only
the professionals working at the centre, but all of those who have worked
with us continuously, helping us to reinvent many of the programmes
and practices that the Museum has undertaken.

In general terms, the Museum's work has concentrated on four areas:
the Collection, the public activities, the Museum's organisational structure
and the invention of spaces for mediation with social agents and
movements.

The MACBA Collection is contemporary. This contemporariness does
not only entail chronological time, but also that which concerns and
transforms these times. As Hannah Arendt and Giorgio Agamben have said,
the contemporary divides time into what is 'no longer' and what is 'not yet',
establishing a particular relationship with both the past and the future;
the contemporary can cite a moment in the past and render it current at
any time. We can only think of the contemporary by splitting it into different
times, introducing into its temporal element an essential break with
homogeneity. The contemporary person is the one who, by dividing and
interpolating time, is capable of transforming it and connecting it to other

times; he or she is able to interpret history in a whole new way, to cite it based on a need that is determined not by one's own judgment, but by an undeniable exigency.[1]

Our times are characterised by a crisis that is not circumstantial, but systematic. As clearly as the Soviet world disappeared following 1989, we are currently witnessing what might be the end of the neo-liberal formulation that has dominated the planet in recent decades. We are faced, then, with an increasingly wide range of possibilities, and it is crucial to analyse the present, its multiple origins and the options it provides for the immediate future. Generally speaking, the Collection that we are presenting here revolves around four historical concepts: a) the forties and fifties, the swan's song of modernity; b) the rupture of the sixties and seventies; c) the critical and theatrical practices of the eighties; d) the current world, after the fall of the Berlin Wall.

A collection constitutes the core of a museum, and the MACBA Collection has experienced constant growth. This volume, as well as some of the works reproduced in *Itinerary*, brings together acquisitions since 1998.[2] Once again, this collective effort has been based on the trusting collaboration between the Museum and the artists. The support of collectors who have ceded their collections – people like Ute and Reinhard Onnasch, Sandra Alvarez de Toledo and Jordi Soley, among others – has also been crucial. Though their works are not included in this book, they have appeared in different presentations of the Collection. Such presentations take place periodically and allow us to delve into certain aspects of the Collection as a whole. For example, in the presentation in 2004, we emphasised what, following Édouard Glissant, we termed 'orality', in reference to the expanded cinema of David Lamelas and Hélio Oiticica, as well as the 'theatricality' of Jeff Wall and Dara Birnbaum. In the presentation in 2006, on the other hand, we focused on certain current practices related to the archive, the relational object, narratology, the performative and political activism.

1 See Giorgio Agamben, *Què vol dir ser contemporani?* Barcelona: Arcàdia, 2008, p. 18.
2 *MACBA Collection. Itinerary* (Barcelona: MACBA, 2002) was published in order to show MACBA acquisitions from 1998 until 2002, including works in the Collection that came from the Generalitat de Catalunya, the Ajuntament de Barcelona and the Fundació MACBA. The introduction to that book attempted to analyse our institutional parameters during those years. This publication begins where that one left off.

We have, on occasion, been criticised for our lack of interest or for our commitment to the local scene. It is true that we never believed that the Museum should be a place to represent a supposed artistic identity. Nor have we understood the Museum as a platform for possible recognition from abroad. Both of those positions entail an exclusive and regressive identity-based vision of culture, one criticised in the first introduction to the Collection.[3] On the other hand, the city has been a constant presence in our planning and activities. Similarly, we have always been aware of the historical moment in which our proposals are made.

Museums must edify epistemological paradigms that allow us to understand and question the world in which we live, choosing certain options over others. It is not gratuitous that a show like *Art and Utopia. Restricted Action* took place in 2004, three years after *Antagonisms* and, more importantly, after having implemented The Agencies (an authentic experiment in 'agency-making' and activism). In 2000 and 2001, the anti-globalisation movement was at its height, and direct action was the most effective means of intervening in the social fabric. The events of 11 September 2001 and the resulting military escalation (strangely and significantly bound to a growing market pressure on art) called for a strategically 'outward bound' withdrawal, to use Pasolini s fitting phrase. Our response was an exhibition project that revolved around Mallarmé and his notion of restricted action. *How do we want to be governed?* (2004), on the other hand, was related to another historical moment, a consequence of the earlier ones. In it, social negotiation and education were considered resources and culminated in the involvement of the PEI[4] in creating a new image for Barcelona, *The Universal Archive.*

Each exhibition has formulated a different way of thinking about the Museum. *Antagonisms* consisted of a series of case studies, adjusted to the studio system used in The Agencies. *Art and Utopia. Restricted Action,* on the other hand, privileged a heterogeneous group of historical works in which paper, magazines and alike played a dominant role. These works

3 Manuel J. Borja-Villel: *MACBA Collection. Itinerary*, op. cit., p. 13.
4 The Independent Studies Program took shape gradually on the basis of seminars that Beatriz Preciado, Xavier Antich, Manuel Asensi, Miren Etxezarreta, Marcelo Expósito and Enric Berenguer gave on the museum's activities. The PEI is geared towards transversal, non-curricular education but questions the discursive practices of the museum and of the art institution in general. It has been central to MACBA and its meaning in recent years.

were geared towards finding a multiplicity of micro-stories as opposed to forging an absolute and exclusive grand narrative. The exhibition *How do we want to be governed?* went beyond the Museum itself, to three very different locations: a high school, an old factory and a cultural centre, all located in the currently very 'central' neighbourhood of Besòs.

The structure of this volume reflects the logic of the Museum itself. On the one hand, Jorge Ribalta offers an analysis of MACBA's public programmes, as well as its education and areas for political action. On the other, Kaira M. Cabañas gathers and relates the central core of acquisitions from 2002 until 2007. Lastly, my text deals with the bases of what was defined at a certain point as the MACBA model, while also attempting to build bridges to the Museo Nacional Centro de Arte Reina Sofía and the Fundació Antoni Tàpies.

CONTENTS

Manuel J. Borja-Villel

19 THE MUSEUM QUESTIONED

Kaira M. Cabañas

**41 CONTEMPORARY RETURNS:
A SELECTION OF NEW ACQUISITIONS, 2002–07**

**43 Other Modernisms: Informel and Concrete, Documentary and Experimental.
The Forties and Fifties**
Roberto Rossellini. Brassaï. Henri Michaux. Jean Dubuffet. Lucio Fontana.
Antoni Tàpies. Jorge Oteiza. Néstor Basterretxea. Pablo Palazuelo. Helen Levitt.
Robert Frank. Joan Colom. Oriol Maspons and Julio Oubiña. Xavier Miserachs.
Ramón Masats. Francesc Català-Roca. Guy Debord. Samuel Beckett.

**79 Discursive Turns: Language, Institution, Cinema.
The Late Fifties to Seventies**
Öyvind Fahlström. Philip Guston. Nancy Spero. Bruce Nauman. Aspen. VALIE EXPORT.
stanley brouwn. Marcel Broodthaers. Hans Haacke. Dieter Roth. Gordon Matta-Clark.
Dara Birnbaum. Vito Acconci. Joan Jonas. Malcom Le Grice. Anthony McCall.
David Lamelas. Hélio Oiticica, Neville d'Almeida. Grupo de artistas de vanguardia.
Grup de Treball. Pere Portabella. Muntadas. Joan Rabascall. Francesc Abad.
Eugènia Balcells. Eulàlia Grau. Vídeo-Nou. Joaquim Jordà. Carlos Pazos. Jo Spence.
Martha Rosler. Hans-Peter Feldmann. Isidoro Valcárcel Medina.

**157 Spatial Order and Disorder: Architecture, Photography, Popular Culture.
The Late Seventies and Eighties**
Manolo Laguillo. Dan Graham. Jeff Wall. James Coleman. Ulrike Ottinger.
Raymond Pettibon. Mike Kelley, Paul Mc Carthy. Juan Muñoz. Jon Mikel Euba.
Jordi Colomer. Sergio Prego. Ibon Aranberri. Cristina Iglesias. Mabel Palacín.
Peter Fischli/David Weiss.

**189 Participation: Archives, Documentaries, Relations.
The Nineties and the 2000s Decade**
Agustín Parejo School. Pedro G. Romero. Marcelo Expósito. Ursula Biemann.
Chantal Akerman. Andreas Siekmann. Alice Creischer. Harun Farocki.
Allan Sekula. David Goldblatt. Alejandra Riera, Fulvia Carnevale. Krzysztof Wodiczko.
Dias & Riedweg. Maja Bajevic. Danica Dakic. Fikret Atay. Frank Hesse.
Deimantas Narkevicius. Rosalind Nashashibi. Peter Friedl.

Jorge Ribalta

224 EXPERIMENTS IN A NEW INSTITUTIONALITY

267 LIST OF WORKS REPRODUCED

THE MUSEUM QUESTIONED

Manuel J. Borja-Villel

In a society such as ours, where the difference between production and reproduction is ever slighter, and the typical actor in the post-Fordist capital system is one who carries out intellectual or symbolic work, art and the museum, as the primary stage on which it is played out, have acquired an unprecedented centrality. It comes as no surprise that the literature on the theme of the museum is abundant and that congresses and events are constantly being held to debate its boundaries and its functions.

Work today is no longer based around the Fordist working class, and is now superabundant, as a multitude of cognitive, communicative and perceptive acts that cannot be represented by or reduced to traditional units of measurement. These days, we can no longer apply rules to a field in which work and intellect are distinguishable; they have ceased to be so. This has also led to a rift between production and ethical values, giving rise to numerous cases of opportunism, one of the characteristics of the neo-liberal hegemony of recent decades, which have seen the gradual transformation of the public sphere into the sphere of publicity. The art institution is totally immersed in this general organisation where knowledge and information are factors of wealth. The museum, the ancient temple of the muses, idealised and idealising, has become a space of consumption and consensus.

Emerging in the sixties as a way of placing art in the discursive framework by means of which the dominant social formations exercise their power, institutional critique has not always grasped the new circumstances in which the society of the general intellect and cognitive work has subsumed the artistic phenomenon. Consequently, many of the studies and analyses of the museum conducted are rather melancholic, not to say nostalgic, in tone. They fail to recognise that the museum is based on a discourse that necessarily implies a narrative fact (the stories we tell or show by means of a series of works, events or documents), as well as publics that appropriate these narratives for themselves, questioning them in accordance with expository mechanisms situated between the two. If we were to describe the museum graphically, it would be represented by an equilateral triangle in which the first side indicates the narratives, the second, the intermediation structures, and the third, the publics. Studies and theories about narrative structures and mechanisms abound. However, no convincing theory of publics and education has yet been presented. This may serve to explain the pessimism of some recently published essays. They analyse artists' proposals and exhibition formats, but not what it is exactly that constitutes the specific pragmatics of the museum.

Today, the museum is a place that generates new forms of sociability. If, rather than a place of control and exclusion, we want it to be a democratic space, its laws must be shared by everyone who visits them. Hence the imperious need to move from a modern archaeology of knowledge to a postmodern praxis – that is, to gain an understanding of the comprehensive scope of the museum as a discursive phenomenon in its own right, its place in today's society and the resistance models it can offer.

This approach presents us with two models. The first might be regarded as that of the modern museum, which emerged in the twenties and thirties, peaked after the Second World War and reached crisis point in the seventies. The second is the type of museum that began to thrive in the eighties, with globalisation and the emergence of culture as spectacle. This model is actually an evolution of the first, in the same way that the postmodern condition is both the consequence and the further development of Fordism.

We begin with the museum of modern art, particularly embodied by New York's MoMA during the period in which it represented the essential issues of the modern age and supplied the model for many arts centres. What were its narratives? What form did they take? How were they conveyed? What was their target public?

As countless specialists have observed, its narratives were historicist in nature, set within a continuous chronological development that charted its course as an infinite return to origins and therefore tended to conceal any ncompatibilities.

This was a linear, evolutionist history that began with Post-Impressionism, continued with Cubism and Surrealism, and ended with the dawn of Abstract Expressionism and the painting of the late fifties. It was quite certainly an exclusive narrative. Anything that digressed from the task of achieving a series of given formal objectives was considered primitive, derivative or directly insignificant. The progression of art aimed to achieve the purity of the artistic species, and anything that hindered this end was considered defective. This segregation applied not only to the art of other cultures or geographical areas, but also to other disciplines. This takes us across the board to the theatre and literature, two of the great anathemas of modernity. The artwork is autonomous, and the system it produces tends to universalise and, ultimately, psychologise knowledge. The modern museum saw to it that the shortest possible distance existed between thought and speech – that is, that the act of passage appeared solely as a link between the two, with thought constituting a truth clothed in signs and rendered visible by words.

The way in which these narratives were transmitted to the public was based on transparency and immediacy. It could not be otherwise, since the spectator was faced with immanent truths. If we were capable of removing everything that could obstruct our view, if we were to present art with total transparency and without interference, the significance of it, its *reality*, would be apprehended automatically by the spectator, who would then become a passive factor. The white cube or, rather, the idea of it, was the appropriate architecture for this type of work, and a form of pedagogy founded on access was its educational method. This was André Malraux's understanding when, in 1947, he published his imaginary museum. Malraux decontextualised the artistic object with a view to determining its meaning by juxtaposing photographic details. All the issues relating to history and context gave way to visuality and were subordinate to style. In this museum of the imagination, rather than being evidence of the past or of what has been, photography was used to abstract objects from their surroundings and create a uniform, seamless continuum. 'They [the objects] have lost their colours, textures and relative dimensions... each one, in short, has lost practically everything that was specific to it – except the common style, which is what thereby gains by far the most.'[1] Art moves from a real

1 André Malraux, *Œuvres complètes.* Paris: Éditions Gallimard, 2004, p. 212.

to an ideal world where images exist freed of the material reality of objects and actions.

Western culture has emphasised sight over the other senses and annulled any phenomenological aspect. The stance adopted by Malraux is, in fact, a metaphor. We are dealing not with vision, but with an idea of it, as the idealist vision is not authentic. This would be possible only if any kind of representative mediation had disappeared, if we were to address the self-present, the identical, that which is, always. But we know that this is impossible, since we cannot rid ourselves of the mediation of language.[2] Our only act of freedom is to recontextualise and reconfigure what has already been said. Further, our expressions do not always correspond with what they are trying to say. This is why the notion of spectator has been so insignificant for the modern museum, and the reason why the relation between the spectator, his space and time, and the work has not been analysed adequately: it has simply not existed, in the absence of a separation between the world and that which spectators thought they were seeing. There was no translation. It was a de-individualised gaze that denied appearances, beyond time and space, and was total and complete, also denying particularity and diversity.

The radical critique of the prevalence of this viewpoint erupted systematically in the second half of the twentieth century, a foremost role being taken by Belgian artist Marcel Broodthaers with his *Peintures littéraires* and, above all, his fictitious museum, founded in 1968. In one of his manifestations, which took place in 1972 at the Städtische Kunsthalle in Düsseldorf, Broodthaers presented 266 objects representing eagles, on loan from 43 'real' museums and numerous private collections. In age, these objects ranged from the Oligocene to the present. Exhibited in display cases or hung on the walls, or placed on shelves, each object was accompanied by a caption that read: 'This is not a work of art.' This formula, which Broodthaers obtained by uniting two conflicting concepts (one provided by René Magritte: any work of art forms part of a sign system that is a construction; the other deriving from Marcel Duchamp: the choice of an object as a work of art is arbitrary and its meaning is determined by the actual discourse in which it is set), was used to completely oppose cultural history and, taking the eagle as a model, to manifest its

2 Kaja Silverman, *World Spectators.*
Stanford, Calif.: Stanford University
Press, 2000, p. 2.

contextual nature. The 'eagle' collection defies integration into a new system, thereby revealing its artificiality. 'The concept of the exhibition,' wrote Broodthaers, 'is based on the identity of the eagle as idea and of art as idea.' But the result of the 'eagle as idea' is, in this case, such a vast range of objects (from paintings to comic strips, from fossils to typewriters, from ethnographic objects to logotypes) that, like Borges's mythical library, they can only be brought together in the discourse.[3] As in the case of the Argentine writer, what it did was to question the bases underlying this juxtaposition, which is revealed to be discursive and dependent on various historic paradigms. By means of his ready-mades, Duchamp made us see that the function of the museum consisted in declaring that the objects housed within were art. Broodthaers's captions extend this proposal. By stating, 'This is not a work of art,' the designation of any other object as art becomes arbitrary, mere representation.

The idea of the museum as a neutral receptacle in which are laid out a series of works that are perceived by the public without interference is rather utopian. An exhibition consists of an intersection of text, practice and place. And it is precisely at this juncture, in this intertextual network, that the work of art takes its place. We could say simply that an exhibition is, on the one hand, a discursive practice that includes the evaluation, selection and organisation of a series of works that are shown in galleries and museums. On the other, it is a system of meanings comprising a group of statements or expressions: that of the works. These meanings are simultaneously 'trapped' by the exhibition's titles, categories and comments, and 'freed' and disseminated by means of the actual process that organises them. Nor should we forget that an exhibition takes place in a fundamentally open space-time arrangement, in which the spectator can follow an argument, or stop and go back as and when he considers fit.

An exhibition can never be read as a single text. There is a whole series of implicit texts that have to be brought out in the exhibition, which thereby, in relation to the artwork, becomes a kind of paratext. The museum or gallery, its history, collection and building, the way the objects are exhibited, the captions and the way the layout is organised all form part of the 'message' that the spectator takes away with him when he visits a show. They also constitute the baggage with which the spectator enters the museum. The museum's role as an

3 Douglas Crimp, *On the Museum's Ruins*. Cambridge, Mass.: The MIT Press, 1993.

index – that is, as an indicator that an object is a work of art – and its active part in the discourse of an exhibition cannot be denied. The artwork is not conceived as a closed book with a complete universal truth, but as an open reality with a network of meanings that is set within the context of the exhibition.

Museums certainly have a historical dimension that makes them respond to the social conditions of the time. They form part of a power structure that generates and masks given relations between individuals and social groups. As Gilles Deleuze might say, commenting on Foucault, power is exercised rather than held. Power not only acts by means of ideology, it also creates it. The discourse is not solely the translation of conflicts and systems of domination, it is also the medium for and by means of which it is striving. The discourse is linked to desire and power, and the principles of exclusion of the discourse that serve to obtain this power are well known. On the one hand, there are those that are external to the actual discourse, such as the separation between madness and reason, or lies and truth. These are based on an institutional framework: schools, libraries, laboratories, etc. Then there are the internal principles: analysis, which limits the random nature of interpretation, and norms, which shape the disciplines and the conditions of use of the text.

One of the corollaries of the enlightened ideas underpinning the present-day museum was that education in itself could be a motive for change and improvement. However, it is impossible for the universal knowledge that corroborates a rule and a given power to also serve to overthrow them. By showcasing the products of specific historical moments in a single continuum, the museum fetishises them, thereby increasing, to quote Walter Benjamin, 'the burden of the treasures that are piled up on humanity's back. But it does not give mankind the strength to shake them off, so as to get its hands on them.' The museum thereby serves to reinforce the established order, eliminating any possibility of otherness.

While seeking to universalise a homogenising history, the belief was that the museum should comprise neutral spaces that did not interfere with the artwork: four walls, overhead lighting and two doors, one for people coming in and the other for those going out. The building and the works it houses are thereby separated from the city of which they form part, the process is suppressed and, despite vaunting objectivity, they respond to a given power structure. When the MoMA was remodelled in the mid-eighties, it was decided that the rooms housing the permanent collection should be of an intimate scale, not so much because this was more neutral, but because it promoted an idea of modern art that corresponded to the private collection. William Rubin, then director of the department of painting and sculpture, said: 'Retaining the spirit of the old museum particularly means keeping the intimate spaces that depend on a rather low ceiling, not much higher than that of an apartment, and restricted volumes. We might also consider whether, even in the case of large paintings (and some of those by Monet, Pollock and Rothko are considerable), they should be exhibited in small rooms. To which the answer is yes… Whereas Renaissance or baroque art is public art, produced for churches or palaces…, after Manet and the Impressionists we are dealing with a more private art. The paintings are intended for artists' studios or, most especially, for the apartments of enthusiasts [and collectors].'[4]

While Broodthaers revealed the discursive nature of the museum, other artists such as Hans Haacke also questioned its idealistic condition. As far back as 1963–65, with his *Condensation Cube*, Haacke addressed the material reality of the gallery walls that 'frame' the artwork. The effect of condensation on a transparent cube rendered visible what the gallery sought to conceal: its walls and limits. At the same time, however, this work introduced something that was to become very important in his subsequent work: the real-time process. The museum ceased to be an ivory tower to become part of reality. In a piece produced six years later, *Shapolsky et al. Manhattan Real Estate Holdings, a Real-Time Social System, as of May 1, 1971* (1971), Haacke placed on show in a museum a body of 'information' (the list of real-estate holdings of the Shapolsky family) that blurred the line between the art world and the 'exterior'. The story goes that this work was censored by Thomas Messer, then director of the Guggenheim Museum, because Shapolsky was supposedly a museum trustee. What Messer considered intolerable, however, was the inclusion of a document in a place reserved exclusively for ideas. Haacke made an issue of the gallery's autonomy and neutrality. The separation between the space of the street and the museum ideal was completely reformulated.

There is a long list of artists whose work has not found an appropriate place in the modern institution and whose aesthetic perception was reduced almost

4 Quoted in Thomas West, 'Circé dans les Musées – Réflexions sur sept nouveaux musées en Europe et aux États-Unis,' *Les Cahiers du Musée national d'art moderne*, 17–18, 1 March 1986.

exclusively to the visitor wandering around the rooms. There was until very recently no place for either Lygia Clark's therapy or Krzysztof Wodiczko's anti-utopian design. The need for a new approach was evident. The non-stop construction of new museums and arts centres in recent years, and all the trends embracing other cultures, which became known as multiculturalism, provided further corroboration.

The exclusive conception of the museum of modern art has been replaced in recent years by another, apparently inclusive one that still lacks any real dialogue with the Other. The universal subject reappeared, not rejecting difference, but annulling it. Whereas previously it was difficult to see, say, Cézanne and Atget together, now it became habitual to find the French artist alongside Rineke Dijkstra, or Matisse next to Marlene Dumas, despite the fact that they have nothing in common. Any attempt at comparison is cancelled out from the outset by the totality of the approach, and the pedagogical practice is not merely questioned, it is actually concealed by the purely formal diversity of the contents. Panofsky's pseudomorphosis has never been so widespread.

Organising exhibitions or collections without taking into account the role of the institution in the society of which it forms part can easily produce the opposite results to those hoped for: rather than transforming our environment, it reinforces the *status quo*. Miami's Margulies Collection is an obvious example. Its works are of a radical bent: photographs of social and political content, Thomas Hirschhorn's return to a culture of waste materials, transgression and gender in Paul McCarthy, etc. The collection is massive, laid out like a warehouse (its public space was once termed 'storage'); yet ultimately, in organisation it is an imitation of what we can experience at the Art Basel Miami Beach. This very common stance is cynical and doubly conformist, in that its subordination to power and the market is clothed in modernity and rebellion. Multiculturalism and modish cultural studies have merely represented a manifestation of this false openness that responds to an economy of multinationals, where consensus has replaced the political act seen as antagonism and negotiation.

The process of globalisation is more strongly in force today than ever. More than in any other period, the flows of capital have acquired a global dimension and determined our perception of the world and the way it is organised. But this is not a new phenomenon: late twentieth-century globalisation is, after all, a continuation of nineteenth-century colonialism. Today, like a hundred years ago, capitalism's voracious conquest of new places for production and consumption continues unbounded. Now, however, the conquered territories are no longer the remote continents that Conrad and Kipling described; they are the space where we live out our private lives, our space of freedom and creation. As the geographical horizons of expansion dwindled, life itself emerged as a whole new vein to be mined. The extraction of formulas for the production and consumption of life experiences in their various manifestations has in recent decades been a fundamental objective for capitalism, as well as motive for ambiguity. On the one hand, in order to meet its ends, it has to promote research, which has increased the possibility of improving life. On the other, the focus of capitalism is not life, but investment, promotion and commercialisation with the aim of generating capital. Singular forms of subjectivisation are encouraged, but only in order to reproduce them, segregating them from their connection with life and transforming them into merchandise, or what Suely Rolnik would call *prêt-à-porter* identities.

To what system of functioning does the museum respond? What are the mechanisms governing it? Does the fact that it is immersed in a broader political organisation mean that its activity merely contributes to its consolidation? For example, there is no concealing the fact that despite what can only be supposed to be the best efforts of those in charge, some of our institutions promote a degree of instability in the workplace. A museum cannot act politically without being aware of its own position as a prime nucleus of social reproduction and a revitalising agent of districts and tourist attraction. In this context, it is logical that the space of intermediation (side b of the triangle), unlike the case of the modern museum, should be based not on access, but on labelling and marketing. The public's needs are created by media campaigns, but the idea is that this public should re-cognise the artwork or, rather, an interchangeable image of the artwork. We are presented with an out-and-out aesthetic of silence, which, as J. G. Ballard tells us, ultimately turns into 'selective madness', a form of self-inflicted authoritarianism, which, despite being manifestly different, has parallels with the fascism of other times. Now, as then, we are faced with a culture of oblivion, in which there is no censure because everything is consumable: 'At the cash desk there is no yesterday, no history to be relived, only an intense transactional present.'[5]

The danger facing us lies in an order that tends to simplify singularity, depriving individuals of their psychical specificity. In our society, the human being runs the risk of being trivialised. Everyone seems to adapt to a standard hierarchy of the image expected of him or her. At the same time, individuals are facing up less to their own responsibilities. The purpose of culture is a highly problematic issue today. Culture as rebellion – that is, culture as a liberating element – runs the risk of disappearing and being turned into a product for consumption. The separation between the public and the private sphere is becoming increasingly vague. Rather than a public, we are dealing with audiences, which, conversely, can be measured and quantified in purely economic terms.

Ours is a time of crisis that, according to Immanuel Wallerstein, is systemic. This is why it is important for museums to create historical paradigms that help us to a better understanding of the world in which we live. We need to understand the present in relation to the past and consider the possibilities that the future holds in store for us. The museum has an obligation to point out some paths rather than others, and rather than being technical or dictated by formal rationality, this choice must entail what Max Weber termed *substantive rationality*. When 'anything goes' is the norm, in the general confusion of ideas this choice or series of choices may be perceived as rigid, elitist or dogmatic. We often hear gloomy voices calling for a new style of eclecticism as a way of safeguarding a supposed democratisation of culture. However, substantive rationality is quite the opposite; it is the exercise of reconciling what we learn from science and morality, and always involves an ethical choice.

Most of humankind is the South of which Enrique Dussel speaks, constituting the 'other face' of modernity.[6] This South is not situated in a pre- or postmodern period, the time previous to a modern age that will be realised by applying the same criteria that served for Europe and the United States. It is not a less evolved stage in the same process. Quite the opposite; we live in a world where the centre presupposes the periphery and *vice versa*; and the

5 J. G. Ballard, *Kingdom Come*. London:
4th Estate – HarperCollins, 2006.
6 See Enrique Dussel and Karl-Otto Apel,
Ética del discurso y ética de la liberación.
Madrid: Editorial Trotta, p. 144.

development of the former is totally related to that of the latter. The problem
lies in the fact that this other modernity is subordinate; it has no say. It obeys
the rules of the Western European world, since they have been declared universal.
Our laws and our moral doctrine tend to justify their own principles from
the inside. Slavery, for example, would be unfair in the bourgeois system, but fair
in a pro-slavery society; paid work is unfair in socialism because it robs the
worker of the surplus value of his labour, but not in capitalism. The only way of
breaking with this discursive order is if the instrumental reason is accompanied
by an ethical criterion, which is always exterior to the established power and
allows the Other to question Totality. Rather than denying the community, this
exteriority discovers it as a place of convergence of persons and groups who are
free to disagree.

We often imagine an artistic construction in which the Other speaks to
us, which is not actually the case. When art pedagogy is institutionalised,
art becomes pure rhetoric directed against what is perceived as social chaos.[7]
The museum and the city become a kind of republic of letters, and the artist
a national patriarch. It is not enough to represent the Other, it is necessary to
find forms of mediation that are both models and specific practices of new forms
of solidarity between the intellectual and subordinate communities, and with
the various collectives that constitute social movements.

Interpellation, the act of speaking that gives a voice to those who are outside
our discursive construction – that is, outside our system of intelligibility – becomes
a necessarily ethical position. It requires a degree of exteriority, of being other,
different to the official institutional community, which only defends its own
interests. The act of interpellation, since it always emerges from outside the
prevailing law, by definition opposes consensus and exclusive history, and its line
of argument is always radical and rarely accepted. Whereas the official discourse
declares the dominator of the centre completely innocent of possible acts of cruelty
committed in the periphery during modernity, interpellation will denounce them.

The modern conception of history has its origins in the Enlightenment,
in the pure reason of Kant, which starts out from an idealistic, Euro-centric
worldview. The modern age began with Europe's expansion in the world and the
centrality it conferred upon itself, in keeping with which it not only dominated

7 John Beverley, *Against Literature*.
Minnesota: University of Minnesota Press,
1993.

the world system, it also ignored the existence of the Other. Europe imagined its particular history as though it were universal, and what it achieved as a power centre it attributed to its own creativity, as a closed, autonomous, self-referring system. It never defined itself as a centre of hegemony that controlled information, processed learning and built the institutions that allowed a greater accumulation of wealth in the metropolis, with the systematic exploitation of the periphery.[8] By passing this over, it also glossed over the violence of European colonisation.

Yet what happens if we replace the *ego cogito* of Descartes with the *ego conquiro* of Hernán Cortés? We see that the modern age began not in the eighteenth century, but in the sixteenth century with the conquest of the Americas by the kingdoms of Spain and Portugal. This was the moment of what Marx called primitive accumulation, when today's world organisation began to take form. This being the case, we have to think that there are multiple modernities, not just one, and that they are interdependent, with different impulses and the potential to start at different times. We also have to recognise that, in the field of art, one of these forms of modernity, at least the one related with the Latin American world, began with the baroque – that is, with a theatrical culture, based on multiplicity and folding. In this way, the significance of artistic manifestations such as those of Lygia Clark, Hélio Oiticica or Gego lies in the fact that they are vital not so much to an understanding of the modernity imposed by Europe and the United States, but to apprehending other aesthetic and political practices.

What stance should we adopt in the face of a past in which we do not recognise ourselves and a present that we do not like? What is the function of the museum in the contemporary world? Is there an alternative to the modern museum or the museum that responds to the culture of the spectacle? I would like to think so. The museum moves between subversion and absorption, contemplative passivity and active breakaway, the state and the masses, creation and the market. On the one hand, it is true that it is very difficult to see artistic forms as being able to bring down borders; on the other, it is equally true that they serve to move them. At a time when all arts centres have entered into an endless spiral of ever larger buildings and franchises, when capitalism has reached a point of inexorable expansion, perhaps the time has come to fold,

8 Dussel, p. 223.

in the sense in which Pasolini used the term: a turn not inwards, but outwards. Attention to the fragile life of bodies, hostility towards the objectification of our existence and the explicit manifestation of the disappearance of a border between public and private would be some of the most interesting political elements.

To continue the model we established at the start, the proposed alternative would be based on three aspects:

  – One or more alternative narrative(s) to modern history.
  – New forms of intermediation.
  – The consideration of the spectator not as a passive subject or a consumer, but as an agent, a political subject.

Numerous cultures tend to base the history of their art and literature on foundational texts that, since they define the nature of their specific community, are to some extent regarded as sacred, absolute and exclusive. They constitute the foundation of what was, at the time, perceived as a community under threat, based on the segregation of any kind of divergence. This was probably the origin of the major narratives underlying the dominant nineteenth- and twentieth-century ideology. According to Édouard Glissant, these narratives, deriving from an epic source, practically taken down in dictation from the gods, are intimately linked to the closed object, transcendence, corporal immobility and a kind of tradition of consecution, which we call linear thinking.[9] Today, conversely, it is no longer possible to guarantee this type of formal unity, unthinkable in a world that has shrunk and where there is a peremptory need to invent multiple forms of relation that challenge our mental structures. What I propose, then, is a relational identity that is not single and atavistic, but rhizomatic, having a multiple root.

This involves being open to the Other and addressing the presence of other cultures and ways of proceeding in our own practices, without fearing a hypothetical danger of dissolution.

In societies without a foundational myth, the notion of identity is established not so much by a great na(rra)tion, or a territory, as by the interweaving of relations between various subjects. Evidently, the poetics of the relation cannot be understood without reference to the notion of place. But this is conceived not as a static territory as much as a series of vectors and lines of force. The

9 Édouard Glissant, *Introduction à une poétique du divers*. Paris: Éditions Gallimard, 1996.

centre-periphery dependence loses all meaning; and the centre makes no claims
on the periphery, such a frequent occurrence in our country. The relation does not
tend from the particular to the general, or *vice versa*, but from the local to the
world-totality, which is not universal and homogeneous but plural. The traditional
political view was based on the capacity to perceive an environment and at once
transcend it, which is how ninetennth-century nationalisms were constituted,
but today the constant flow of images that are posited in the magma of our
relations means that the perception-transcendence correspondence has changed.
Now, we are from a place in a different way. 'We no longer belong to a position,
a tradition, a party. The urge to participate or form part of a project is fading.
Yet this separation from one's roots, far from relinquishing the sense of belonging,
merely strengthens it; the impossibility of being ensconced in a lasting context
disproportionately increases adherence to the most fleeting here and now. What
clearly comes to light is, in short, belonging as such, no longer qualified by
"to what". This sentiment has become directly proportional to the absence of
a privileged, protective something to which to belong.'[10] Evidently, this cannot
be applied as an omnilateral simultaneous affirmation to all prevailing orders,
and all rules and games; it is, rather, a question of reformulating histories and
mediations that make us reconsider our 'belonging'.

History has ceased to be written as though it were made up of large
continents, to become a kind of archipelago. The author thereby enters into tension,
seeking to reflect and relate at once with his or her community and with the
world. Art seeks at once the absolute and its opposite – that is, writing and
orality. There is no longer a single voice issuing its narrative from a privileged
platform; instead, we are immersed in a multiplicity of micro-narratives that has
produced a new cartography of art. New York can no longer be said to have
stolen the idea of modern art from Paris, because the idea emerges in multiple
places and because there is nothing to steal, just relations to establish and render
visible. Artists who, in traditional historiography, might have been considered
secondary, derivative or simply late developers, such as Georges Vantongerloo,
Pablo Palazuelo or Jorge Oteiza, achieve their greatest complexity. For example,
we understand that the work of an artist such as Palazuelo has little to do with
the quests of modernity but a great deal with the fragility and *expansiveness* of

10 Paolo Virno, *Virtuosismo y revolución.*
La acción política en la era del
desencanto. Madrid: Traficantes
de sueños, 2003, p. 73.

the oral. His works require the participation of the spectator, who is invited
to discover the rhythms and forms of his own body in the rhythms and
forms with which the artist presents him. He has to appropriate them, recreate
them and even reproduce them as he looks at them. Without this dimension,
his paintings and drawings would be seen as mere decoration.

The poetics of the relation and diversity materialises in the open work,
the transversality of art and poetry, the immanence of orality, bodily
movement or the indeterminacy of expanded cinema. The function of the
artist or curator is not so much to produce objects or narratives that provoke
a reflex response on the part of the spectator as to enable him to recreate
his own aesthetic experience. Art is, primarily, experience, and if the
spectator does not retain it, it is lost. The involvement of the spectator is,
then, essential, as is his capacity to seize and repeat this experience.

The oral has to do with the event and with theatricality, which
challenges the visibility device of the white cube. But this does not mean
that it should be replaced by its opposite, the black box. Whereas in the
former, the spectator remains passive and separate from the work of art,
in the latter he is submerged into the cinematographic space, absorbed
by the screen and unable to maintain a distance. These two stances are
interchangeable, as they do not take into account the specificity of the
time and space in which the artwork is exhibited. The space and time of
the theatre are, conversely, relational: they exist because there is a spectator.
This was particularly the case with Tadeusz Kantor, Jerzy Grotowski
and Samuel Beckett, not to mention Antonin Artaud. For Artaud, the word
theatrical lost its ontological importance and became a sign that shared the
stage with other signs. The stage ceases to be a 'substantial' place and
creates its own limits in the interplay of relations of the performance.

Ultimately, such plays are like the other face of modern art. Whereas
art promised to make people happy without considering the spectator,
the theatre is only possible thanks to him. Theatricality keeps its promise
of modern liberation by means of the insurrection of the spectator and the
crossing of institutional limits. As Artaud announced, the theatre frees
in the social sphere the pathologies that are generated by the violence of

this normalised life that it is our lot to bear: 'Perhaps the theatre's poison, injected into the social body, disintegrates it.'[11]

Publics are created around texts. The texts, however, are neither neutral nor politically aseptic. By their very nature, they exert an influence on us. There is a close link between them and the way we see our destiny. Foundational narratives determine and, to a large extent, give meaning to the lives of their 'inhabitants', which they model and constrain. We cannot help interpreting our lives in accordance with these texts. If a cultural institution accords its publics the capacity of agent, it is saying that these texts have the capacity to be compared with others, as well as translated and reconsidered. It is precisely by means of this process that we can free 'our destiny'.

How is memory created on the basis of orality? Collecting objects often means transforming them into merchandise. How can events be staged without being fetishised? How to create a museum that does not monumentalise what it explains? The answer lies in conceiving of the collection as an archive. Both museums and archives are repositories from which many stories can be taken and updated. The archive, however, 'de-auratises' them, as it places documents, artworks, books, magazines and photographs on the same level. It shatters the aesthetic autonomy that separates art from its history, redefines the link between object and document, offers the opportunity of discovering new territories beyond the plans of fashion or market, and involves a plurality of readings. The correspondence generated between the artistic phenomenon and the archive produces displacement, drift, alternative narratives and counter-models. It returns to us knowledge and the aesthetic experience, as well as the possibility of apprehending a historic moment in a way that is comparable to Peter Weiss's explanation in *The Aesthetics of Resistance*.

The archive is a *topos*, a place and a *nomos*, a law, as it has the power to interpret the archived elements that speak and recall that law, and call for its observance.[12] The archive not only guarantees the physical safety of the deposit and the support, it also has a hermeneutic authority over them. Archive science must therefore include the theory of this institutionalisation – that is, of the rule that is first written in it and of the law that authorises it. It is this law that establishes firm boundaries, whether we are dealing with family or state law,

11 Antonin Artaud, *Le Théâtre et son double*. Paris: Éditions Gallimard, 1938. English edition: *The Theater and Its Double*. New York: Grove Press, 1994.
12 Jacques Derrida, *Mal d'archive. Une impression freudienne*. Paris: Éditions Galilée, 1995. English edition: *Archive Fever: A Freudian Impression*. Baltimore, Md.: The John Hopkins University Press, 1995.

the bonds between the secret and the non-secret, or, which amounts to the same, between the private and the public, be it the law of property or right of access, of publication or reproduction, of classification or of order. Effective democratisation is always measured by this essential criterion: participation in and access to the archive and its constitution and interpretation.[13]

Collecting is a need; it forms part of our deepest desires and it is a form of knowledge. But we must not forget how the first museums were built and the way in which the Louvre, the British Museum and others swelled their legacies. The holdings of national galleries have often been gathered as though they were plunder. At a given moment, they all took great pains to have the most prized treasures, be it the Elgin Marbles or the bust of Nefertiti. And these have continued, in recent years, to become tourist attractions, the neo-colonial fate of artworks accumulated by former empires. We have to understand, however, that our collections are not ours; they belong to humankind. Conservators, museum directors, restorers and so on are merely their custodians, not their owners. Earlier, I referred to the importance of creating a body of narratives that intertwine like rhizomes; this is also the sense that should be accorded to collections. Letting the Other have his say means giving him the capacity to archive and rethink his own history, to tell it to us. One solution would be to constitute a universal archive, a kind of archive of archives, which would serve not only to challenge the concept of ownership but also to let those with no voice have their say and know that it is heard.

Stories require a community to pass them on, minds in which to reproduce, a fertile medium that allows them to evolve. If they are not to maintain their auratic nature, narratives have to question the notion of author and renounce the idea of the Romantic genius. Rather than conceiving of history as a succession of great figures, or even as the nomadic individual of this multicultural moment, we have to see it as a throng of supporting actors, the anonymous seething mass of events, destinies, movements and vicissitudes.[14] The author is a vehicle by means of whom a community's 'library' seeks to replicate itself.

It is important for these histories to multiply and circulate as much as possible. Whereas our society's economic system is based on scarcity, which allows art objects to achieve exorbitant values, the new narrative is based on

13 Ibid.
14 'What we want is the education, emergence and movement of the multitude, which has nothing to do with the mass, a homogenous block to be mobilised or a "black hole" to be stimulated by means of surveys.' Ibid.

excess, on an organisation that escapes the criterion of the count. In this case, those who receive the stories are richer, for sure, but those who give (tell) them are not poorer. This involves constituting federations of free communities, a bottom-up process that speaks more of autonomy than of a state power-seizure. It is no longer a question of educating a nation/state uniformly in order to prepare, at best, revolution or, at the worst, consensus. Nor is the idea to avoid ties with institutions, but to establish networks and discover new fields for differing practices. It is not enough to say that the mass media lies or to complain about the way consensus is engineering and imposed; we have to manage its lies, by offering myths and preconstituting the terrain on which the facts are distorted, with the aim of redressing this distortion and producing displacements of meaning.[15]

Intrinsically linked to the formation of publics, education is a major pending issue in museography today, as important as the narratives proposed by the museum, or more so. Indeed, it is the popularisation of arts centres in recent decades that has highlighted just how pressing an issue it is. We often hear debates about low standards of education and how we are 'forced' to address ever less educated spectators. Yet it is also true that no other time has seen this vast circulation of information or such apparent ease of access to culture. Museums continue their inexorable race towards the highest visitor figures. What until fairly recently was a space reserved for specialists and the muses has become a meeting place, a prime place to develop relations and social activity. So how is it possible that, precisely when entertainment and free time are associated with formative experience, education is at such a low ebb? Why so much talk of the crisis of culture when never in our recent history have so many people had access to culture?

The problem lies in the fact that pedagogy is still not considered as a potential element of liberation. Most teaching programmes continue to hinder true access to knowledge. Since culture is increasingly becoming an industry, and art, consumer merchandise, it is no wonder that cognition is being replaced by re-cognition. The former aspires to the acquisition of knowledge, and is constantly expanding and difficult to label and consume; the latter is an interchangeable, superficial brand.

15 Ibid.

This is not to undermine the good intentions of those museums that invest considerable effort and resources in bringing art to the public and devise outreach programmes to disseminate the treasures they hold in store. However, these reformist measures have merely served to perpetuate some of the fallacies on which modern pedagogy is based: transparency, progress and education as transmission. As Jacques Rancière points out, this approach is: a) 'obscurantist', because it assumes that the best way to reduce inequality in knowledge is to cut back knowledge itself; b) 'racist', because it supposes that people from working-class backgrounds or underprivileged groups should receive a less abstract and cultural education, and c) 'infantilising' in its maternal conception of the school or education area.[16]

The modern age conceived education as a means of conveying knowledge to those who did not have it and, as such, is based on inequality between those who know and those who do not. It established a separation between research and education, between the artwork and its communication, which assumed and perpetuated the distance between educator and spectator. However, knowledge is not necessary for teaching, nor is the explanation vital to the learning process. Explanation is the myth of pedagogy. Instead of eliminating incapacity, it creates it. And it does so, in part, by creating a time structure of delay, consubstantial to modernity: 'a little further along', 'a little later', 'a few more explanations and you'll see the light'.[17]

A pedagogy of emancipation presupposes that one 'ignorant person' teaches another. An ignorant person will not be able to teach given contents to another ignorant person, but he can help him to find a path – his own – and to associate apparently diverse things. Rather than a quest for the purity of the primitive or an acultural state, this kind of pedagogy demonstrates the liberating faculty of culture, the capacity we all have to rediscover and redefine knowledge.

Emancipating education is based on a relationship of equality. It is a two-way relation, involving not only the will of the 'teacher' who wishes to address an interlocutor, but also that of the interlocutor in search of emancipation. Intelligence does not exist where there is only aggregation, the reflection of one mind in another. Intelligence exists when each acts, explains what he is doing and offers the means to verify the reality of his actions. This is a proposal that

16 Jacques Rancière, *Le Maître ignorant. Cinq leçons sur l'émancipation intellectuelle*. Paris: Éditions Fayard, 1987. English edition: *The Ignorant Schoolmaster. Five Lessons in Intellectual Emancipation*. Stanford: Stanford University Press, 1991, p. XIV.
17 Ibid., p. XX.

promotes both duality and community. Rather than the absorption of one mind
by another, it allows their interrelation, at the same time maintaining the identity
of each.

In this form of education, the artwork is a key element in that it constitutes
a link between the artist and the spectator, or between two or more spectators.
Idealism places the word above the object. Plato manifested his doubts as to the
validity of the written word, whose materiality was merely a shadow of the idea.
The discourse of books was, for him, both excessively silent and loquacious,
and distracted the mind from its real objective: the idea. The materiality of the
book and of the object or artistic phenomenon is precisely the opposite.
It redresses the hierarchy of minds, allows the relation between two *ignorant
persons* and serves to establish new relations that cancel out the stultifying
action of intellectual and moral instruction based on transmission, explanation
and prohibition. It also establishes forms of play that are capable of changing
the game and generating new ways of seeing the world. It is an active element
with which we create and re-create the world in which we live. More than
adaptation, implying submission, to our environment, playing, poetry and art
make us feel alive and ease passage from one space to another.

The ongoing quest for truth has certainly hindered a radical change in
education and stood in the way of a solution to the dilemma that has
overshadowed much so-called political art since the late-nineteenth century up
until the present day, torn between political engagement and the quest for
beauty. It is not that the artwork represents an immutable truth exterior to the
subject; it is an enigmatic signifier whose radical ambiguity allows and even
demands mobility of relations, the contingency of beings and things.

The artistic experience is a transitional phenomenon, because it generates
an illusion in the spectator that prompts him to relate with others and with an
environment that, though exterior, is not perceived as alien. It makes us see
ourselves both as subjects and objects of the perception of others, creating
new and liberating spaces of sociability. It is logical to think 'that the task
of reality-acceptance is never completed, that no human being is free from
the strain of relating inner and outer reality, and that relief from this strain
is provided by an intermediate area of experience… which is not challenged

(arts, religion, etc.).'[18] This calls for a certain right to opacity, to the absence of a need to 'understand' the Other – that is, to reduce him to the model of our own existence in order to live with him. The opacity of any work of art, rather than impeding knowledge, offers the promise of new knowledge and expands our field of epistemological appropriations. The problem arises when, as a result of authoritarianism, academia or the market, the zones of experience established are closed in on themselves. The result is a pathological society that is probably not so different to the one in which it has fallen to our lot to live.

18 D. W. Winnicott, *Playing and Reality*.
London: Pelican Books, 1974, p. 15.

CONTEMPORARY RETURNS:
A SELECTION OF NEW ACQUISITIONS, 2002–07

Kaira M. Cabañas

This volume builds upon *MACBA Collection. Itinerary*, which was published in 2002.
In so doing, the task of the present publication is not to present a comprehensive
overview of the entire MACBA Collection, but rather to demonstrate how the Museum
has sought to initiate new narratives and histories of art through its acquisitions
in the years 2002–07. These newly acquired works thus function in tandem and in
tension with the work that the Museu d'Art Contemporani de Barcelona (MACBA)
has amassed since its founding in 1995 – only a small portion of which is represented
here. In what follows, the Collection has been divided into loose chronological
sections that broach specific critical concerns, including the possibility of charting
'other' modernisms and the modalities of participation evinced by contemporary art.

If the modernist museum as instantiated in The Museum of Modern Art (MoMA)
was originally premised on the linear evolution of art and the purity of artistic
mediums, the MACBA instead opens its Collection to multiple histories and cultural
formations, while also embracing the transversality and cross-contamination between
media from painting to poetry, sculpture to theatre. Moreover, the MACBA's various
presentations of its Collection have aimed to demonstrate how the return to a
specific moment – be it through a new acquisition or an exhibition – always entails
a modification of how we have come to understand that moment in the present,
thereby reframing its issues and stakes.

To understand a collection's formation as a discursive function is to resituate
the question of art's autonomy and a collection's representativeness in order to
speak to the field of possibility, historical contingencies and social relations that gave
rise to the collection itself as well as its eventual elaboration and critique through
subsequent acquisitions and exhibition programmes. Michel Foucault describes the
effect of such returns:

We return to those empty spaces that have been masked by omission or concealed in a false image and misleading plenitude.... It follows naturally that this return, which is a part of the discursive mechanism, constantly introduces modifications and that the return to a text is not a historical supplement that would come to fix itself upon the primary discursivity and redouble it in the form of an ornament which, after all, is not essential. Rather, it is an effective and necessary means of transforming discursive practice.[1]

Along the lines of Foucault's discussion of discursive practice, a collection *always already* entails a recursive structure, but few institutions have engaged this recursivity with such openness, self-reflexivity and rigor.

Even as some of the new acquisitions represented here 'return' to the forties and fifties, sixties and seventies, and eighties in order to build upon the Collection, they do so in a way that tellingly wrestles with contemporary practices. The MACBA Collection may in part attempt to 'represent' the art historical past but it does so – and this is crucial – against the backdrop of the present institutionalisation of certain artistic practices and aesthetic debates more generally: from the status of documentary work to the rise of what has come to be termed 'relational' aesthetics. It is through its attention to a constantly shifting cultural and political terrain, both past and present, that the MACBA Collection does not solely express, represent, imitate or even champion a single history of modern and contemporary art. In presenting its repository of artworks as a site of interpretation and contestation, the MACBA's strategy has been to propose how a collection, and an institutional one in particular, might be productively put to use.

[1] Michel Foucault, 'Qu'est-ce qu'un auteur?', *Bulletin de la Société française de philosophie*, year 63, no. 3, July–September 1969, pp. 73–104. English edition: Michel Foucault, 'What is an Author?', in Donald F. Bouchard (ed.), *Language, Counter-memory, Practice: Selected Essays and Interviews by Michel Foucault*. Ithaca, N.Y.: Cornell University Press, 1977, p. 135.

Other Modernisms: Informel and Concrete, Documentary and Experimental. The Forties and Fifties

In the immediate aftermath of the Second World War, artists in Europe struggled
with the memory of technology's destructive potential. Their attempts to cope with
the past – or what in German is called *Vergangenheitsbewältigung* – developed
alongside unprecedented industrial development and economic growth: the
devastation of war was replaced (and repressed) by enthusiasm for the various
countries' economic booms. The works in the MACBA Collection pertaining to this
historical moment probe critical questions, including: How do aesthetic practices
register historical experience and trauma? Where does one locate the criticality of
a work vis-à-vis its historical context? How do we interpret the discontinuity between
the narratives of documentary practice and the retreat into painterly abstraction
in the late forties and fifties?

While institutions such as MoMA have long championed the predominance of
American Abstract Expressionism in the post-war moment, Art Informel abstraction
was the dominant mode of painterly production in Europe at this time. By the early
fifties, the 'informel', a term launched by Michel Tapié in *Un art autre: où il s'agit
de nouveaux dévidages du réel* (1952), was used variously to describe painting that
emphasised the opaque, physical materiality of the medium (e.g., Jean Dubuffet,
Jean Fautrier) or spontaneous expression (e.g., Georges Mathieu). Moreover, it was
generally understood within the terms of France's liberation from German
occupation, the Vichy regime, the Stalinist threat and aesthetic 'liberation' from the
dictates of Socialist Realism. In this historical context, the visible expressivity of Art
Informel suggested the artist's freedom from traditional painterly criteria, while the
work's gestural nature also signified the singular subjectivity and existential presence
of the painter. What is more, the work of many of the artists associated with Art
Informel belies American critic Clement Greenberg's neo-Kantian insistence on

medium specificity (i.e., painting's flatness), which was later subtended by his endorsement of a visualist ideality for modernist painting. Indeed, the hegemony of Greenbergian modernism at this time was challenged in the exhibition *Be-Bomb: The Transatlantic War of Images and All That Jazz. 1946–1956*, curated by Serge Guilbaut and Manuel J. Borja-Villel and presented at the MACBA in 2007.

Regarding the artists represented in the MACBA Collection, Jean Dubuffet turned to the depths of the psyche as a creative force and became the spokesperson, collector and practitioner of Art Brut in 1945. Dubuffet's insistence on a regression to childhood and other 'primitive' states can be read as a symbolic resistance to the 'blight of urban industrial life and the new consumer culture' in the post-war moment.[2] Like the Surrealists before him, his work shares with Brassaï's photographs of graffiti an insistence on creativity at the margins of institutionalised culture, while Dubuffet's creative 'regression' also presents the dialectical counterpart to the concurrent insistence on realism as in the films of Roberto Rossellini described below. With its thick impasto and combination of materials such as asphalt and mud, Dubuffet's work elicited strong negative reactions from his contemporaries. In the MACBA Collection, *Le chien jappeur* demonstrates the artist's rejection of painterly illusion in favour of the materiality of paint and the use of different materials toward expressive ends.

The work of Antoni Tàpies has similar recourse to different materials, and his prolific production from the forties to the present was the subject of a major retrospective at the MACBA in 2004. Tàpies's early work includes recurring motifs – from esoteric signs and self referential calligraphy to ambiguously rendered bodies – that were informed by his early contact with different 'primitivisms', including children's art, the art of the insane, the work of Surrealists and the photographs of graffiti by Brassaï. By 1954, all apparent figuration disappeared and he produced what was referred to at the time as *matiériste*, or matter painting (a tendency to which Dubuffet is also aligned). Characterised by the composition of surfaces with dense textures and a predominance of earthy colours – which often include sand, marble dust and coloured earth – works such as Tàpies's *Pintura ocre* (1959) and *Forma blanca* (1959) create the effect of a geological formation or a wall. For Tàpies, it was key that the object did not exist apart from its constituent

2 Benjamin H. D. Buchloh, 'From Detail to Fragment: Décollage Affichiste,' *October*, no. 56, Spring 1991, p. 102.

>
Be-Bomb: The Transatlantic War of Images and All That Jazz. 1946–1956, 2007

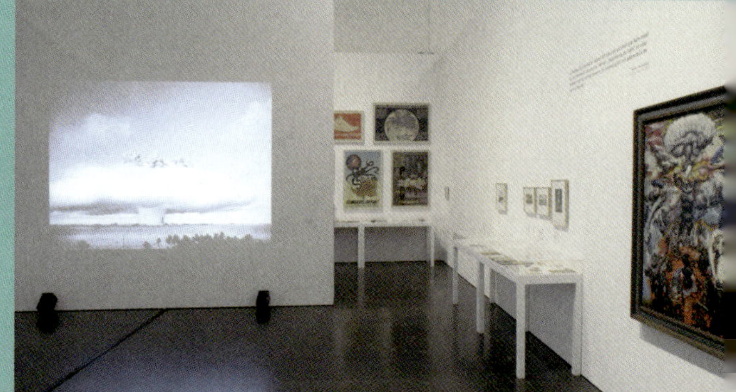

matter, which was its 'subject'. Such work, in which fissures and cracks do not describe a particular object, is to be perceived as matter in a state of constant change and is informed by scientific discussions (in the wake of the atomic bomb) that stimulated new interest in the status of matter and energy.

Also aligned with Art Informel (but not its *matiériste* version) is the work of Henri Michaux. A poet and a painter, Michaux spoke of drawing as liberation from words. Even so, his drawings and paintings exhibit a calligraphic character that often suggests illegible writing. In 1950 Michaux returned to his earlier use of ideograms in a series of India ink drawings – a representative sample of which forms part of the MACBA Collection. Subsequently, between 1955 and 1962, he experimented while working under the influence of the drug mescaline. The results of these experiments were obsessively detailed when compared to the calligraphic economy of his earlier work.

Moving from artists working in France to Italy, Lucio Fontana became the founder of Spatialism and published the *Primo manifesto dello spazialismo* in 1947. Two years later, in 1949, Fontana literally pierced the canvas with his *Buchi* and created his first *Ambiente spaziale*. The perforated works constitute the series known as *Concetti spaziali*, one of which is included in the MACBA Collection. Traditional pictorial illusionism here gives way to the introduction of real space and a dense accretion of sand mixed with paint on the surface of the canvas. By 1958, Fontana took his *Buchi* perforations to the extreme, slashing his canvases with a knife in his first *Tagli*, which form the series *Concetti spaziali-attese*.

In addition to those associated with Informel painting, other artists at this time developed a constructivist aesthetic. In the case of Jorge Oteiza's sculptures, by fusing the interior and exterior spaces of his work, he increasingly began to create interstitial spaces in the pursuit of contrast between zones of light and shadow. *Conjunción dinámica de dos pares de elementos curvos o livianos* (1957) in the MACBA Collection is a work from Oteiza's mature period. Here he explores how a volume can be produced through the 'non-occupation' of space. While the work may seem to be informed by an *a priori*, almost mathematical, logic, it is nevertheless driven by a desire to maintain vital content in his work. The perceptual experience of Oteiza's structures depends on a phenomenological mode of

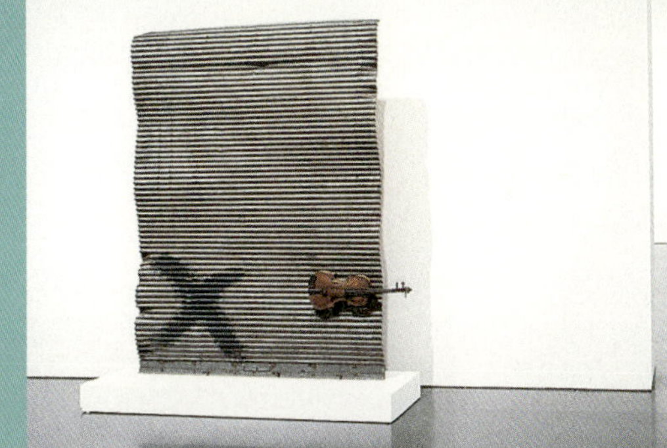

Antoni Tàpies. Retrospective, 2004

perception whereby one cannot derive any 'pure' thought cleaved from the tactile and material world and thus the work's physical presence. While Oteiza's writing displays a certain mysticism, his search for the Absolute is always framed in relation to art's social function: '[Art's] main objective is to engender in life (for all) an instantaneous imagination as a public (political) service from the realm of sensibility.'[3] By 1959, Oteiza ultimately abandoned sculpture and devoted himself to the theory of art and the study of Basque cultural identity.

Like Oteiza, Pablo Palazuelo is a singular artist whose work cannot be easily accommodated within a dominant history of art in the West. Moreover, they both share a rejection of rationalist abstraction that assumes a correspondence between what one thinks and what one sees. In the case of Palazuelo, he explains, 'Geometry is central to me in that it is the measure of matter. Measuring is a way of exploring, and you explore in order to try to know the unknown.'[4] Rather than take geometry as a given, what is crucial to Palazuelo's work are the relationships *between* the forms, participating in what he calls an 'organic geometry' or at times a 'transgeometry' (*transgeometría*). Where Oteiza's work emphasises gaps and empty spaces (hence also the 'silence' attributed to his work),[5] in drawings such as *Estudio para 'Alborada'* (1950) and gouaches such as *Cosas olvidadas IV* (1952), Palazuelo works to '*collaborate* in the act of [form's] appearance'.[6] In so doing, his work encourages a relational and embodied perception on the part of the viewer, instantiating a 'performative geometry' that he shares with Latin American modernists like Gego and Lygia Clark.[7]

With these works, the MACBA Collection offers alternative understandings of modernism and its presentation of *matiériste* and constructivist inflected work challenges the predominance of American Abstract Expressionism. The Collection seeks to demonstrate and give voice to other modernisms at odds with the dominant historiography of art and criticism in the United States and the teleological underpinnings of Greenbergian modernism. To be sure, this line of questioning also informs the acquisition of works by American artists such as Philip Guston, who as early as 1960 spoke of the 'impurity' of painting during a public discussion (in which Ad Reinhardt and Robert Motherwell also participated) and whose work is represented in the following section.

3 Jorge Oteiza, *Quousque Tandem…!* Alzuza, Navarra: Fundación Museo Jorge Oteiza, 2007, p. 5. The Spanish reads: 'Su razón última es de desembocar (para todos) en la vida con una imaginación instantánea como servicio público (político) desde la sensibilidad.'
4 See Palazuelo's 1995 statement reproduced in *MACBA Collection: Itinerary*. Barcelona: MACBA, 2002, p. 43.
5 See Manuel J. Borja-Villel, 'Jorge Oteiza, silencio y misticismo', *El País*, 21 October 2008.

6 See the introduction by Manuel J. Borja-Villel and Teresa Grandas in *Palazuelo: Working Process*. Barcelona: MACBA, 2007, p. 7.
7 I take 'performative geometry' from the title of my essay 'Gego's Performative Geometry', in Nadja Rottner and Peter Weibel (eds.), *Gego, 1957–1988: Thinking the Line*. Ostfildern-Ruit: Hatje Cantz, 2006.

The role of the photographic document in the twentieth century was most recently taken up in the MACBA's 2008 exhibition *Universal Archive. The Condition of the Document and the Modern Photographic Utopia*, which was curated by Jorge Ribalta. Since its invention in 1839, photography has been claimed as constituting a universal language, and it has been championed historically on precisely these grounds. Photography became an updated version of a Rousseau-like dream: a return to an originary communication prior to modern alienation and linguistic dispersion. With photography, this dream was considered technologically realised through the medium's capacity to perfectly redouble presence and yield it to the immediacy of visual perception. These claims were also echoed in the fifties when, in his own defence of the medium, Edward Steichen explained: 'Long before the birth of a word language the cavemen communicated by visual images. The invention of photography gave visual communication its most simple, direct, universal language.'[8]

Inspired by the work of Cartier-Bresson and Walker Evans, Helen Levitt produced the first works of her artistic career with a 35 mm camera. The street life and people in New York's disenfranchised neighbourhoods became the main subject of her photography and film. *In the Street* (1945–46 [1952]), a silent documentary film produced in collaboration with James Agee and Janice Loeb, was shot with a hidden camera and depicts the harsh realities of Harlem through scenes of children at play and their parents.[9] The film's shots are loosely juxtaposed, reporting on the neighbourhood's residents through what Siegfried Kracauer described as an 'unconcealed compassion'. Levitt's work taps into a history of documentary practice – be it photography or film – that was committed to the representation of the working class at a time when photography would increasingly become an instrument of ideological manipulation. The latter was perhaps nowhere more evident than in Steichen's promotion of American values against the encroaching threat of communism through MoMA's most widely circulated exhibition and catalogue, *The Family of Man* (1955).

Alongside Levitt's film, the MACBA Collection also includes, among other works, *NYC Sagamore Cafeteria* (1948) and *14th of July 1948. Day becomes night...* (1948) by Robert Frank, who was similarly influenced by the work of Walker Evans as he too worked within a documentary modality that was premised on realism and the corresponding representation of minority groups and classes. But in the end Frank's

8 Here photography both returns to and transcends 'primitive' pictographic language. Edward Steichen, 'On Photography', *Daedalus* 89, no. 1, The Visual Arts Today, Winter, 1960, pp. 136–37.
9 Levitt also worked with James Agee and Janice Loeb on the documentary film *The Quiet One* (1949) directed by Sidney Meyers. Previously, Levitt had also worked as an assistant to the director Luis Buñuel on the editing of documentaries.

photographs provided a more biting critique – one critic described them as displaying 'brutal sensitivity'.[10] His book *The Americans* of 1959 was reviled at the time for its display of the country's racism, excessive materialism and empty patriotism.

In Catalonia, Joan Colom, along with Francesc Català-Roca, Xavier Miserachs and Oriol Maspons, formed the 'new avant-garde' in photography according to the critic Josep Maria Casademont. In 1958, Colom began taking photographs in the neighbourhood known as the Barrio Chino in Barcelona, capturing scenes of social marginality, prostitution and its protocols, and other residents, such as the children who lived in and roamed the neighbourhood's streets. Informed by the photo-reportage of Paris and New York photographers like Cartier-Bresson, Brassaï, Walker Evans and Garry Winogrand, Colom's work differs from theirs in that his photographs were taken in a semi-occult fashion: he hid the camera in his hand and, without looking through the lens, literally shot from the hip. Colom's film, *El carrer* (1960) takes up similar subjects in an alternative medium. Organised under the double principle of 'seriality' and the 'sketch', the film disavows conventional montage and instead groups shots into figurative and thematic blocks. Together these 'sketches' capture forms of popular expression. In its 30 minutes, the film offers, according to Santos Zunzunegui, 'a different world to look at and at once an *other* place from which to look'.[11]

The city devastated by the war is the subject of Roberto Rossellini's *Germania anno zero* (1947), the final film in his famed neorealist trilogy (the first two are *Roma, città aperta* and *Paisà*). In *Germania anno zero*, Rossellini shot on site in post-war Germany and, as with many neorealist films, used mainly local, non-professional actors. The film dramatises the stakes of this historical moment in Europe, conveying the reality and destruction shortly after the end of the Nazi regime in Germany. As with his photographic counterparts working in the US and Europe, Rossellini's neorealist content focuses on the lives of the poor and working class and illustrates the economic hardship and social conditions of post-war Italy and Europe in general.

Just as photography and film were harnessed toward a 'realist' aesthetic premised on their indexicality as well as a commitment to socio-historical representation, so too are these mediums the domain of avant-garde experimentation, perhaps nowhere

10 As cited in Joel Eisinger, *Trace and Transformation: American Criticism of Photography in the Modernist Period*. Albuquerque: University of New Mexico Press, 1995, p. 131.
11 See Santos Zunzunegui, 'Hacer (ver) la calle', in *Joan Colom: Fotografías de Barcelona, 1958–1964*. Madrid: Fundación Telefónica, 2004, p. 54. The original Spanish reads: 'un mundo diferente al cual mirar como un lugar *otro* desde donde mirarlo.'

more marked than in Guy Debord's *Hurlements en faveur de Sade* (1952) and Samuel Beckett's *Film* (1965). Informed by his exposure to Lettrist cinema, Debord's film consists of a soundtrack spoken by Debord and fellow artists: the screen remains white when a voice is heard and, alternatively, when no one speaks the screen is black. With a total running time of 75 minutes, only about a quarter of the work contains light and sound. For the final 24 minutes the viewer sits in total darkness and silence. Yet *Hurlements* was not only an attack on the iconic properties of film – and thus at odds with the contemporary turn to 'neorealism' in Italy and the subsequent development of *cinéma vérité* in France – but also called the particular viewing relations the cinematic context enforces into question, shifting the terms of film's analysis away from a consideration of the medium's ontology (as with André Bazin) and toward a critique of the institutionalisation of cinematic viewing experience. This line of experimentation was subsequently taken up in a generation of artists and filmmakers largely associated with 'expanded cinema'.

In contrast, Samuel Beckett's only venture into the medium, tellingly titled *Film*, takes as its point of departure Bishop Berkeley's theory *Esse est percepti* (to be is to be perceived). Written in 1963 and filmed in New York in the summer of 1964, *Film* was directed by Alan Schneider and features Buster Keaton. The film, which has no dialogue, stages Berkeley's theory as a drama by splitting the main character's role into a performance of the act of seeing, E, and the state of being seen, O. In Beckett's words: 'It will not be clear until the end of the film that the pursuing perceiver is not extraneous but the self.'[12]

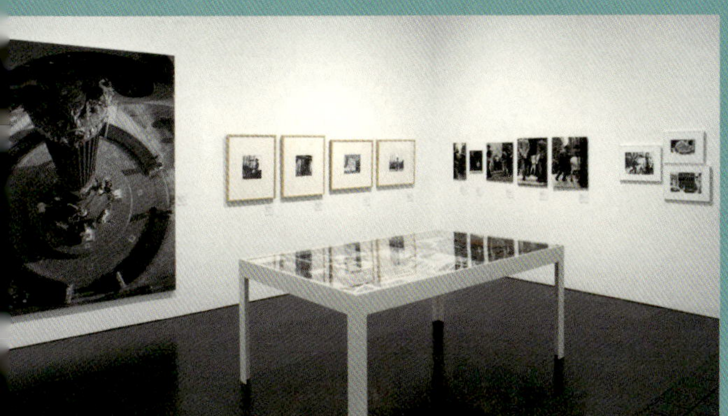

12 Maurice Harmon (ed.), *No Author Better Served: The Correspondence of Samuel Beckett and Alan Schneider*. Cambridge, Mass.: Harvard University Press, 1998, p. 167.

<
Universal Archive. The Condition of the Document and the Modern Photographic Utopia, 2008

Quando le ideologie si discostano dalle leggi eterne della morale e della pietà cristiana che sono alla base della vita degli uomini, finiscono per diventare criminale follia.
Persino la prudenza dell'infanzia ne viene contaminata e trascinata da un orrendo delitto ad un altro non meno grave, nel quale, con la ingenuità propria dell'innocenza, crede di trovare una liberazione dalla colpa.

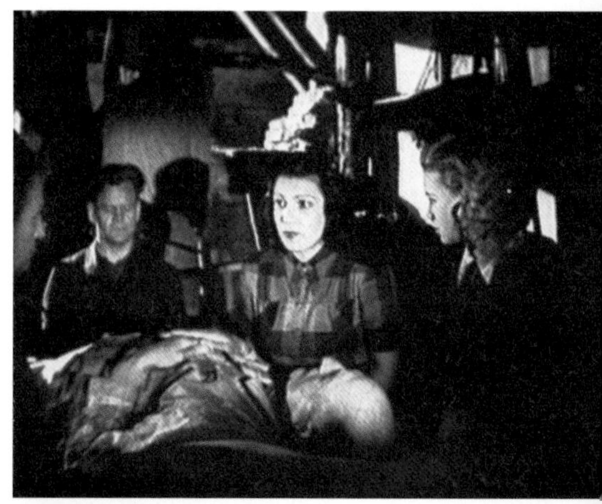

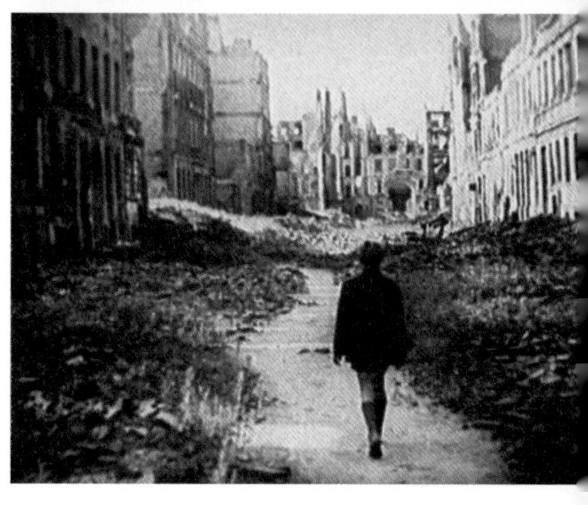

Roberto Rossellini
Germania anno zero, 1947
35 mm film transferred to video,
b/w, sound, 75 min
Motion Pictures, S.A.

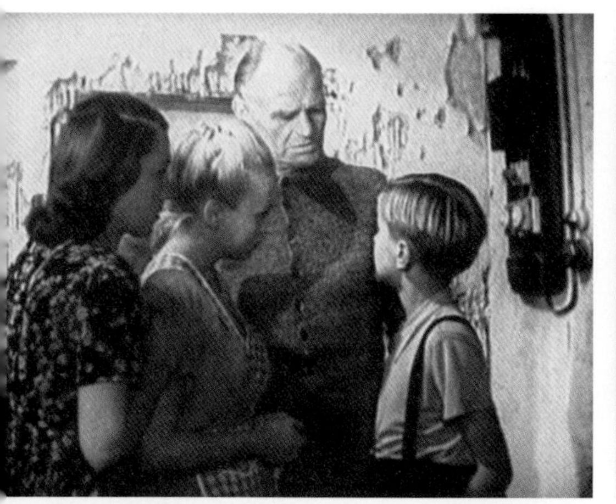
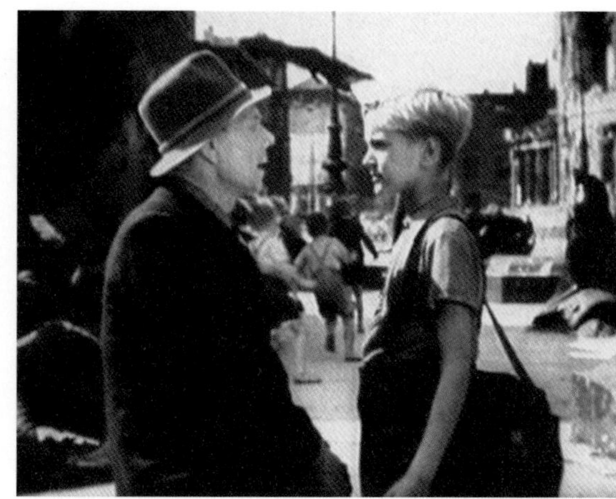
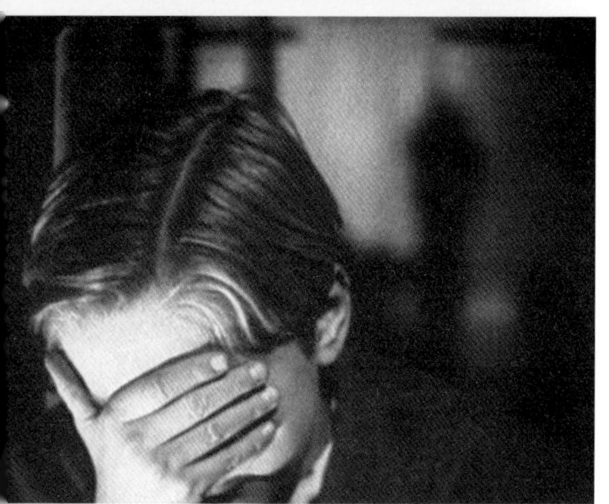
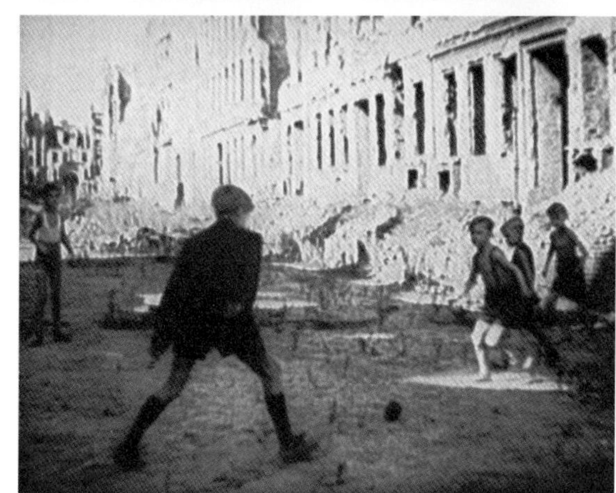
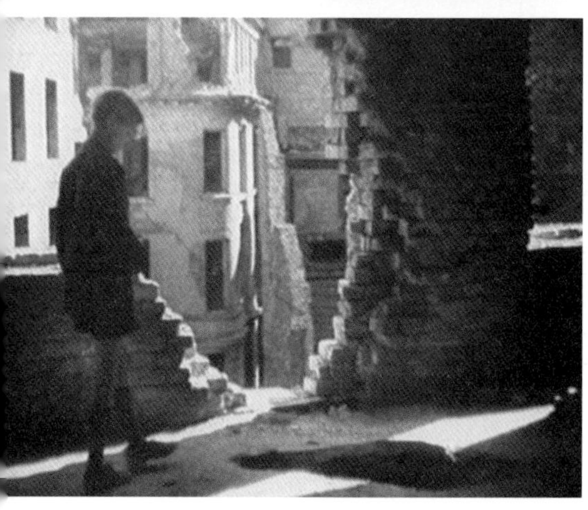
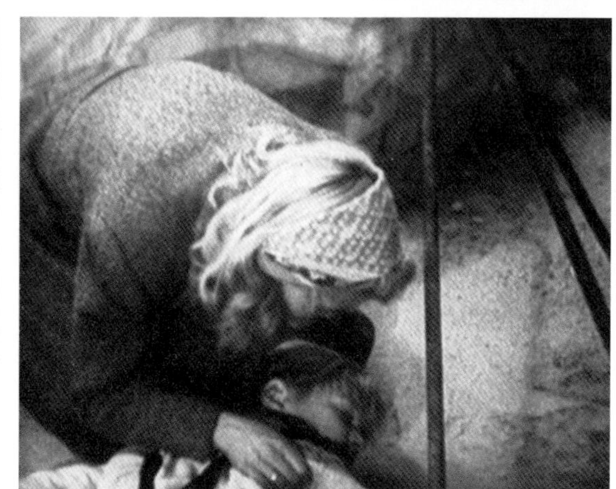

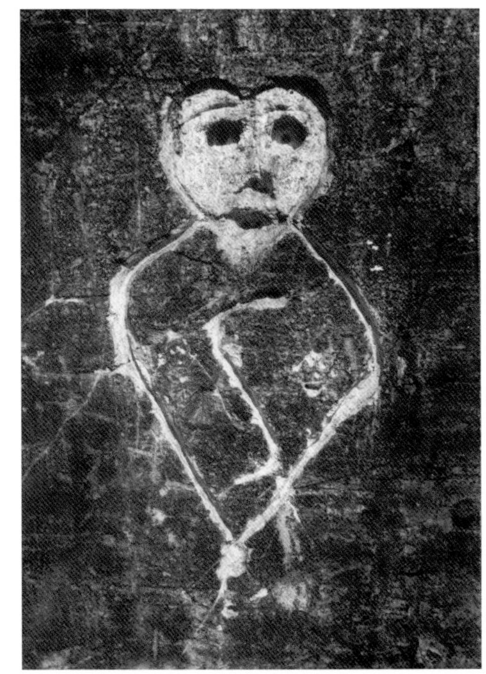

Brassaï
Untitled. Graffiti
Series VIII 'La Magie'
Ca. 1930. Print run ca. 1950
Silver-salt photograph
39 × 29.5 cm

La femme (Passage Prévot). Graffiti
Series VI 'L'amour'
Ca. 1930. Print run ca. 1950
Silver-salt photograph
50 × 40 cm

Untitled. Graffiti
Series III 'Naissance du visage'
Ca. 1930. Print run ca. 1950
Silver-salt photograph
50 × 39.5 cm

Untitled (rue Médéah). Graffiti
Series IV 'Masques et visages'
Ca. 1930. Print run ca. 1950
Silver-salt photograph
40 × 29.5 cm

Untitled. Graffiti
Series VII 'La mort'
Ca. 1930. Print run ca. 1950
Silver-salt photograph
50 × 40 cm

Petit lutin à la jupe triangulaire. Graffiti
Series IX 'Images primitives'
Ca. 1930. Print run ca. 1950
Silver-salt photograph
50 × 40 cm

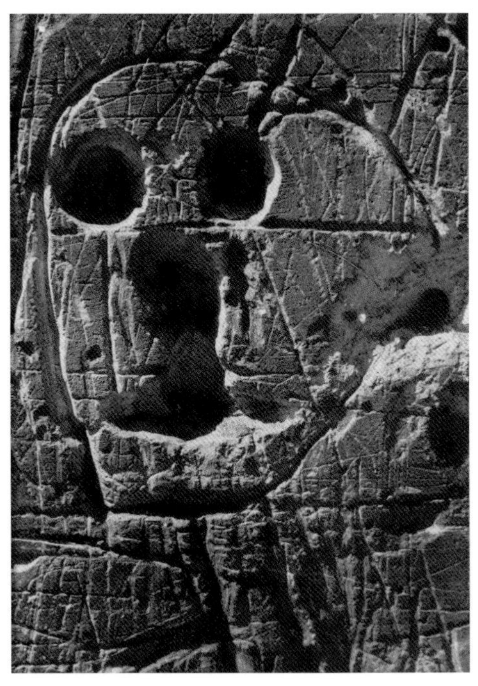

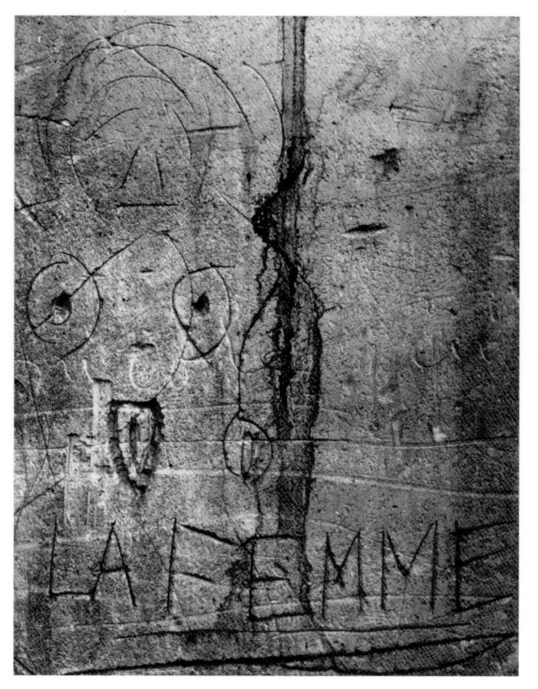
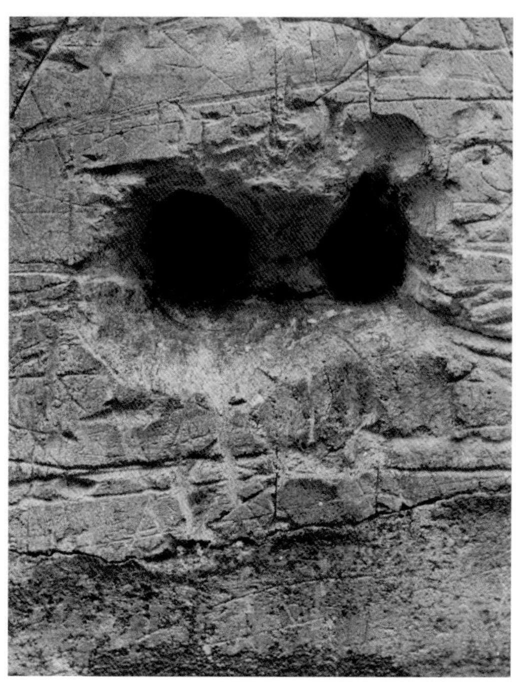
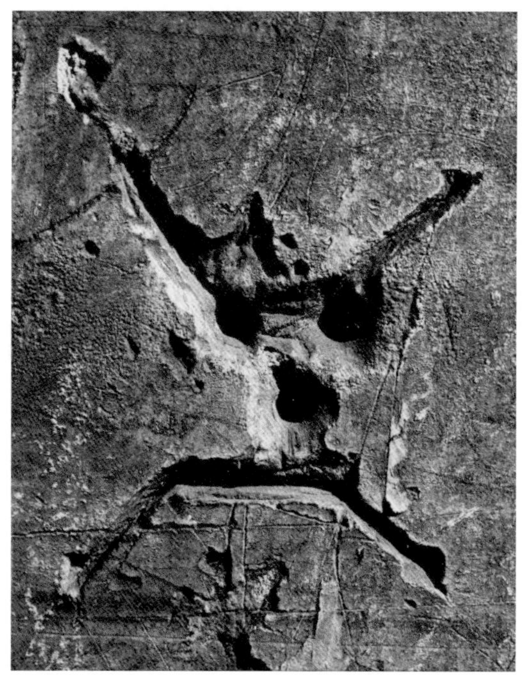
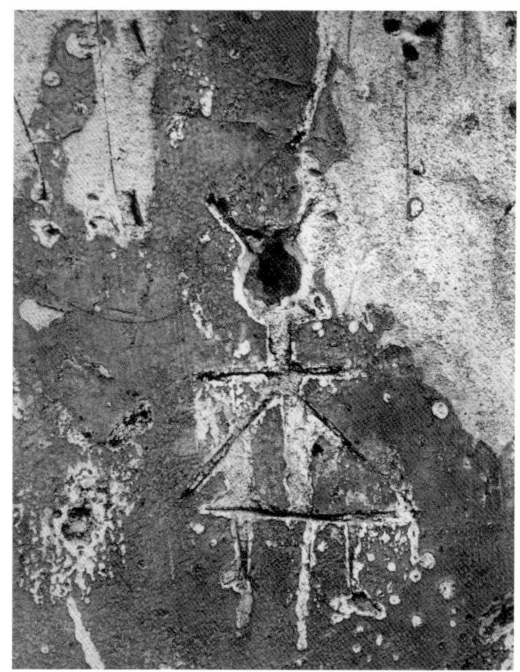

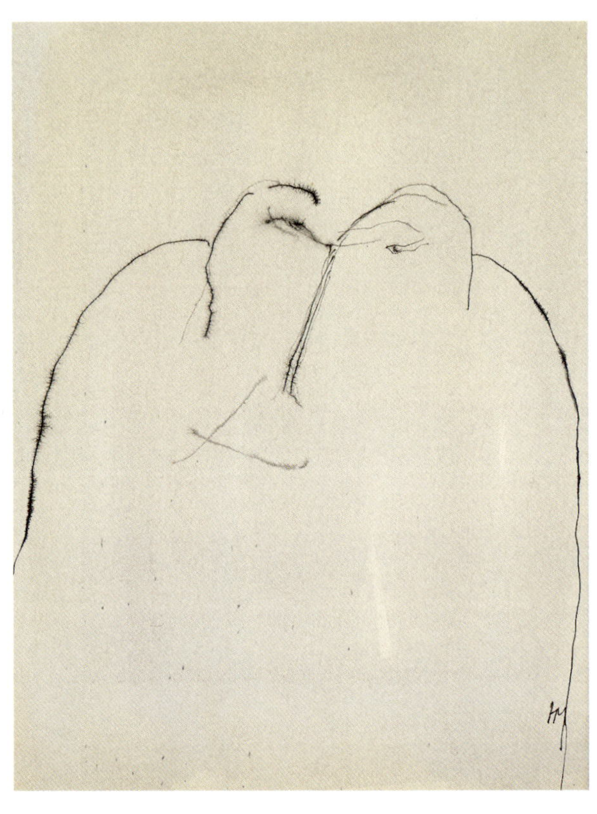

Henri Michaux
Untitled, 1948
Ink on paper
32.5 × 24.5 cm

Untitled, 1948
Watercolour on paper
39.5 × 28.2 cm

Untitled, ca. 1979
Watercolour on Japanese paper
51 × 31 cm

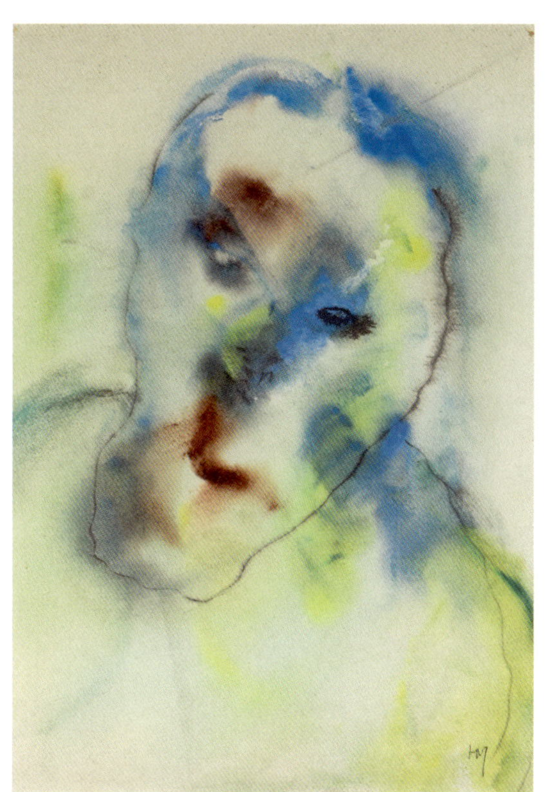 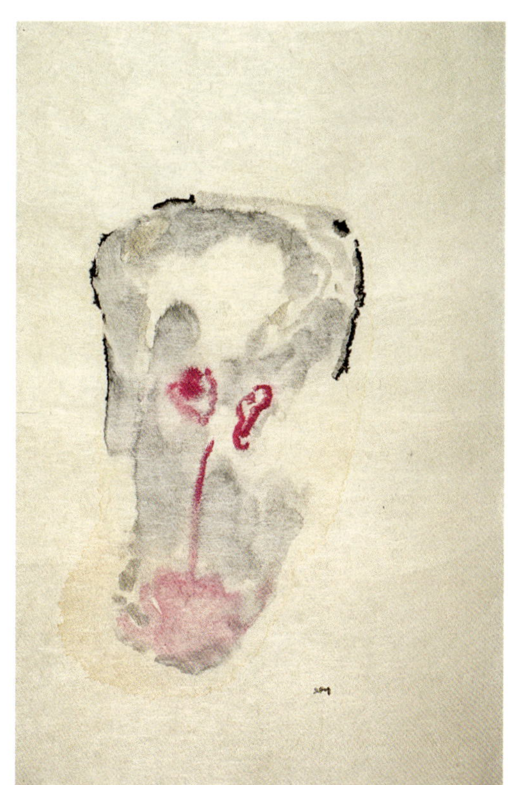

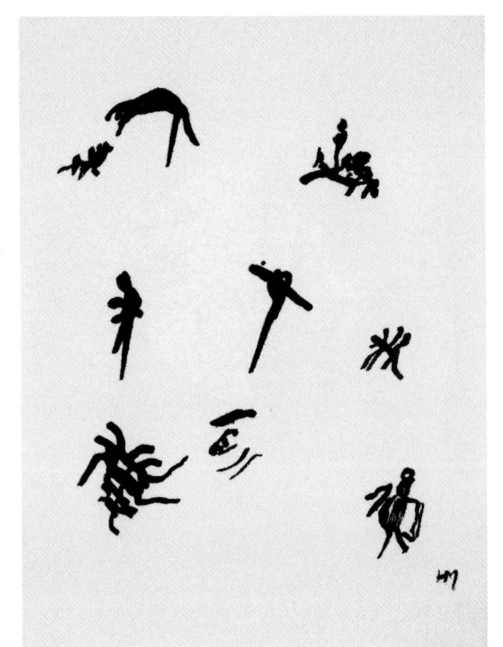

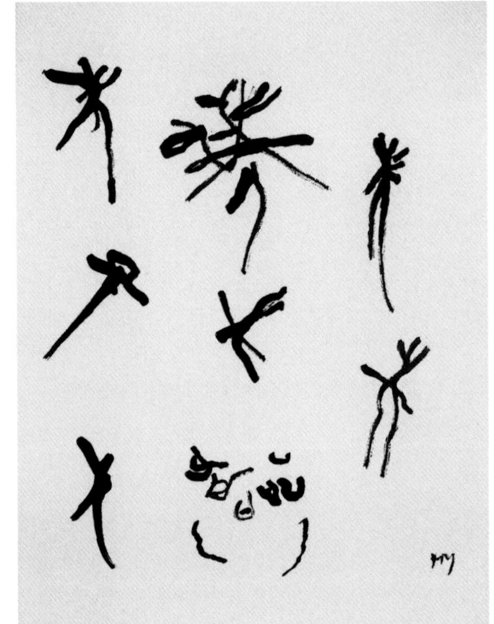

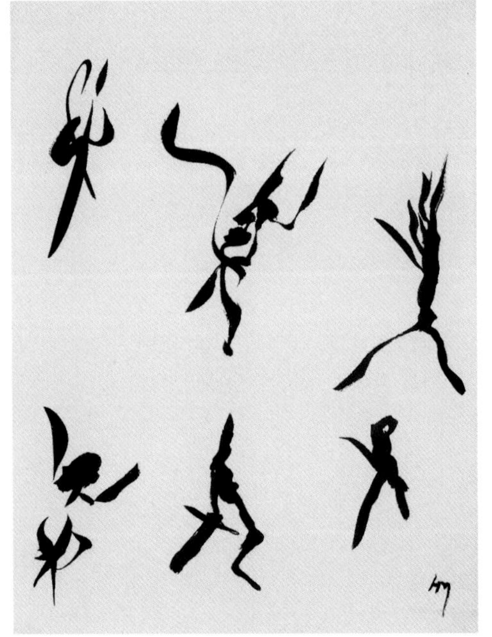

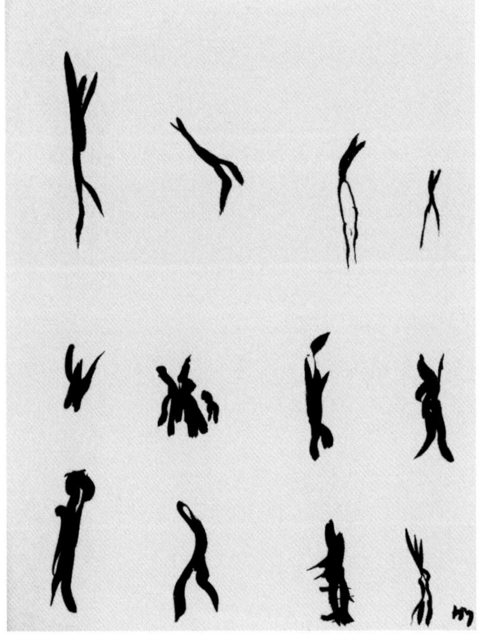

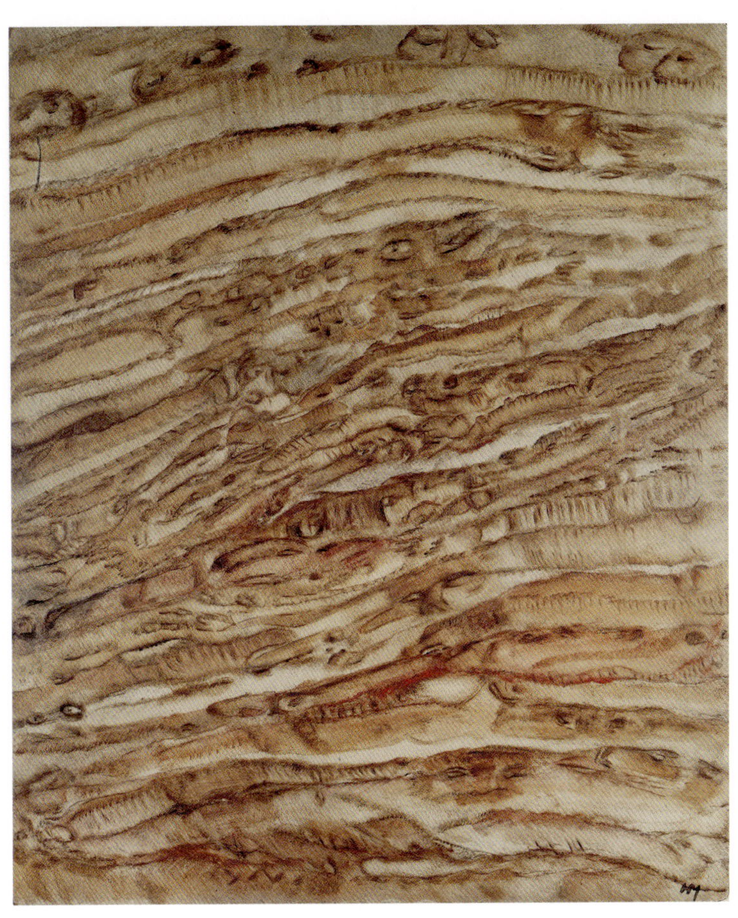

Henri Michaux
Untitled, 1950
India ink on paper
31.5 × 23.5 cm

Untitled, 1950
India ink on paper
34.5 × 24 cm

Untitled, 1950
India ink on paper
31.5 × 24 cm

Untitled, 1950
India ink on paper
31.5 × 24 cm

Untitled, ca. 1955
Oil on wood
54.5 × 45.5 cm

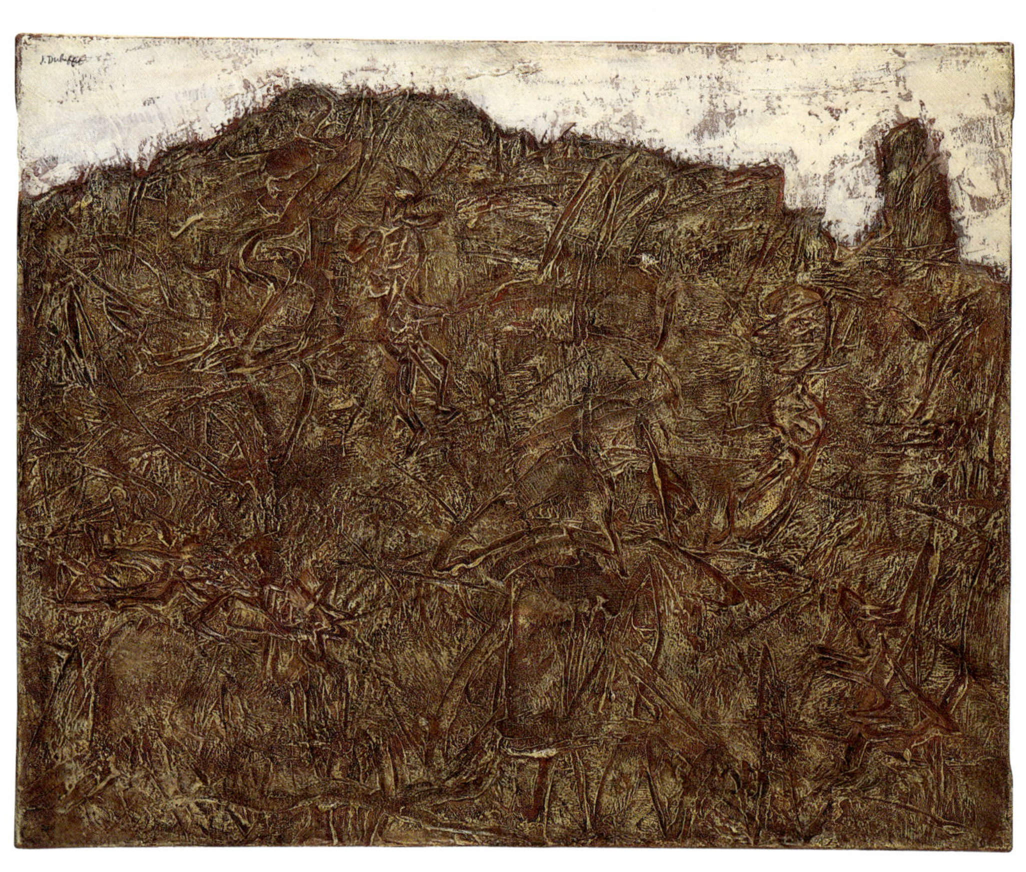

Jean Dubuffet
Le chien jappeur, 1953
Oil on canvas
72.6 × 92 cm

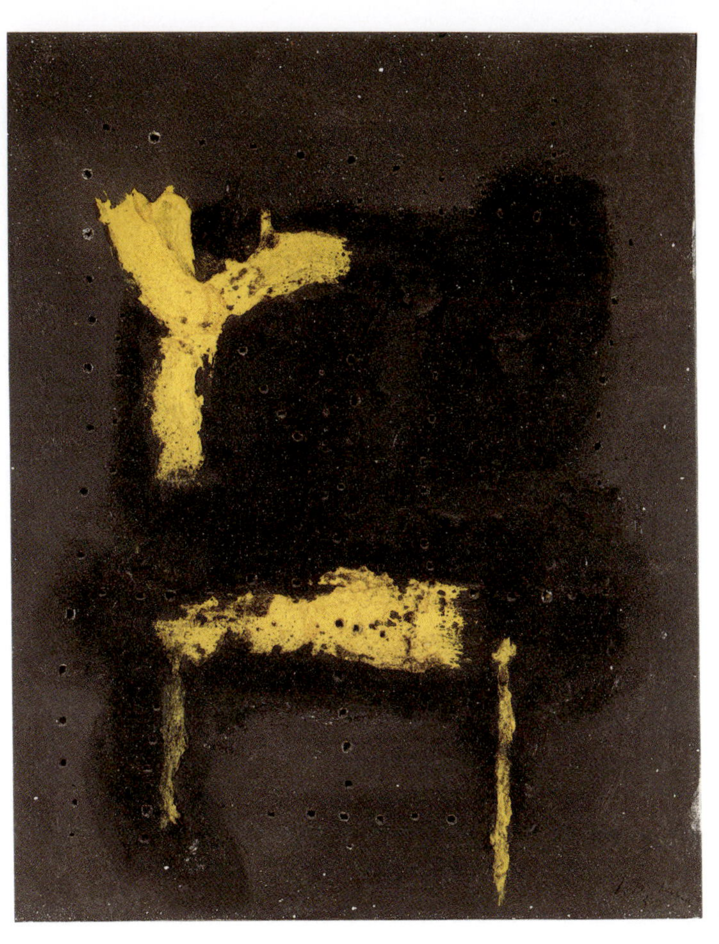

Lucio Fontana
Concetto spaziale, 1957
Acrylic and marble dust on canvas
74.2 × 61 cm

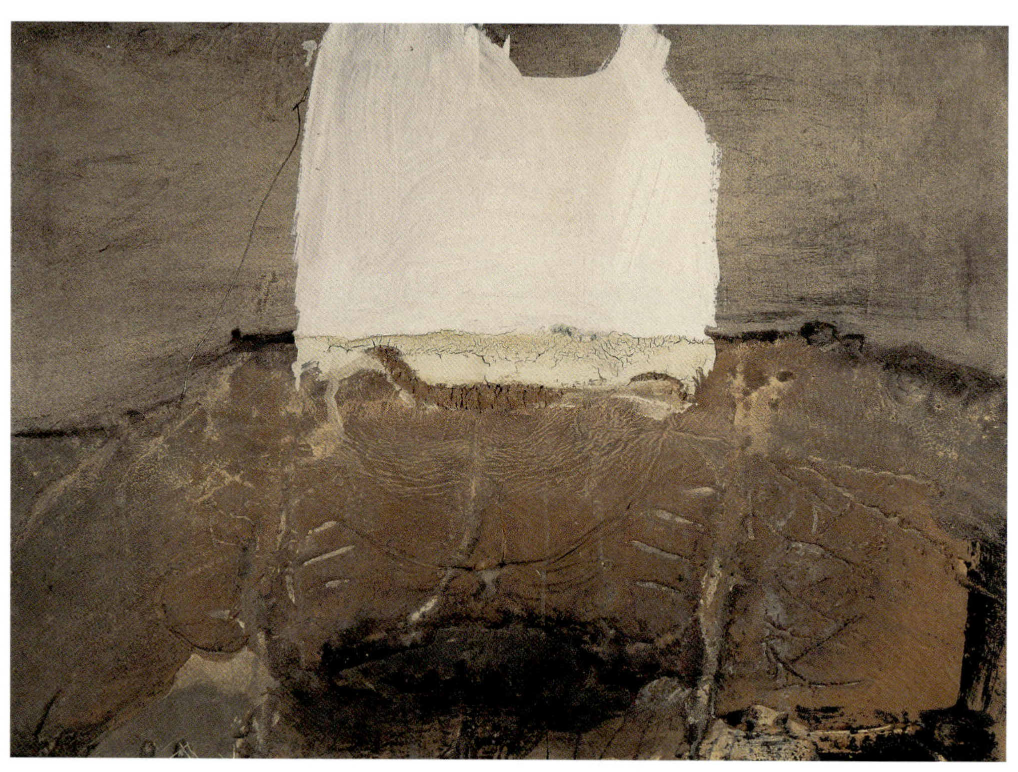

Antoni Tàpies
Forma blanca, 1959
Mixed media on canvas
81 × 116 cm

Negre amb dos entallaments, 1962
Mixed media on canvas mounted on wood
202 × 177 cm

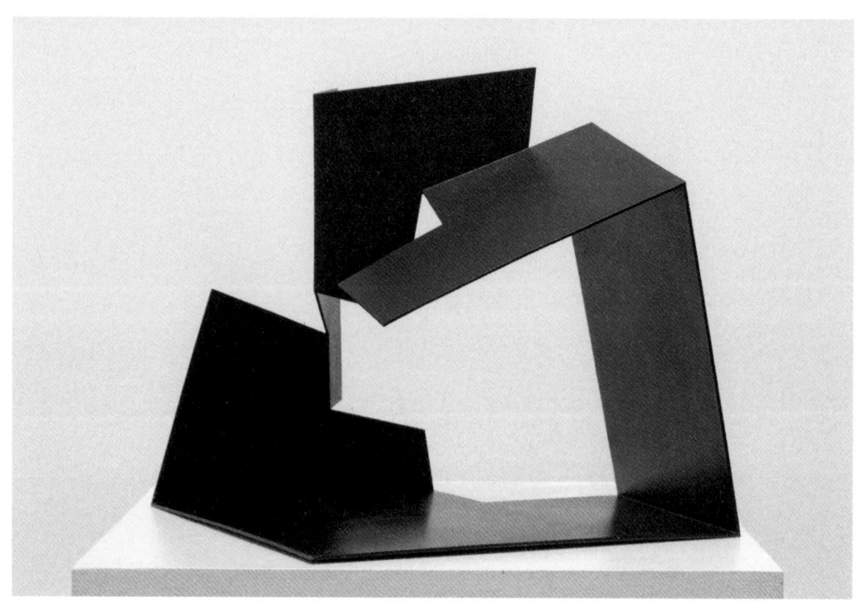

Jorge Oteiza
Desocupación no cúbica del espacio, 1959
Steel
40 × 43.8 × 38 cm

Néstor Basterretxea
Operación H, 1963
35 mm film transferred to video,
colour, sound, 11 min 49 s

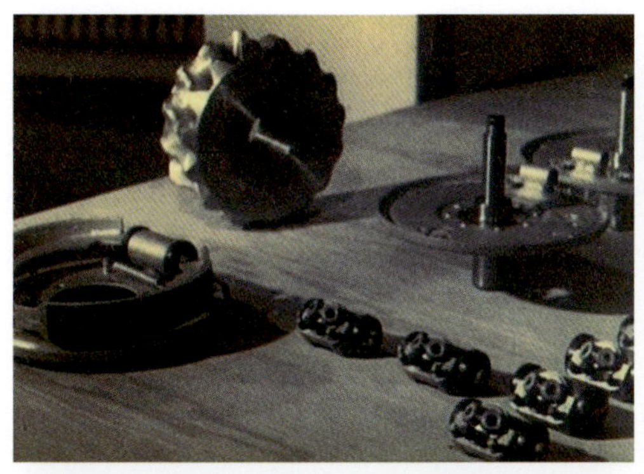
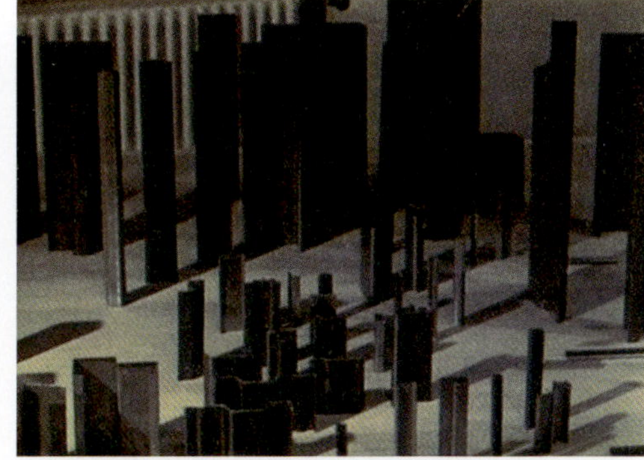
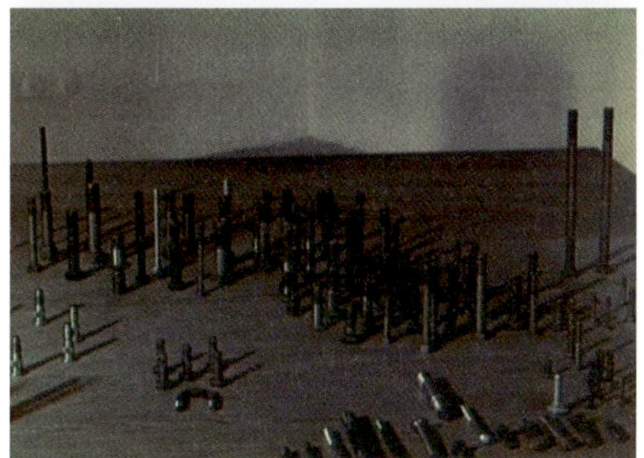
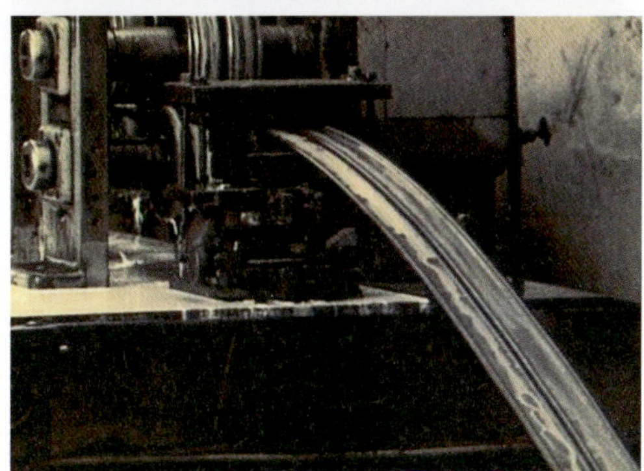
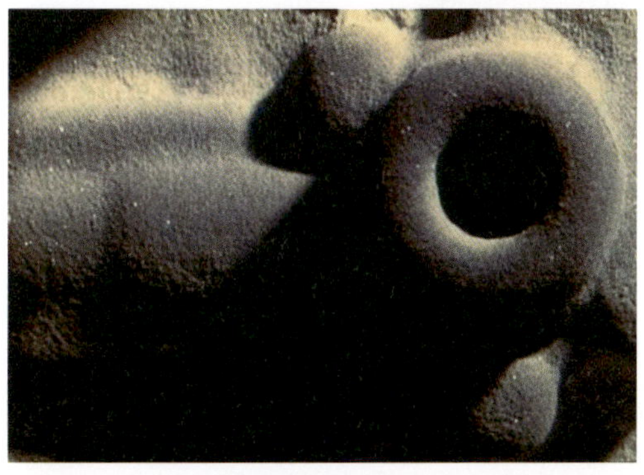
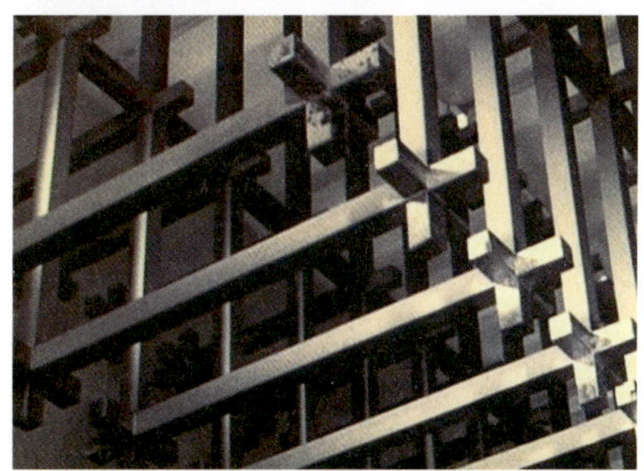
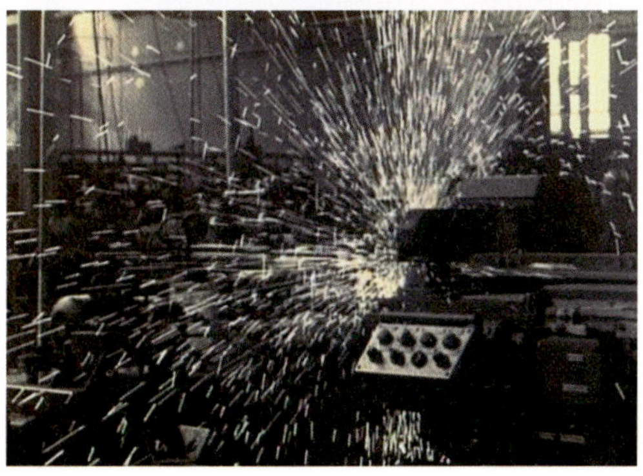
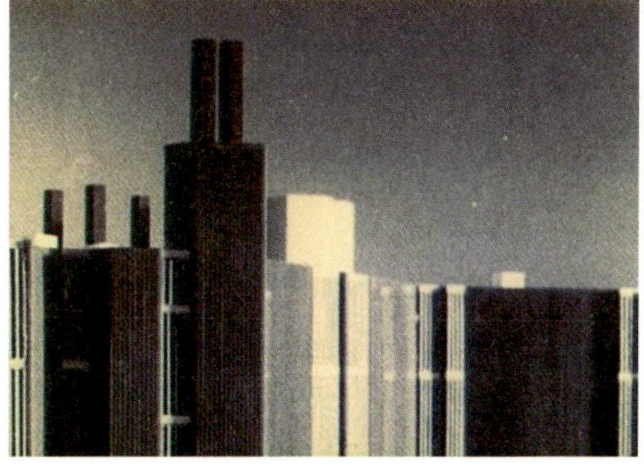

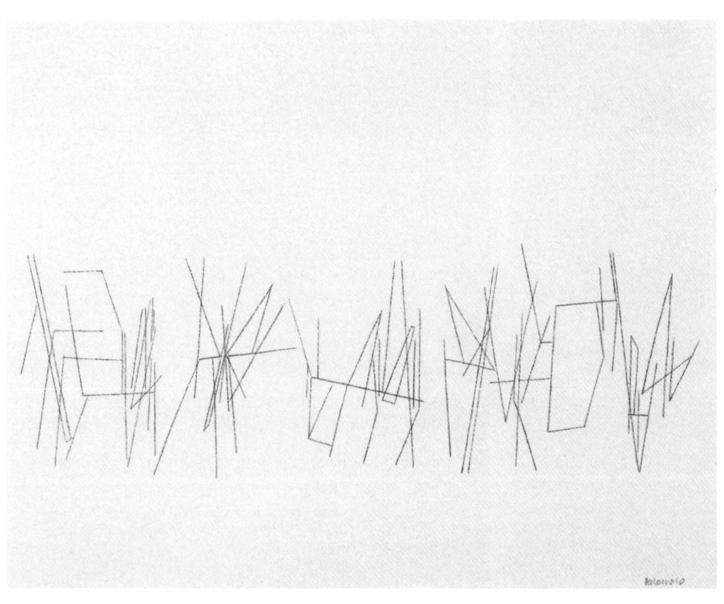

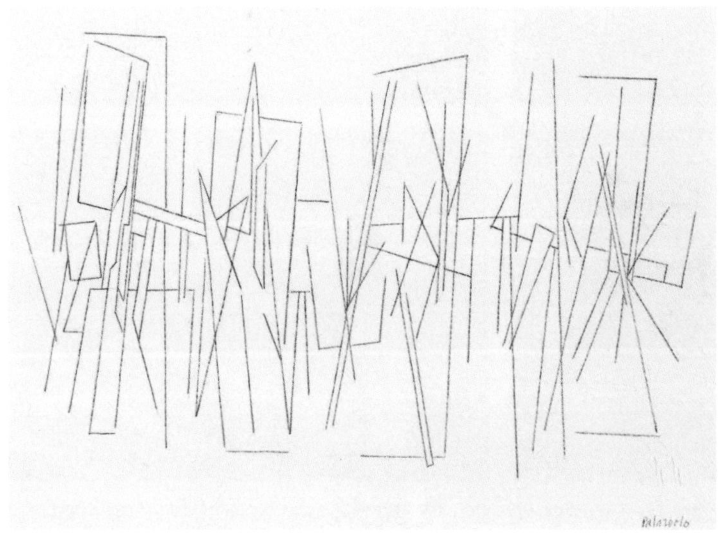

Pablo Palazuelo
Estudio para 'Alborada', 1950
Pencil on paper
50 × 65.5 cm

Estudio para 'Alborada' (2), 1950
Graphite on paper
29.5 × 41 cm

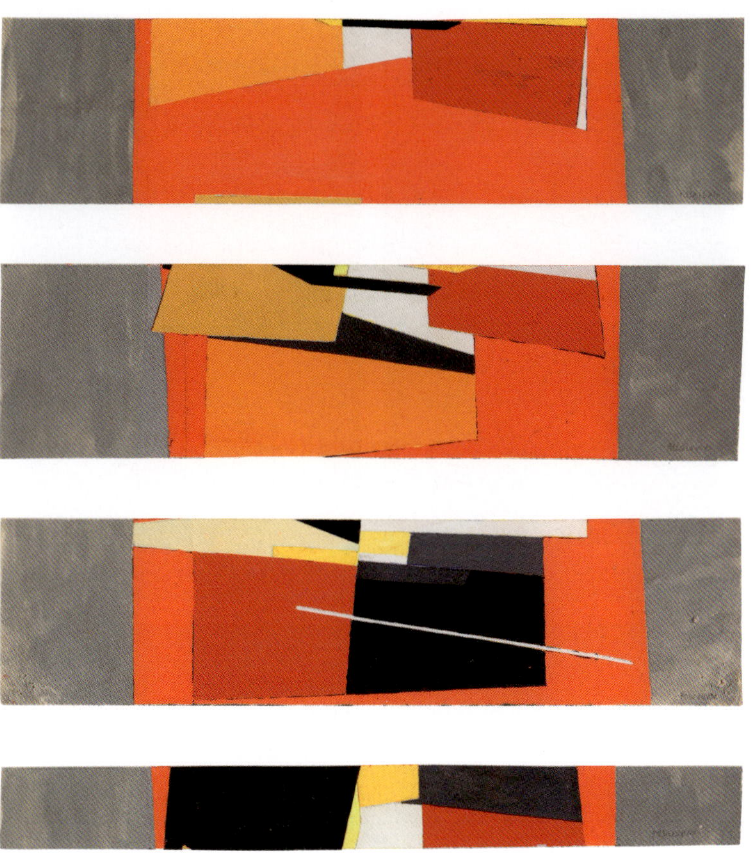

Horizontal I, 1952
Gouache on paper
9 × 36.5 cm

Horizontal II, 1952
Gouache on paper
9.2 × 37 cm

Horizontal III, 1952
Gouache on paper
9 × 37 cm

Horizontal IV, 1952
Gouache on paper
4.1 × 35.7 cm

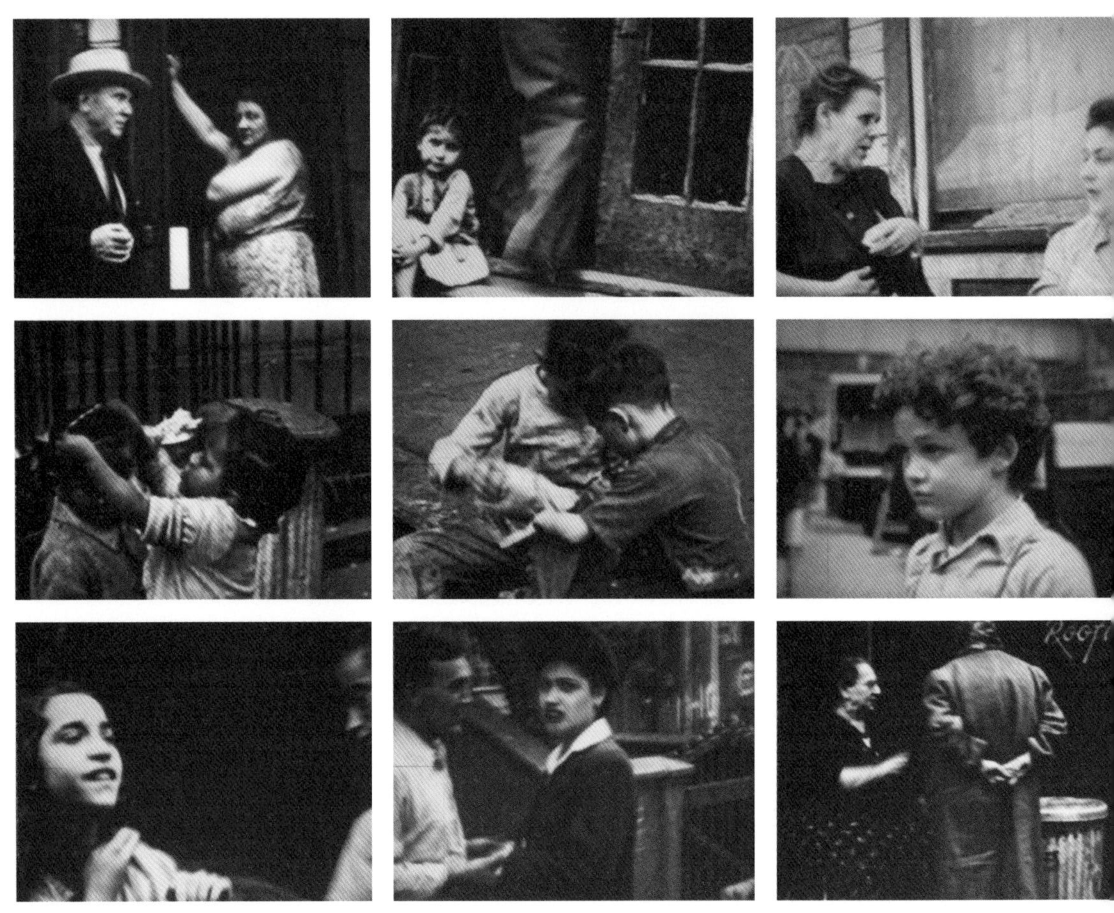

Helen Levitt
In the Street, 1945–46 (1952)
16 mm film transferred to video, b/w,
silent, 15 min, and sound recording
Co-creators: James Agee and Janice Loeb
Piano: Arthur Kleiner

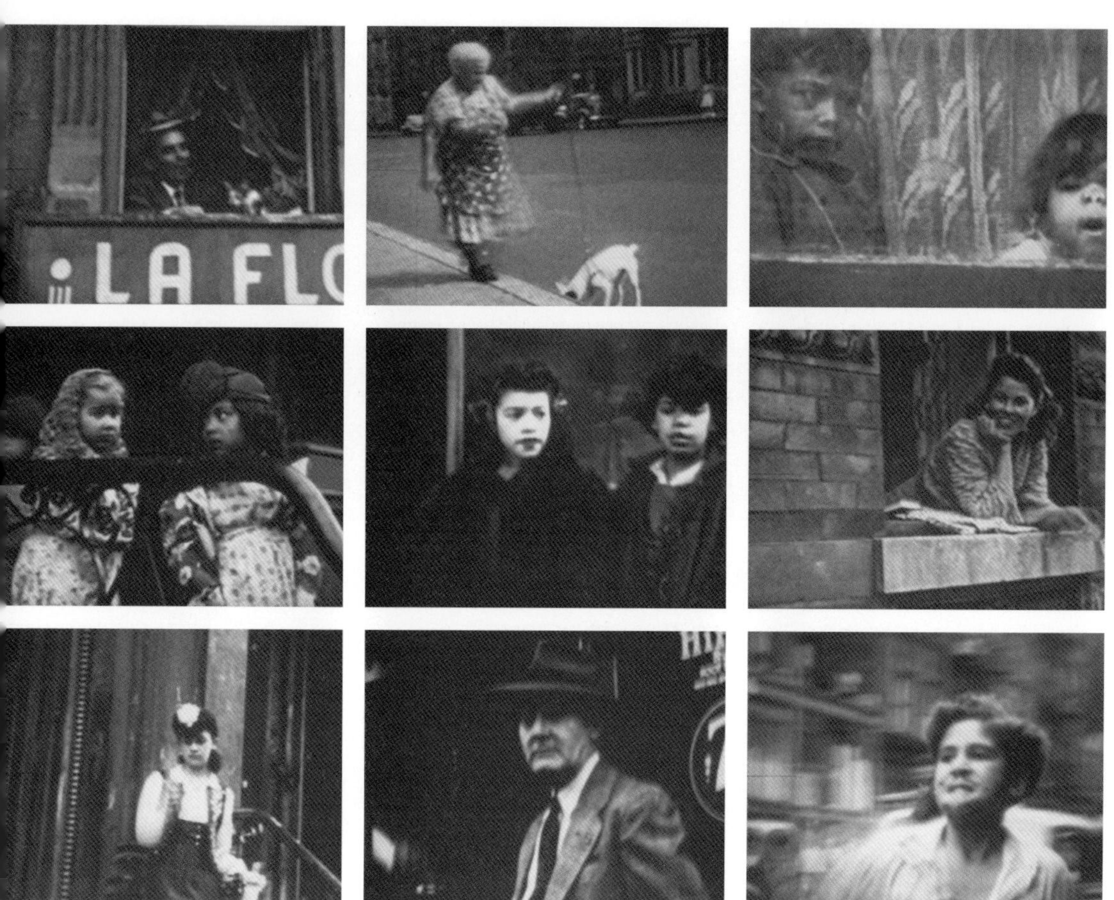

¡ LA FLO

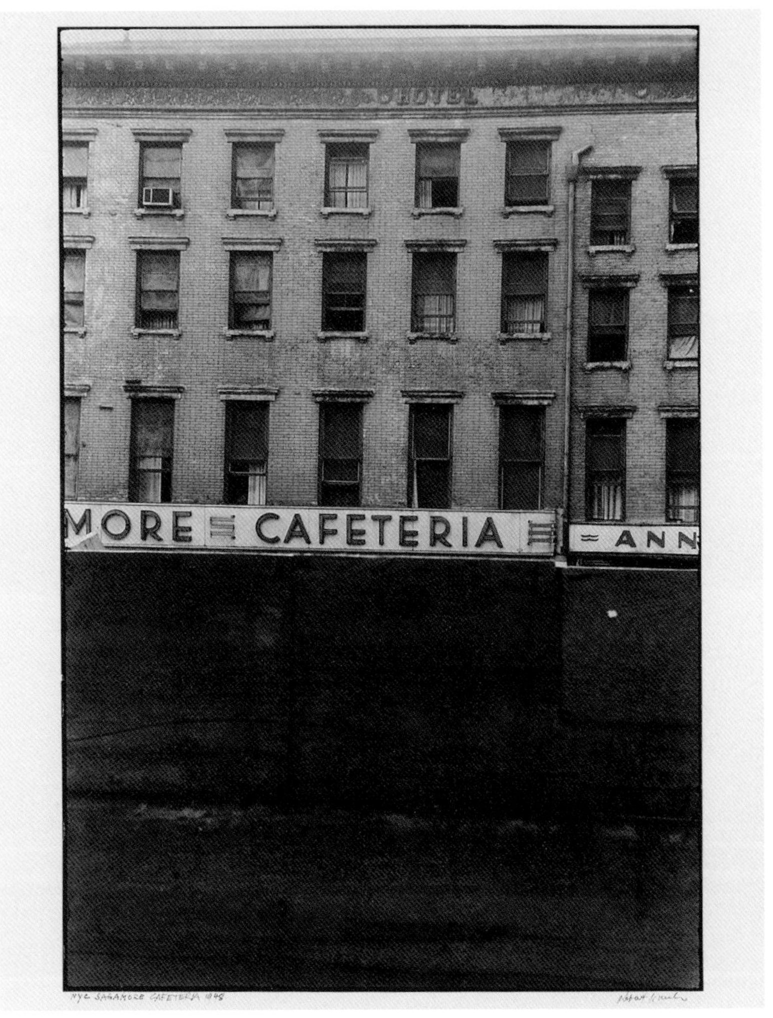

Robert Frank
NYC Sagamore Cafeteria, 1948
Silver-salt photograph
50.4 × 40.4 cm

14th of July 1948. Day Becomes Night..., 1948
Silver-salt photograph
35.5 × 48 cm

Mallorca, 1951
Silver-salt photograph
27.7 × 25.4 cm

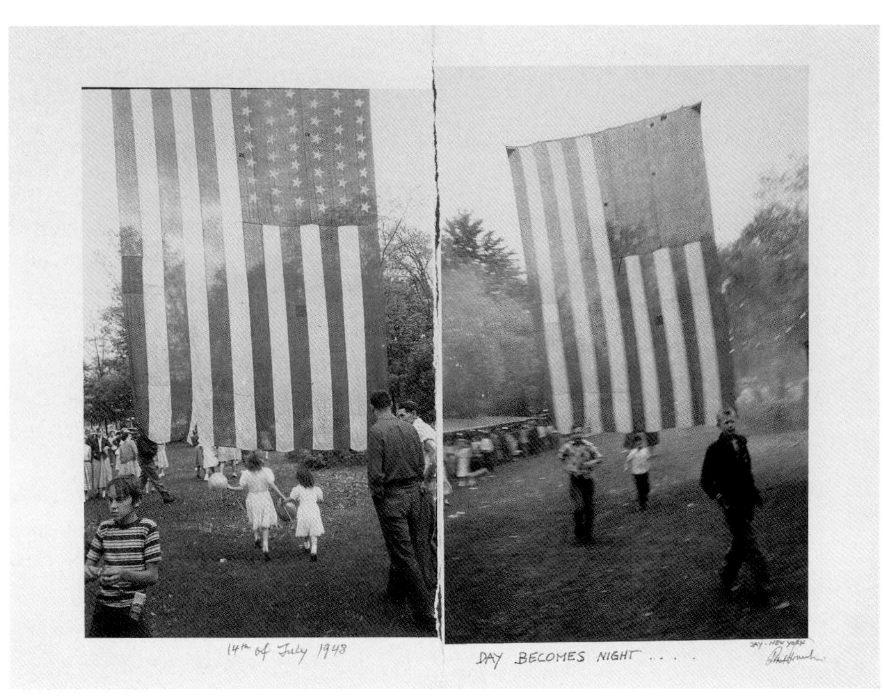

14ᵗʰ of July 1948

DAY BECOMES NIGHT . . . .

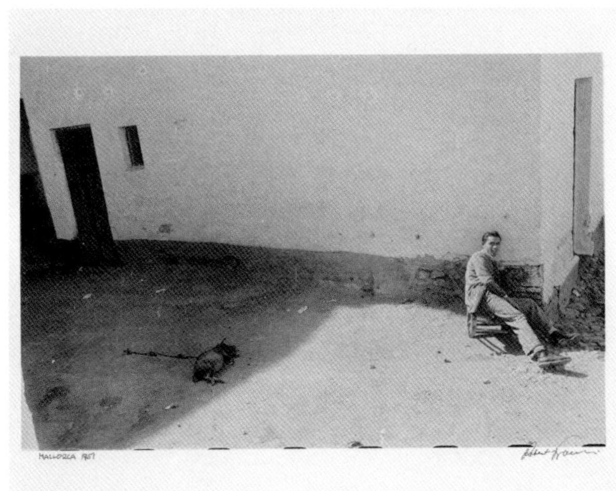

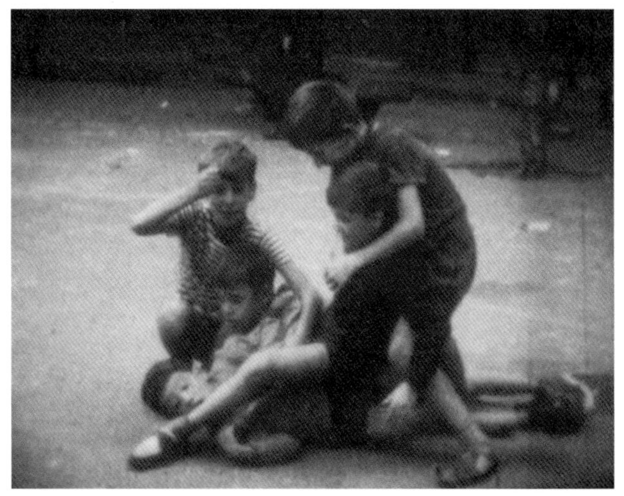

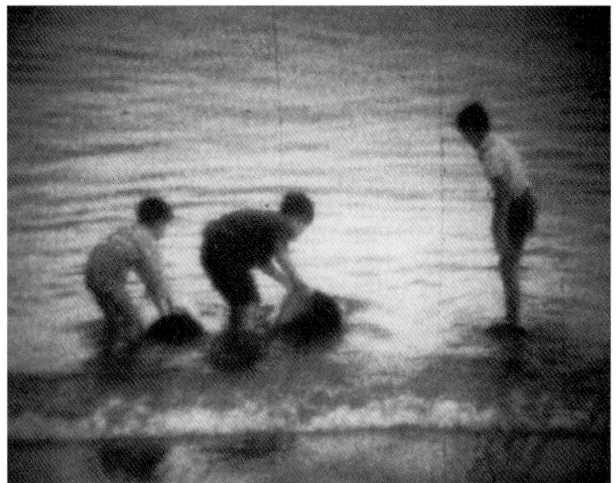

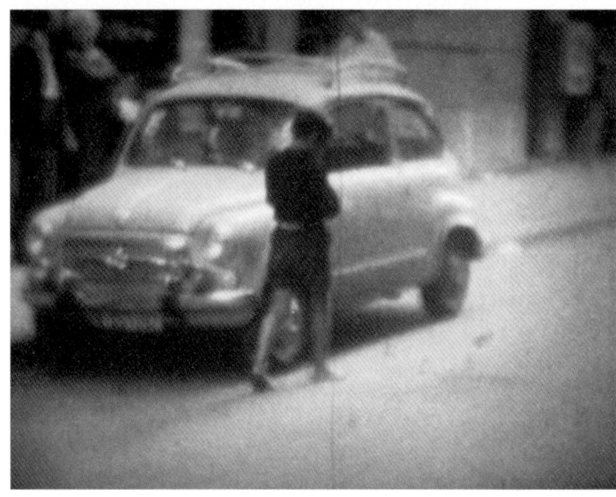

Joan Colom
El carrer, 1960
Single-channel video, b/w, silent,
30 min

70

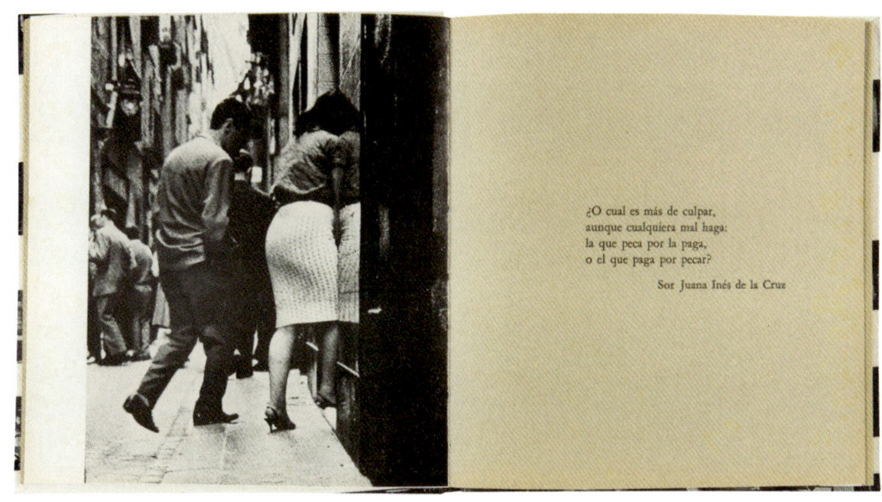

*Izas, rabizas y colipoterras: drama con
acompañamiento de cachondeo y dolor de corazón*
Book
23 × 22 cm
Barcelona: Lumen, Palabra e Imagen, 1964
With text by Camilo José Cela

para los niños ricos, el comercio; para los niños que no lo son, el comercio en el que se despacha al fiado. Ahora toca trepar por las fachadas. Dos son las filas de casas, cada una de ellas alzándose sobre su acera: la de la moto con sidecar y la del cajón del heladero. En ésta, dos abejas se asoman al balcón. Si se llaman Pepita y Paquita Sedano Tamarón, vale lo que se va a decir; si no, sobra todo lo que se dirá: ya es sabido que, a veces, fallan las fuentes históricas y se arman unos bochinches de cien mil pares de diablos (o de pelotas, a elegir). Pepita y Paquita cantan zarzuelas. Pepita y Paquita van algo estreñidas. A Pepita y a Paquita las plantaron los novios, etc. Pasemos a la otra acera, a la de la moto con sidecar. La abeja con calva de cura que se asoma al balcón del segundo de la primera casa, se llama Joaquín, a secas. Si no se llama Joaquín, a secas, cae por su base el cuento. Joaquín, a secas, fue maestro antes de que lo pusieran en la calle por republicano. Joaquín, a secas, tuvo amores con la señora de un coronel de carabineros que se llamaba Leonorcita Mayoral. La Leonorcita era algo bestia e indiscreta, aunque de buen ver y palpar, y Joaquín, a secas, cuando se hartó, la mandó a paseo y volvió al buen camino del que jamás debiera haberse apartado. La abeja de pelo blanco que se asoma al balcón del primero de la segunda casa, es la abuela de los dos niños del portal. No es porque nosotros lo digamos, ni porque lo diga ella, pero lo cierto es que los lleva muy curiosines y bien puestos. La abeja que se asoma al balcón del primero de la tercera casa, queda ya algo lejos para que se le pueda leer la historia en las rayas de la frente.

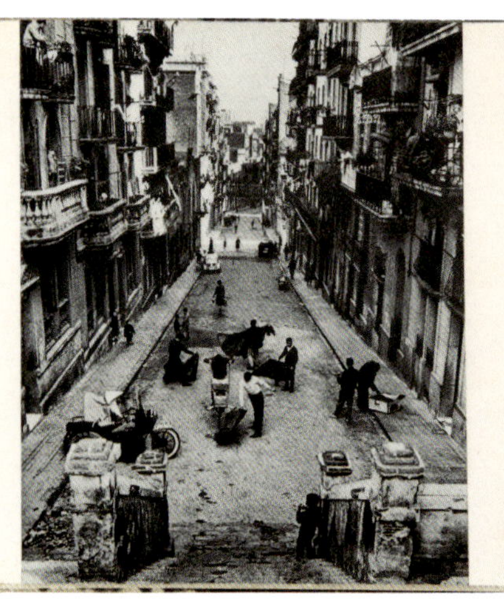

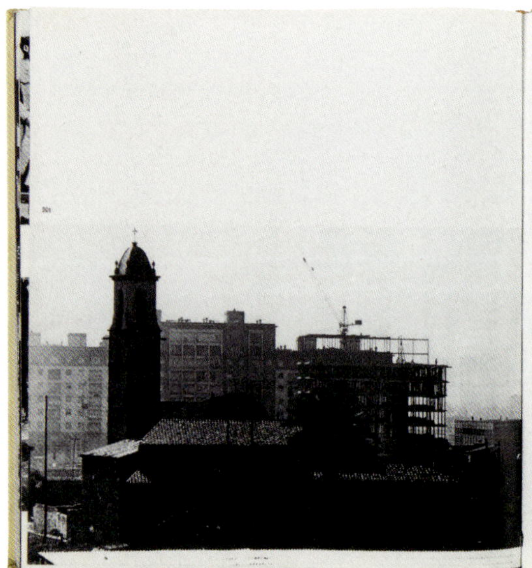

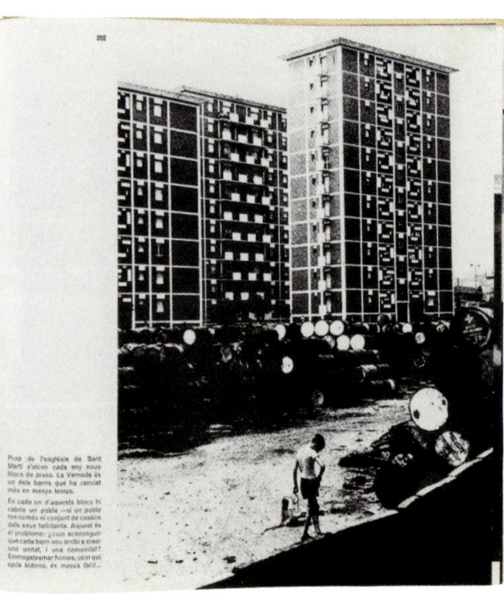

Oriol Maspons and **Julio Oubiña**
Toreo de salón: farsa con acompañamiento de clamor y murga
Book
23 × 22 cm
Barcelona: Lumen, Palabra e Imagen, 1963
With text by Camilo José Cela

Xavier Miserachs
Barcelona blanc i negre
Book
33.3 × 31.2 cm
Barcelona: Aymà, 1964
With a prologue by Joan Oliver
and texts by Josep Maria Espinàs

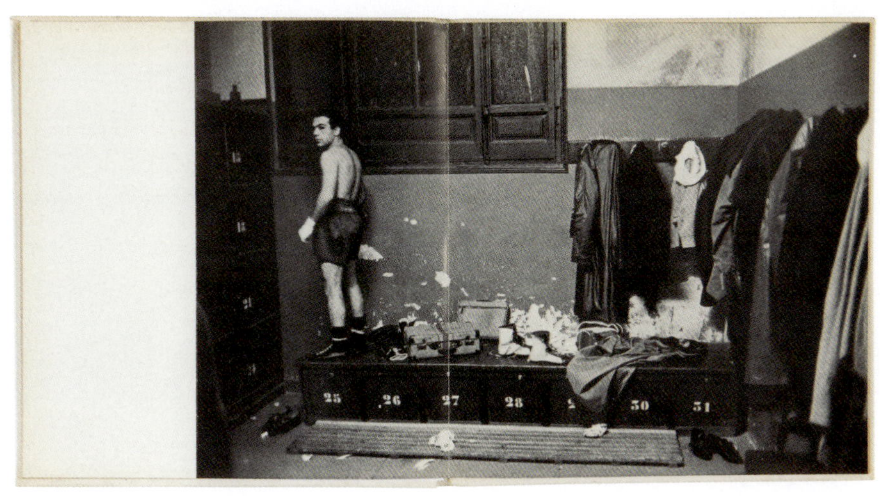

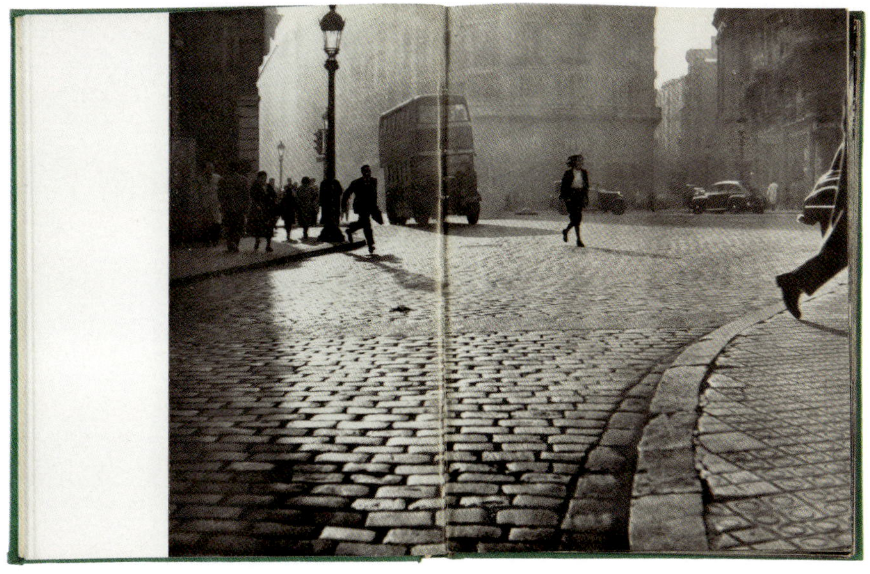

Ramón Masats
Neutral Corner
Book
23 × 22 cm
Barcelona: Lumen, Palabra e Imagen, 1962
With text by Ignacio Aldecoa

Francesc Català-Roca
Barcelona
Book
29 × 23 cm
Barcelona: Barna, 1954
With text by Luis Romero

«Il n'y a pas de film. Le cinéma est mort. Il ne peut plus
y avoir de films. Passons si vous voulez au débat.»

Guy-Ernest Debord

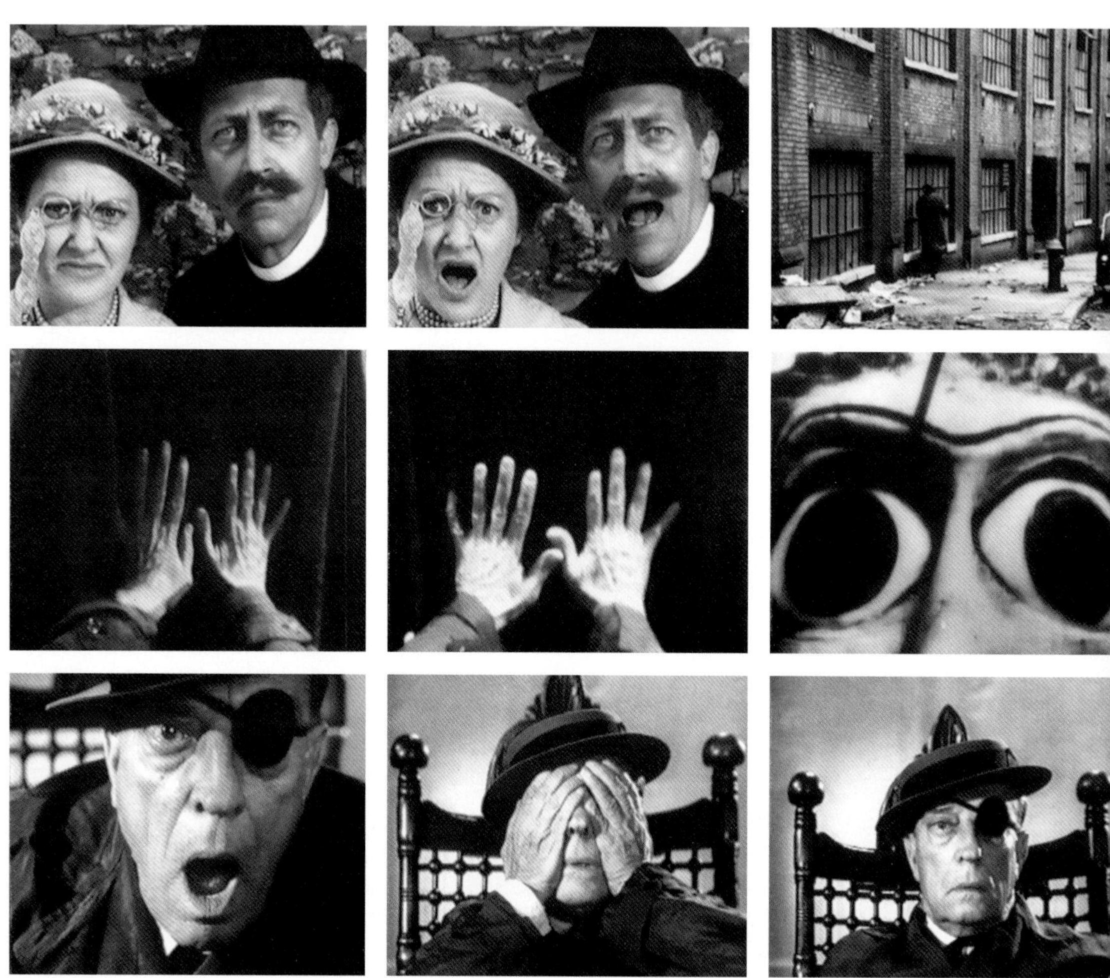

Samuel Beckett
Film, 1965
16 mm film transferred to video,
b/w, silent, 20 min
Produced and distributed by Barnet Rosset

<
Guy Debord
Hurlements en faveur de Sade, 1952
Single-channel video, b/w, sound, 64 min

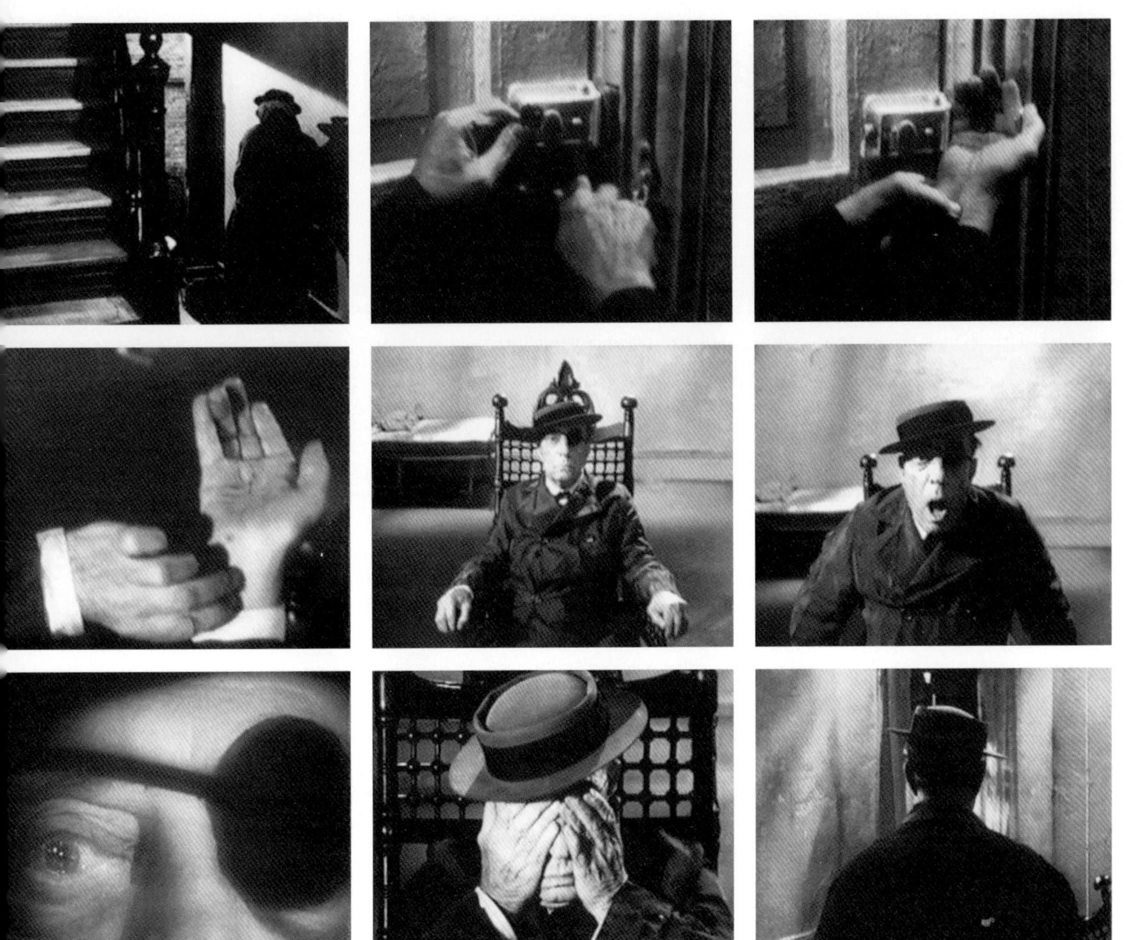

Discursive Turns: Language, Institution, Cinema.
The Late Fifties to Seventies

From the late fifties through to the seventies, artists explored the various modalities
of spoken and written language, be it through Fluxus event-scores or by engaging
in discursive practices that were socially, institutionally and historically pertinent.
While contemporaneous with the widespread development of structuralism in the
humanities, the works incorporated into the MACBA Collection present alternatives
to the dominant understanding of language as a system as well as the assumption
in communication theories that mass media served as neutral transmitters of
information.[13] As pertains to the history of Conceptual art in particular, the Collection
provides a more inclusive theoretical framework that draws out the complex
interrelationships between artistic experimentation, geopolitical context and identity.
In this way, it challenges Joseph Kosuth's tautological version of Conceptual
art – i.e., art as idea as idea – but also Conceptual art's status as an 'aesthetics of
administration'.[14]

The conditions that determine visual communication and art's institutions
came increasingly to bear in the work of artists in the wake of May 1968. At this
time, some artists, such as Marcel Broodthaers and Hans Haacke, took art's
institutions as their subject and object, while others challenged cinema's
conventions through film and video practices that activated the live context of
viewing, thereby transforming cinema into a site of multiple and heterogeneous
experiences.

By the late fifties, painters, poets, sculptors and publishers increasingly moved
toward dissolving the distinction between art and life, and participated in
international artist groups such as Fluxus. Dieter Roth's books, like his Fluxus
contemporaries and Dick Higgins's Something Else Press, use language and
the page as alternative sites for art production. In addition, by using food as a

13 See the critique of communication
theory in Jean Baudrillard, *For a Critique
of the Political Economy of the Sign*.
St. Louis: Telos Press, 1981, esp.
pp. 178–81; trans. Charles Levin.
14 Benjamin H. D. Buchloh, 'Conceptual
Art 1962–69, From the Aesthetic of
Administration to the Critique
of Institutions', *October*, no. 55, Winter
1990, pp. 105–43.

sculptural material (in particular, dairy products such as cheese and yogurt, which curdle and mould) and including these in his books, Roth's interest in organic transformation became part of his consistent strategy to subvert the mechanisms of art's commercialisation. This strategy also extends to his sculpture and reliefs such as the *Untitled (Kleiner Schimmelhaufen)* (1968) in the Collection. This attitude of challenging art's commercialisation is also echoed in the work of his contemporary George Brecht whose *Water Yam*, originally published in 1963, is represented in the MACBA Collection (Brecht was also the subject of a 2006 exhibition at the MACBA curated by Julia Robinson and Alfred Fischer and organised by the Ludwig Museum, Cologne). Designed by George Maciunas and typeset by Tomas Schmitt, this artist's multiple is one of Fluxus's most representative works, and includes a large number of printed cards with instructions known as 'event-scores'. These scores, contrary to Conceptual art's emphasis on ideation, use language as a means by which to enact the slippage between a general schema (or system) and its specific realisations in the everyday.[15]

The desire to subvert a general schema is taken up specifically in the work of stanley brouwn, who was exposed to Fluxus in Amsterdam's art scene at the beginning of the sixties. Among other activities, brouwn engages various ways of measuring his environment. To move from point A to point B is a basic daily activity for which brouwn devised his own subjective measurement units (the 'sb-foot', the 'sb-ell' and the 'sb-step'). In this way, he counters the universally adopted metric system or other, often obsolete, units of measure; his work *ten steps* (1975) derives from such a process.

In this context, one of brouwn's quotes is also particularly relevant: 'Publications are lasting exhibitions.'[16] This statement is pertinent in relation to the MACBA's acquisition of *Aspen*, the multimedia magazine in a box conceived by Phyllis Johnson. Published between 1965 and 1971, each of *Aspen*'s ten issues were delivered to the subscribers in a box that contained materials produced on diverse supports: printed material, sound recordings, reels of Super 8 film, etc. Each number had a different designer and editor and dealt with subjects ranging from mass media and Pop art to Fluxus and the arts of Asia. Some of the leading artists of the twentieth century counted among its contributors, including Marcel Duchamp, John Cage and Stan VanDerBeek.

15 See Liz Kotz, 'Language Between
Performance and Photography', *October*,
no. 111, Winter 2005, pp. 3–21.
16 See brouwn's statement as cited on
www.macba.cat/controller.php?p_action=
show_page&pagina_id=29&inst_id=22000
(accessed December 2009).

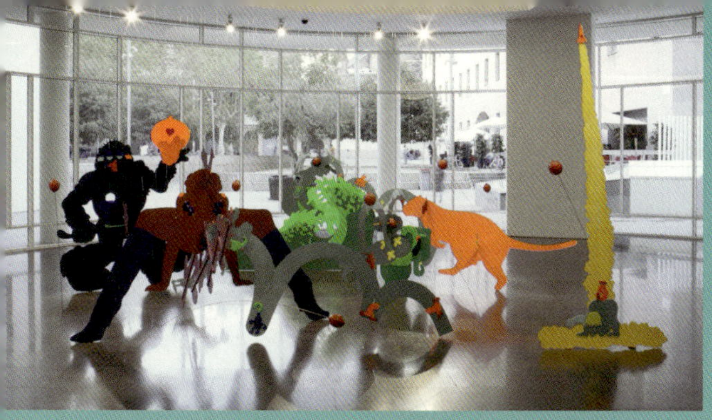

Öyvind Fahlström, 2000

In this historical context, Öyvind Fahlström's work is quite singular. Despite his longstanding involvement with a 'technological/conceptual' aesthetic, Fahlström was also profoundly concerned with *iconography* in his work. Certain images appear again and again in diverse forms and are culled from various sources, including comics, magazines, documentary films and newspapers. A crucial event for understanding his work occurred when Hal Glicksman showed him a series of *Zap* comic books during a visit to Los Angeles in March 1969. The first issue of *Zap* appeared in October 1967 and was circulated as an underground publication out of San Francisco. *Zap* featured comic strips by artist Robert Crumb, among others. The first issue, no. 0, provided not only a rich catalogue of images for Fahlström, but also the title of his work *Meatball Curtain (for R. Crumb)* (1969), which forms part of the MACBA Collection. Unlike the Pop artists with whom he is often associated, Fahlström's use of comic-strip figures is filled with complex mythological content. In addition to the various works included in the Collection, the Öyvind Fahlström Archive is also housed at the MACBA.

If artists associated with Fluxus used language and the page as alternative sites for artistic production, a subsequent generation self-reflexively made an artistic practice out of reframing institutional frames. In 1968 Marcel Broodthaers founded the *Musée d'Art Moderne, Département des Aigles, Section XIXième siècle*, a four-year project that initially began in the artist's studio in Brussels. As a 'fictive' institution, Broodthaers's Musée nevertheless engaged in the discursive activities of a real one: as the museum's 'director' the artist circulated *lettres ouvertes* stamped with the 'official' name and address of the Musée, organised inaugural speeches, exhibitions of its various sections, as well as publicity campaigns.[17] In the summer of 1972 at the Städtische Kunsthalle in Düsseldorf, Broodthaers presented the museum's 'Section des Figures' under the title *The Eagle from the Oligocene to the Present*. Amassing 266 works that represented eagles, the exhibition borrowed objects from 43 'real' museums and private collections, including Broodthaers's own. Displayed in glass cases or hung on the wall, each eagle (from its presence in banal objects such as postage stamps to its uses in military iconography and advertising) was accompanied by a small plastic plaque that replaced the conventional exhibition label with the statement 'This is not a work of art' printed in English, French or German. As remarked by Broodthaers, the statement 'This is not a work of art' derives from 'a formula obtained by the contraction of a concept by Duchamp and an antithetical concept by Magritte'.[18] But he critically elaborates the implications of these earlier strategies by shifting the stakes from what objects can or cannot legitimately be called art to the institutional authority that underwrites museum classification and display. This critique is instantiated in his museum labels and their relationship to his rather absurd presentation of eagles from all media and genres, both high and low. With his shift from art producer to administrator and his cultivation of a series of museum fictions, Broodthaers draws attention to the language and institutions within which art and its discourse is framed.

Part of the editions by Marcel Broodthaers in the MACBA Collection relates to his project *Le Corbeau et le Renard* (1967), which, inspired by an eponymous poem by La Fontaine, was originally presented and rejected at Knokke, the International Festival of Independent Film in Belgium. Here Broodthaers replaced the conventional screen for the film's projection. He explains: 'In order to integrate text and object, I would have to print on the screen the same typographic characters I had used in the film.'[19] In this way, his work in cinema provided Broodthaers with a new writing model, whereby he affirms: 'For me, films are the continuation of language. I began with poetry, then plastic arts and finally cinema, which brings together various elements of art. That is to say: writing (poetry), objects (plastic arts) and image (film).'[20] The work thus engages the legacy of poetry in the visual arts and the work of Stéphane Mallarmé more specifically, a subject taken up and

17 See Benjamin H. D. Buchloh's entry for '1972a', in Hal Foster, Rosalind Krauss, Yve-Alain Bois and Benjamin H. D. Buchloh (eds.), *Art Since 1900: Modernism, Antimodernism, Postmodernism*. New York: Thames and Hudson, 2004, pp. 549–53.
18 Marcel Broodthaers, 'Ten Thousand Francs Reward', trans. Paul Schmidt, *October*, no. 42, Autumn 1987, p. 47.
19 Ibid., p. 36.

20 See Broodthaers's statement as cited on www.macba.cat/controller.php?p_action= show_page&pagina_id=70&inst_id=16063 (accessed December 2009).

explored in the exhibition *Art and Utopia. Restricted Action* curated by Jean-François Chevrier and presented at the MACBA in 2004.

If, alongside his poetic action, Broodthaers conjured strategic museum fictions, Hans Haacke turned to pure facts and deployed the visual presentation of data through his use of statistics, graphs and surveys in order to emphasise the 'functional dimension of the aesthetic construct' and take 'the relations of power as the subject of his constructs'.[21] Jointly acquired with The Whitney Museum of American Art, the MACBA's Haacke acquisition, *Shapolsky et al. Manhattan Real Estate Holdings, A Real Time System, as of May 1, 1971* (1971), includes a map of the Lower East Side and Harlem, 142 data sheets next to photos of urban properties and 6 charts on business transactions. The work exploits the evidentiary character of documentary photography in order to trace the ownership of these slum properties to corporations that include members of the Shapolsky family or that had real estate dealings with them. These 'facts', which reveal the Shapolsky real estate group as a 'slumlord' hiding behind various corporation names, ultimately resulted in Guggenheim Director Thomas Messer's cancellation of Haacke's solo exhibition at the Museum that same year. In doing so, Messer claimed he had removed 'an alien substance that had entered the art museum organism'.[22] Given Messer's adamant stance, it is often assumed that members of the Guggenheim Board of Trustees had investments in Shapolsky properties, although there is no evidence to support this claim.

While artists such as Marcel Broodthaers and Hans Haacke revealed art's imbrications in epistemic and economic formations, other artists turned more specifically to experimentation between cinema and the visual arts – be it in the materialist aesthetics of structural film or the heterogeneous practices of what has come to be termed 'expanded cinema'. In the sixties the materiality of film became the self-reflexive subject and object of film practice, as fixed camera position, flicker effect, loop printing and re-photography off the screen became structural film's defining techniques.[23] This anti-illusionist bent took various forms – from Michael Snow's 'movement of the camera as the movement of consciousness'[24] to works such as Malcom Le Grice's *Berlin Horse* (1970), which 'attempts to compare some of the paradoxes of the relationship between

21 Benjamin H. D. Buchloh, 'Hans Haacke: Memory and Instrumental Reason', *Art in America* 76, no. 2, February 1988, pp. 97–108, 157–59.
22 As cited in *'Obra Social': Hans Haacke*. Barcelona: Fundació Antoni Tàpies, 1995, p. 72.
23 See P. Adams Sitney's discussion of structuralist film in his *Visionary Film: The American Avant-Garde 1943–2000*. New York: Oxford University Press, 2002, p. 348.
24 See Annette Michelson's, 'Toward Snow' in *Artforum* 9, no. 10, June 1971, pp. 30–37.

the "real" time experienced when making the film, with the "real" time experienced when the film is screened'.[25] Here, each filmmaker emphasises film's materiality, uncoupling film from both narrative and illusionism. Also at this time, some independent filmmakers who did not necessarily identify themselves as 'artists' began to consider film's sculptural dimensions through an attention to film's emulsion, the sound of the projector and the space between projector and wall. In this vein, Anthony McCall's *Line Describing a Cone* (1973) works with a projector and light to create an immaterial cone in space. First shown in the context of 'independent film', *Line Describing a Cone* has only been more recently displayed in art museums in tandem with the growing interest in the 'projected image' in contemporary art.[26]

Other works in the MACBA Collection similarly aligned with 'expanded cinema' include David Lamelas's *Film Script (La manipulación del mensaje)* (1972), which offers a number of ways to interpret key narrative elements through its disruption of sequence in the three slide projections presented alongside the film. VALIE EXPORT's *Cutting* (1967) deals with the technique of 'cutting' or editing. In this work, EXPORT dramatises the materiality of the projection screen, which variously appears as a paper, a cloth T-shirt and a naked body, while she manipulates these materials in order to explore forms of communication and mediation. With *Attack Piece* (1975), Dara Birnbaum shows the material filmed during a performance between her and a number of actors (among them Dan Graham). One monitor presents the static images shot by Birnbaum with a 35 mm camera in self-defence against her 'attackers'. The second monitor shows the moving images taken by the 'intruders' who were using a Super 8 camera.

While there is much debate about what terms such as 'expanded cinema', 'film beyond its limits', 'paracinema' (and even 'structuralist film') designate, each of these works opens up questions concerning the spectator's construction of time and space relations. In so doing, they activate the spaces of cinema and narrative as well as other contexts of media reception, including television and video. These works offer an alternative perspective on film production, the construction of social space and the modalities of cultural communication. In its recourse to various materials and supports, 'expanded cinema' shifts away from structural film's emphasis on the materiality of the medium to more explicitly socialised

25 See Le Grice's statement as cited on
www.macba.cat/controller.php?p_action=
show_page&pagina_id=29&inst_id=19563
(accessed December 2009).
26 See, for example, the catalogue of
the exhibition curated by Chrissie Iles,
*Into the Light: The Projected Image in
American Art, 1964–1977*. New York:
The Whitney Museum of Art, 2001.

acts of seeing and ultimately visitor participation, as seen in works such as Hélio Oiticica and Neville d'Almeida's *CC3-Maileryn. Quasi Cinema (a Block-Experiment in Cosmococa-Program in Progress)* of 1973.

Other artists such as Bruce Nauman and Vito Acconci also eventually turned to film and video after their respective beginnings as a painter and poet. Nauman quickly abandoned painting and from 1966–70 created photographs, imprints, casts and linguistic signs that were self-reflexive investigations of the artist as author. During this period, he turned to considerations of behaviour, documenting himself in video while performing everyday non-spectacular actions such as walking, pacing and jumping. *Art Make-Up* (1967–68) in the MACBA Collection consists of four related films in which Nauman applies a successive layer of coloured make-up (white, pink, green and finally black) to his face and upper torso. While he masks himself literally, the title implies that he also 'makes himself up'.

   In his first poetic works from the mid-sixties, Acconci treated the blank page as a space where he could act, using words as material for movement and the page as a container. Later on, his actions moved from paper to gallery space, evolving into performances in which Acconci reflected on his own physical and psychological being. In one of his earliest films, *Three Frame Studies* (1969), Acconci performs a series of actions – running in a circle, jumping, pushing another man – in which the physical limits of the action refer to the boundaries of the film frame itself.

Conceptual art inaugurated a paradigm shift in art from materials to ideas, images to concepts, objects to subjects. In North America it is often understood in relation to what Lucy Lippard famously termed the 'dematerialisation of the art object'. Yet the works in the MACBA Collection challenge this dominant understanding of Conceptual art in order to resituate its varied practices within a larger field of negotiation in the production of artistic and social meanings. This proposes differential models of Conceptualism that respond to local and international politics. For example, the collective project *Tucumán Arde* is one instance of a politicised Conceptualism in Latin America. In 1968 a group of artists, journalists and sociologists in Buenos Aires and Rosario (Argentina),

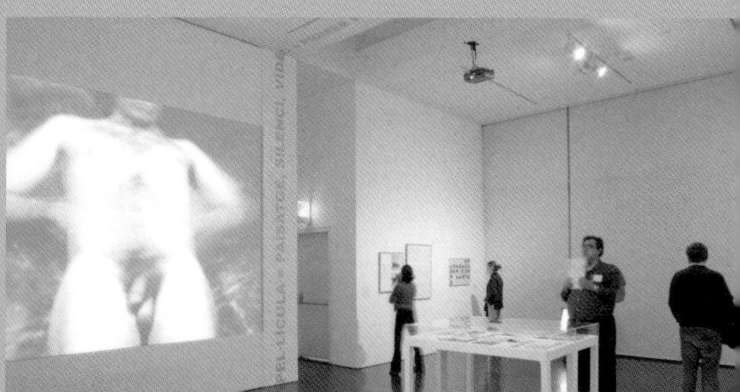
>
Vito Hannibal Acconci Studio, 2004

including Graciela Carnevale, León Ferrari, Roberto Jacoby and Norberto Puzzolo, began a project to investigate the consequences of neoliberal economic policies in Latin America. With their action *Tucumán Arde*, they aimed to expose the crisis in Tucumán through an analysis of 'Operativo Tucumán', which was launched by the Argentine dictatorship in 1966. *Tucumán Arde* acted outside of official communication channels in order to condemn the crisis in the region. In the words of one of the group's members (whose prints also form part of the MACBA Collection), León Ferrari: '*Tucumán Arde* used art to do politics. Many conceptual artists and certain examples of contemporary political art use politics as a theme for doing art.'[27]

A politicised Conceptualism also defines Grup de Treball, who worked from 1973 to 1975 and marked a turning point in Catalan culture. As with *Tucumán Arde*, their work was collective and moved away from conventional artistic practices in order to engage art's social function. Their brief contribution, well defined and documented in the MACBA Collection and in the museum's 1999 exhibition *Grup de Treball*, occurred during an unstable political climate defined by the increased repression of the final years of the fascist regime. At this time, Pere Portabella also became a key figure in the development of an independent, clandestine cinematographic practice that was intimately linked to his political opposition to the dictatorship. His films in the MACBA Collection, including *Vampir-Cuadecuc* (1970) and *Umbracle* (1971–72), together with his participation in the Grup de Treball were radical interventions in the cinema and art worlds.

In the historical context of Spain's transition to democracy, the work of Muntadas takes as its point of departure a critical analysis of communication media and the forms of transmission. At a time when the Spanish state only had one official television station, which was controlled by Franco's regime, Muntadas created *Punt d'informació. Cadaqués Canal Local* (July 1974) and *Punto de información. Barcelona Distrito Uno* (October 1976). Both these works contrasted with the dominant public television in order to work in a determinate place and its community. With *Punto de Información. Barcelona Distrito Uno*, Muntadas used an art gallery, in this case the Galería Ciento in Barcelona, to present documents related to his previous work but also as a base of operations for developing an alternative television. This work attempts to develop a neighbourhood (or district) television, extending

27 See Ferrari's statement cited on
www.macba.cat/controller.php?p_action=
show_page&pagina_id=29&inst_id=19583
(accessed December 2009).

from the Born (former central market area) to the popular Rambla. For the site of transmission, Muntadas chose a small bar in La Barceloneta (the maritime quarter) in which the TV was oriented toward its public on the terrace. In this way, as Eugeni Bonet explains: '[Muntadas] keeps one foot in the field of art and tries to firmly place the other in public space and in communication media.'[28]

Formed in 1977, the video collective Vídeo-Nou actually borrowed Muntadas's portapack before acquiring their own equipment. Carles Ameller, one of the group's members, defined Vídeo-Nou as 'the first independent video collective in the Spanish state that worked in the field of social intervention so as to realise the contextual use of electronic communication media'.[29] Attempting to contribute to the decentralisation of power, their main goal was the reappropriation of communication media so that various local communities in Barcelona could become agents of their own representations through what the group called 'acciones de video sociológico/video de animación social' (sociological video actions/social mobilisation video). Their work, in addition to other artistic and political initiatives in Spain, was presented in 2005 in the context of *Desacuerdos. Sobre arte, políticas y esfera pública en el Estado español* (Disagreements. On Art, Politics and the Public Sphere in Spain), a research project and exhibition-event programme produced by the MACBA in collaboration with other institutions throughout Spain.

While she produced some of her seminal work at the time of Conceptual art's rise to prominence, Nancy Spero's practice established an alternative, or what Benjamin H. D. Buchloh calls 'other', modernist tradition. Her work at once articulates a critique of New York School painting and also develops a model of language at odds with the analytic propositions of Conceptual art. Her series of *Artaud Paintings* (1969–70), a sample of which was acquired by the MACBA, testifies to her simultaneous infiltration of painting with writing as well as her development of writing's somatic dimensions. As Buchloh maintains in his pioneering text on her work: 'The countersublimatory impulse operates thus throughout Spero's work, consistently negating the privilege of the pictorial over the literary just as much as it defaces the triumphant claims of the "language" of Conceptual art.'[30]

Other female artists similarly developed a politics of language, while nevertheless deploying the visual vocabulary of conceptualism (e.g., photography,

28 See Eugeni Bonet, 'La televisión, de frente y de perfil', in *Muntadas: La construcción del miedo y la pérdida de lo público*. Granada: Centro José Guerrero/Diputación de Granada, 2008, p. 19. The original Spanish reads: '[Muntadas] mantiene un pie en el terreno del arte y trata de hincar el otro en el espacio público y en los medios de comunicación.'
29 See Carles Ameller, 'Por una comunicación contextual. La experiencia de Vídeo-Nou/Servei de Video Comunitari', in *Banda aparte*, no. 16, October 1999, p. 46. The original Spanish reads: 'como el primer colectivo de vídeo independiente del Estado español que trabaja en el campo de la intervención social potenciando el uso contextual de los medios de comunicación electrónicos.'
30 Benjamin H. D. Buchloh, 'Spero's Other Traditions' (1996), reprinted in *Nancy Spero: Dissidances*. Barcelona: MACBA, 2008, p. 86.

alternative supports such as magazines and video, the 'look' of information, and seriality) in order to probe the construction of gender and the politics of representation. In her influential video *Semiotics of the Kitchen* (1975), Martha Rosler begins her demonstration of kitchen utensils in alphabetical order (from 'apron' to 'tenderiser') in the style of a seemingly straight TV feature. Through her deadpan presentation, Rosler addresses the inherent violence of 'the Woman in the kitchen' through the alphabet as system. In demonstrating women's instrumentalised position, Rosler ultimately turns herself into a tool.

Subject of the exhibition *Jo Spence. Beyond the Perfect Image* curated by Jorge Ribalta and Terry Dennett in 2005, the work of Jo Spence plays a crucial role in the debates surrounding photography and the critique of representation. More specifically, Spence explores the ways that social identities are constructed through the still image. As author and model, she deploys photography as a catalyst of rebellion and therapy in the face of the symbolic violence resulting from the dominant images produced by and for mainstream culture.

This section ends with *Numax Presenta...* (1980), a film by Joaquim Jordà. The film describes the self-management experience of a group of workers (also the film's producers) at Numax, an electronics factory in Barcelona. The film captures the workers' attempts to stop the factory from being shut down by its owners. The film alternates between black and white scenes of the workers' assemblies and individual narrative accounts, and the portrayal of the owners' hypothetical viewpoint filmed in colour and presented in an exaggerated theatrical mode. In this way, the film juxtaposes two antithetical contents (i.e., the workers' and owners' positions) as well as two aesthetic registers (i.e., the black and white of 'documentary' with the staginess and mannered expression characteristic of bourgeois theatre). While it begins as a militant film, *Numax Presenta...* ends with the workers opting to end the strike and have a party, thereby signalling a new epoch when factory work becomes less relevant in the struggle against capitalism. April 1979 was the month of Antonio Negri's imprisonment for his participation in *Autonomia Operaia* in Italy. According to Negri, the seventies represent the decade when capitalism is redirected from the factory to broader forms of social organisation, and hence from a Fordist to the service-information economy that has

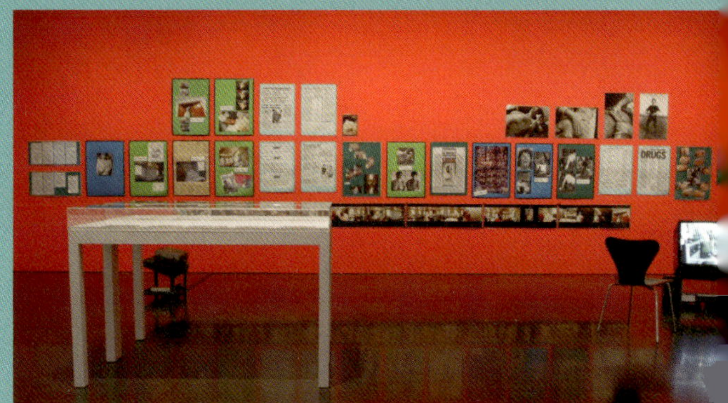

>
Jo Spence. Beyond the Perfect Image, 2005

increasingly come to define the present. Reflecting on *Numax Presenta...* in 2004, Negri explains: 'The new form of work, the new capital no longer generates power without wealth, it produces power and cooperation. If the power of work is born of the spirit, it cannot live in forms that are not free. In *Numax Presenta...* all these things were beginning.'[31]

[31] Antonio Negri, as cited in a lecture at Arteleku on 20 April 2004. See www.universidadnomada.net/IMG/pdf/ Negri_arteleku.pdf (accessed December 2009).

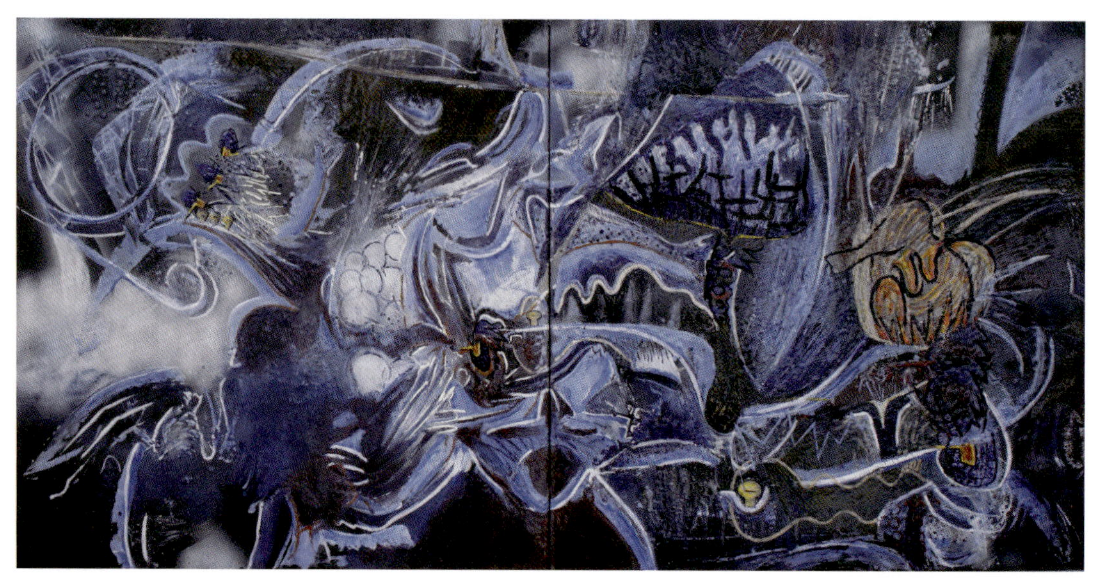

Öyvind Fahlström
Restaurangblandning I (Himlar och Klyftor), created
in March-April 1961 / *Restaurangblandning II
(Soluppgång - Solnedgång)*, created in April-May 1961
Enamelled metal panels
Diptych, 4 pieces at 100 × 100 cm each

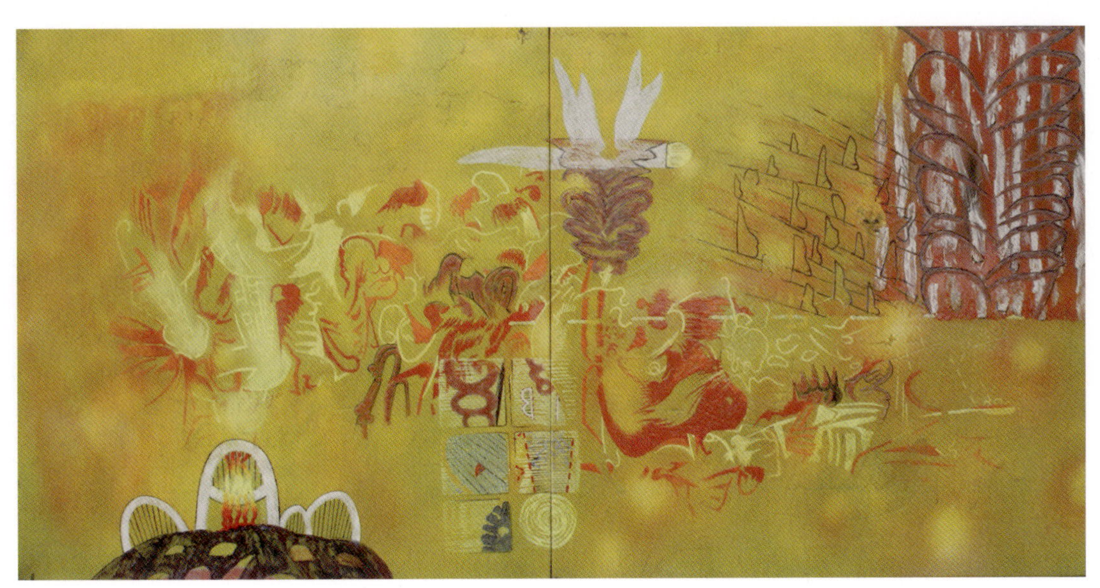

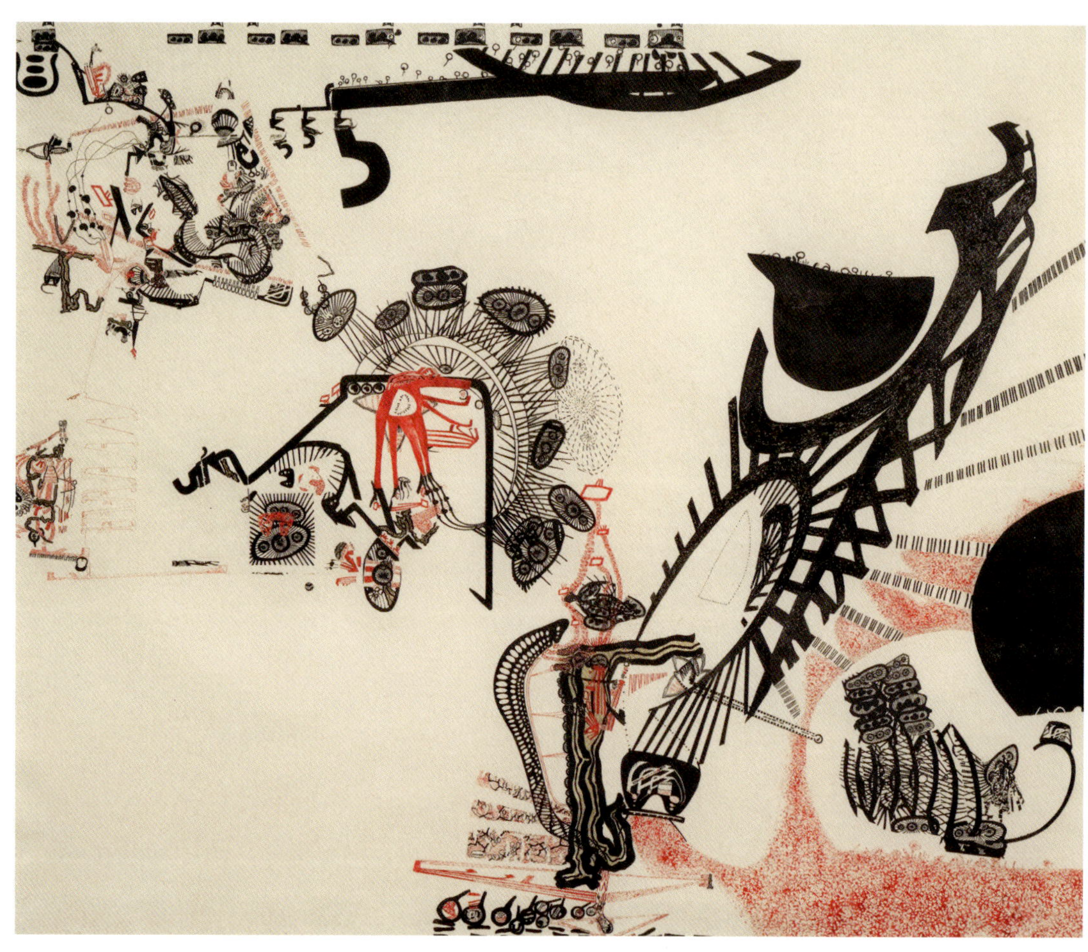

Öyvind Fahlström
Andra kalaset på 'Edlund', 1956
Marker, felt-tip pen and coloured ink on paper
121 × 147.5 cm

Mao-Hope March, 1966
16 mm film, b/w, sound, 4 min 50 s
Director, producer and sound editor: Öyvind Fahlström
Camera and montage: Alfons Schilling
Interviewer: Bob Fass

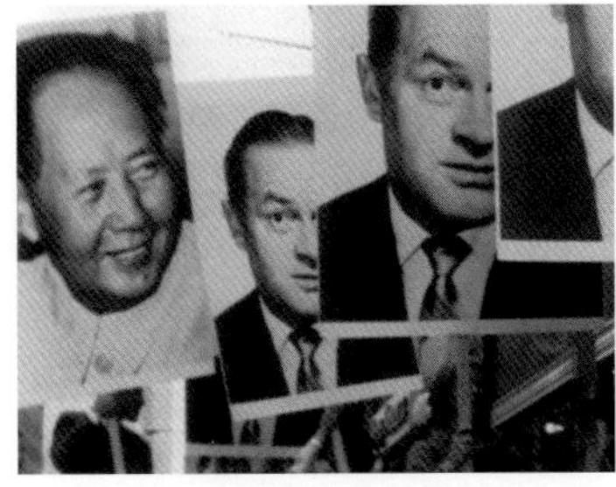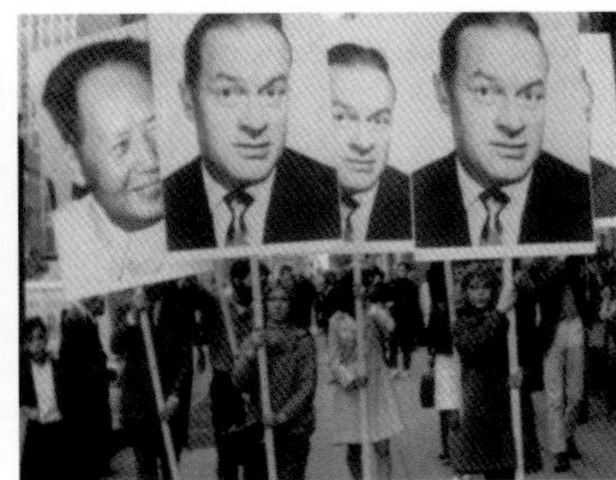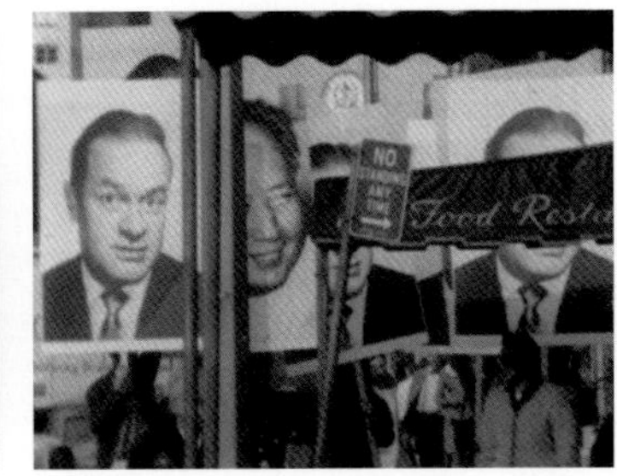

MAO-HOPE MARCH, 1966

Wait a second! Let me see. I don't know.
That isn't Bob Hope but I don't know
who he is. I like Bob Hope, that's for
sure.
Are you happy generally?
Oh yes, I love the television.
What makes you happy?
Television, because I'm very lonesome
without....
Are you happy?
Very tough question. Up and down.
How about you, sir? Are you happy?
Yes, I just came back from Mexico.
Why not? I went all through the States
to Mexico, why shouldn't I be happy?
I went on that $99 thing that
Greyhound gave out. I took every day
the world what it was. So why shouldn't
I be happy? And with this Bob Hope
thing, I think it's a publicity campaign
because he was on TV the other day
and probably his book that he did or
something about Russia.
And what's the connection with Mao Tse
Tung?
The connection? That I wouldn't know
now. Let's say he's in town for some sort
of publicity, that's all.
Is Mao in town?
Bob Hope.
Oh, I thought you meant that Mao Tse
Tung was in town.
No. Well not that I know of.
Was it a strike against something? Are
they protesting somebody? They're
running Bob Hope for some kind of
political office?
There's somebody else's picture there,
too.
Yeah, I don't recognize the other fellow.
Recognize Bob Hope, though.
Who's the other fellow?
What is that? The Chinese general
marshal? Whatever the fella's name is.
Is that a Japanese? Is he Korean?
What do you call it? President, General,
whatever he is....
Who is he?

I see Bob Hope!
Am I happy? Sure, I'm the happiest
person in the world.
Why?
Why? I've got my good health, I work,
have a nice family, so why shouldn't
I be happy?
What do you make out of that? Do you
know?
I don't say. They're all sick in the head,
maybe.
Are you a happy man?
Certainly! Do I look happy, huh?
Why?
Because I live the type of life I do.
What type of life is that?
The type that you don't.
Why are you happy?
No troubles, nothing to bother me.
Nothing to worry about, right? I work,
enjoy life....
You know, it really stops you, you know.
It makes you sort of stop and wonder
what is he running for? Because if you
notice that most of these actors are
going into politics now, like Ronald
Reagan, for instance.
Whose pictures are they?
Bob Hope and I'm not sure of the other
person, but it's, I think it's Mao Tse Tung.
Is there some kind of connection?
I hope not.
The only thing I can think of is that
they're inferring that Bob Hope is
a communist, but....
I wish I knew! Maybe the cops could
help. I don't know. I was just thinking,
maybe we ought to call Bob Hope
and tell him about it.
If you know his number....
I can get it.
Does it make you unhappy?
Very! It doesn't make you happy, does
it? Doesn't make you very happy,
does it?
You seem to be unhappy.
Wouldn't you be? Well, tell me. Let me
ask....

Are you unhappy?
Yes, very!
Well, I think something political,
political going on with a picket line.
Are you generally a happy man?
All the time.
What makes you happy?
The whole world.
Is there anything that makes you
unhappy?
Nothing.
Are they all pictures of Bob Hope?
Yeah.
No, no, there's one different. I don't
know. One looks like what's-his-name
from China.
The premiere, right? Chu? Is it Chu?
Was it Chu?
Was it the premiere from China? Is it?
Huh?
My boy is Bob Hope. I like Bob Hope.
I don't like the other guy.
Are you happy?
Very happy.
Why?
Because I love this country and I love
the people here and I'm very happy.
Are we on television?
No.
Bob Hope for president! Bing Crosby
vice-president!
Is that Mao Tse Tung?
That's right!
Bing Crosby vice-president!
What's it all about?
I wouldn't know.
Can I ask you a question?
Yes, sir.
Are you happy?
Yes, sir.
What makes you happy?
What makes me happy? Seeing
Bob Hope up there, for president.
That's right! Make Bing Crosby
vice-president. That's right! Bing
Crosby vice-president! That's right!

Transcription: Sharon Avery-Fahlström

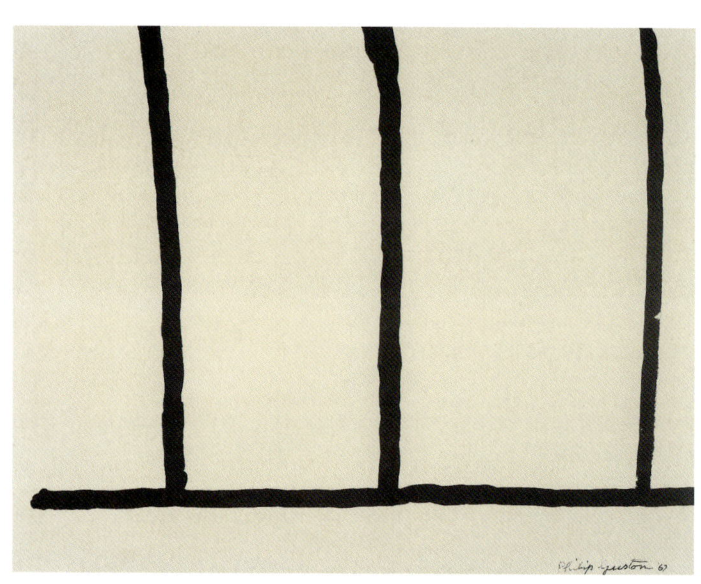

Philip Guston
Horizon, 1967
Ink on paper
44.5 × 58 cm

Mark, 1967
Ink on paper
33 × 41.5 cm

Edge, 1967
Ink on paper
34.5 × 40.5 cm

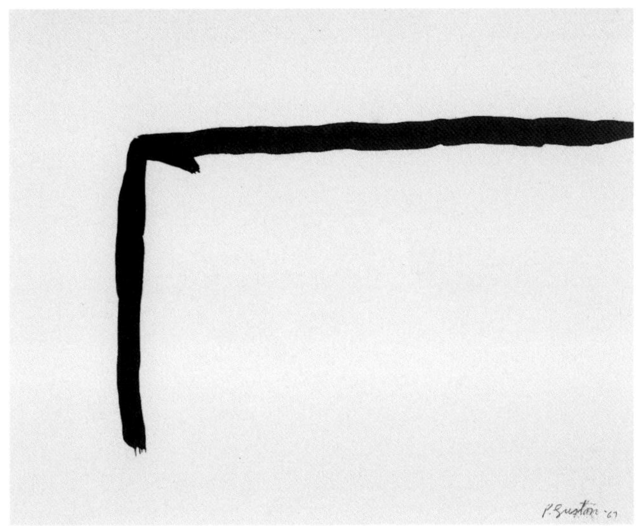

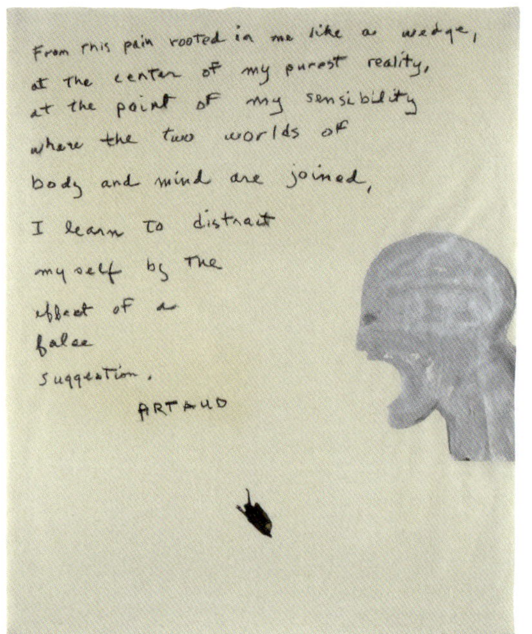

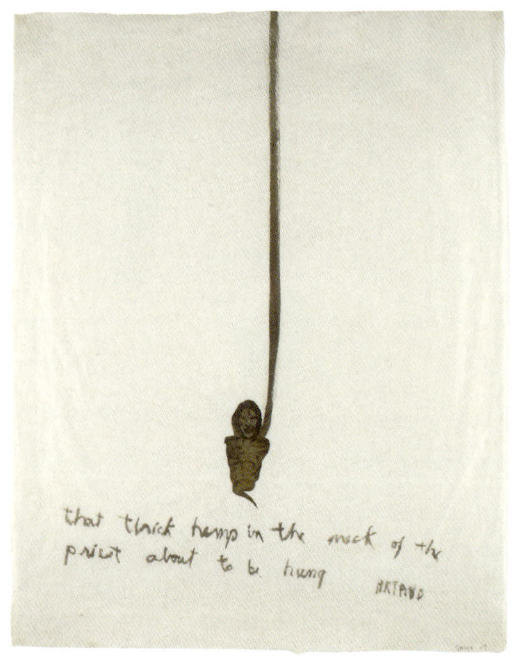

Nancy Spero
Artaud Painting – From this pain..., 1969
Gouache, ink and collage on paper
63.5 × 52.7 cm

*Artaud Painting – That thick hemp in the neck
of the priest about to be hung*, 1969
Gouache, ink and collage on paper
62.9 × 50.8 cm

Artaud Painting – Un nœud d'asphyxie centrale, 1970
Gouache, ink and collage on paper
62.2 × 49.5 cm

*Artaud Painting – Une fatigue de commencement
du monde*, 1970
Gouache, ink and collage on paper
61.6 × 49.5 cm

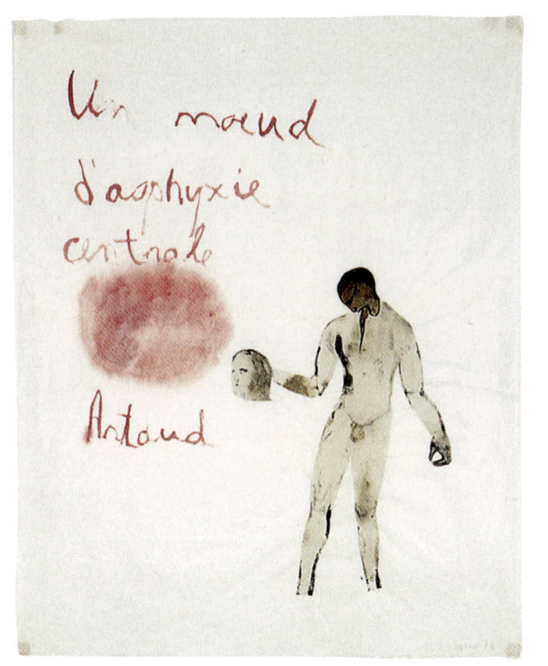

Un nœud
d'asphyxie
centrale

Antaud

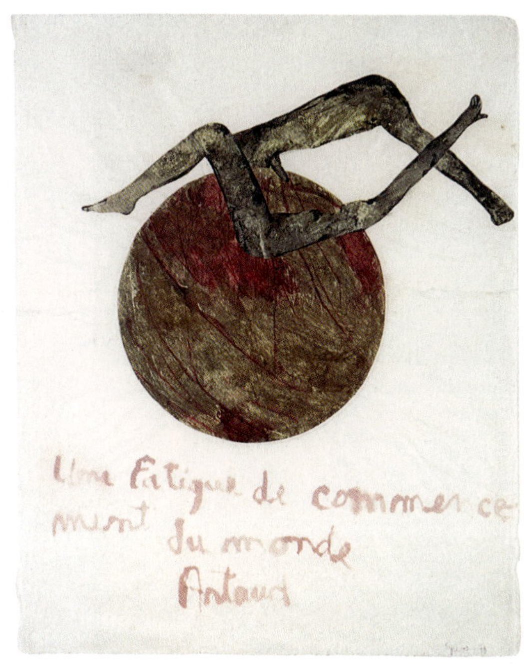

Une fatigue de commence
ment du monde
Antaud

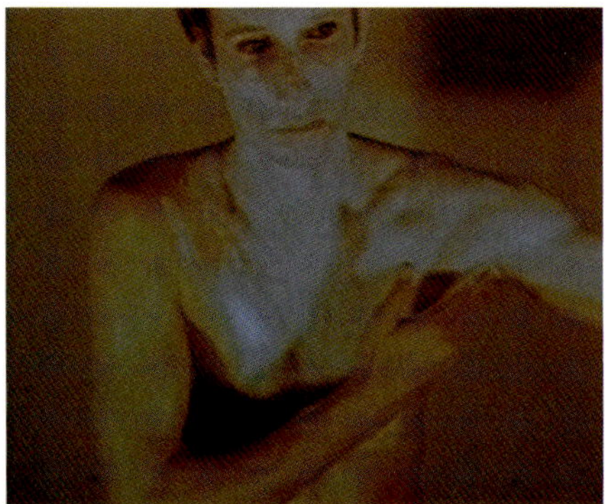

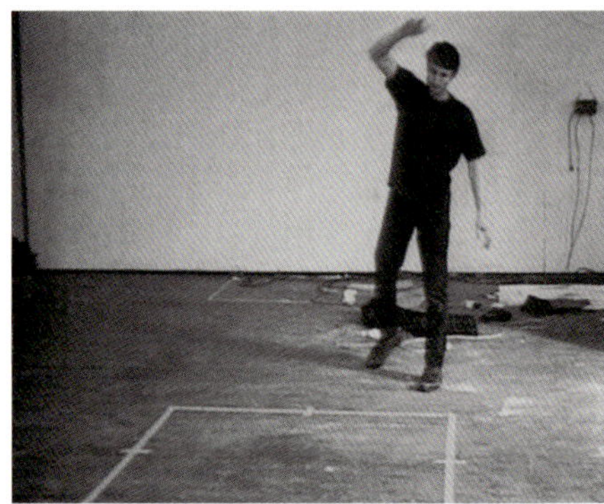

Bruce Nauman
Art Make-Up, 1967–68
16 mm film transferred to video,
colour, silent, 40 min

*Bouncing Two Balls Between the Floor
and Ceiling with Changing Rhythms*, 1968
16 mm film transferred to video,
b/w, sound, 10 min

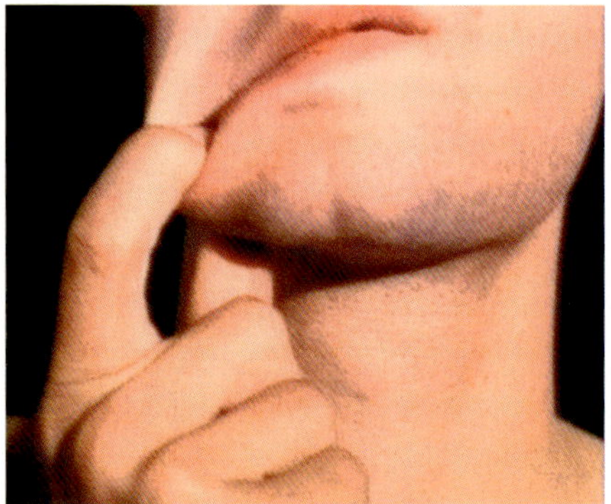

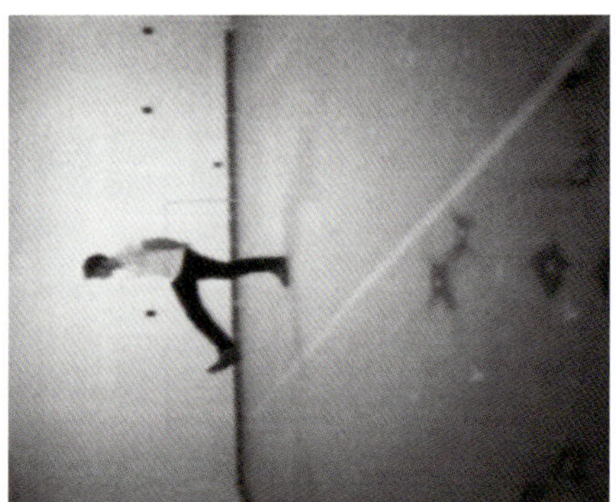

Pinchneck, 1968
16 mm film transferred to video,
colour, silent, 1 min 54 s

Slow Angle Walk (Beckett Walk), 1968
Single-channel video, b/w, sound, 60 min

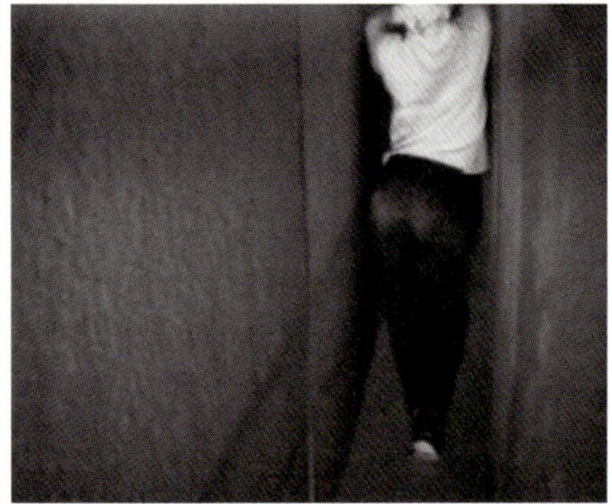

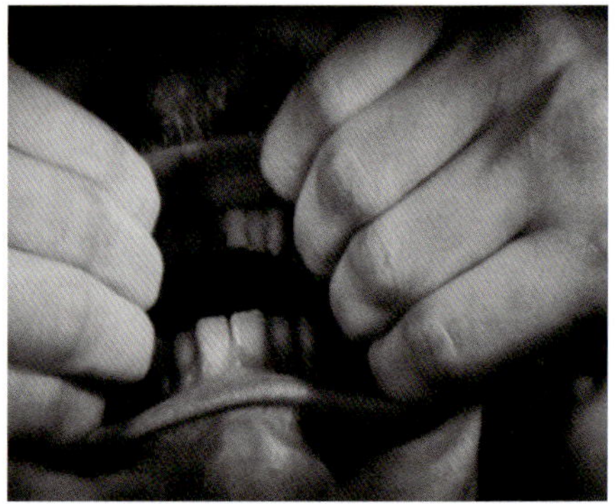

Walk with Contrapposto, 1969
Single-channel video, b/w, sound, 60 min

Pulling Mouth, 1969
Single-channel video, b/w, silent, 8 min

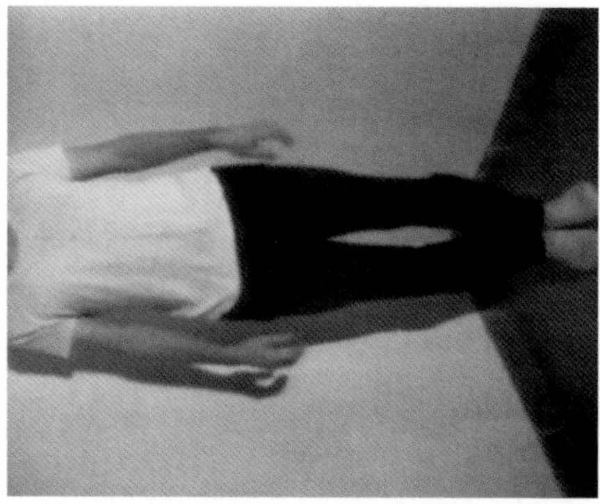

Bouncing on the Corner no. 1, 1968
Single-channel video, b/w, sound, 60 min

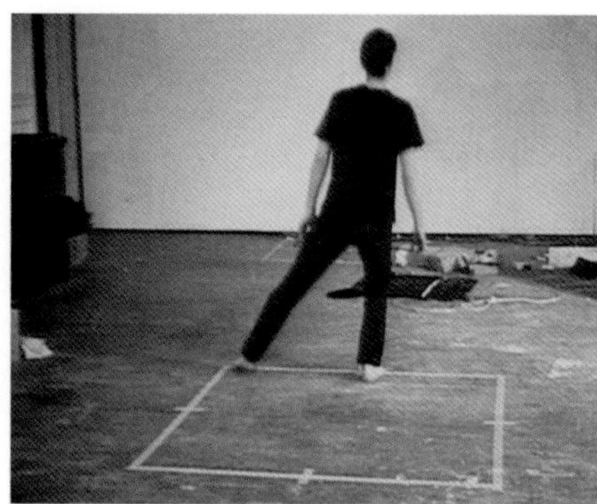

*Dance or Exercise on the Perimeter
of a Square (Square Dance)*, 1968
16 mm film transferred to video,
b/w, sound, 10 min

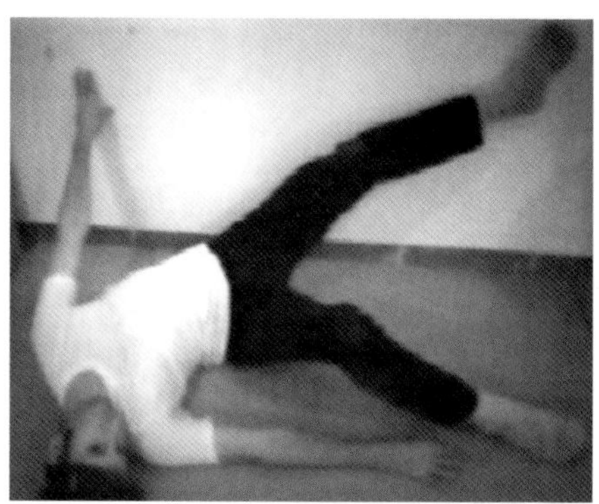

Wall/Floor Positions, 1968
Single-channel video, b/w, silent, 58 min 31 s

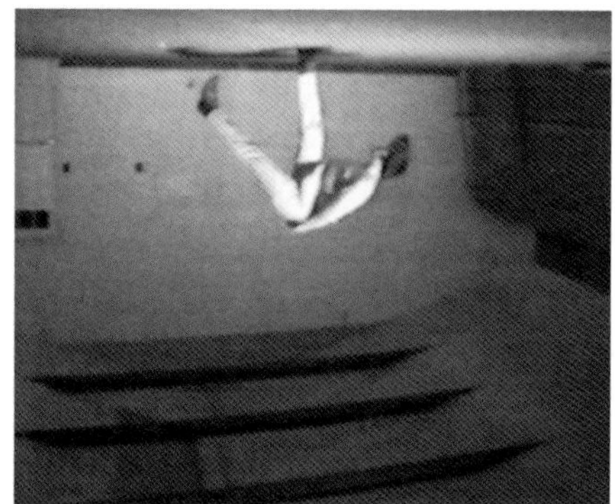

Revolving Upside Down, 1969
Single-channel video, b/w, sound, 61 min

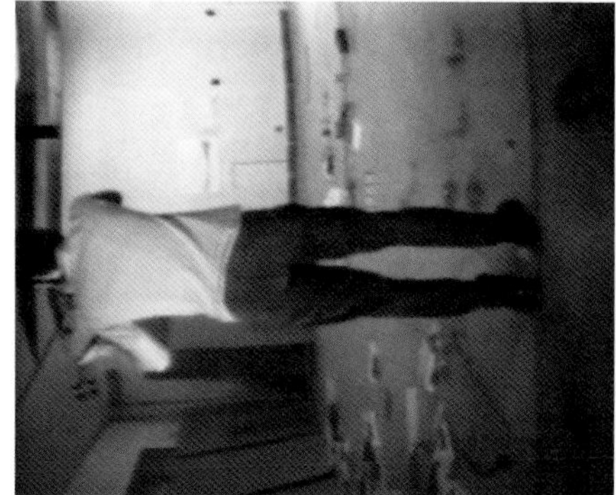

Violin Tuned D.E.A.D, 1969
Single-channel video, b/w, sound, 60 min

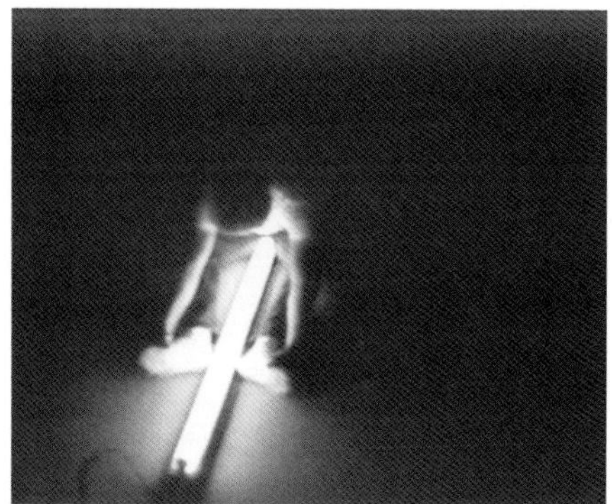

Manipulating a Fluorescent Tube, 1969
Single-channel video, b/w, sound, 62 min

contents

B = LUFURUBUD

$28 = 1 + 4 + 5 + 8 + 10$

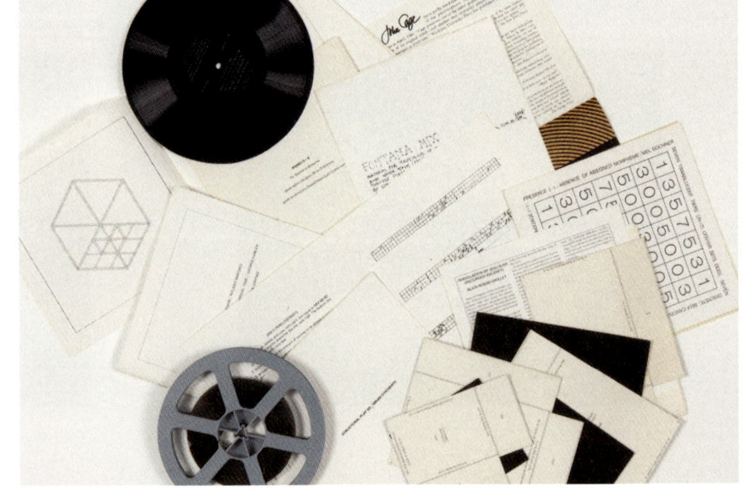

Aspen
*Aspen. The Multimedia Magazine
in a Box, no. 5 + 6, The Minimalism
Issue*, 1967
Publication, diverse elements
Edition and design: Brian O'Doherty
Published by: Phyllis Johnson,
Roaring Fork Press, NYC

book	essays	The Death of the Author/Roland Barthes/trans. Richard Howard
book		Style and the Representation of Historical Time/George Kubler
book		The Aesthetics of Silence/Susan Sontag
record	fiction	Text for Nothing #8/Samuel Beckett/read by Jack MacGowran
record		Nova Express/excerpts/William Burroughs/read by the author
record		"Now the shadow of the southwest column" from Jealousy/Alain Robbe-Grillet/read by the author
record	music	Fontana Mix-Feed/John Cage/realized by Max Neuhaus
record		The King of Denmark/Morton Feldman/Max Neuhaus (percussion)
boards	sculpture	The Maze/Tony Smith
film	films	Rhythm 21 (1921)/Hans Richter
film		Lightplay: Black-White-Grey (1932)/Laszlo Moholy-Nagy (excerpt)
film		Site (1964)/Robert Morris/Stan VanDerBeek (excerpt)
film		Linoleum (1967)/Robert Rauschenberg (excerpt)
record	interview	Merce Cunningham
record	documents	The Creative Act (1957)/Marcel Duchamp/read by the author
record		Some texts from A L'Infinitif (1912-20)/Marcel Duchamp/read by the author
record		Four poems from Phantastische Gebete (1916)/Richard Huelsenbeck/read by the author
record		The Realistic Manifesto (1920)/Naum Gabo/Noton Pevsner/read by Gabo
print		The Russian Desert: A Note on Our State of Knowledge/Douglas MacAgy
record		Space, Time and Dance (1952)/Merce Cunningham/read by the author
print	poetry	Conditionnement/Michel Butor/trans. Michael Benedikt
print		Poem, March 1966/Dan Graham
print	data	Serial Project #1/Sol LeWitt
print		Seven Translucent Tiers/Mel Bochner
print		Structural Play #3/Brian O'Doherty
print		Drawings for The Maze/Tony Smith
print		Score for Fontana Mix-Feed/John Cage/Max Neuhaus
print		Score for The King of Denmark/Morton Feldman
print		Translation of Jealousy (recorded excerpt)/Alain Robbe-Grillet/trans. Richard Howard

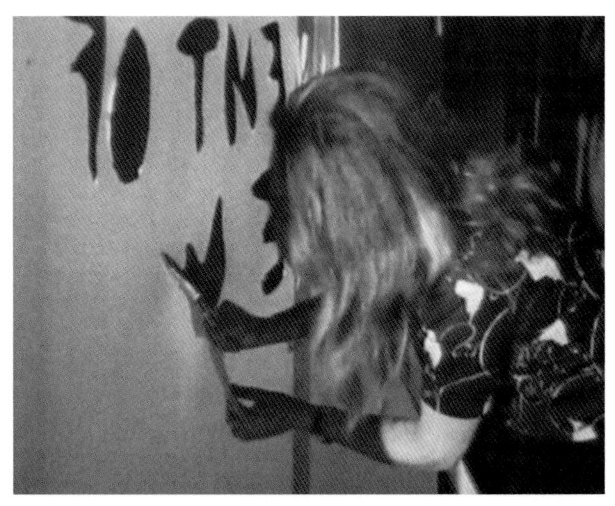

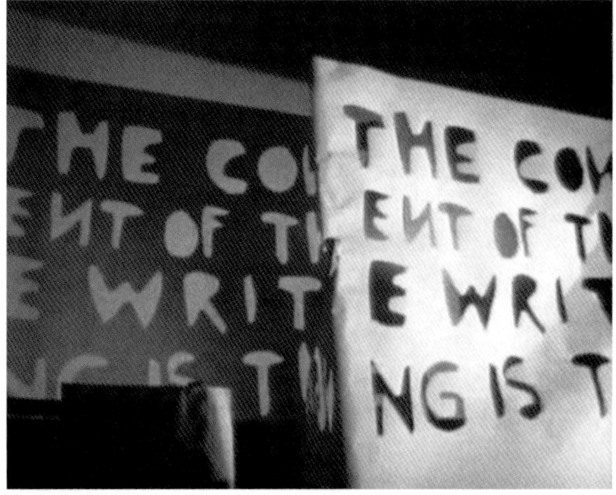

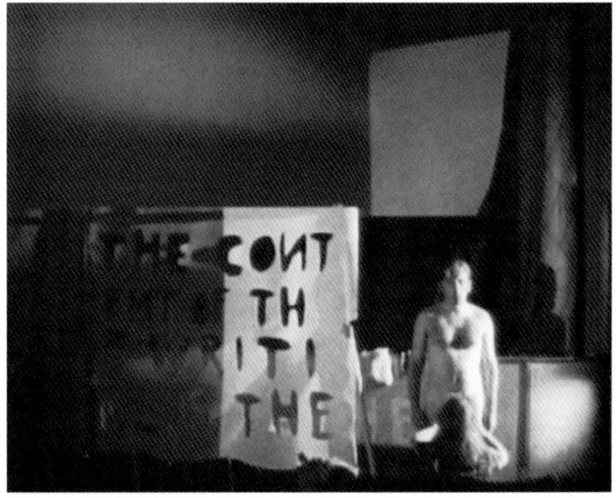

VALIE EXPORT
Cutting, 1967
Single-channel video, b/w, sound,
1 min 41 s

102

stanley brouwn
book
ten steps
1975

10 blocks of text at 100 × 1 mm (1000 mm) on each page;
the distance from each step is marked in red.

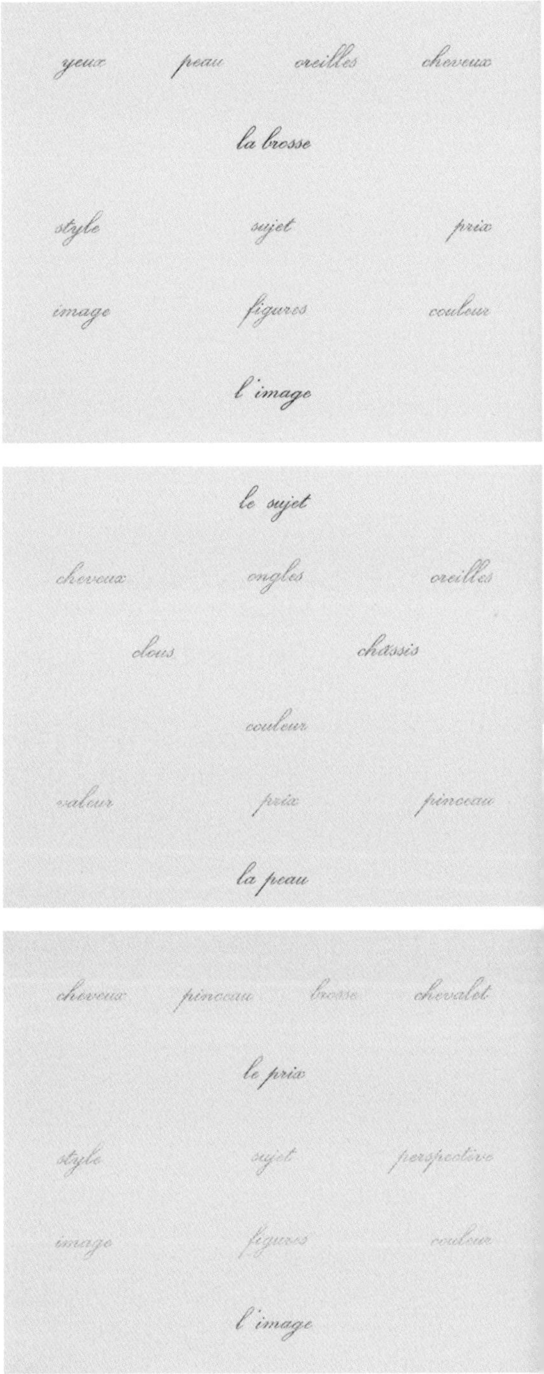

Marcel Broodthaers
L'art et les mots, 1973
Typographic print with acrylic on canvas
9 pieces at 79.4 × 99.7 cm each

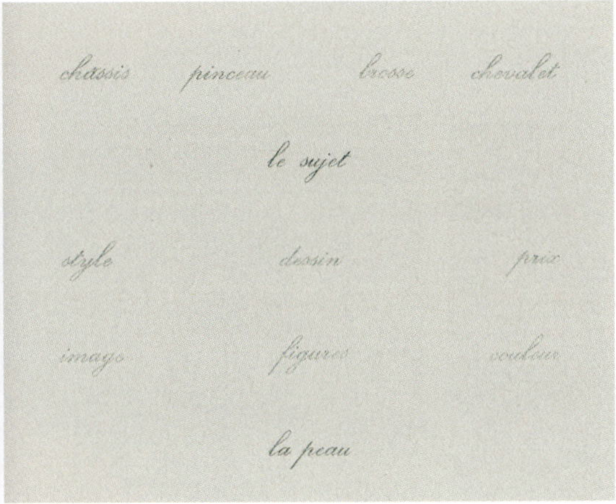

chassis   pinceau   brosse   chevalet

le sujet

style   dessin   prix

image   figures   couleur

la peau

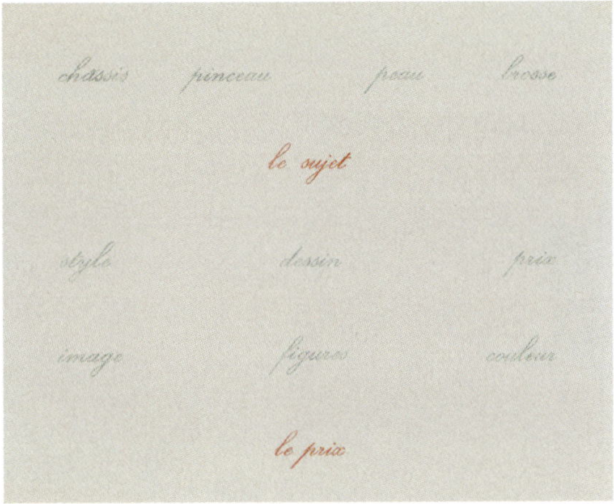

---

chassis   pinceau   peau   brosse

le sujet

style   dessin   prix

image   figures   couleur

le prix

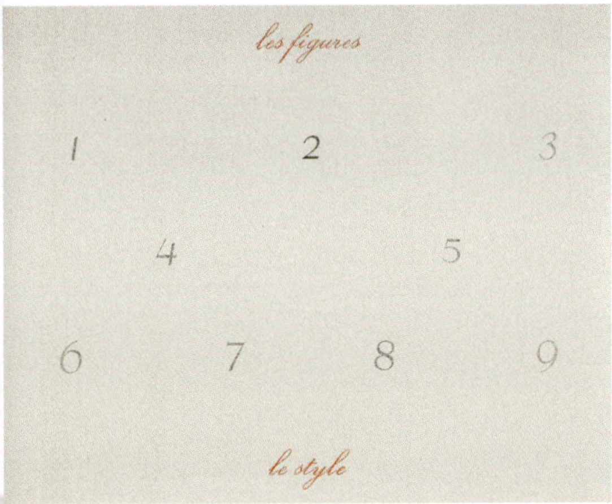

---

les figures

1   2   3

4   5

6   7   8   9

le style

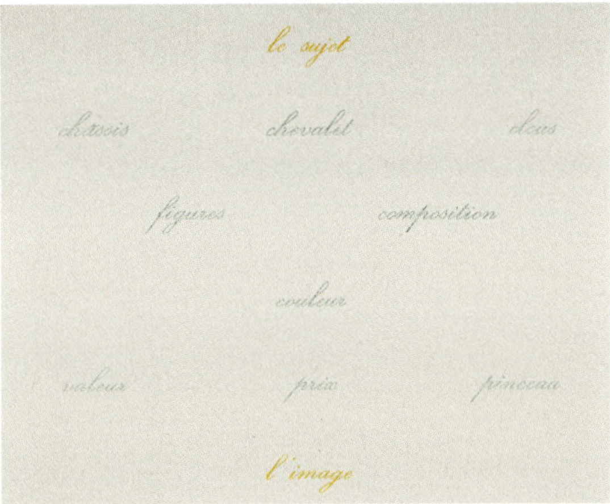

---

le sujet

chassis   chevalet   clous

figures   composition

couleur

valeur   prix   pinceau

l'image

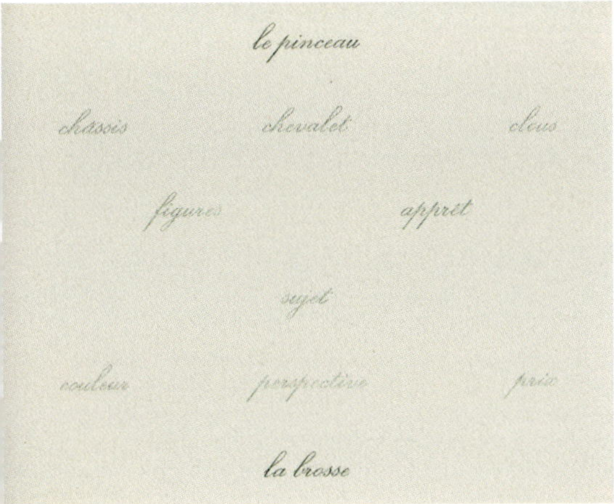

---

le pinceau

chassis   chevalet   clous

figures   apprêt

sujet

couleur   perspective   prix

la brosse

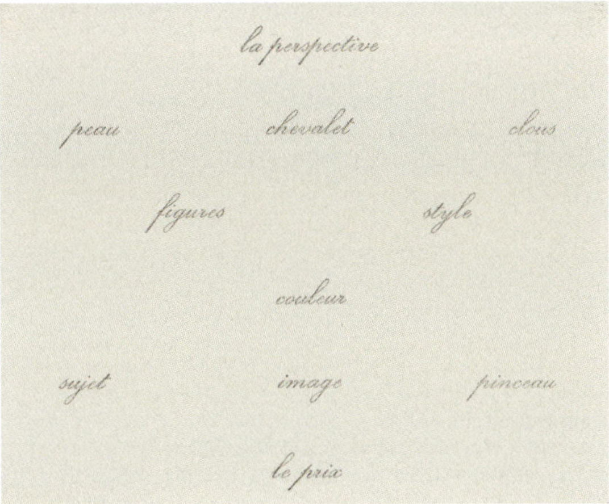

---

la perspective

peau   chevalet   clous

figures   style

couleur

sujet   image   pinceau

le prix

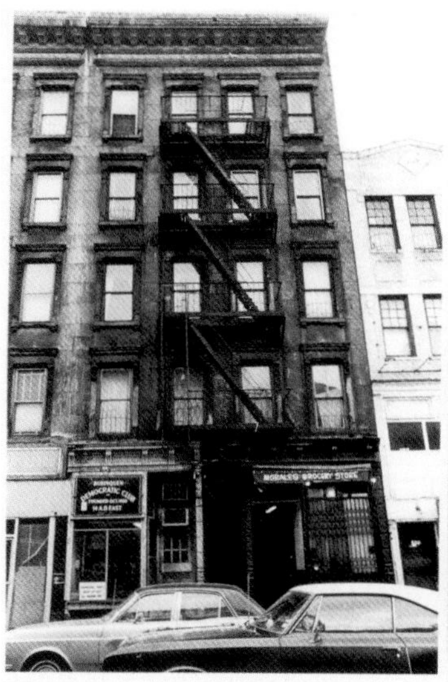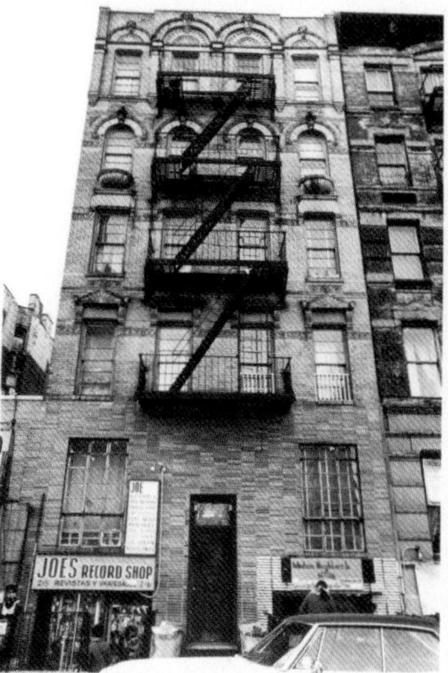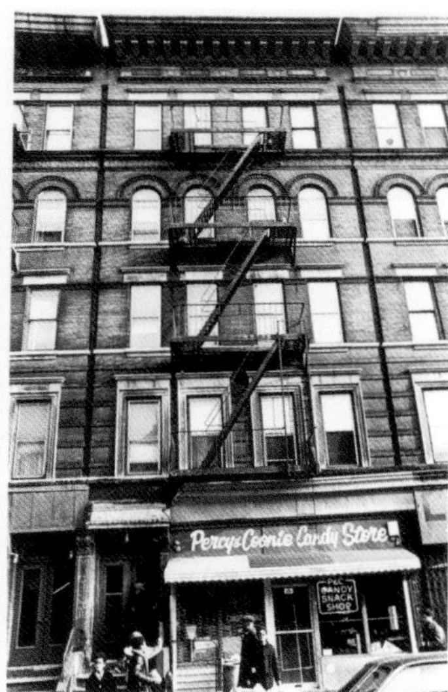

1681 Madison Ave.
Block 1617 Lot 20
27 x 70' 5 story walk-up old law tenement

Owned by Callipari Construction Corp., 608 E 11 St., NYC
Contracts signed by Ernest Callipari, Pres.('39/41/63/69)
                    Anna Callipari, President ('63)
                    Harry J. Shapolsky, President('42)
Principal Harry J. Shapolsky(according to Real Estate
Directory of Manhattan)

Acquired 8-11-1967 through foreclosure from
Zalchek Realty Corp., 44 E 21 St., NYC, defendant

$5 100.- mortgage at 5 1/2 % interest, 4-20-1961, due
4-17-1975, held by the City of New York

Assessed land value $8 600.-, total $20 000.- (1971)

215 Madison St.
Block 271 lot 41
26 x 100' 5 story walk-up apt. bldg.

Owned by 128 Realty Corp., 608 E 11 St., NYC
Contracts signed by Harry M. Gruber, Pres.(55/7/60/3/4/7)
                    Harry J. Shapolsky, Secretary ('55)
                    Alfred Fayer, Vicepresident ('60)
Principal Harry M. Gruber(according to Real Estate Direc-
tory of Manhattan)

Acquired 4-9-1954 from One Fifty Four Realty Corp.,
608 E 11 St., NYC,
contracts signed by Harry M. Gruber('54/60/64)
                    Harry J. Shapolsky, Secretary('46/51)
                    George Greenberger, Vicepresident('61)
Principal Harry J. Shapolsky(according to Real Estate
Directory of Manhattan)

$50 000.- consolidated and extended mortgage at 6% interest,
11-29-1967, due 11-28-1977, held through assignment, 2-9-1972,
by One Fifty Four Realty Corp.

Assessed land value $7 200.-, total $76 000.- (1971)

492 Manhattan Ave.
Block 1947 Lot 19
25 x 70' 5 story walk-up old law tenement

Owned by Eighth Realty Estate Inc., 608 E 11 St., NYC
Contracts signed by Harry J. Shapolsky, President ('65)
                    Sam Shapolsky, President ('59)
                    Martin Shapolsky, President ('57)
                    Harry J. Shapolsky, Secretary('69)
                    Alfred Fayer, Vicepresident ('58)
Principal Harry J. Shapolsky(according to Real Estate
Directory of Manhattan)

Acquired 8-17-1967 through foreclosure from
492 Manhattan Realty Corp., 51 Chambers St., NYC,defendant

$5000.- mortgage at 6% interest, 5-23-1969, held by
102 W 115 St. Realty Corp., 608 E 11 St., NYC,
Harry J. Shapolsky, President

Assessed land value $6 000.- , total $15 500.- (1971)

Hans Haacke
*Shapolsky et al. Manhattan Real Estate Holdings,
a Real-Time Social System, as of May 1, 1971*, 1971
Maps, graphs, typewritten pages, silver-salt photographs,
and explanation panel
Various dimensions

3 photographs, 25.4 × 20.3 cm each; 3 typewritten pages,
25.4 × 20.3 cm each; 1 graph, 61 × 50.8 cm

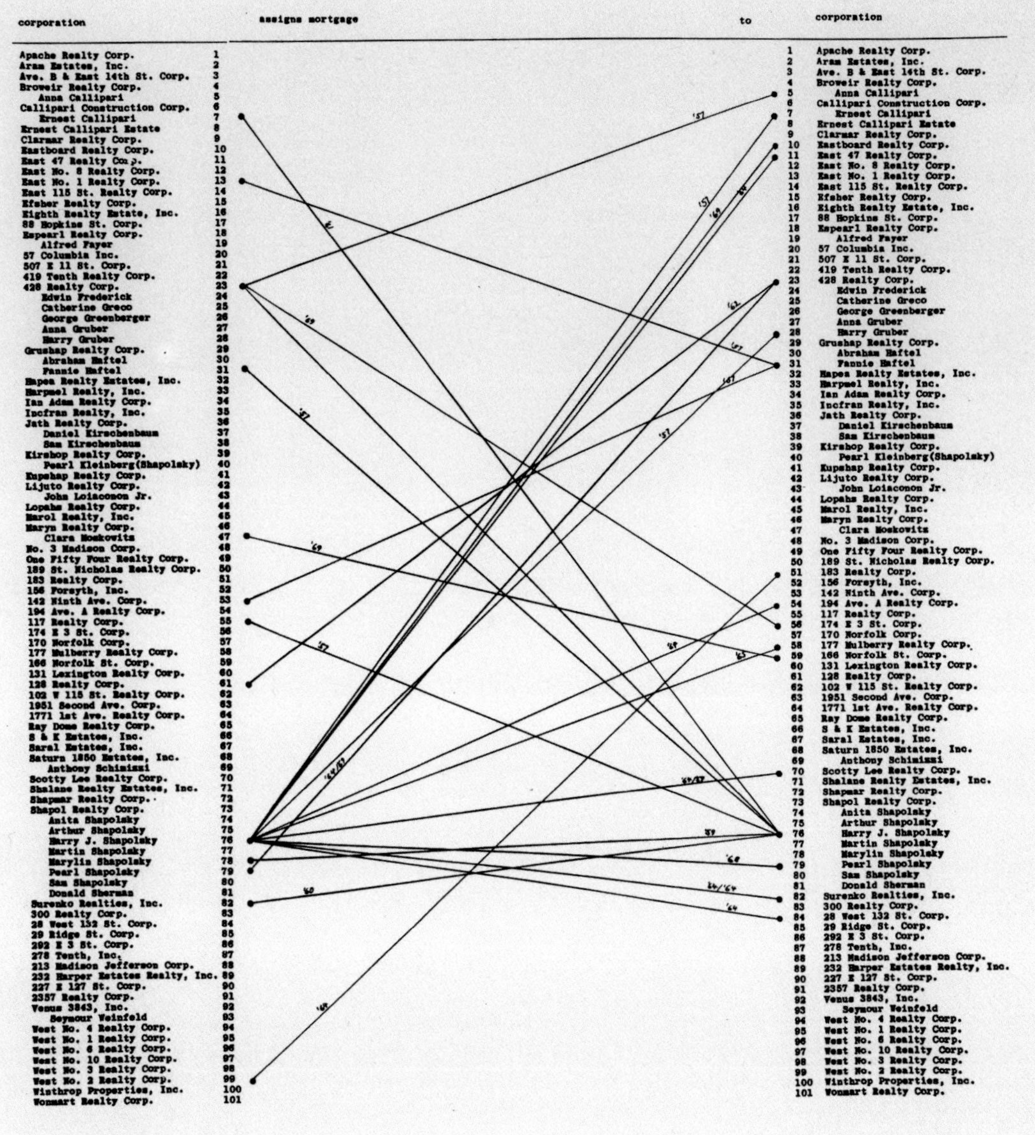
Apache Realty Corp. — 1
Aram Estates, Inc. — 2
Ave. B & East 14th St. Corp. — 3
Broweir Realty Corp. — 4
Anna Callipari — 5
Callipari Construction Corp. — 6
Ernest Callipari — 7
Ernest Callipari Estate — 8
Clarmar Realty Corp. — 9
Eastboard Realty Corp. — 10
East 47 Realty Co. — 11
East No. 8 Realty Corp. — 12
East No. 1 Realty Corp. — 13
East 115 St. Realty Corp. — 14
Efsher Realty Corp. — 15
Eighth Realty Estate, Inc. — 16
88 Hopkins St. Corp. — 17
Espearl Realty Corp. — 18
Alfred Fayer — 19
57 Columbia Inc. — 20
507 E 11 St. Corp. — 21
419 Tenth Realty Corp. — 22
428 Realty Corp. — 23
Edwin Frederick — 24
Catherine Greco — 25
George Greenberger — 26
Anna Gruber — 27
Harry Gruber — 28
Grushap Realty Corp. — 29
Abraham Haftel — 30
Fannie Haftel — 31
Mapes Realty Estates, Inc. — 32
Harpuel Realty, Inc. — 33
Ian Adam Realty Corp. — 34
Incfran Realty, Inc. — 35
Jath Realty Corp. — 36
Daniel Kirschenbaum — 37
Sam Kirschenbaum — 38
Kirshop Realty Corp. — 39
Pearl Kleinberg (Shapolsky) — 40
Kupshap Realty Corp. — 41
Lijuto Realty Corp. — 42
John Loisaconon Jr. — 43
Lopahs Realty Corp. — 44
Marol Realty, Inc. — 45
Maryn Realty Corp. — 46
Clara Moskowits — 47
No. 3 Madison Corp. — 48
One Fifty Four Realty Corp. — 49
189 St. Nicholas Realty Corp. — 50
183 Realty Corp. — 51
156 Forsyth, Inc. — 52
142 Ninth Ave. Corp. — 53
194 Ave. A Realty Corp. — 54
117 Realty Corp. — 55
174 E 3 St. Corp. — 56
170 Norfolk Corp. — 57
177 Mulberry Realty Corp. — 58
166 Norfolk St. Corp. — 59
131 Lexington Realty Corp. — 60
128 Realty Corp. — 61
102 W 115 St. Realty Corp. — 62
1951 Second Ave. Corp. — 63
1771 1st Ave. Realty Corp. — 64
Ray Dome Realty Corp. — 65
S & K Estates, Inc. — 66
Saral Estates, Inc. — 67
Saturn 1850 Estates, Inc. — 68
Anthony Schimizzi — 69
Scotty Lee Realty Corp. — 70
Shalane Realty Estates, Inc. — 71
Shapmar Realty Corp. — 72
Shapol Realty Corp. — 73
Anita Shapolsky — 74
Arthur Shapolsky — 75
Harry J. Shapolsky — 76
Martin Shapolsky — 77
Marylin Shapolsky — 78
Pearl Shapolsky — 79
Sam Shapolsky — 80
Donald Sherman — 81
Surenko Realties, Inc. — 82
300 Realty Corp. — 83
28 West 132 St. Corp. — 84
29 Ridge St. Corp. — 85
292 E 3 St. Corp. — 86
278 Tenth, Inc. — 87
213 Madison Jefferson Corp. — 88
232 Harper Estates Realty, Inc. — 89
227 E 127 St. Corp. — 90
2357 Realty Corp. — 91
Venus 3843, Inc. — 92
Seymour Weinfeld — 93
West No. 4 Realty Corp. — 94
West No. 1 Realty Corp. — 95
West No. 6 Realty Corp. — 96
West No. 10 Realty Corp. — 97
West No. 3 Realty Corp. — 98
West No. 2 Realty Corp. — 99
Winthrop Properties, Inc. — 100
Wonmart Realty Corp. — 101

1 — Apache Realty Corp.
2 — Aram Estates, Inc.
3 — Ave. B & East 14th St. Corp.
4 — Broweir Realty Corp.
5 — Anna Callipari
6 — Callipari Construction Corp.
7 — Ernest Callipari
8 — Ernest Callipari Estate
9 — Clarmar Realty Corp.
10 — Eastboard Realty Corp.
11 — East 47 Realty Corp.
12 — East No. 8 Realty Corp.
13 — East No. 1 Realty Corp.
14 — East 115 St. Realty Corp.
15 — Efsher Realty Corp.
16 — Eighth Realty Estate, Inc.
17 — 88 Hopkins St. Corp.
18 — Espearl Realty Corp.
19 — Alfred Fayer
20 — 57 Columbia Inc.
21 — 507 E 11 St. Corp.
22 — 419 Tenth Realty Corp.
23 — 428 Realty Corp.
24 — Edwin Frederick
25 — Catherine Greco
26 — George Greenberger
27 — Anna Gruber
28 — Harry Gruber
29 — Grushap Realty Corp.
30 — Abraham Haftel
31 — Fannie Haftel
32 — Mapes Realty Estates, Inc.
33 — Harpuel Realty, Inc.
34 — Ian Adam Realty Corp.
35 — Incfran Realty, Inc.
36 — Jath Realty Corp.
37 — Daniel Kirschenbaum
38 — Sam Kirschenbaum
39 — Kirshop Realty Corp.
40 — Pearl Kleinberg (Shapolsky)
41 — Kupshap Realty Corp.
42 — Lijuto Realty Corp.
43 — John Loisaconon Jr.
44 — Lopahs Realty Corp.
45 — Marol Realty, Inc.
46 — Maryn Realty Corp.
47 — Clara Moskowits
48 — No. 3 Madison Corp.
49 — One Fifty Four Realty Corp.
50 — 189 St. Nicholas Realty Corp.
51 — 183 Realty Corp.
52 — 156 Forsyth, Inc.
53 — 142 Ninth Ave. Corp.
54 — 194 Ave. A Realty Corp.
55 — 117 Realty Corp.
56 — 174 E 3 St. Corp.
57 — 170 Norfolk Corp.
58 — 177 Mulberry Realty Corp.
59 — 166 Norfolk St. Corp.
60 — 131 Lexington Realty Corp.
61 — 128 Realty Corp.
62 — 102 W 115 St. Realty Corp.
63 — 1951 Second Ave. Corp.
64 — 1771 1st Ave. Realty Corp.
65 — Ray Dome Realty Corp.
66 — S & K Estates, Inc.
67 — Saral Estates, Inc.
68 — Saturn 1850 Estates, Inc.
69 — Anthony Schimizzi
70 — Scotty Lee Realty Corp.
71 — Shalane Realty Estates, Inc.
72 — Shapmar Realty Corp.
73 — Shapol Realty Corp.
74 — Anita Shapolsky
75 — Arthur Shapolsky
76 — Harry J. Shapolsky
77 — Martin Shapolsky
78 — Marylin Shapolsky
79 — Pearl Shapolsky
80 — Sam Shapolsky
81 — Donald Sherman
82 — Surenko Realties, Inc.
83 — 300 Realty Corp.
84 — 28 West 132 St. Corp.
85 — 29 Ridge St. Corp.
86 — 292 E 3 St. Corp.
87 — 278 Tenth, Inc.
88 — 213 Madison Jefferson Corp.
89 — 232 Harper Estates Realty, Inc.
90 — 227 E 127 St. Corp.
91 — 2357 Realty Corp.
92 — Venus 3843, Inc.
93 — Seymour Weinfeld
94 — West No. 4 Realty Corp.
95 — West No. 1 Realty Corp.
96 — West No. 6 Realty Corp.
97 — West No. 10 Realty Corp.
98 — West No. 3 Realty Corp.
99 — West No. 2 Realty Corp.
100 — Winthrop Properties, Inc.
101 — Wonmart Realty Corp.

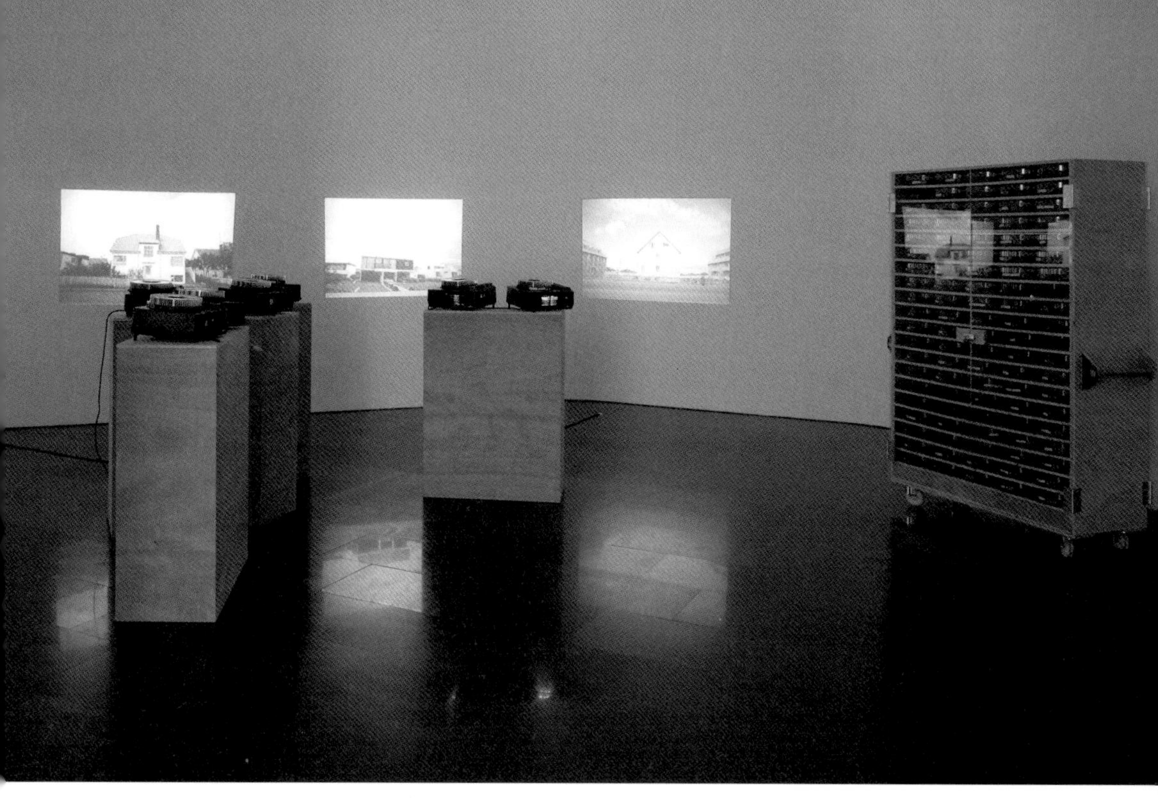

Dieter Roth
Reykjavik Slides, 1973–75, 1990–93
7 slide projections, large glass cases with carousel slide
projectors, photomechanical reproductions on paper
and city map of Reykjavik
Dimensions variable

Intallation view, presentation of the MACBA Collection, 2006

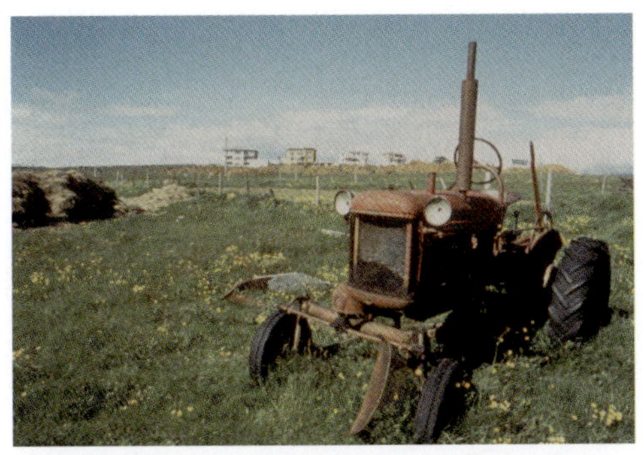
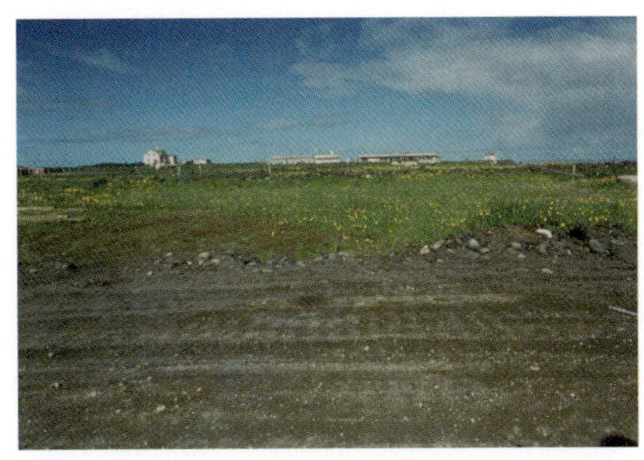
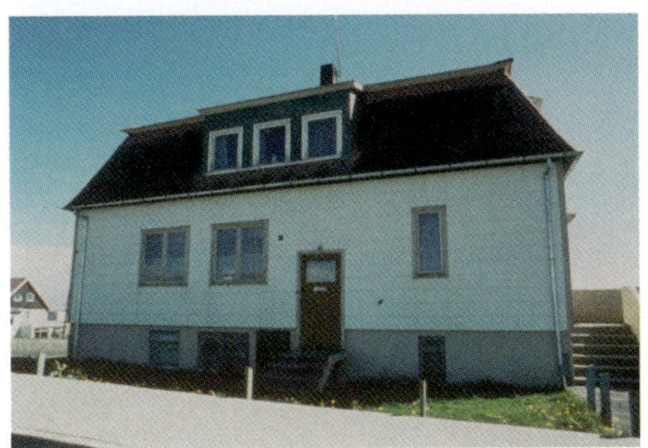
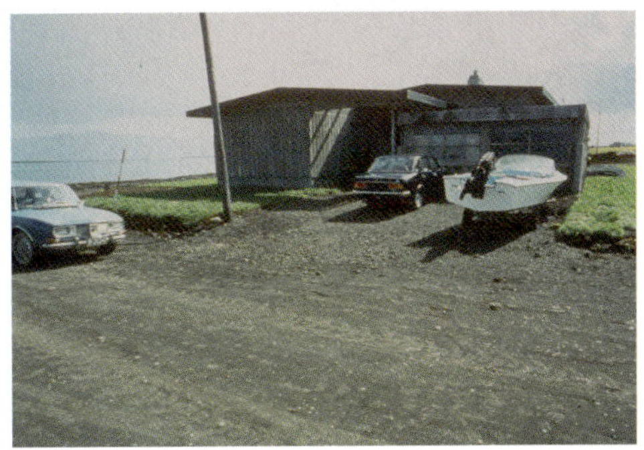
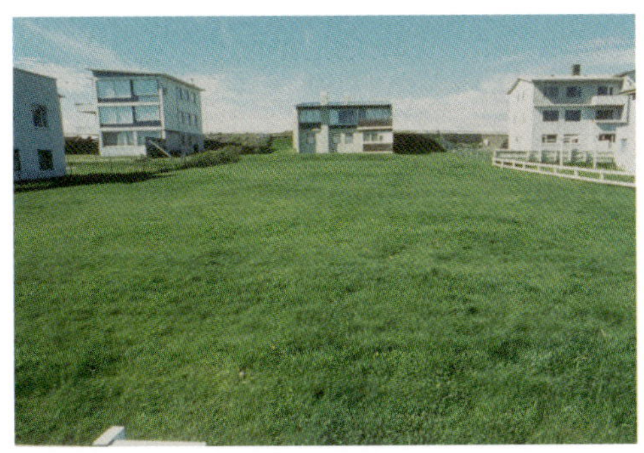
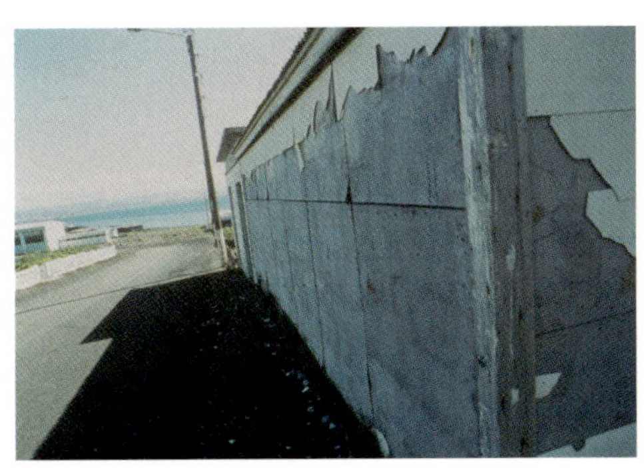
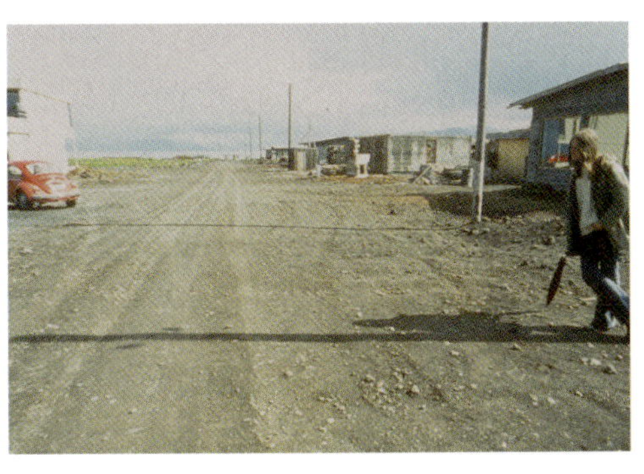
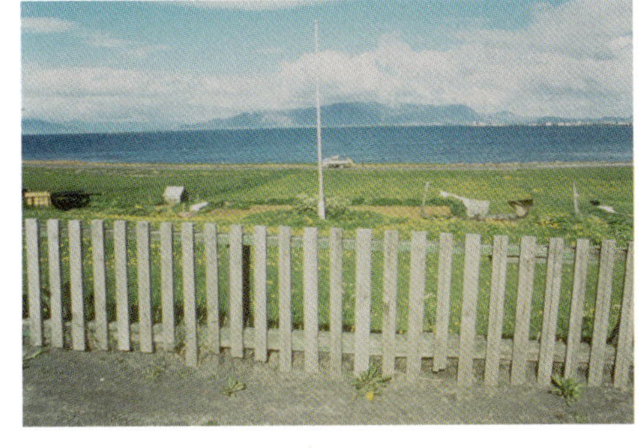

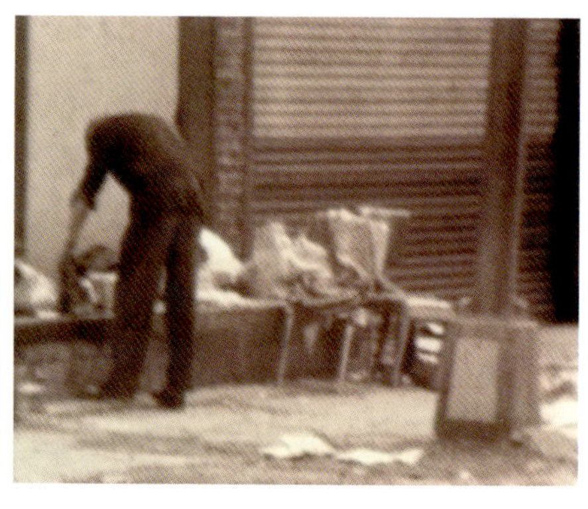

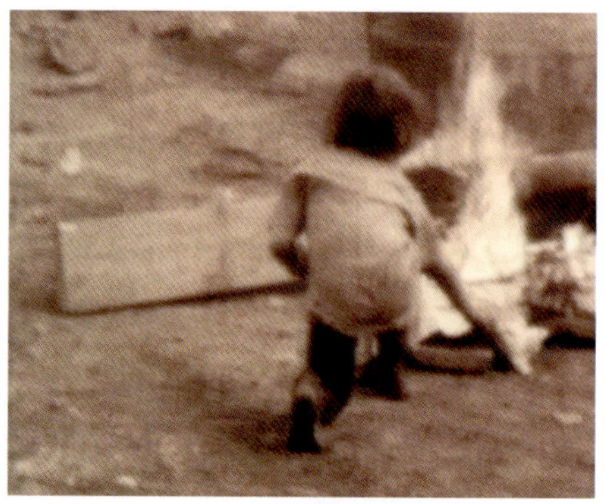

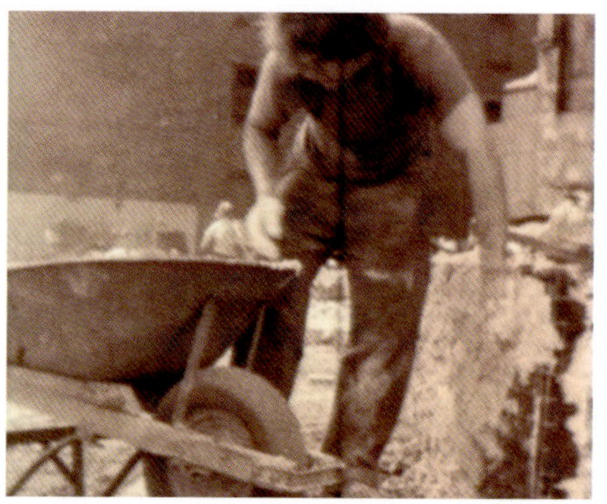

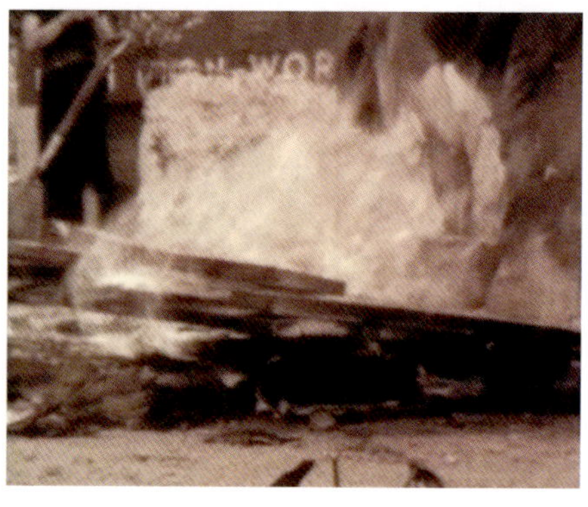

Gordon Matta-Clark
Fire Child, 1971
Single-channel video, colour, silent, 9 min 47 s

Fresh Kill, 1972
Single-channel video, colour, sound, 12 min 56 s

Day's End, 1975
Single-channel video, colour, silent, 23 min 10 s

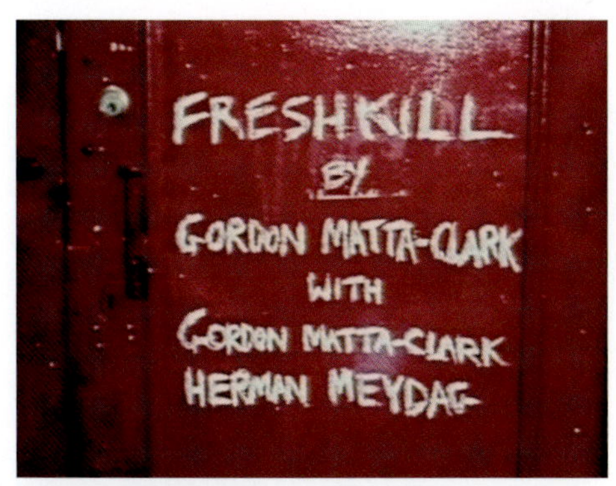

FRESHKILL
BY
GORDON MATTA-CLARK
WITH
GORDON MATTA-CLARK
HERMAN MEYDAG

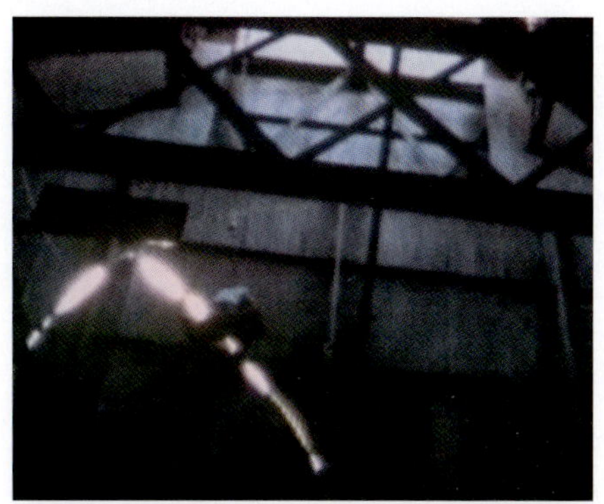
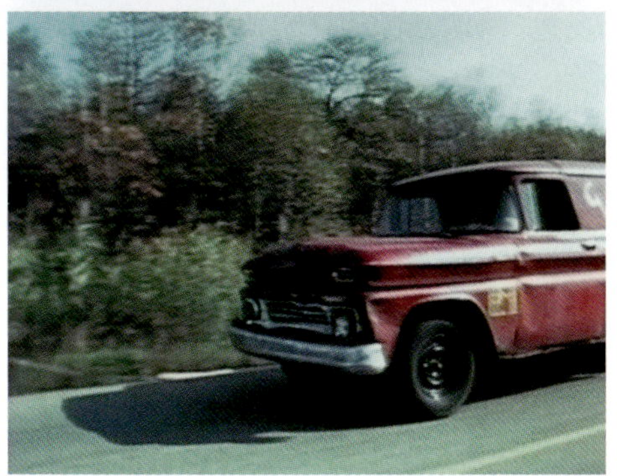
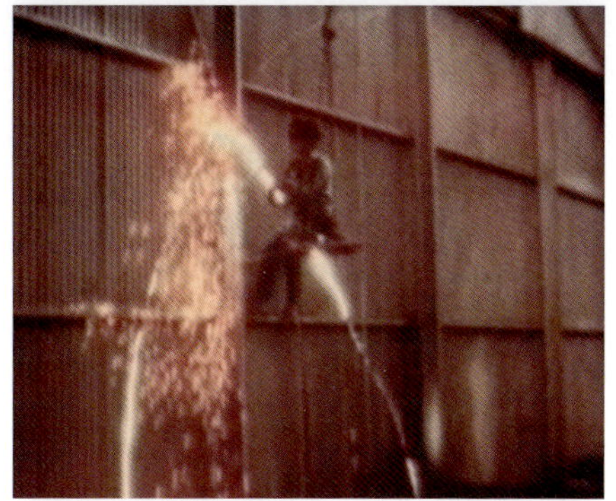
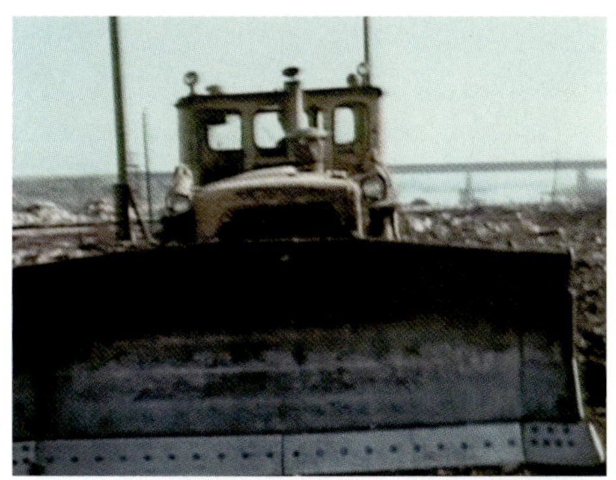
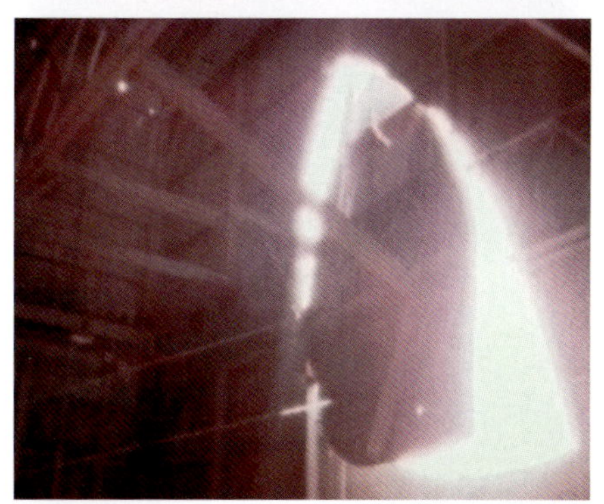
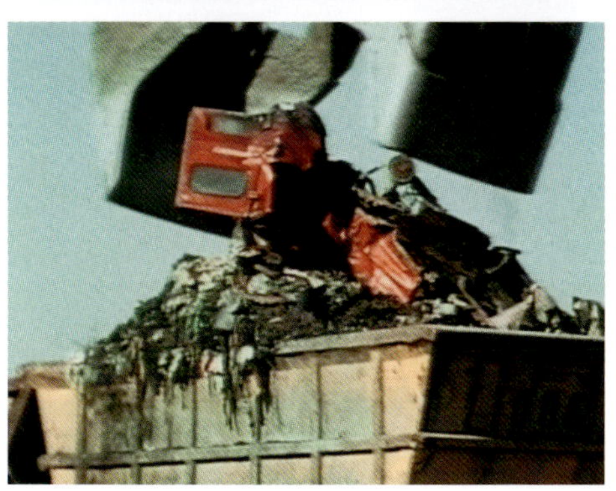
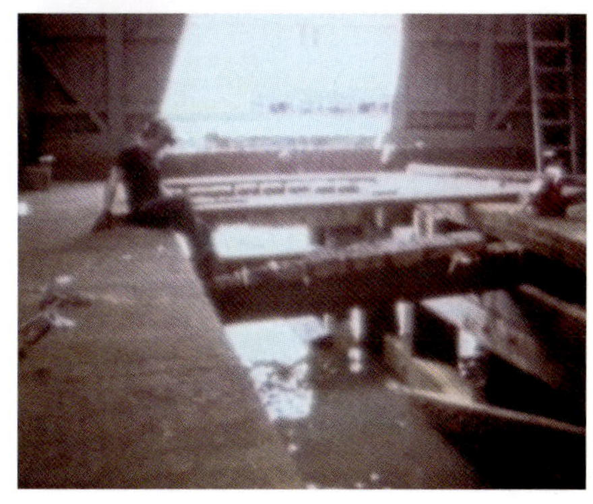

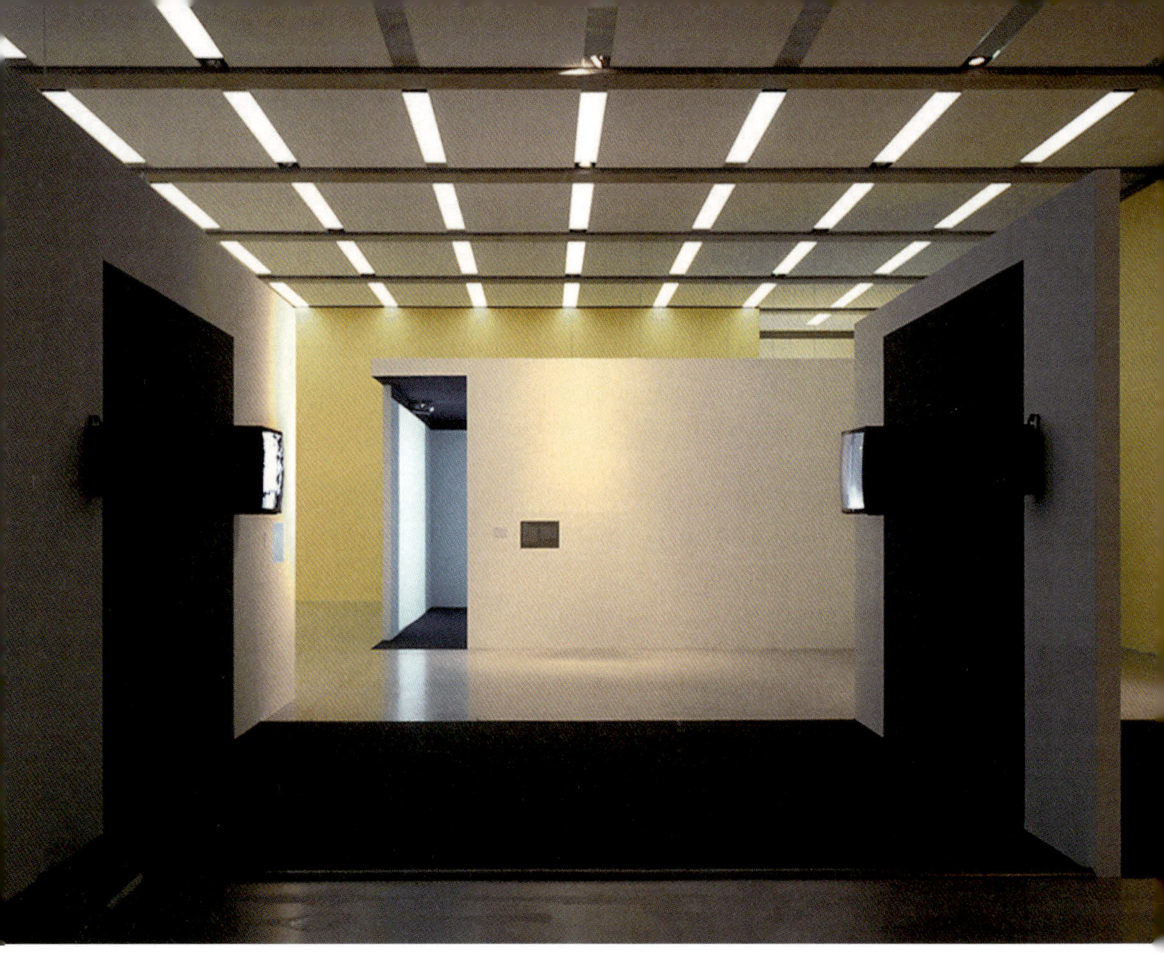

Dara Birnbaum
Attack Piece, 1975
Two-channel video, b/w, sound, 7 min 45 s

Installation view, *X-Screen. Film Installations and Actions
in the 1960s and 1970s*, MUMOK, Museum Moderner Kunst Stiftung
Ludwig Wien, Vienna, 2003

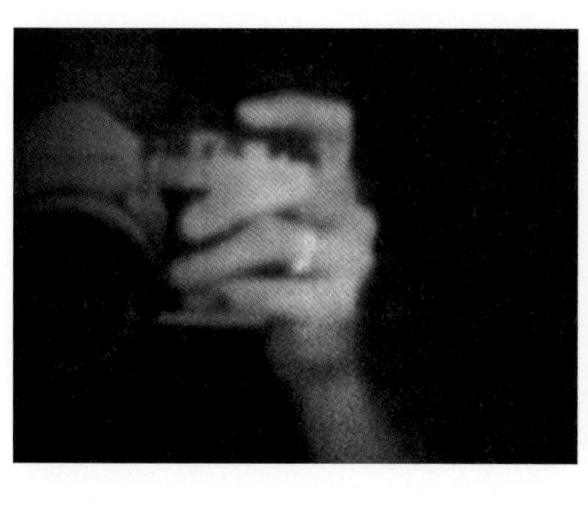
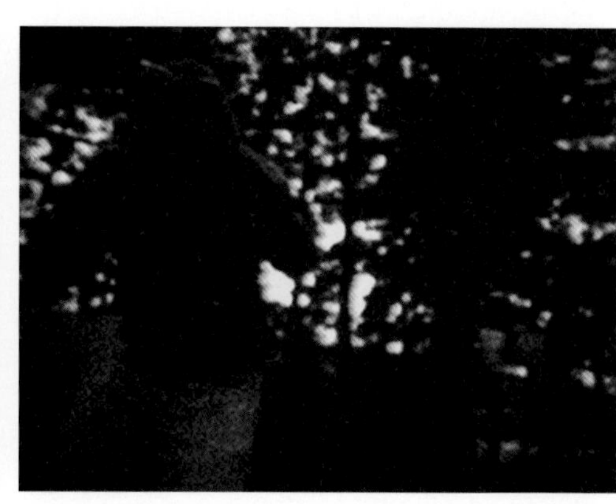
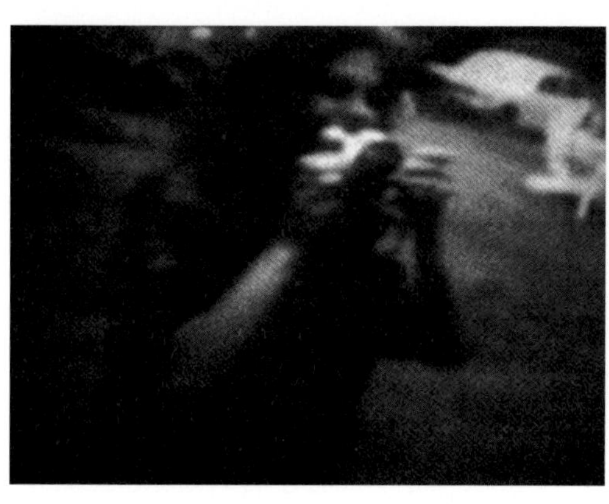
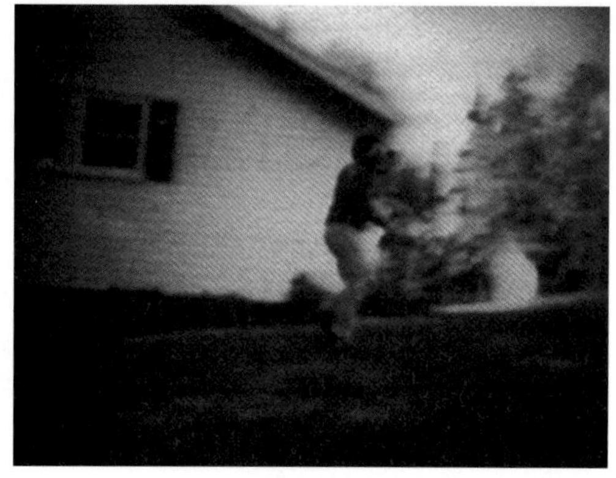
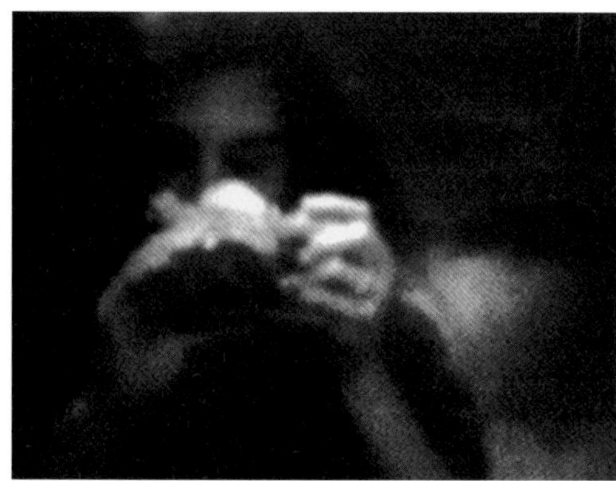
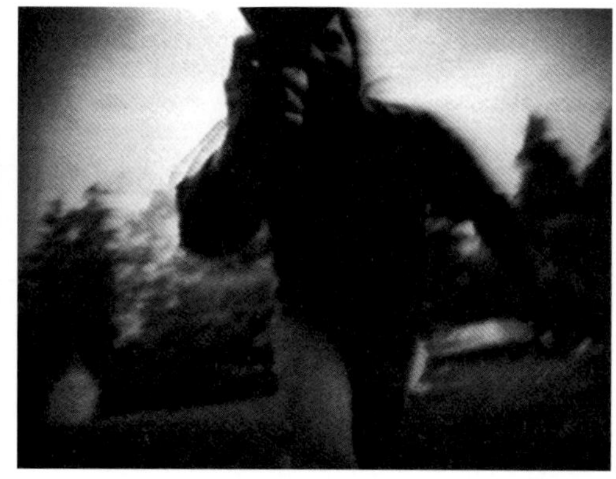

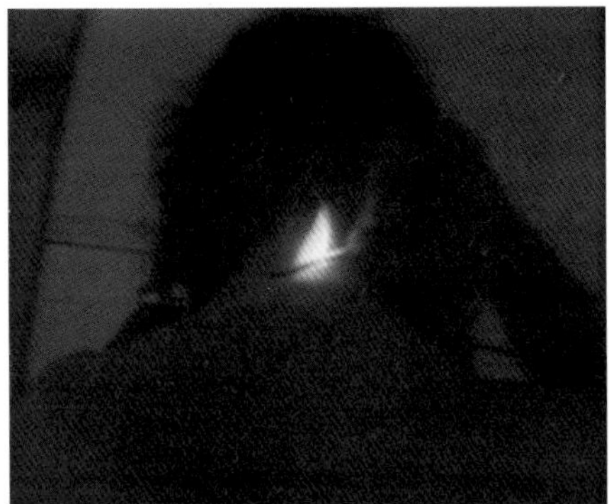

Vito Acconci
Corrections, 1970
8 mm film transferred to video,
b/w, sound, 12 min

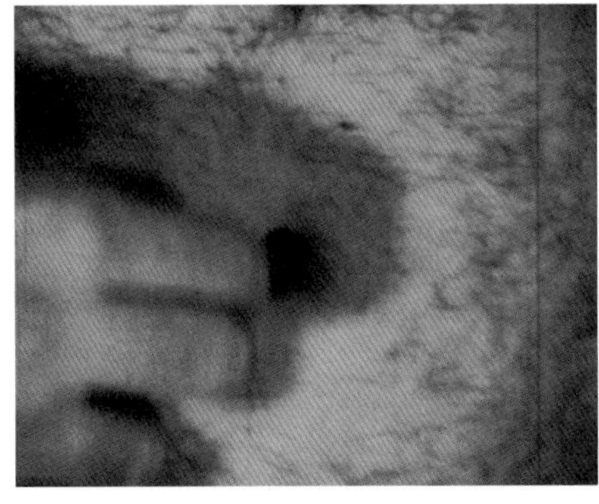

Openings, 1970
8 mm film transferred to video,
b/w, silent, 14 min

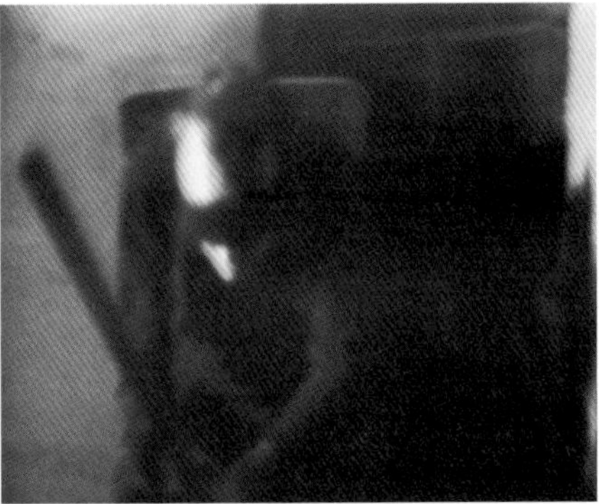

Claim Excerpts, 1971
Single-channel video, b/w, sound, 62 min 11 s

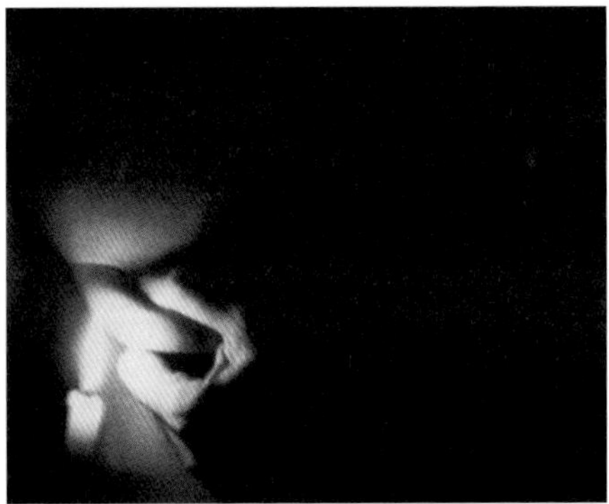

Conversions
1. Light, Reflection, Self-Control, 1971
8 mm film transferred to video,
b/w, silent, 44 min 15 s

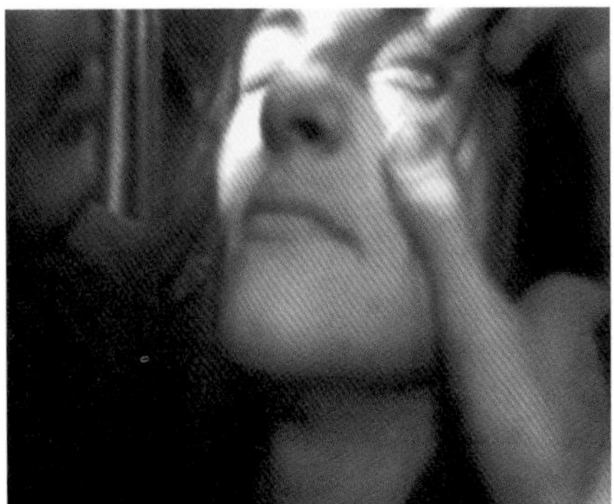

Pryings, 1971
Single-channel video, b/w, sound, 17 min 10 s

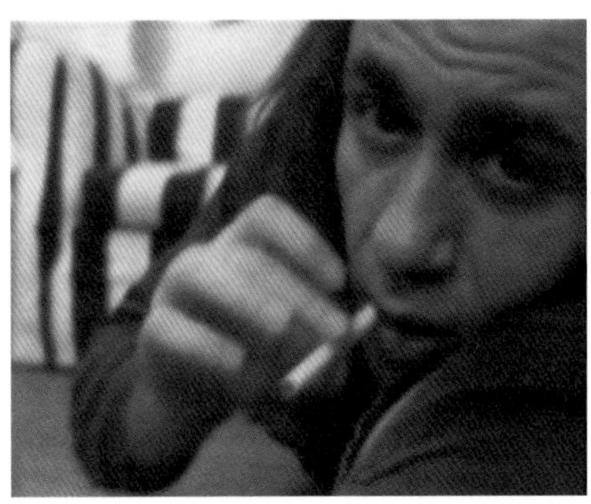

Theme Song, 1973
Single-channel video, b/w, sound, 33 min 15 s

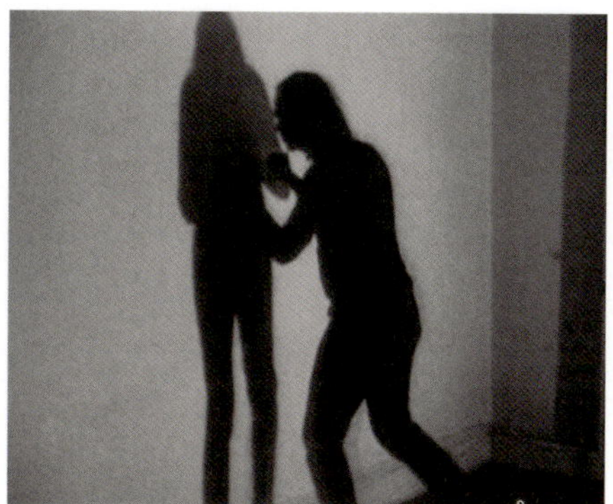

Three Relationship Studies, 1970
8 mm film transferred to video,
b/w and colour, silent, 12 min 30 s

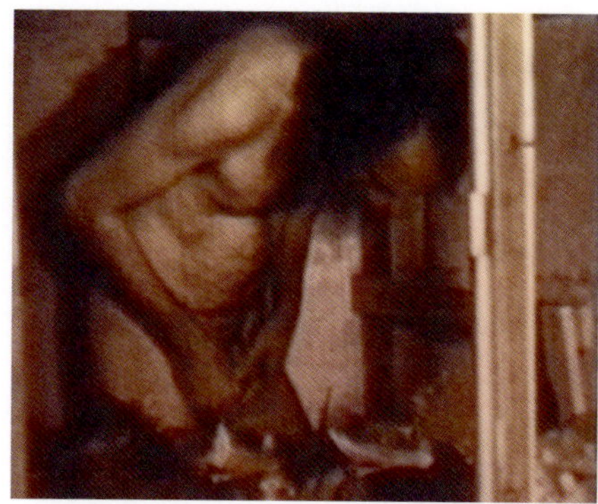

Trappings, 1971
Single-channel video, colour, sound, 8 min

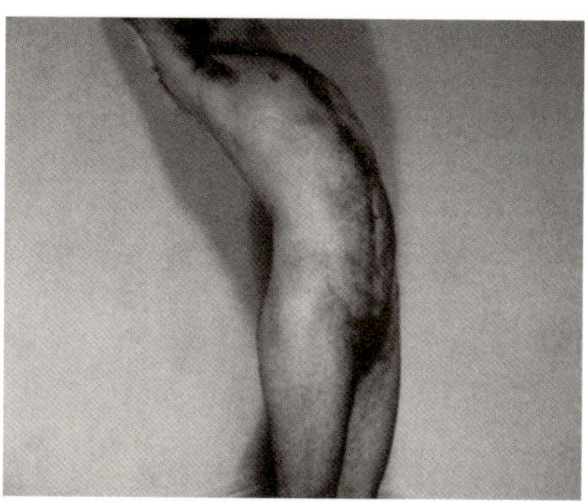

Conversions
2. Insistence, Adaptation, Groundwork,
Display, 1971
8 mm film transferred to video,
b/w, silent, 13 min 45 s

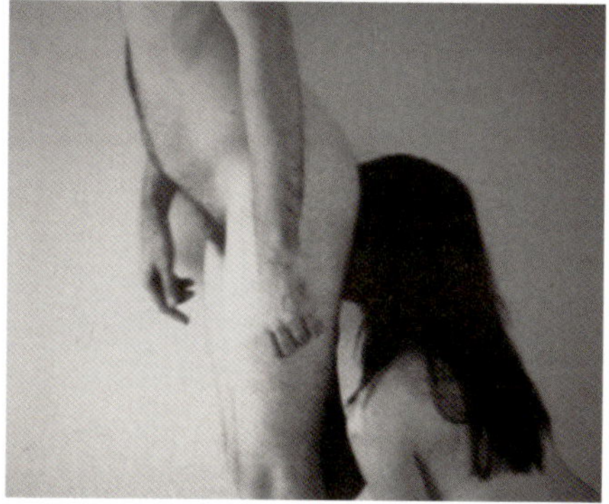

Conversions
3. Association, Assistance, Dependence, 1971
8 mm film transferred to video,
b/w, silent, 7 min

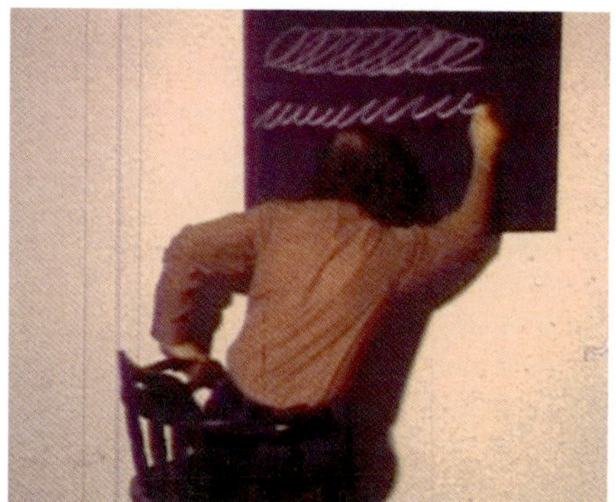

My Word, 1974
8 mm film transferred to video,
colour, silent, 91 min 30 s

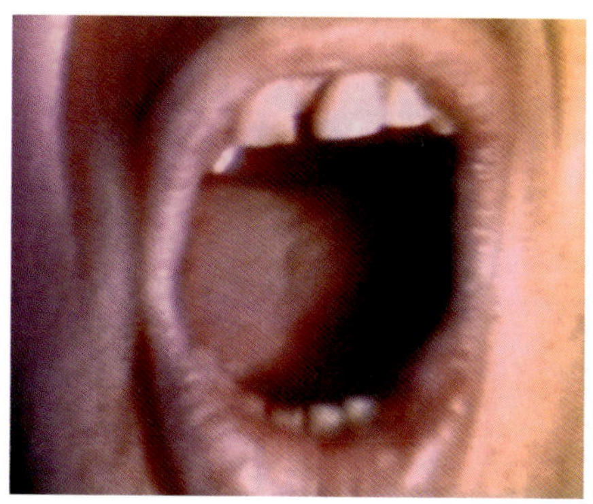

Open Book, 1974
Single-channel video, colour, sound, 10 min 5 s

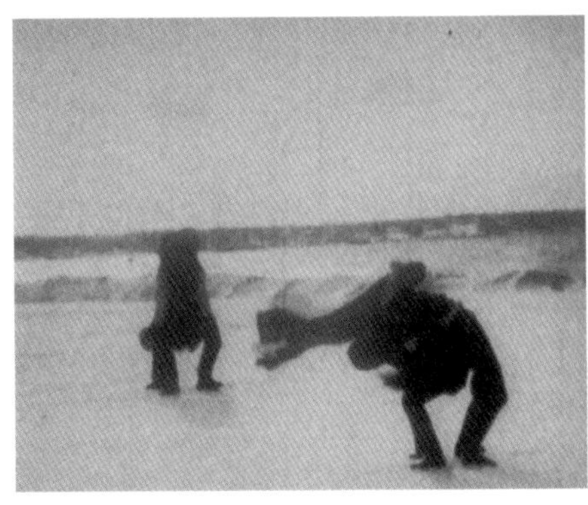

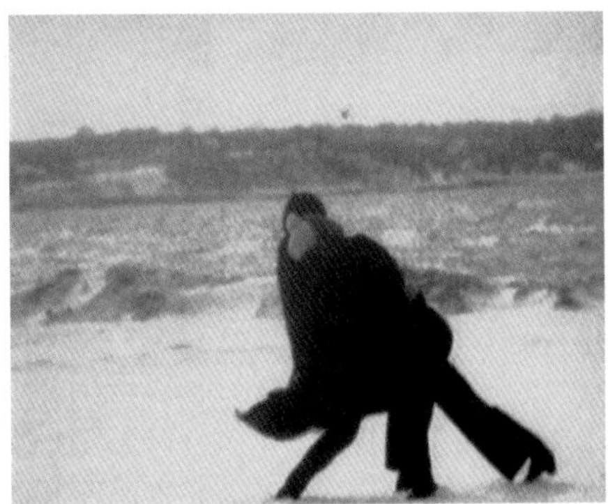

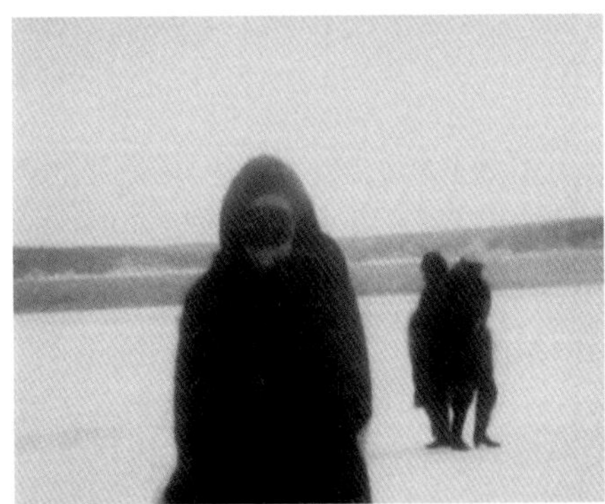

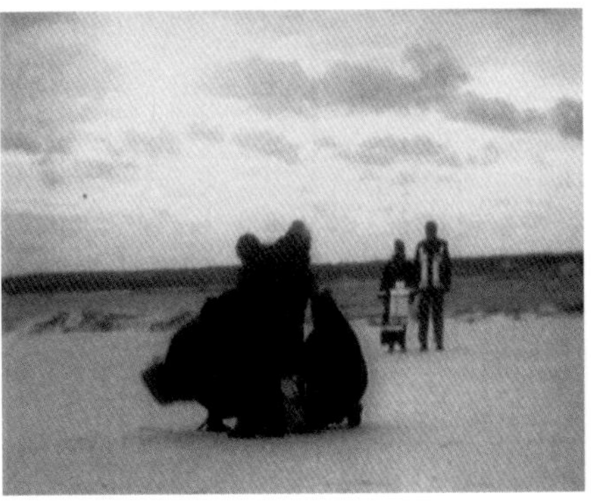

Joan Jonas
Wind, 1968
16 mm film transferred to video,
b/w, silent, 5 min 37 s

Organic Honey's Visual Telepathy, 1972
Single-channel video, b/w, sound, 15 min

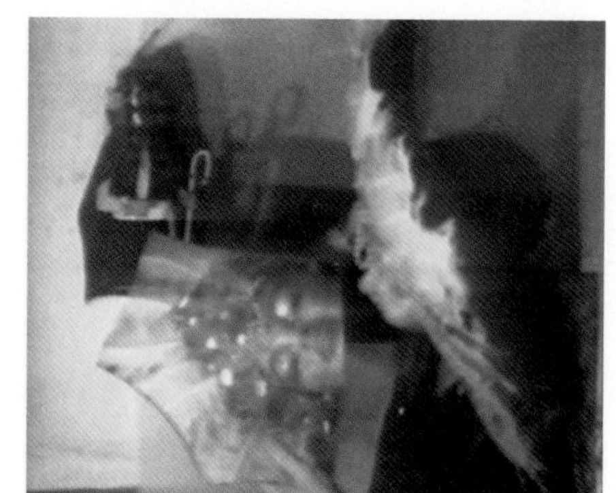

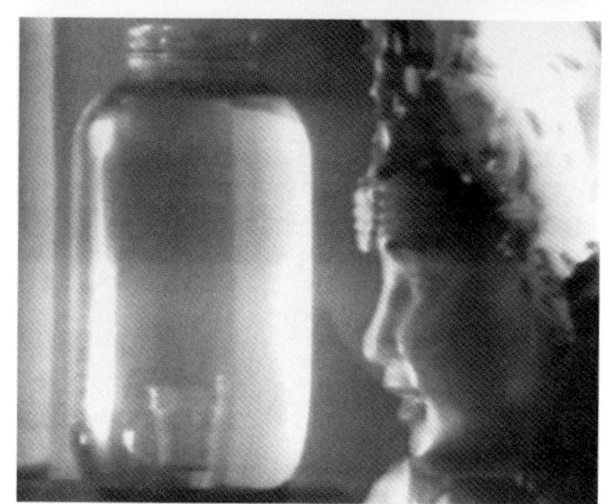

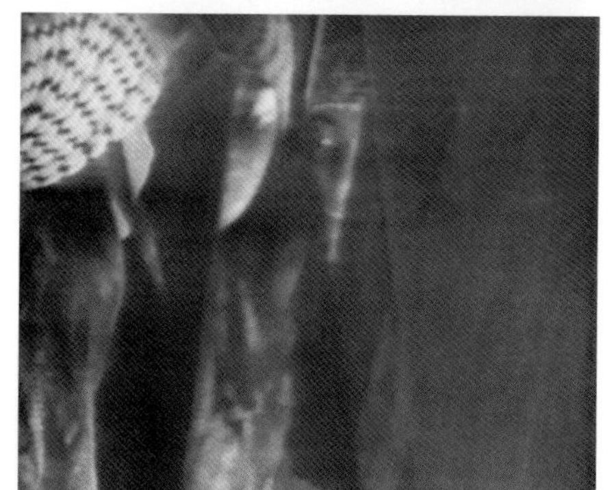

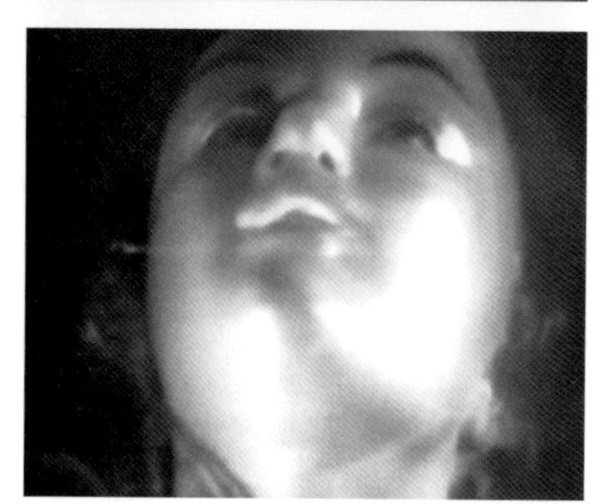

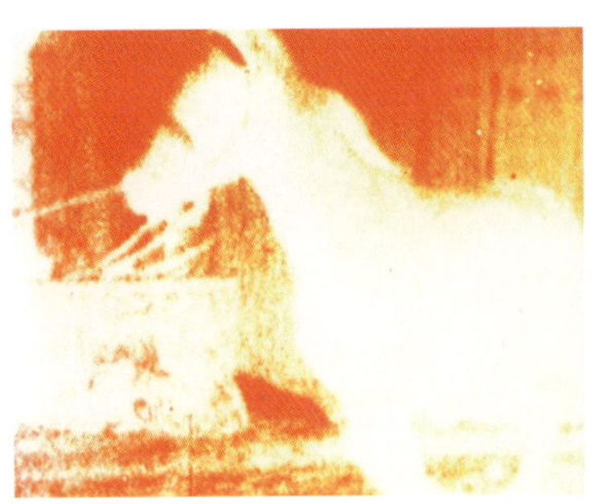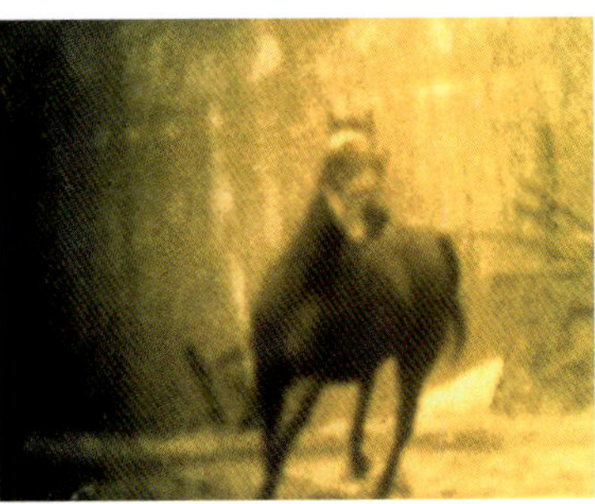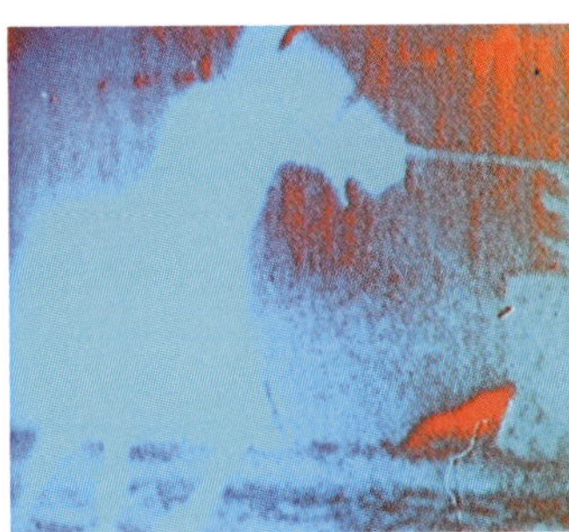

Malcom Le Grice
Berlin Horse, 1970
Double projection, 16 mm film transferred to video,
b/w and colour, sound, 7 min each

Installation view, presentation of the MACBA Collection, 2004

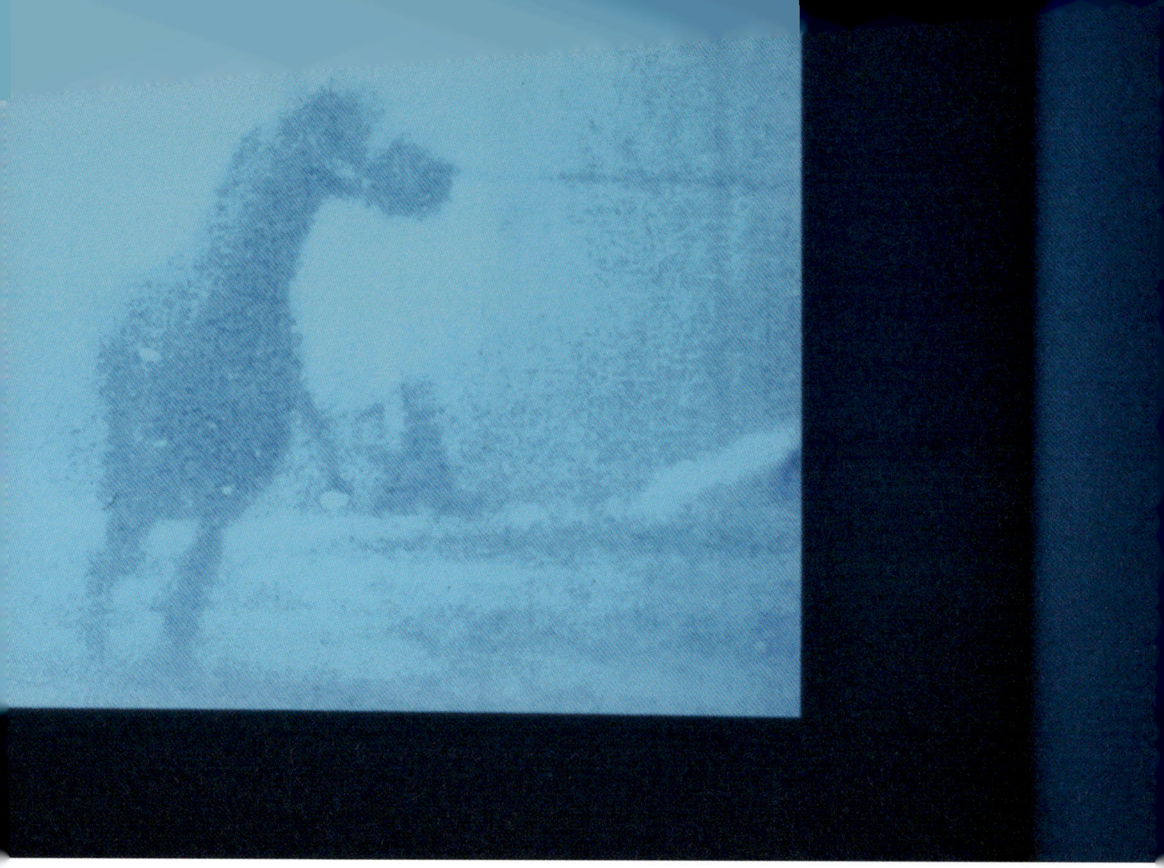

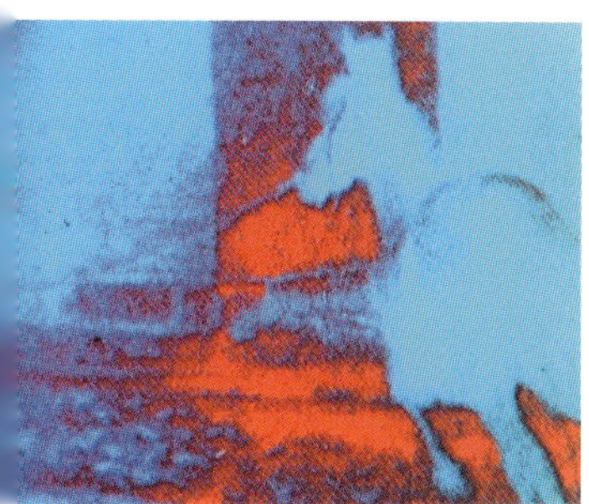 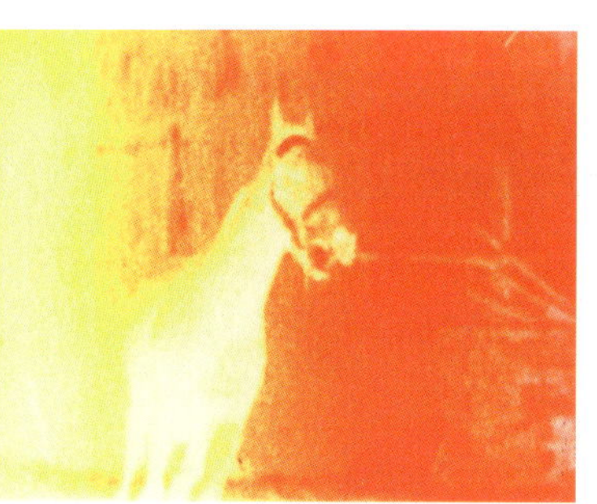 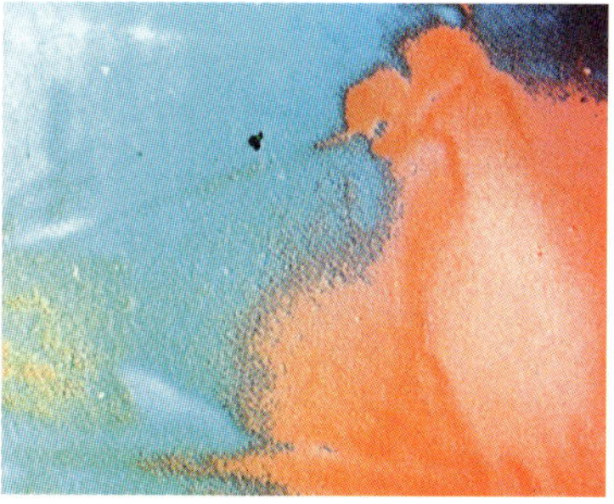

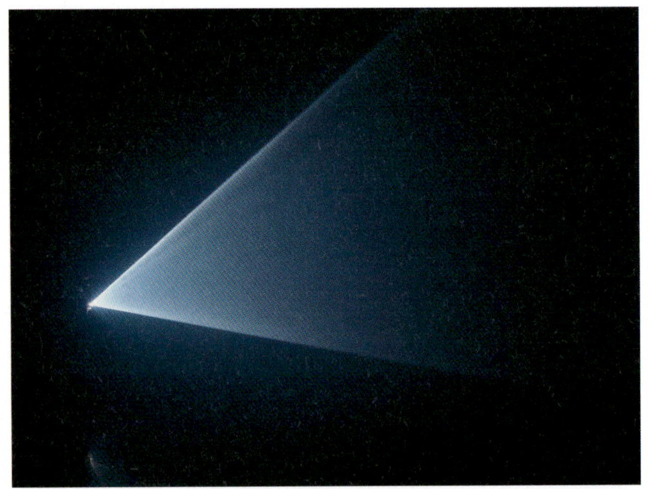

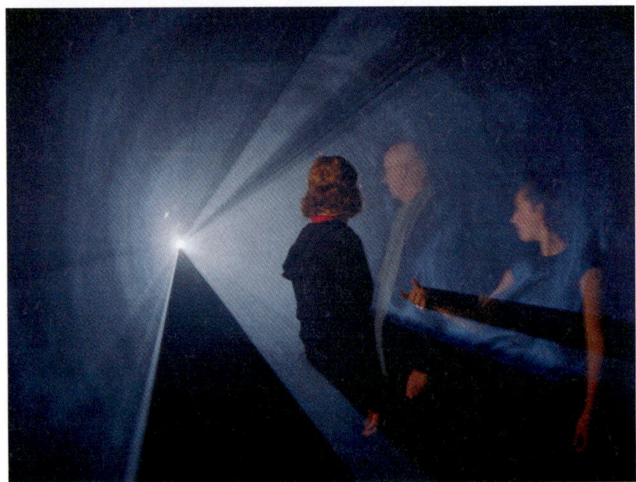

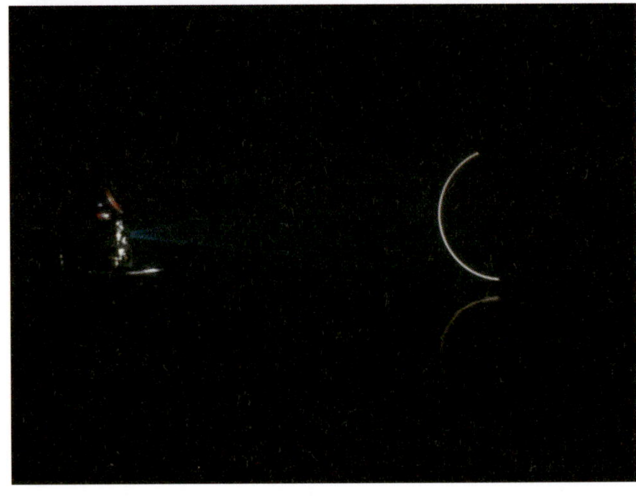

Anthony McCall
Line Describing a Cone, 1973
16 mm film, b/w, silent,
25 min, smoke
Dimensions variable

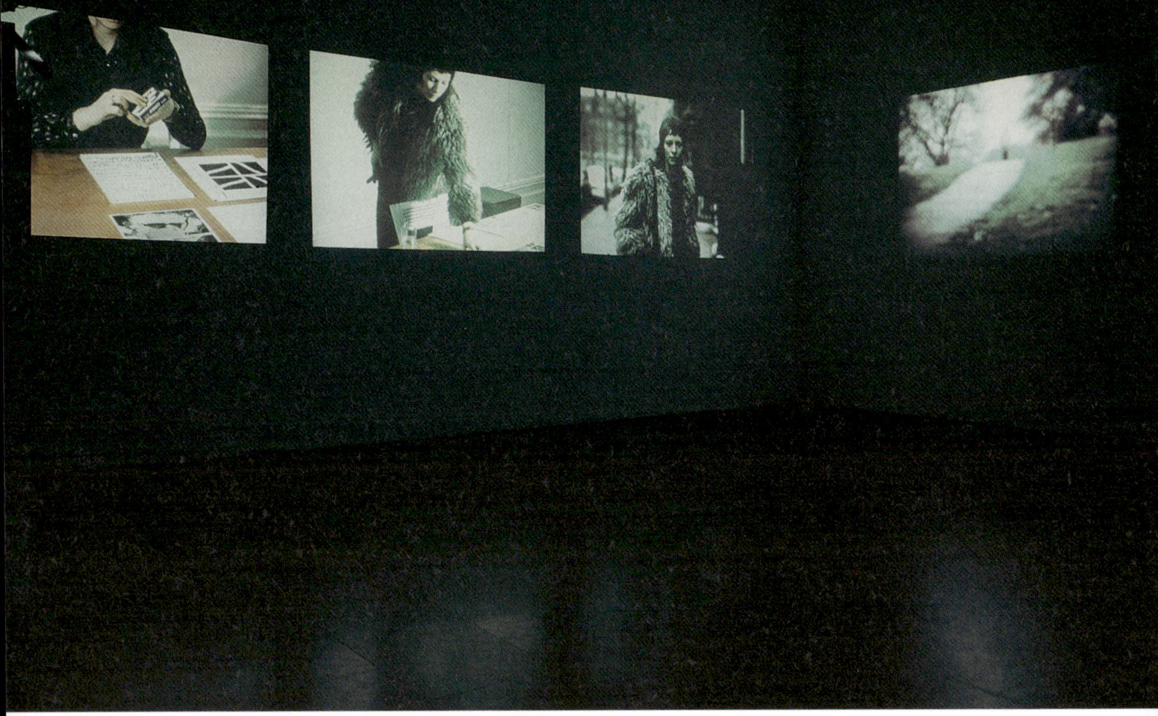

David Lamelas
Film Script (La manipulación del mensaje), 1972
8 mm film transferred to 16 mm film, colour, silent, 10 min,
looped projection and triple slide projection

Installation view, presentation of the MACBA Collection, 2004

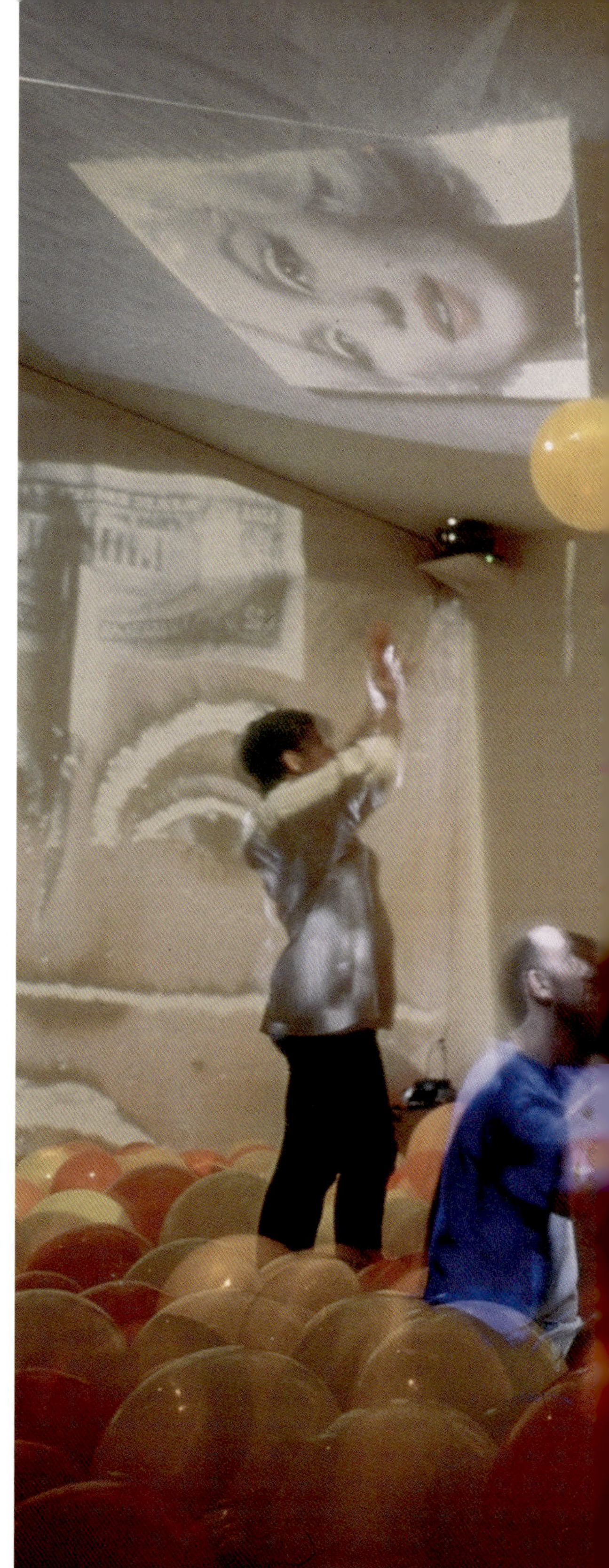

Hélio Oiticica, Neville d'Almeida
*CC3-Maileryn. Quasi Cinema (Block-Experiment
in Cosmococa-Program in Progress)*, 1973
5 slide projections, sound, sand, plastic
and balloons
Dimensions variable

Installation view, Pinacoteca do Estado
de São Paulo, 2003

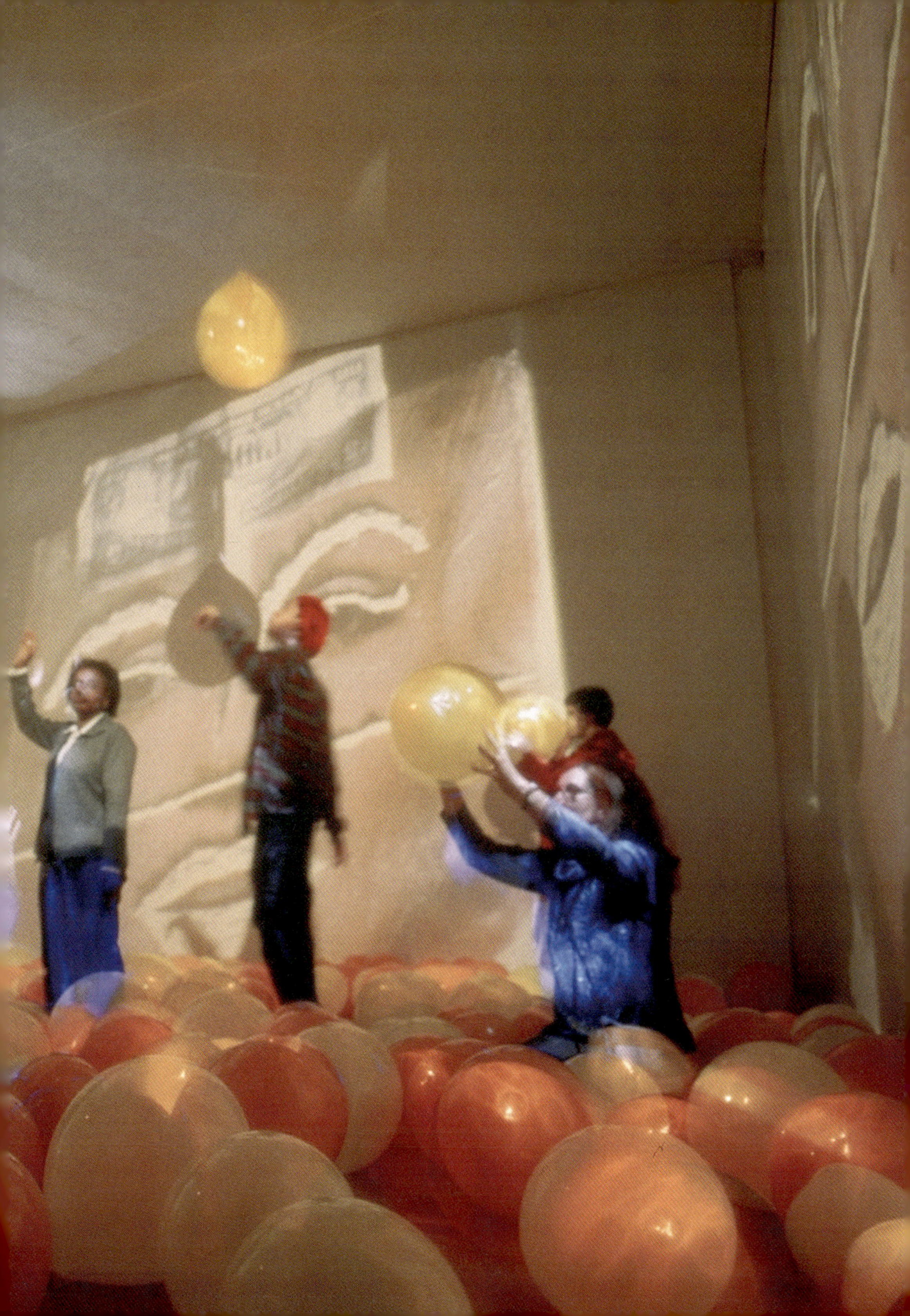

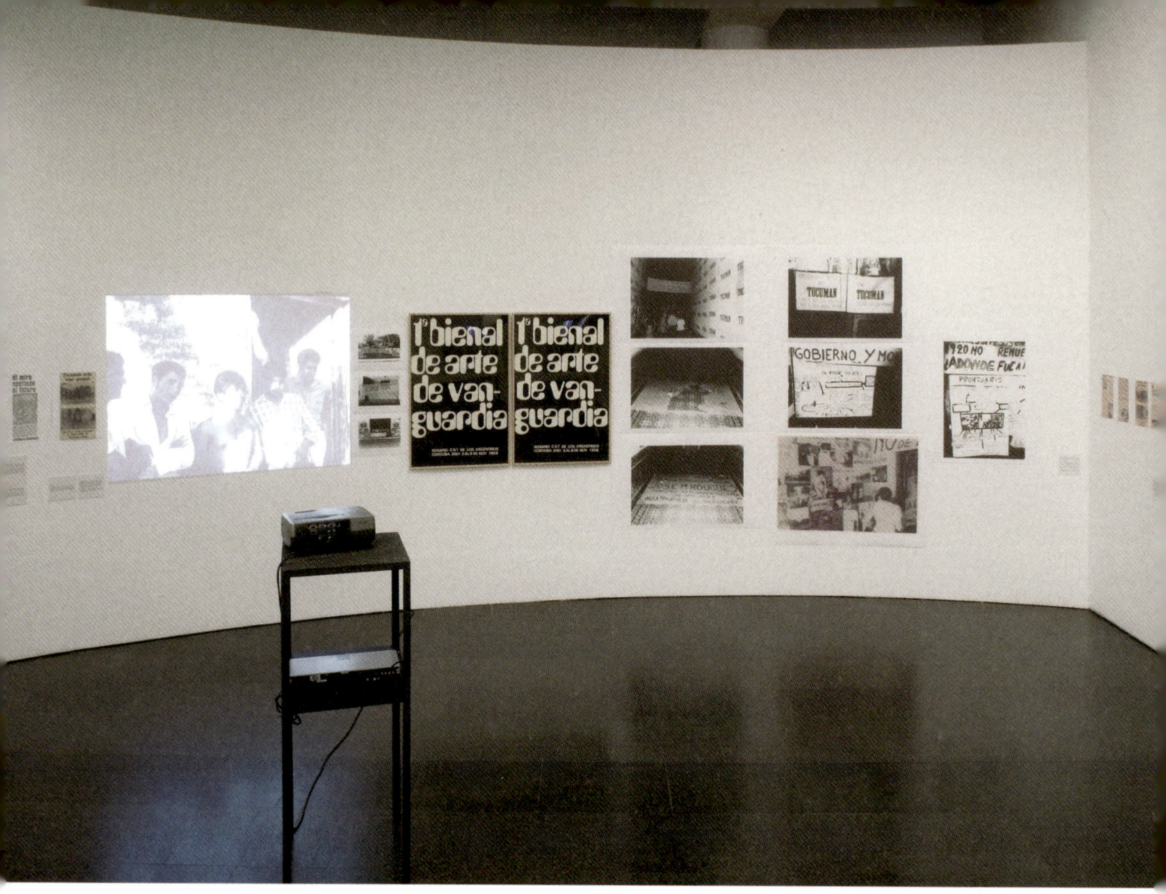

Grupo de artistas de vanguardia
Tucumán Arde Archive. Documentation related
to different actions and works carried out by
this group, 1966–68
Documents, photographs and press cuttings
Various dimensions

Installation view, presentation of the MACBA Collection, 2006

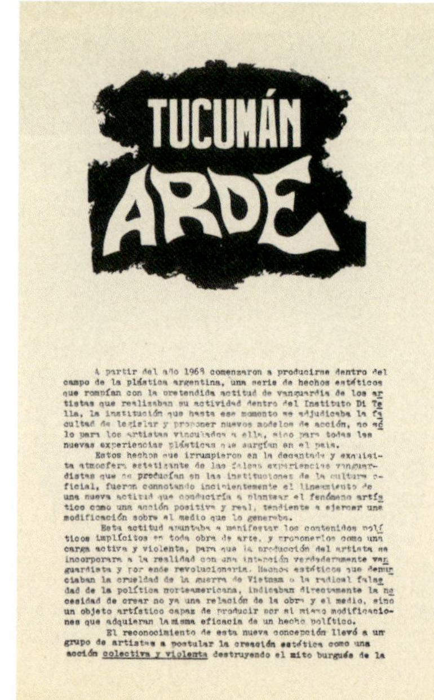

TUCUMÁN ARDE

The year 1968 marked the start on the Argentine arts scene of a series of aesthetic events that broke with the supposedly avant-garde stance of the artists who pursued their activities under the auspices of the Instituto di Tella, the institution that hitherto had taken upon itself the power of legislating and proposing new models of action, not only for the artists associated with it, but for all new artistic experiences to emerge in Argentina.

These events, breaking in on the biased, rarefied, aestheticising atmosphere of so-called avant-garde experiences taking place at the institutions of official culture, marked the start of a new attitude that was to consider the artistic phenomenon as a real, positive action that sought to modify the context that generated it.

This attitude sought to manifest the political contents implicit in any artwork and propose them as an active, violent force, incorporating the artist's output into reality with a truly avant-garde and, therefore, revolutionary intent. Aesthetic acts that denounced the cruelty of the Vietnam War or the radical hypocrisy of US politics were a direct indication of the need to create not a relation between the work and the context, but an artistic object that was capable in itself of bringing about changes with the same efficacy as a political act.

Recognition of this new conception led a group of artists to posit aesthetic creation as an individual act on the part of the artist and the passive role traditionally assigned to art. Deliberate aggression became the form of the new art. Violent action meant possessing and destroying the old forms of an art that were deeply rooted in individual ownership and personal enjoyment of the unique work. Violence became an action that created new contents: it destroyed the system of official culture, setting up against it a subversive culture that incorporated the process of modification, creating a truly revolutionary art.

Revolutionary art is born of an awareness of the present-day reality of the artist as an individual in the political and social context in which he finds himself.

Revolutionary art posits the aesthetic act as a nucleus that incorporates and unifies all the elements that make up human reality: economic, social and political; as a coming together of the ideas of the various disciplines, removing the separation between artists, intellectuals and technicians, and as a unitary action on the part of all of them, aimed at modifying the entire social structure – that is, a total art.

Revolutionary art acts on reality through a process of recruitment of its constituent elements and by means of a lucid ideological conception, based on the principles of materialist rationality.

In this way, revolutionary art manifests itself as a partial form of reality that is incorporated into total reality, destroying the idealistic separation between the artwork and the world, insofar as it serves to truly transform the social structures – that is, a transforming art.

Revolutionary art is the manifestation of the political contents that fight to destroy the outmoded cultural and aesthetic preconceptions of bourgeois society, joining up with the revolutionary forces that battle with forms of economic dependence and class oppression: it is, then, a social art.

The work produced by the Grupo de artistas de vanguardia (Group of Avant-garde Artists) is the continuation of a series of acts of deliberate aggression against institutions and representatives of bourgeois culture, such as the non-participation in and boycott of the Braque Prize, created by the Cultural Service of the French Embassy, which culminated in the arrest of several artists who gave violent expression to their rejection of it.

The collective work produced is based on the current Argentine situation, which has become more radical in one of its poorest provinces, Tucumán, subjected to a long tradition of underdevelopment and economic oppression. The current Argentine government, bent on a detrimental policy of colonisation, has closed down most of Tucumán's sugar mills, the driving force of the province's economy, sowing hunger and unemployment, with all the attendant social consequences. 'Operation Tucumán', devised by government economists, seeks to mask this overt aggression against the working class with false economic development based on the creation of hypothetical new industries financed by US capital. The truth masked by this operation is as follows: it is an attempt to destroy a real, explosive trade union movement that has extended throughout the north-west of Argentina by dissolving groups of workers, which are then fragmented into small industrial operations and forced to emigrate to other areas in search of temporary, poorly paid, insecure employment. One of the serious attendant consequences is the dissolution of the worker's family unit, which is exposed to improvisation and chance in order to subsist. The economic policy implemented by the government in the province of Tucumán serves as a pilot experience to gauge the resistance put up by the worker population so that, once union opposition has been neutralized, it can be applied to other provinces of similar economic and social characteristics.

'Operation Tucumán' is reinforced by 'operation silence', organised by government institutions to

confuse, distort and silence the serous situation
of Tucumán, to which the so-called 'free press' has
submitted for reasons of common class interests.

In the face of this situation, assuming their
responsibility as artists who are committed to
a social reality of which they form part, avant-garde
artists respond to 'operation silence' with the work
Tucumán Arde (Tucumán is burning).

The work consists of the creation of an over-
information circuit to manifest the surreptitious
distortion of events in Tucumán by the media,
the official authorities and the middle classes. The
media are powerful elements of mediation, which
can be used to convey a variety of content; the
positive influence exerted by the media in society
depends on the reality and veracity of the contents.
The information about the events that took place
in Tucumán, provided by the government and the
official media, serves to silence the serious social
problem unleashed by the closure of the sugar
mills and give a false image of economic recovery
in the province, blatantly refuted by the real facts.

To document these facts and unmask their
fallacious contradiction by the government and its
supporting class, the Grupo de artistas de
vanguardia travelled to Tucumán, accompanied by
technicians and specialists, and proceeded to verify
the social reality of life in the province. The process
of the artists' action reached a climax at a press
conference where, with recourse to violence, they
voiced their condemnation of the conduct of the
official authorities and the complicity of the media,
which collaborated in maintaining disgraceful,
degrading social conditions for the worker population
of Tucumán. The artists' action was carried out
in collaboration with student and worker groups,
which thereby contributed to the materialization of
the work.

The artists travelled to Tucumán armed with
comprehensive documentation about the economic
and social problems of the province and detailed
knowledge of all the information compiled by the
media about Tucumán's problems. This report had
previously undergone critical analysis to gauge
the degree of distortion and misinterpretation of the
facts. The next step was to draft the information
collected by the artists and technicians, which was
to serve as the basis for the exhibition presented
at the Centrales Obreras union headquarters.
Finally, the information that the media had produced
about the artists' action in Tucumán will be included
in the information circuit of the first phase.

The second part of the work is the presentation
of all the information collected about the situation
and the artists' action in Tucumán, part of which
will be publicized at trade unions and student and
arts centres, along with the exhibition, which,

in audiovisual and performance format, is taking
place at the Rosario Regional CGT de los Argentinos
union headquarters before travelling to Buenos
Aires.

The over-information circuit, which is basically
intended to challenge the image of reality in
Tucumán produced by the mass media, will
culminate in the third and final phase by producing
third-degree information that will be compiled in a
publication featuring all the processes of conception
and realization of the work and all the documentation
produced, along with a final evaluation.

The stance adopted by avant-garde artists
demands that they should not place their works
in the official institutions of bourgeois culture
and suggests the need to move them to another
context; this exhibition is, then, held in the
headquarters of the CGT de los Argentinos union,
this being the body that represents the class that
is in the vanguard of a struggle whose ultimate ends
are shared by the authors of this work.

María Teresa Gramuglio
Nicolás Rosa

Taking part in this work are:
Ma. Elviara de Arechavala, Beatriz Balbé, Graciela
Borthwick, Aldo Bortolotti, Graciela Carnevale,
Jorge Cohen, Rodolfo Elizalde, Noemí Escandell,
Eduardo Favario, León Ferrari, Emilio Ghilioni,
Edmundo Giura, Ma. Teresa Gramuglio, Martha
Greiner, Roberto Jacoby, José Ma. Lavarello, Sara
López Dupuy, Rubén Naranjo, David de Nully Braun,
Raúl Perez Cantón, Oscal Pidustwa, Estella
Pomerantz, Norberto Puzzolo, Juan Pablo Renzi,
Jaime Rippa, Nicolás Rosa, Carlos Schork, Nora
de Schork, Domingo J.A. Sapia, Roberto Zara.

Rosario CGT de los Argentinos
Córdoba 2061: 3–9 November 1968

NORBERTO JULIO PUZZOLO

27 DE MAYO AL 8 DE JUNIO

La exposición es una serie de sillas iguales, alineadas en filas como la platea de un cine, o como si se las hubiera dispuesto para una conferencia; están dirigidas de manera que si uno se sentara en alguna de ellas, lo único que podría ver sería la calle a través de la vidriera de la sala. La ventana está reforzada visualmente por un marco que colocó el autor para hacer notorio al espectador que forma parte de la obra. El espacio desmesurado de la sala también ha sido incorporado a ella con una jerarquía diferente a la de su vacío natural. Lo que se expone es una obra de Norberto Puzzolo, el más joven de los componentes del grupo de vanguardia rosarino, quien en su corta trayectoria ha demostrado una gran rigurosidad y claridad de ideas.

La visita a esta muestra puede resultar desconcertante para gran parte del público: esto es natural si tenemos en cuenta dos factores: en primer término, que en Rosario la vanguardia no ha expuesto con la frecuencia necesaria como para que el espectador interesado haya podido eslabonar cronológicamente cada etapa del proceso de investigación de los artistas; en segundo término, es también una realidad que el esquema pseudo-estético de la vieja-mala pintura que atesta las galerías locales, sigue en vigencia para gran parte del público. Sin embargo, salvando estos dos obstáculos, queda un tercero, y lo constituye el pensamiento de aquellos que efectivamente o por snobismo se acercan a las muestras de vanguardia: para este tipo de público que, a pesar de su actitud sin prejuicios aparente, mantiene también falsas ideas con respecto al arte, la muestra de Puzzolo resultará monótona y aburrida.

Es posible que esta última opinión se generalice entre parte del público porque esta obra no pretende (como muchas) decorar o explícitamente.

El problema central de la obra puede divi-amenizar la vida burguesa de nadie, sino que está estructurada sobre la base de la problematización de ciertas funciones de la existencia. Si bien toda obra de arte plantea problemas de la realidad —y Puzzolo ya lo ha hecho en sus anteriores trabajos— en esta obra lo logra con mayor materialidad y más dirse en dos temas fundamentales que se interrelacionan: por un lado tenemos la estructura material, con una gran imagen austera conseguida mediante la multiplicación (insistencia) de un mismo elemento (sillas) perfectamente ordenadas según una geometría elemental. Este enorme prisma de sillas actúa sobre el espacio previamente vacío de la sala, transformándolo para la percepción. Por otro lado, el hecho más significante de la muestra reside en que uno, si sigue las directivas de la obra, entra a la sala para mirar hacia afuera; de hecho, nadie dará importancia a esta acción, salvo como mero ensayo lúdico, pero el valor de la obra tanto en la acción como en el aparato desplegado para indicarla.

Esta desproporción entre tema y desarrollo, esta gratitud del aparato desplegado para proponer un "mensaje" aparentemente tan sencillo, se erigen como una formulación desmesurada de una "teoría" de la visión objetiva de la realidad.

Esta obra de Puzzolo es, en varios sentidos, la refirmación de las ideas planteadas en sus últimos trabajos del año pasado. Insisto en ésto porque a partir de la forma —digamos mejor: de su apariencia— podría suponerse que no tiene ningún vínculo con las anteriores. Aclaro que no es mi preocupación encontrar una "continuidad" entre los trabajos de Puzzolo (ésta, si existe, es una consecuencia accidental de la actitud de búsqueda del artista). Me interesa más señalar que esta permanencia de intención (de idea) es una demostración de que, si bien forma y contenido pueden considerarse una misma cosa, o mejor, dos cosas íntimas, dialécticamente relacionadas, a un cambio de la forma no necesariamente corresponde un cambio de contenido.

En esta obra Puzzolo decidió optar por un material diferente del que últimamente usaba; también es diferente la imagen general que resulta de ella, que es más intensa y

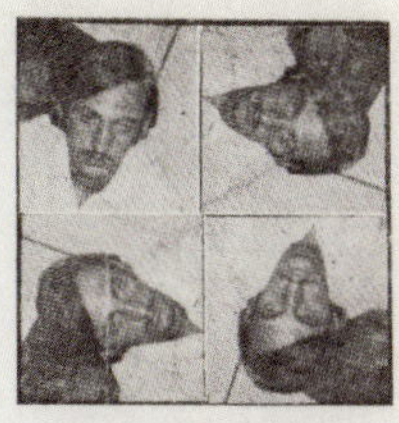

Norberto Julio Puzzolo nació en Rosario en julio de 1948. Estudios de dibujo y pintura con Juan Grela G. y dibujo con Mijalichen. Exposiciones: Galería "El Taller" diciembre de 1966 / Galería "Carrillo" agosto 1967 Rosario / "Pintura Actual Rosario" Colección Slullitel Museo Provincial de Santa Fe agosto 1967 / "Rosario 67" Museo de Arte Moderno Buenos Aires y Montevideo (Uruguay) / "Estructuras Primarias II" Sociedad Hebraica Bs. As. setiembre 1967 / Facultad de Medicina Bs. As. octubre de 1967 / Galería "El Galpón" Santa Fe 1967 / O.P.N.I. Galería Quartier Rosario diciembre 1967 / "El arte por el aire" Hotel Provincial Mar del Plata enero 1968.

más comprometida visualmente con la apariencia normal de la realidad; además, ha cambiado la relación del espectador con la obra, y la de ésta con la realidad, pero el contenido, la idea, es sustancialmente semejante a la de sus obras anteriores, porque si bien ha introducido tantos cambios en los constituyentes de su obra, también ha modificado las relaciones internas de estos elementos entre sí, de manera que el resultado sea, en líneas generales, el mismo de las obras anteriores, pero con mayor eficacia y enriquecido por un planteo más original.

JUAN PABLO RENZI

CICLO DE ARTE EXPERIMENTAL / ROSARIO / 1968

AUSPICIADO POR EL INSTITUTO DI TELLA / CUADROS PUBLICIDAD ENTRE RIOS 730

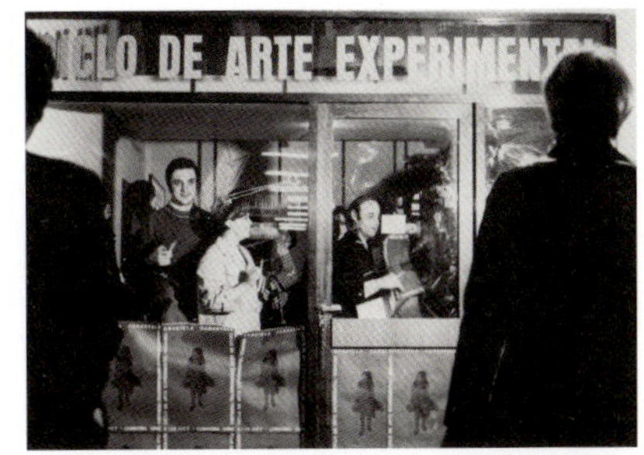

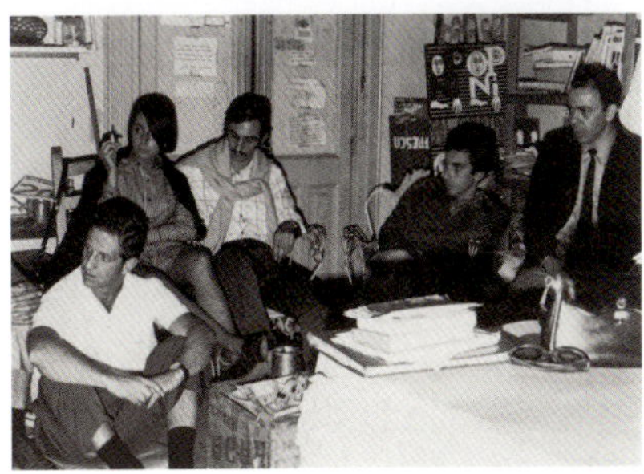

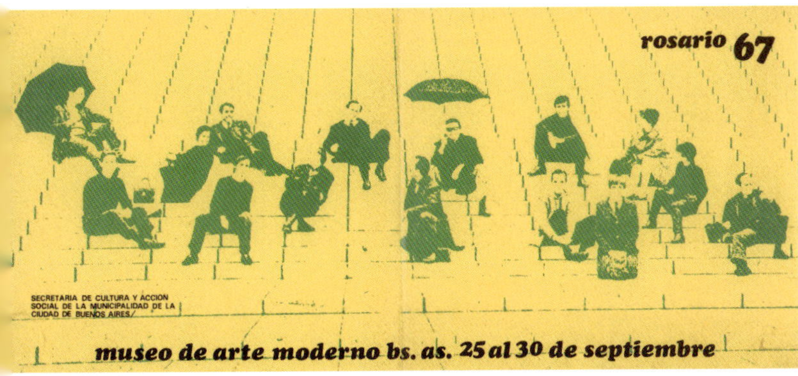

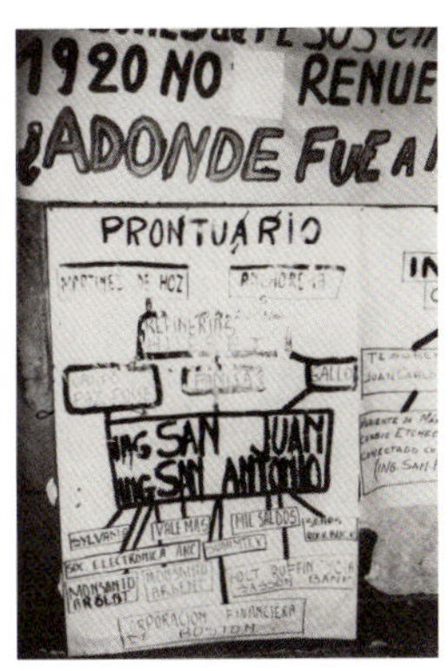

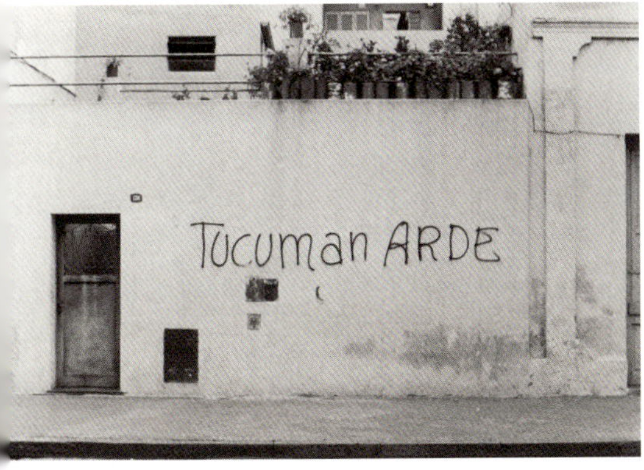

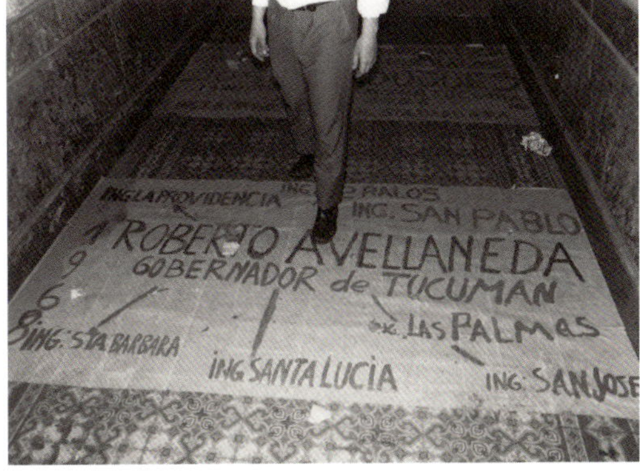

ENCUESTA A 24 GALERIAS DE ARTE DE MADRID
===

----- ¿En que año abrió la galería?   *26 de noviembre 71*

----- ¿Como definiria la linea de su galería?   *De Vanguardia.*

----- ¿Cuales son los artistas que exponen en su galería?   *Navarro Ramón, Montesa, Echauz, Hess, Domingo Sang, Mármol, Ben-Yessef Polit, Marola, Alcoy, …*

----- ¿Con que criterios de selección han escogido estos artistas?   *Teniendo en cuenta que la obra de arte es un medio de expresión y testimonio del momento universal que vivimos.*

----- ¿Está de acuerdo en que la galería desempeña un papel de intermediario entre el artista y el coleccionista?

Sí

----- ¿Esta de acuerdo en que la galería establece y mantiene la plusvalía de la obra de arte?

Sí,

----- ¿Hasta que punto las galerias influyen en la evolución del arte?

La galería mantiene el mecenazgo, imprescindible para la evolución del arte.

----- ¿Concibe la posibilidad de un contacto artista-coleccionista, sin intermediarios?

Sí, pero no lo encuentro interesante para el artista.

----- ¿Admitiria la práctica artistica desligada de un valor de cambio?

Sí, pero me parece una utopía

----- ¿En un contexto domo el nuestro, crea posible un arte sin galerias (plusvalía) y sin coleccionistas (especulación)?

cionista un especulador "a priori". NO. Y ademas, no considero al cole-

----- ¿Ante una transformación real cree que tendría sentido la galería?

Sí, des de el momento que la Galería representa el apoyo del artista y sus intereses.

----- ¿Es rentable su galería?

Espero que algún dia lo sea.

GRUP DE TREBALL de Barcelona

NUEVOS COMPORTAMIENTOS ARTISTICOS

MADRID - INSTITUTO ALEMAN - 20 y 21 MARZO 1974

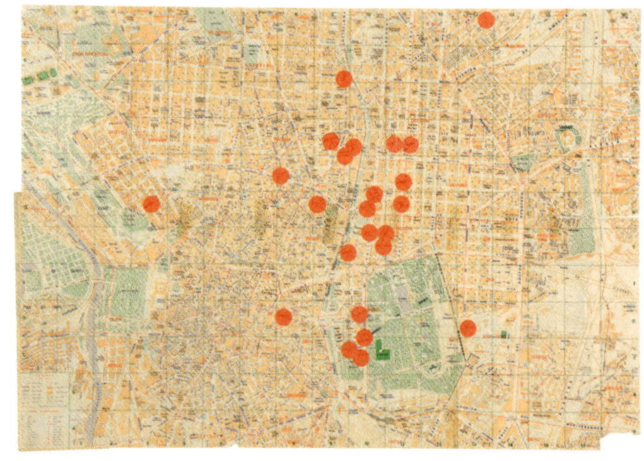

Grup de Treball
Encuesta a 24 galerías de arte de Madrid,
1974
Map of the city of Madrid, sticky labels,
typewritten pages, handwritten pages
and photocopies
Various dimensions

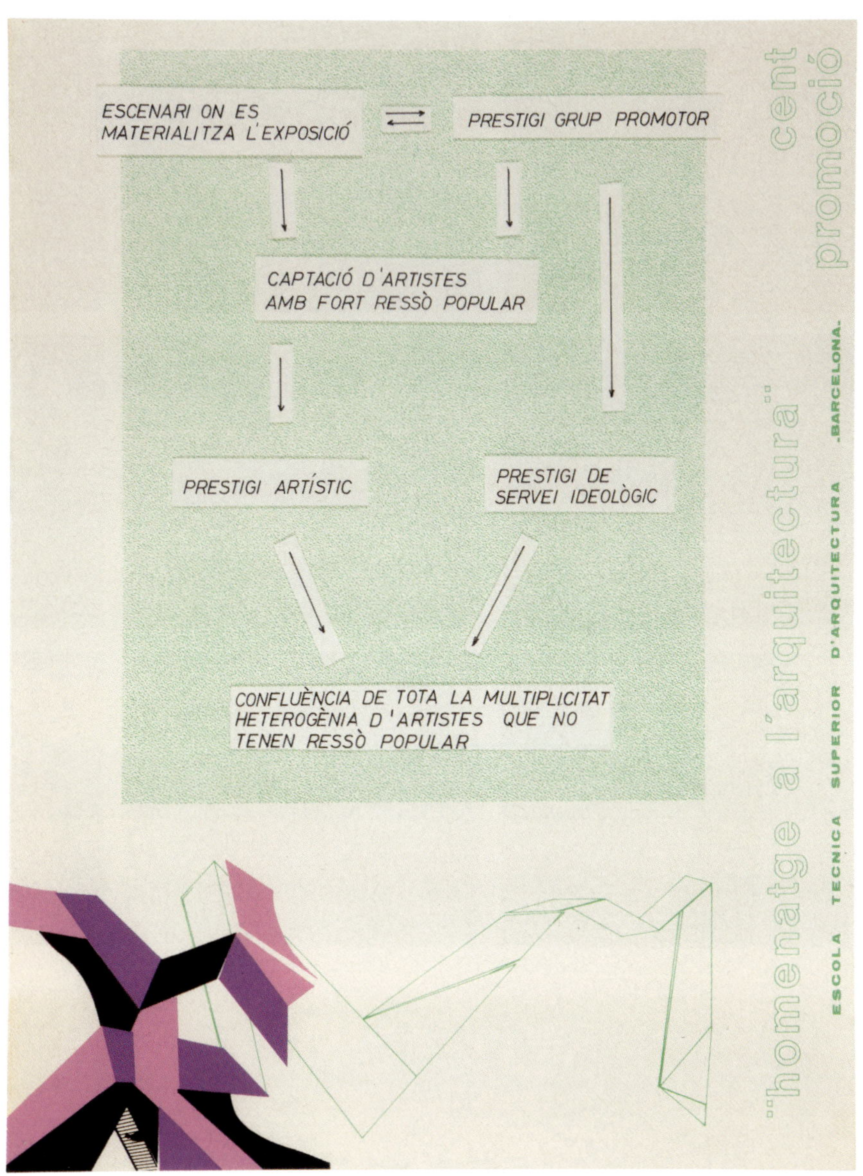

Homenatge a l'arquitectura, 1975
Ink on paper
Various dimensions

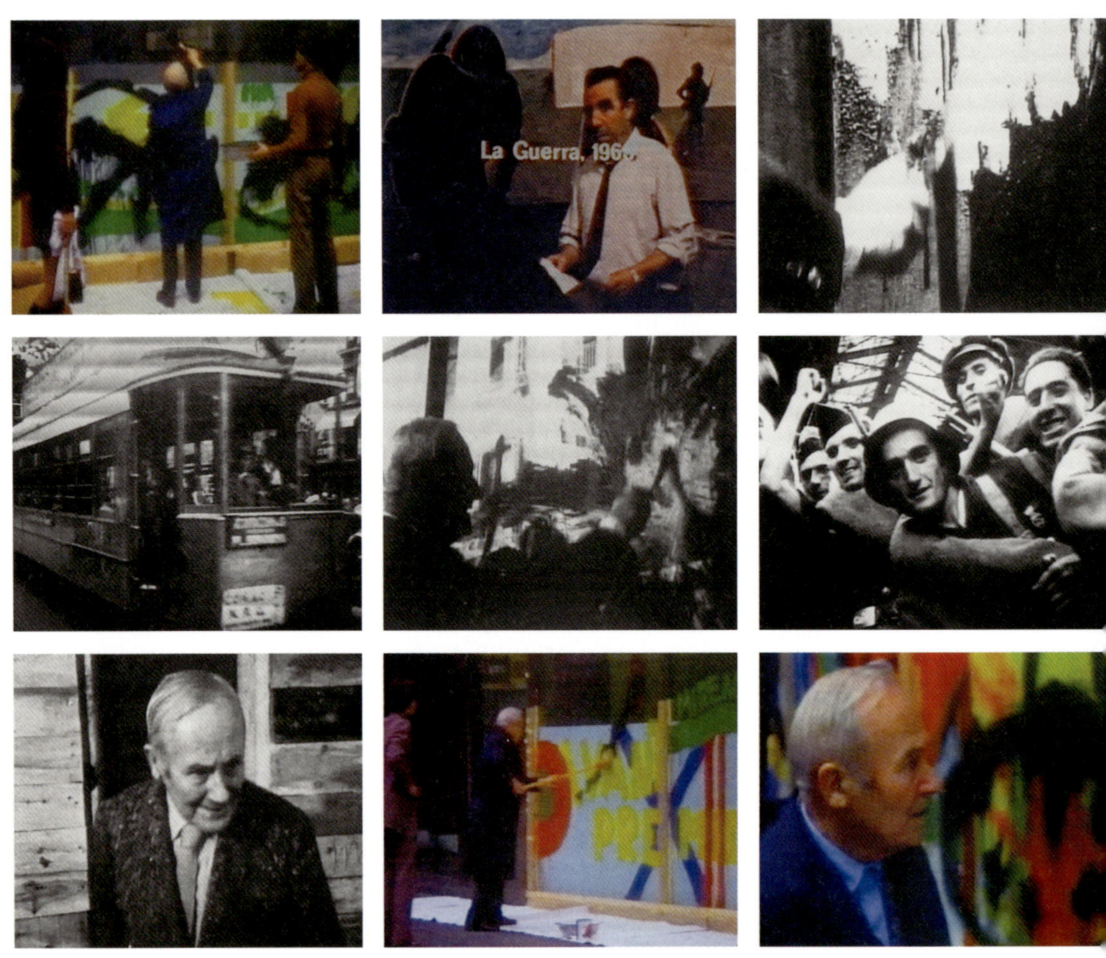

Pere Portabella
Miró, l'altre, 1969
16 mm film, b/w and colour, sound, 15 min
Production: Pere Portabella, Films 59

Informe general, 1976
16 mm film, colour, sound, 173 min
Production: Pere Portabella, Films 59

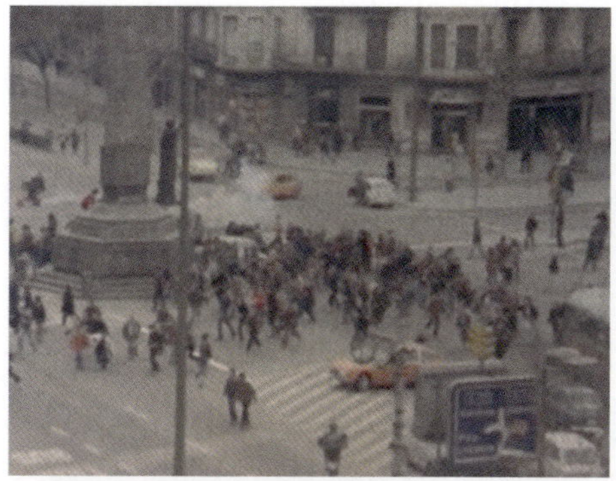
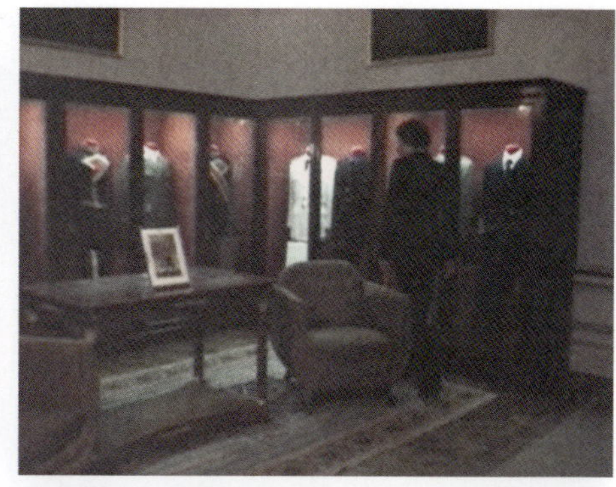
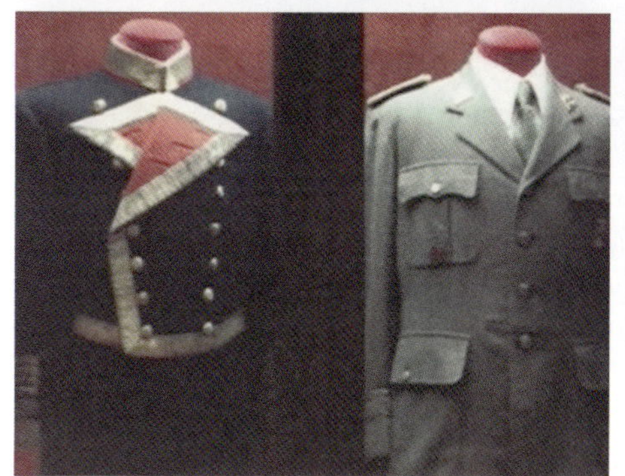
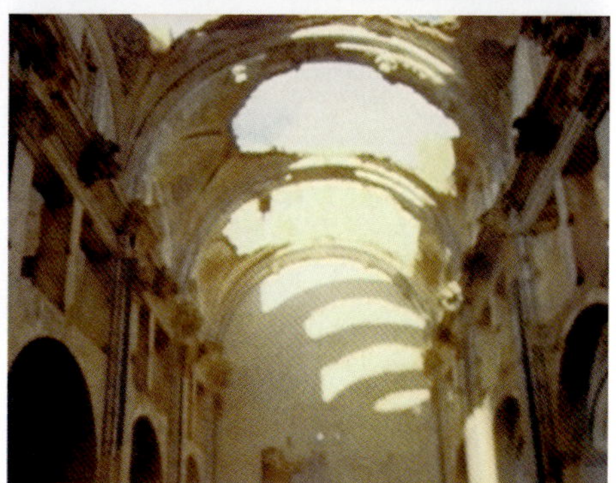
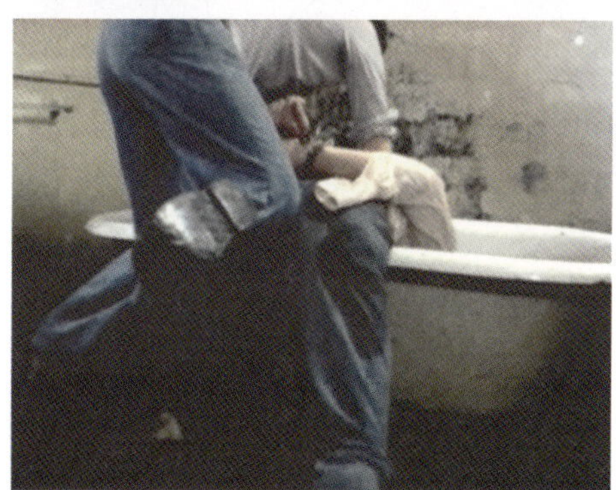

Artículo 12º. Nadie será objeto de injerencias arbitrarias en su vida privada, su familia, su domicilio o su correspondencia, ni de ataques a su honra o a su reputación. Toda persona tiene derecho a la protección de la ley contra tales injerencias o ataques.

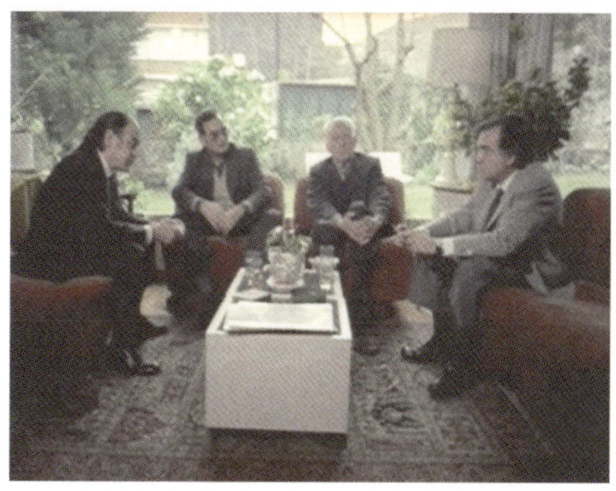
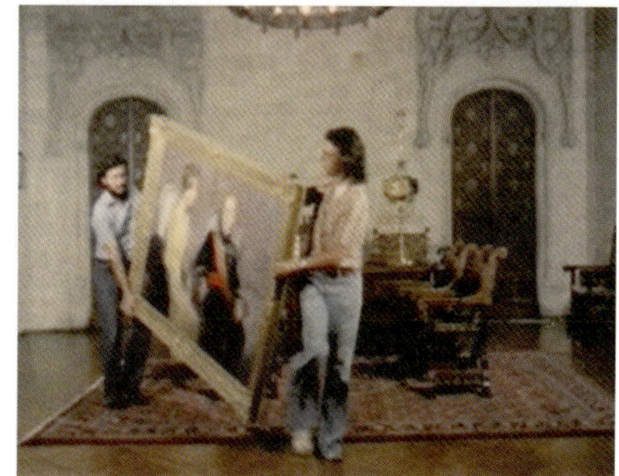

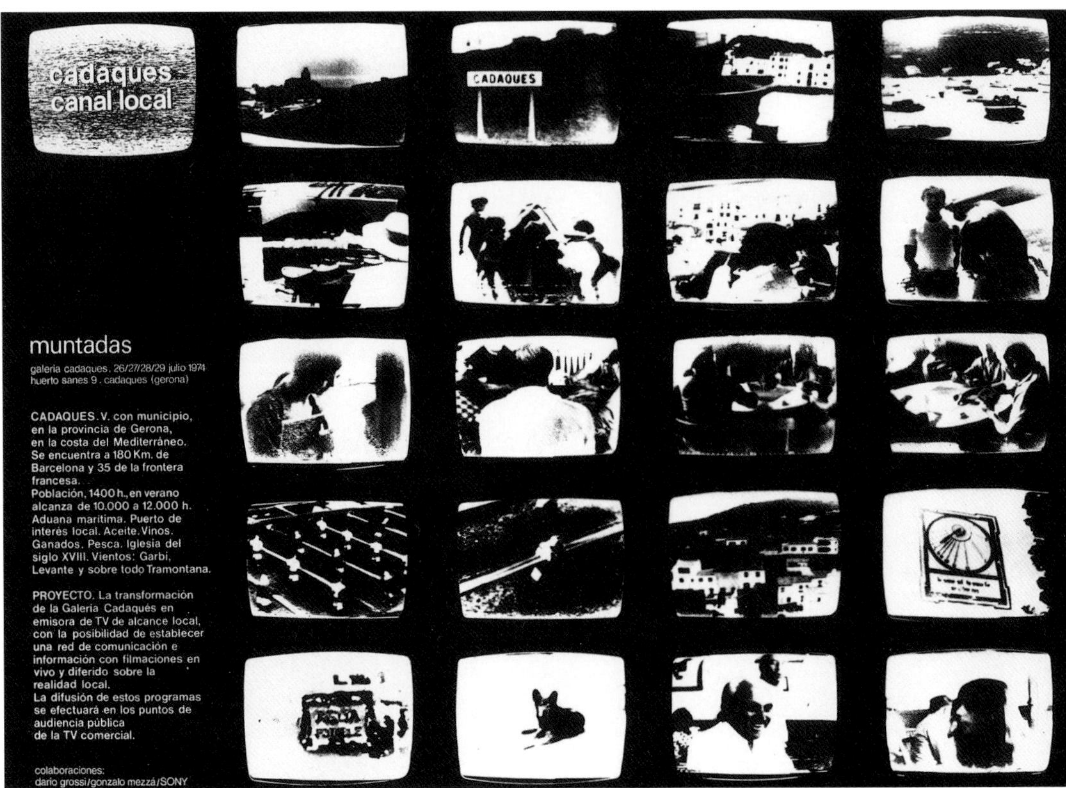

Muntadas
Punt d'informació. Cadaqués Canal Local, 1974
Compilation of video recordings, texts, documents
and photographs, photocopied and blown up
Various dimensions

Poster, 42 × 58.5 cm

Punto de información. Barcelona Distrito Uno, 1976
Documentary video, b/w, sound, 154 min 39 s; photographic
panel, glass table, photocopied documents and photographs
Various dimensions

Document, 29.7 × 21 cm

TVE: primer intento, 1989
Single-channel video, b/w and colour, 38 min 20 s

On Translation: The Audience (Barcelona), 1998 (2002)
Digital print on PVC
2 parts at 230 × 388 cm and 230 × 390.2 cm

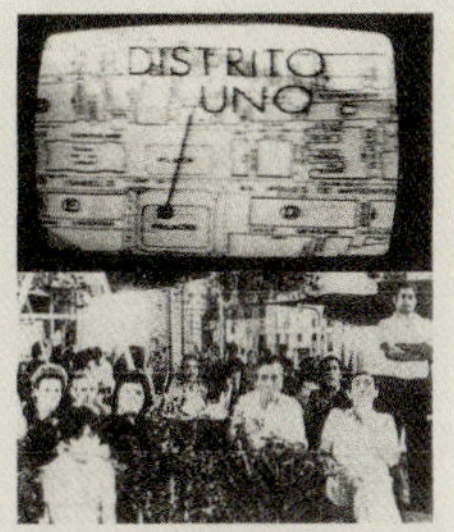

BARCELONA DISTRITO UNO (B.D.U.)

SUPOSÀ LA SEGONA APLICACIÓ DEL MODEL DE POSADA EN PRÀCTICA ADAPTAT A L'ARREL SOCIAL URBANA I ASSOCIATIVA, TOT CONNECTANT AMB ELS MOVIMENTS SOCIALS I POLÍTICS DE LA TRANSICIÓ. B.D.U. VA APROFITAR L'ESPAI DE LECTURA TELEVISIVA PÚBLICA DE LA TERRASSA D'UN BAR-QUIOSC PER A SITUAR-HI UN PUNT DE CONTRAINFORMACIÓ —CANVIANT EL SISTEMA TELEVISIU— I DE COL·LABORACIÓ MICROCOMUNICATIVA QUE ES VA CONVERTIR EN UN PROTOTIP DE TELEVISIÓ DE BARRI.

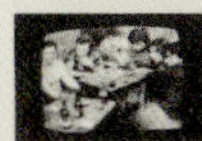
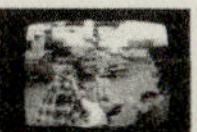
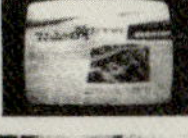

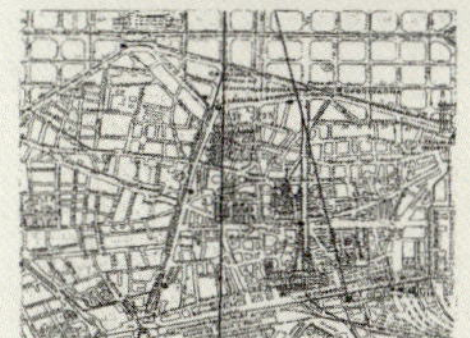

EXPERIÈNCIA DE COMUNICACIÓ

"... los habituales programas habíanse trocado en informaciones de televisión alternativa en las que los protagonistas eran los habitantes del barrio, sus problemas y el mismo barrio. Los vídeos se grabaron con la colaboración de la correspondiente Associació de Veïns."
(Josep Iglesias del Marquet. "Experiencia de comunicación", *Diario de Barcelona*. Dominical del Brusi, 17 d'octubre de 1976).

ALTERNATIVA A LA TV

"De hecho, Muntadas estaba llenando con su actividad artística un hueco que debería corresponder a los propios vecinos, la desenmascaración de la información."
(J.M. Martí Font. "Alternativa a la TV", *El Viejo Topo*. Barcelona, novembre de 1976, p. 66).

EL VÍDEO NOVAMENT

"... tres dies consecutius, per a les quals fou utilitzat el televisor d'un bar-quiosc de la plaça del Palau. El barri, la seva topografia, els habitants i els seus problemes foren el centre del treball, i els espectadors del bar i la gent del barri, el públic de la intervenció."
(Alicia Suárez i Mercè Vidal. "El vídeo novament", *Serra d'Or*, núm. 206. Monestir de Montserrat 1976, p. 45)

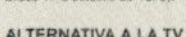
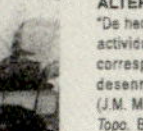

Els col·lectius de barri del Districte 1 de Barcelona van prendre consciència política molt ràpidament i es van organitzar d'acord amb les dinàmiques de les associacions de veïns de l'època de la transició.

La televisió a Espanya quasi no evoluciona, tot i l'acceptació del repte que suposa assimilar els canvis produïts en els darrers dos anys prenent part activa en l'esforç legitimador de la nova democràcia.

S'inicia la transició política. Les Corts Espanyoles aproven la Llei de la Reforma Política. L'índex de productivitat espanyol era el més baix de l'Europa occidental, l'increment del PIB va ser del 3,3% i l'atur de 4,6%.

L'ex-ministre xilè Orlando Letelier és assassinat a Washington. Reunificació oficial de Vietnam del Nord i del Sud. Primeres imatges de Mart. Gran èxit de la pel·lícula Rocky, de Sylvester Stallone

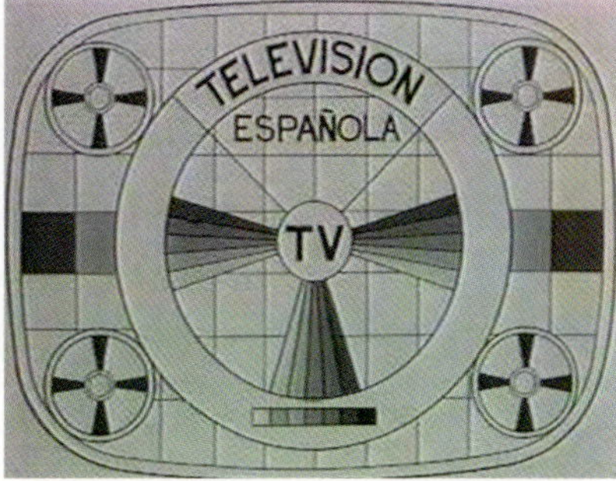

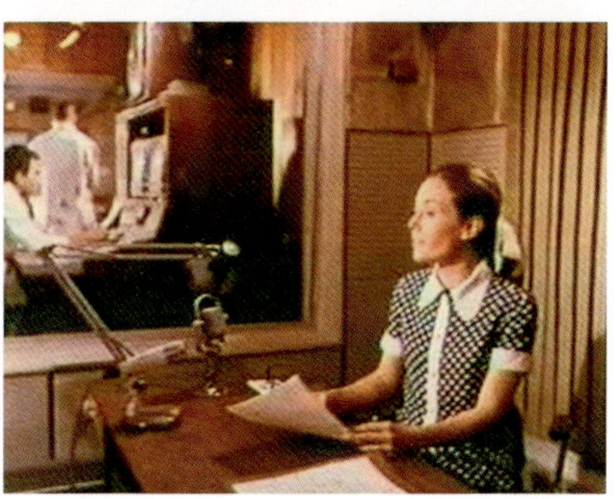

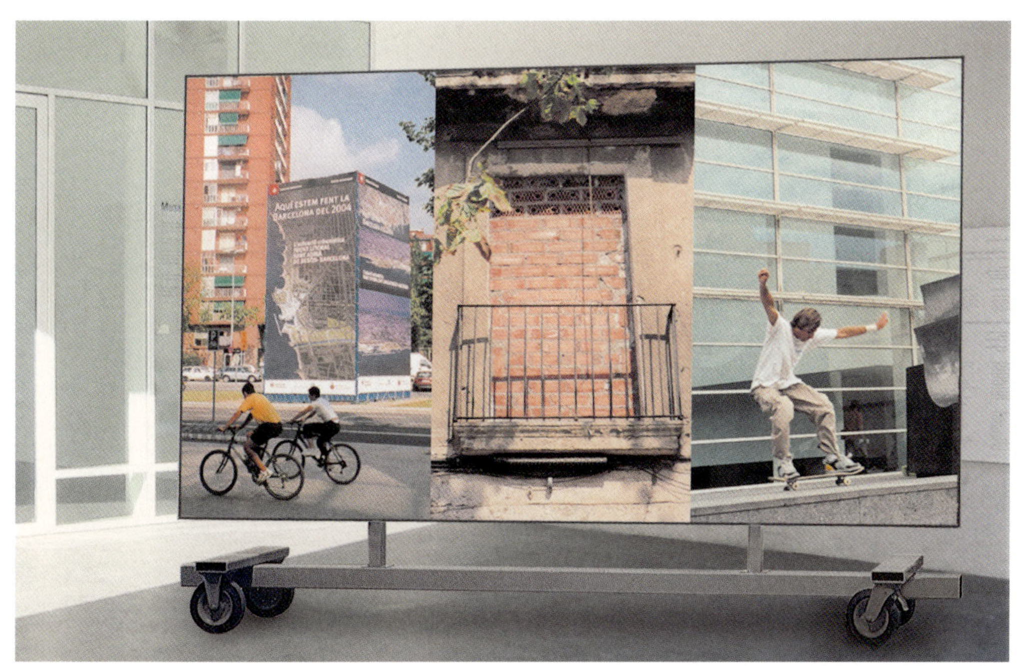

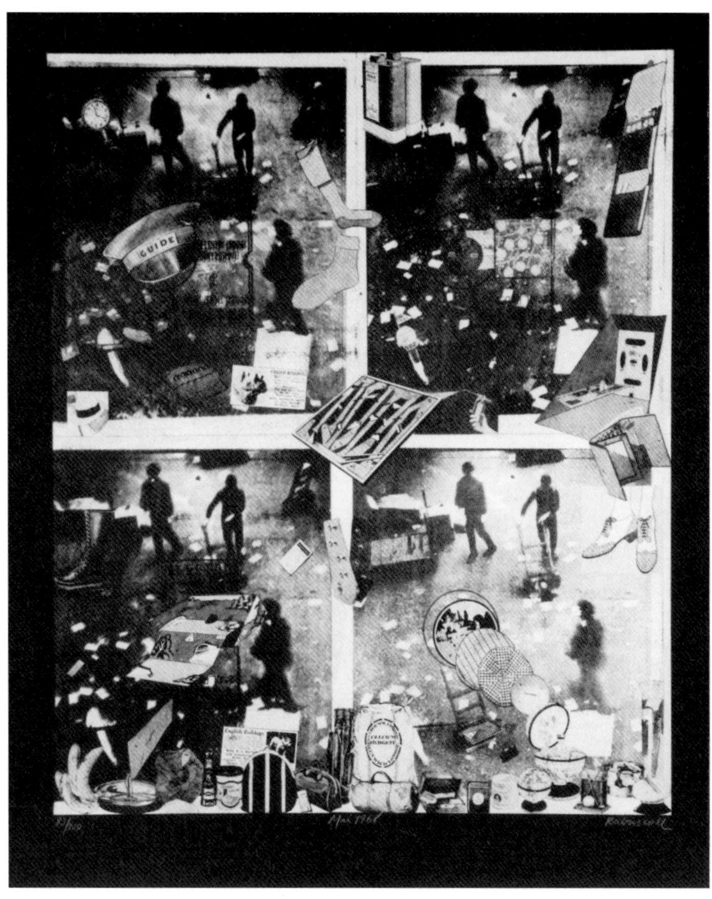

Joan Rabascall
68 mai 1968, 1968
Offset lithography on paper
56 × 47 cm

Gol. Serie: 'Spain Is Different', 1975
Photographic emulsion on canvas
100 × 100 cm

Horario de misas. Serie: 'Spain Is Different', 1975
Photographic emulsion on canvas
50 × 20.5 cm

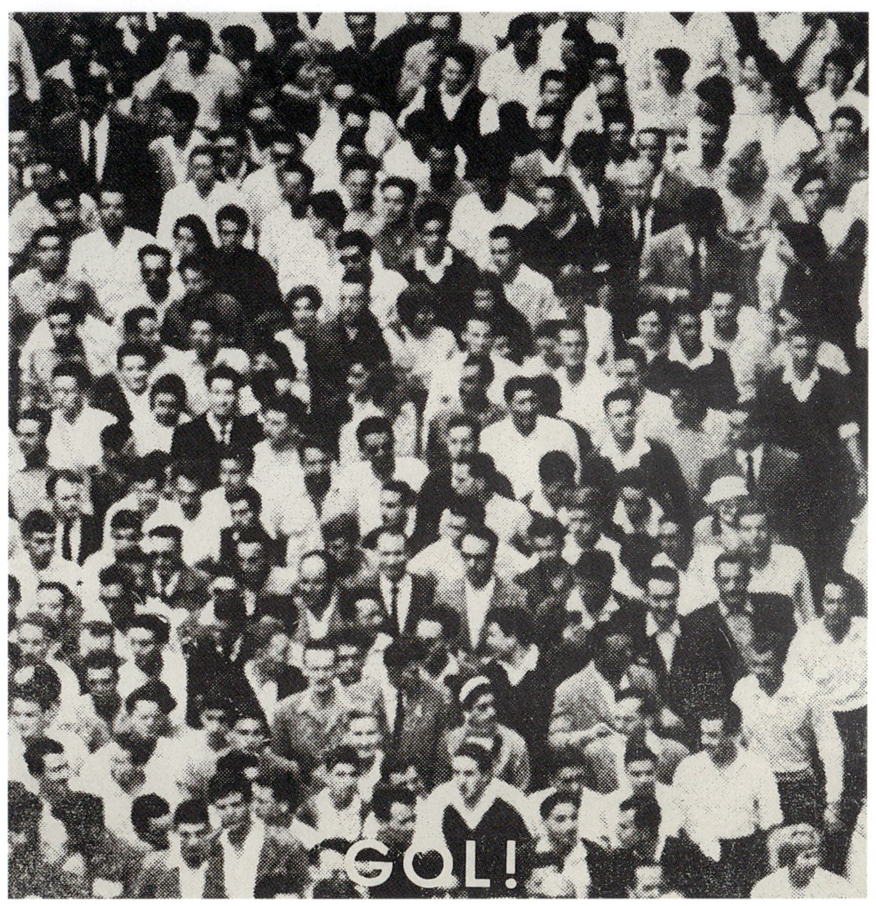

HORARIO DE MISAS

MARZO

S. I. Catedral	festivos	10 h.
S. Pedro	vigilias	19 h.
	festivos	8,12,19 h.
Monast.S.Cristóbal	festivos	9 h.
El Salvador	vigilias	20 h.
	festivos	8,9,10,11,12,19,20 h.
Sta. Cruz	vigilias	17'30,19'30 h.
	festivos	8'30,9'30,10'30,11'30, 12'30,17'30,19'30 h.
San Ciriaco	vigilias	20 h.
	festivos	10'30, 20 h.
San Pablo	vigilias	19 h.
	festivos	9 h.
San Antonio	vigilias	20 h.
	festivos	8,10,12,18'30,19'30 h.
San Rafael	vigilias	20 h.
	festivos	10,17'30 h.
San Mateo	festivos	9'30,12 h.
Sta. Inés	festivos	16'30 h.
Buscastell	festivos	11 h.
Sta. Eulalia		
Puig de Missa	festivos	11 h.
Capilla Monjas	vigilias	19 h.
	festivos	9'30, 19 h.
Cala Llonga	festivos	17 h.
Ntra.Sra.de Jesús	vigilias	19 h.
	festivos	9'30, 19 h.
Puig den Valls	vigilias	19 h.
	festivos	9 h.
Sta. Gertrudis	vigilias	20'30 h.
	festivos	11, 18 h.
San Carlos	festivos	9,11 h.
San Juan	festivos	9,11 h.
San Miguel	festivos	10'30, 17 h.
San Lorenzo	festivos	10'30,17 h.
San José	vigilias	19'30 h.
	festivos	9,12 h.
San Jorge	vigilias	18 h.
	festivos	8, 11, 19'30 h.
San Francisco de Paula	festivos	alterno 9 h.
La Revista		
Aeropuerto	festivos	10 h.
San Agustín	vigilias	20'30 h.
	festivos	10'30, 18 h.
N.S.Carmen, Cubells	vigilias	19 h.
	festivos	16'30 h.
S.Fco.Javier	vigilias	19 h.
	festivos	10,18 h.
N.S.del Pilar	festivos	9'30,17 h.
San Fernando	festivos	16'30,18'30 h.

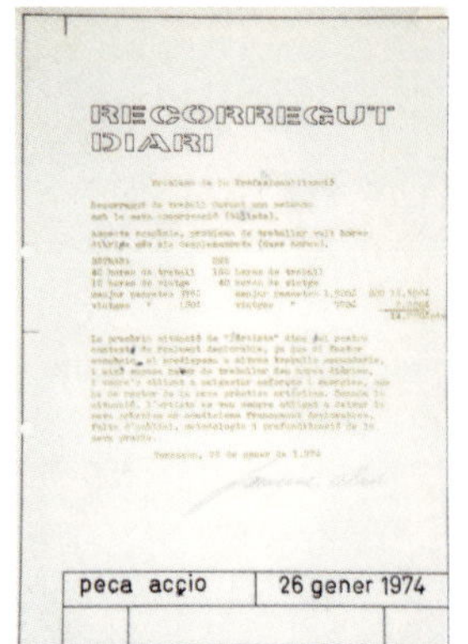

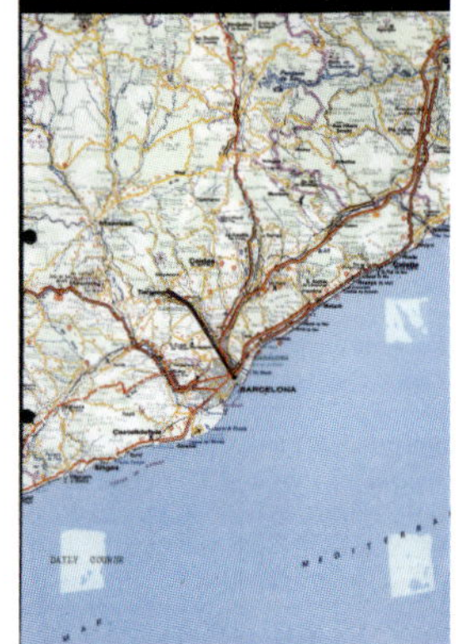

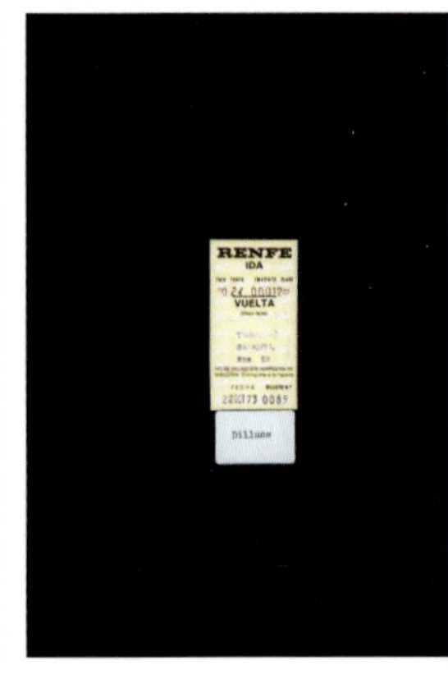

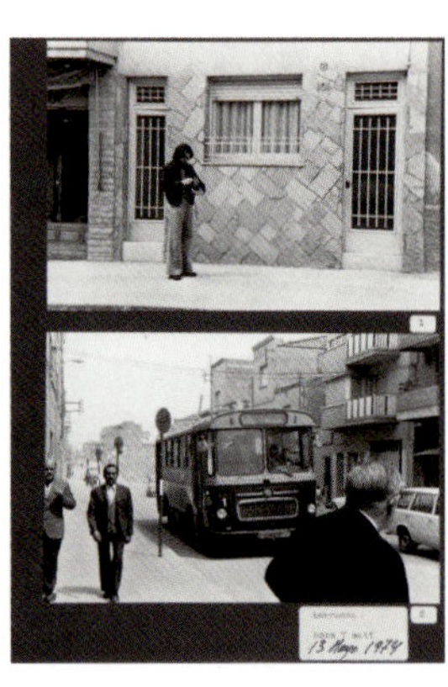

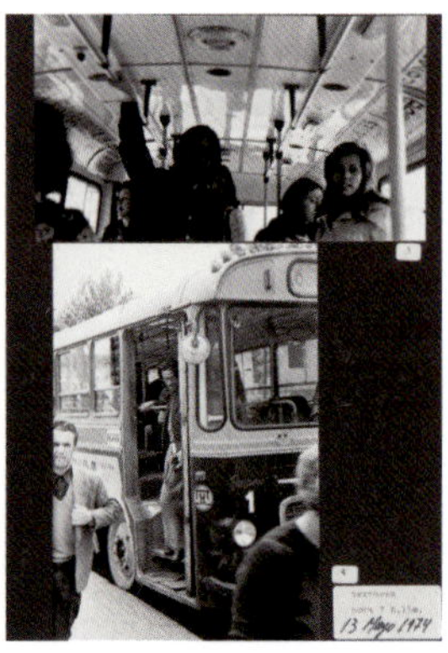

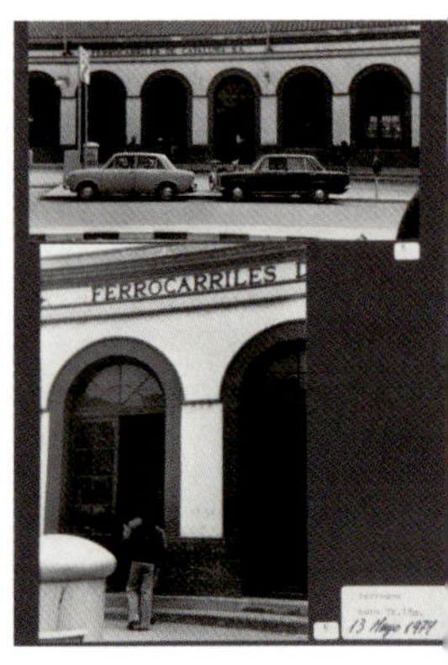

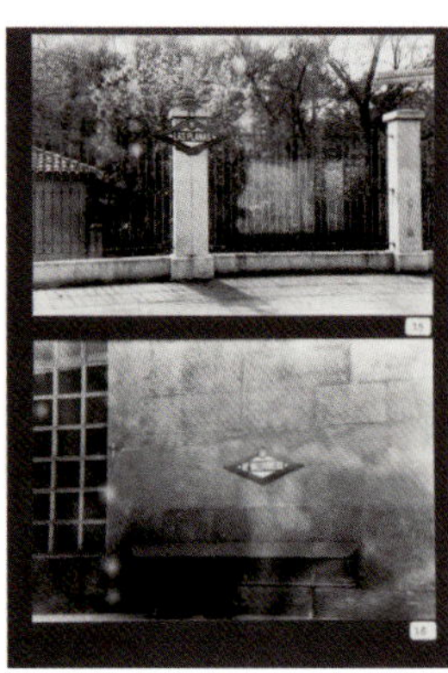

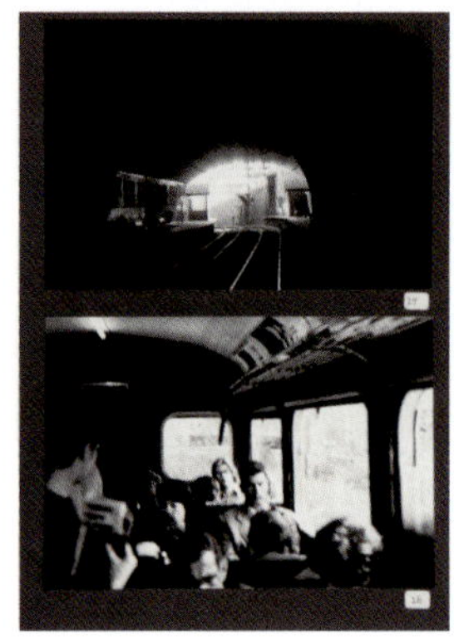

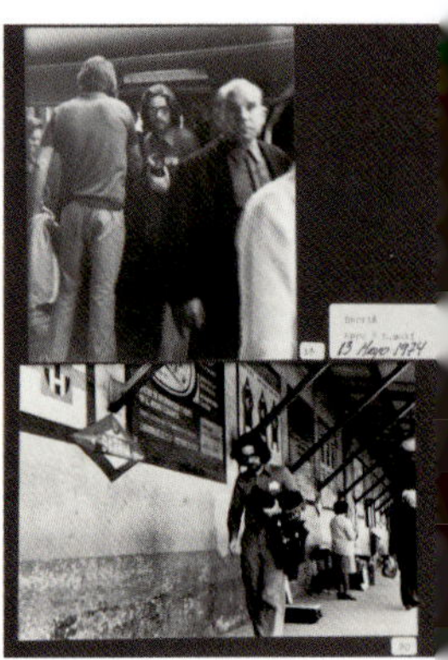

Francesc Abad
Recorregut diari, 1974
Photographs, maps, tickets and sound recording
Various dimensions

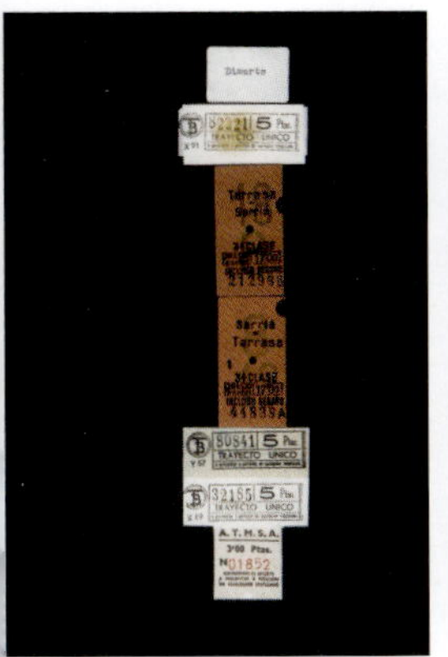

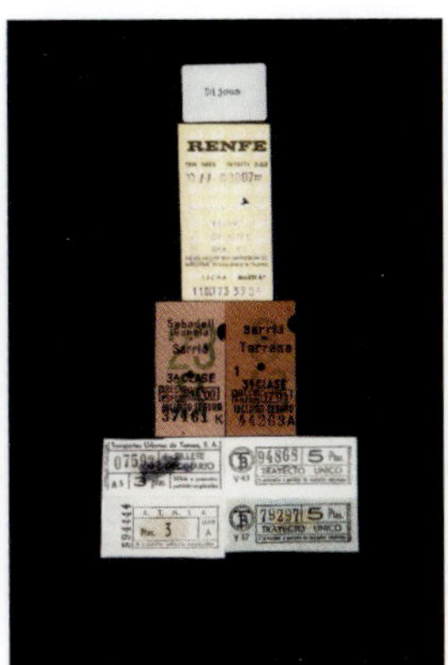
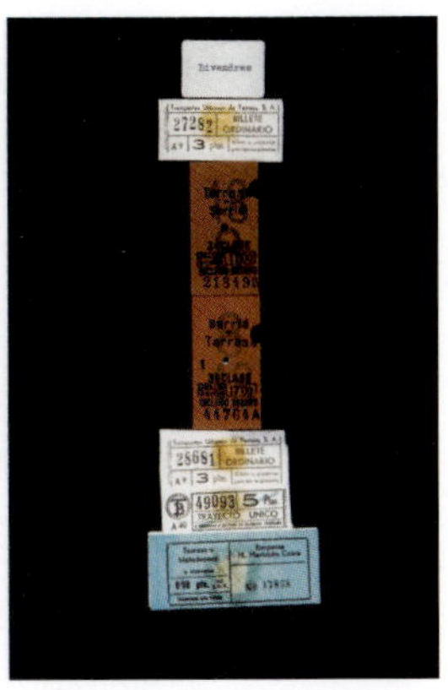
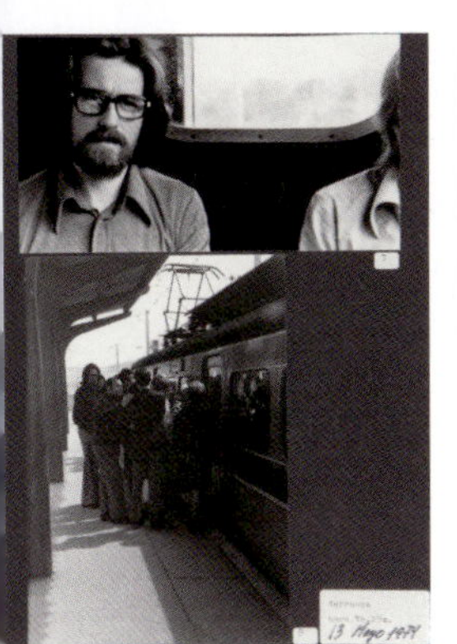
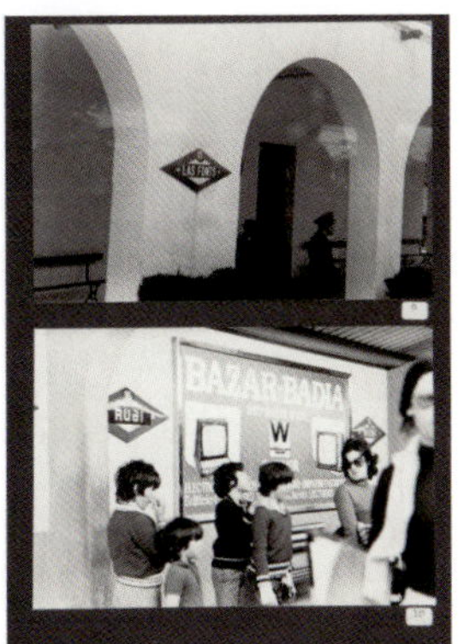
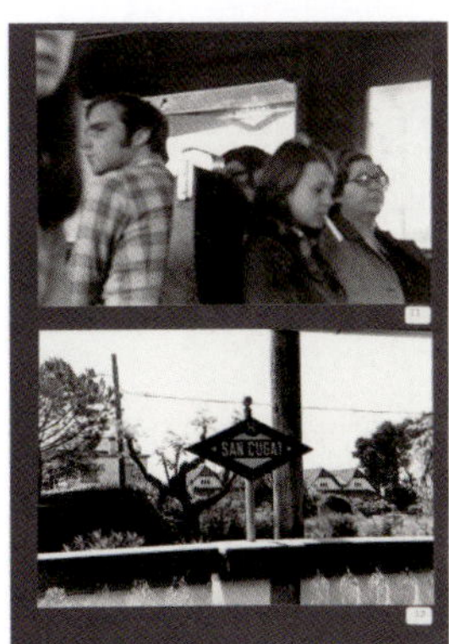
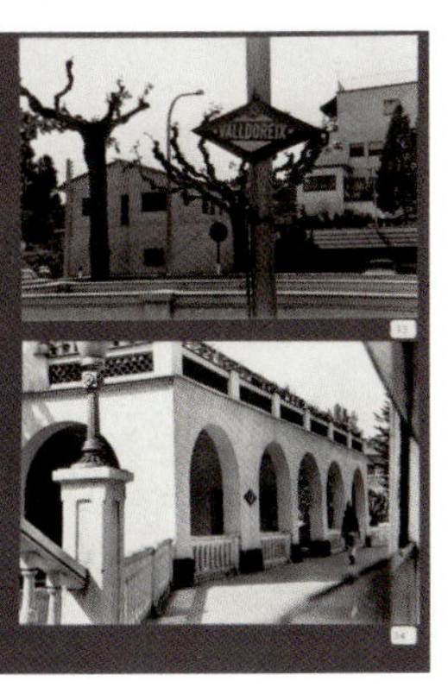
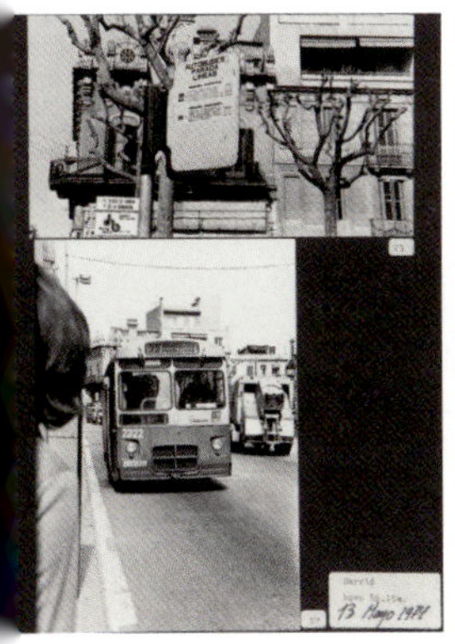
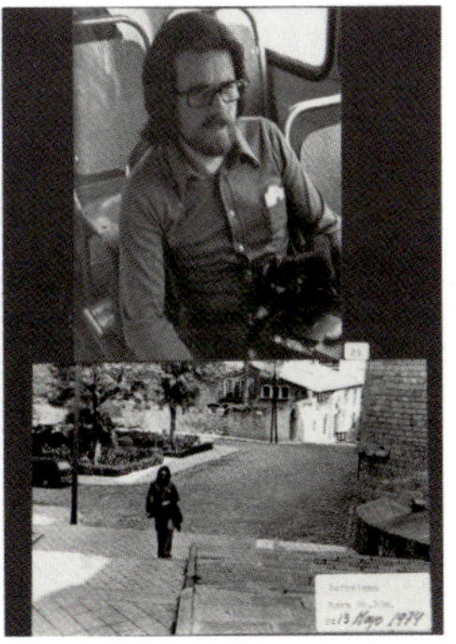
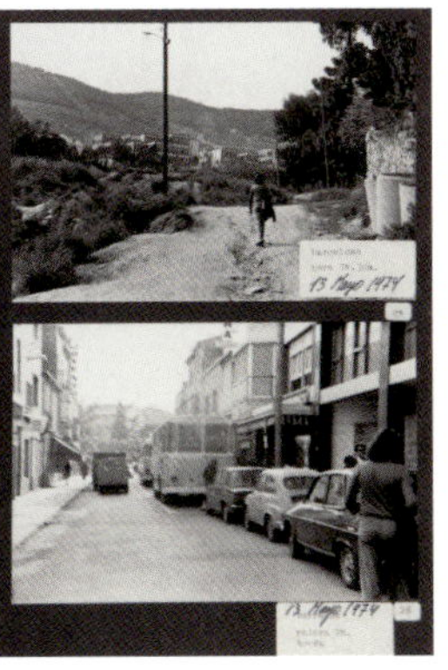

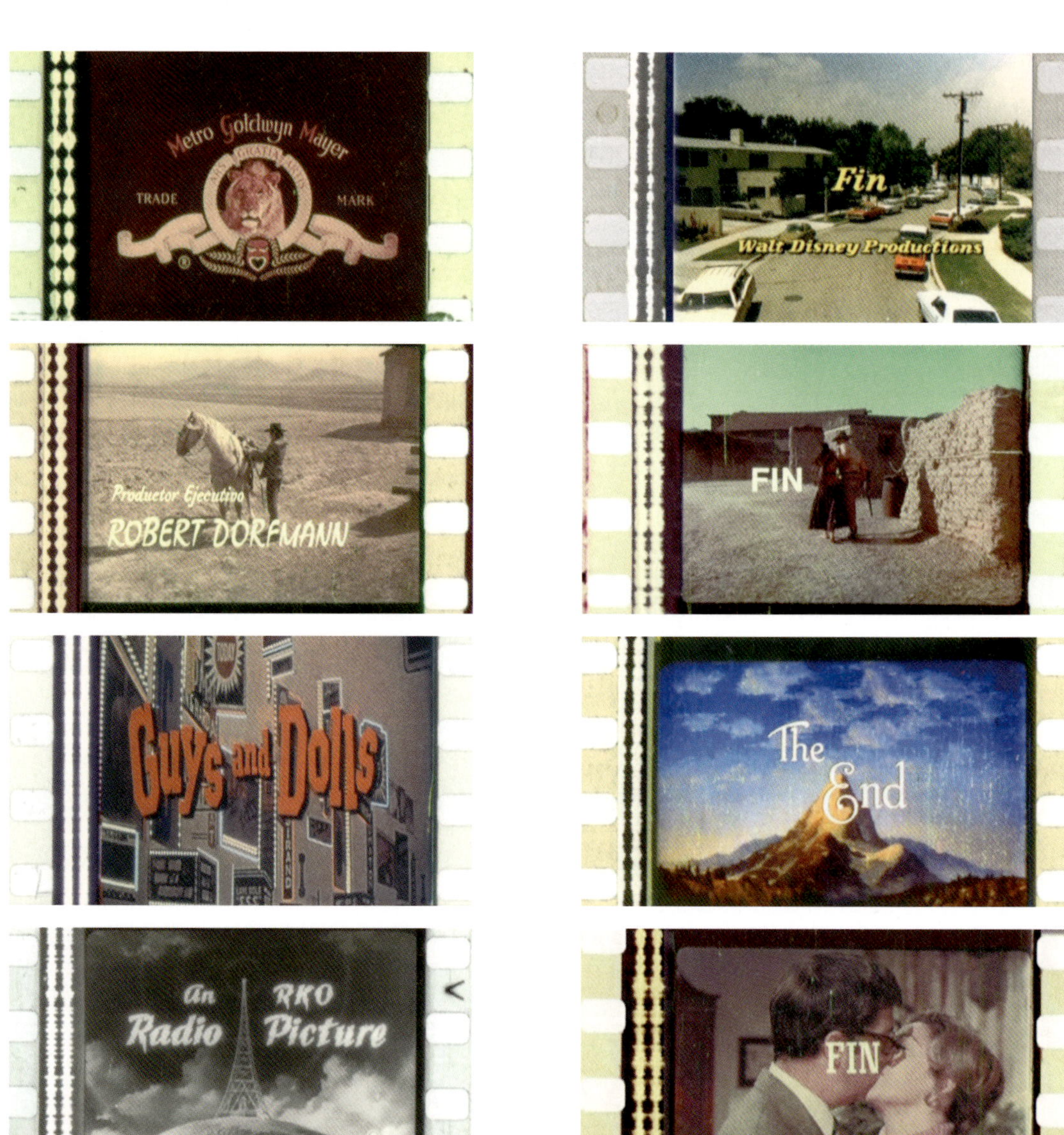

Eugènia Balcells
Presenta, 1977
16 mm film transferred to video,
colour, sound, 9 min 34 s

The End, 1977
16 mm film transferred to video,
colour, sound, 9 min 34 s

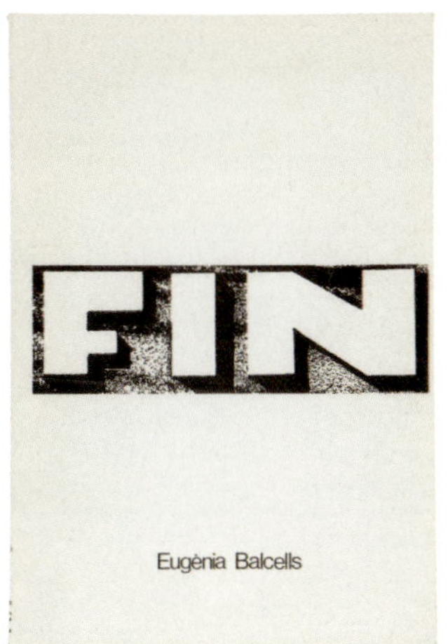

Eugènia Balcells

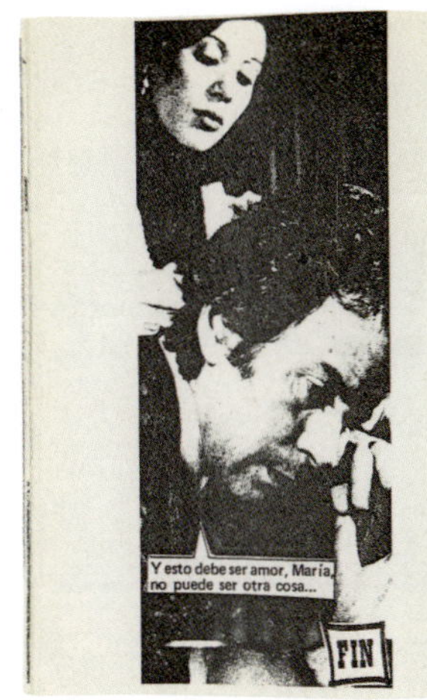

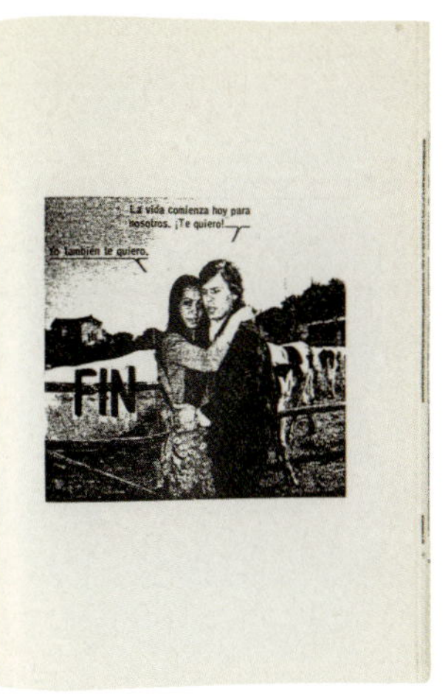

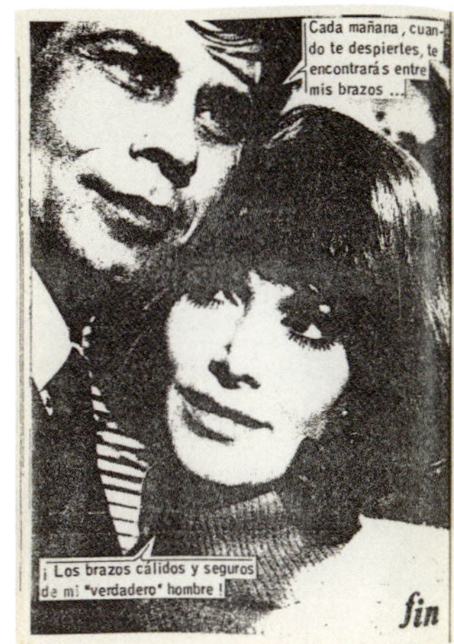

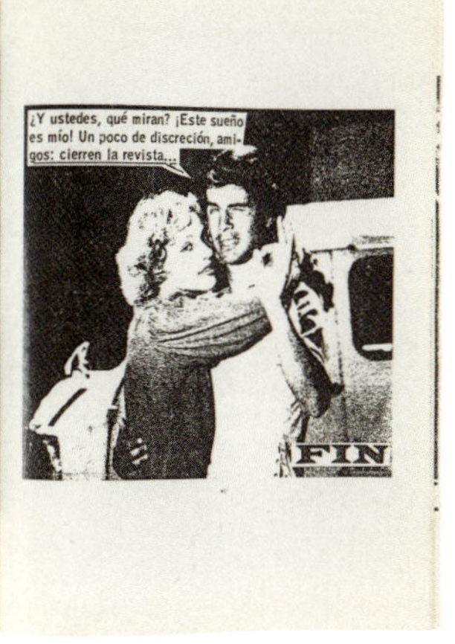

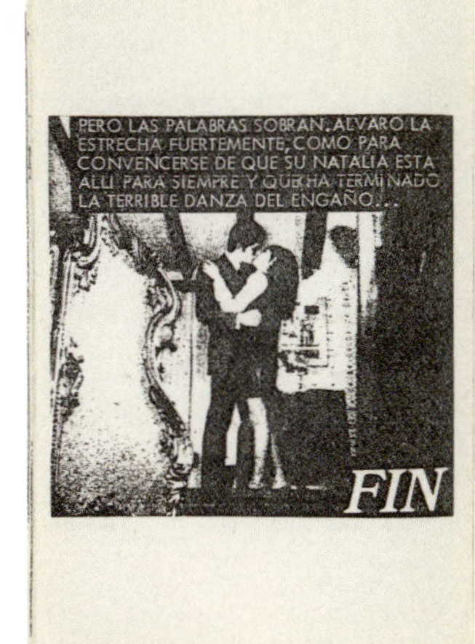

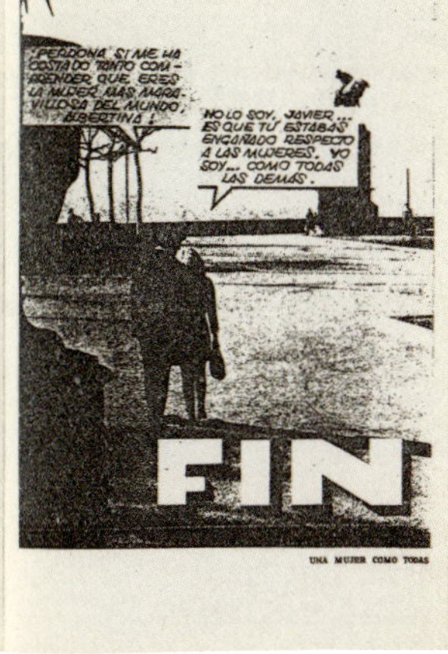

Fin, 1977
Book. Typographic print
on paper
31.2 × 21.7 cm

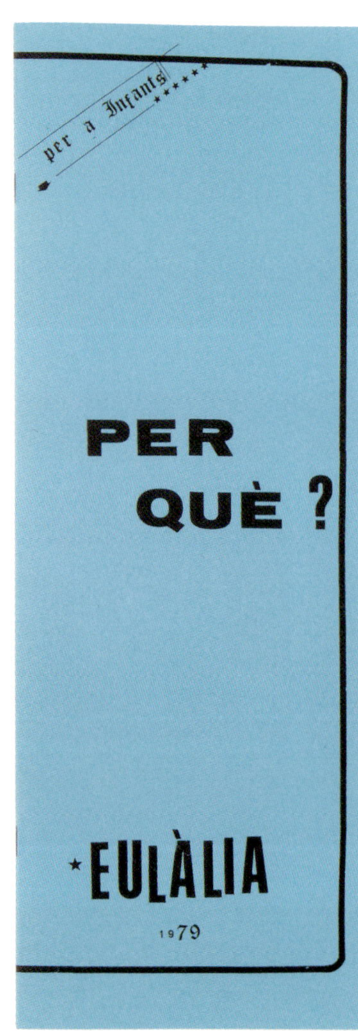

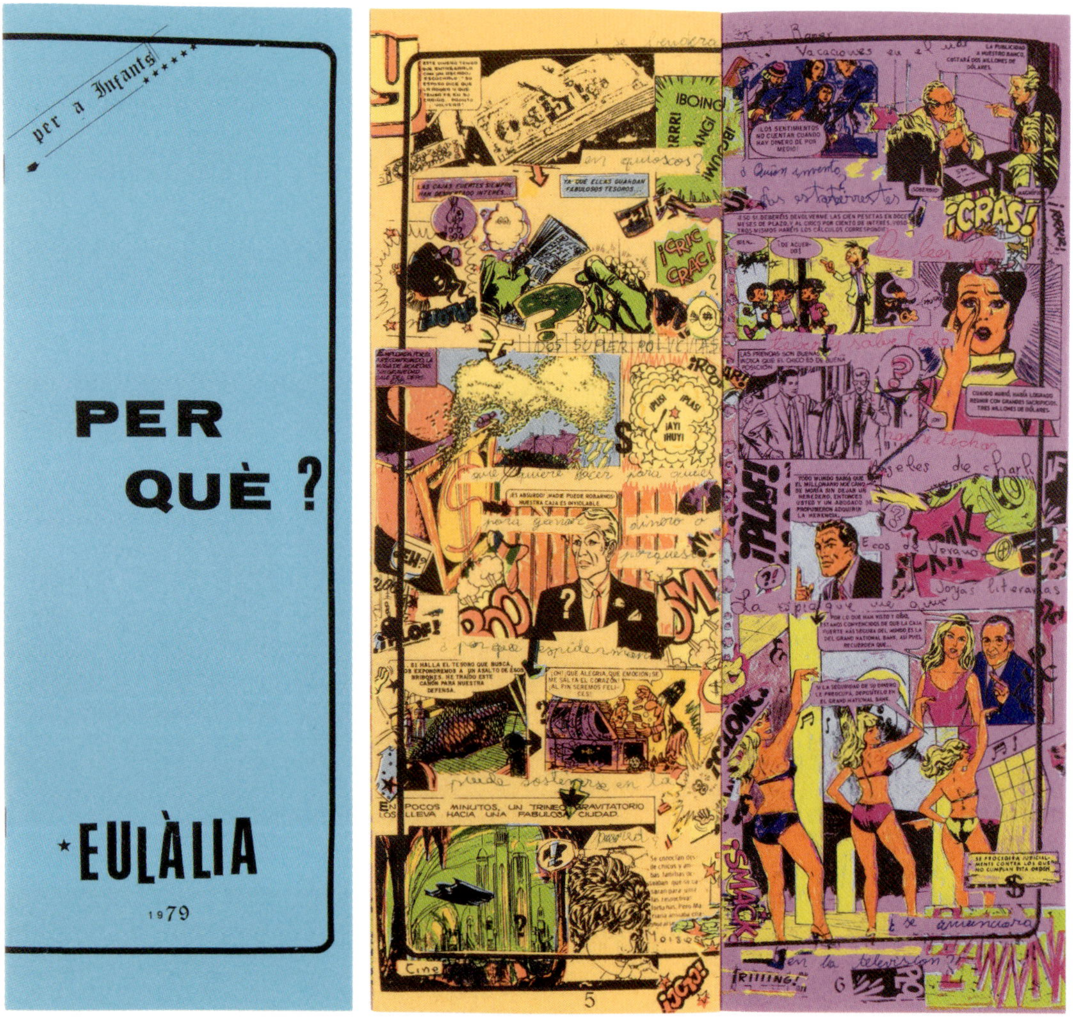

Eulàlia Grau
Per què?, 1979
Leaflet. Print on paper
42 × 15.2 cm

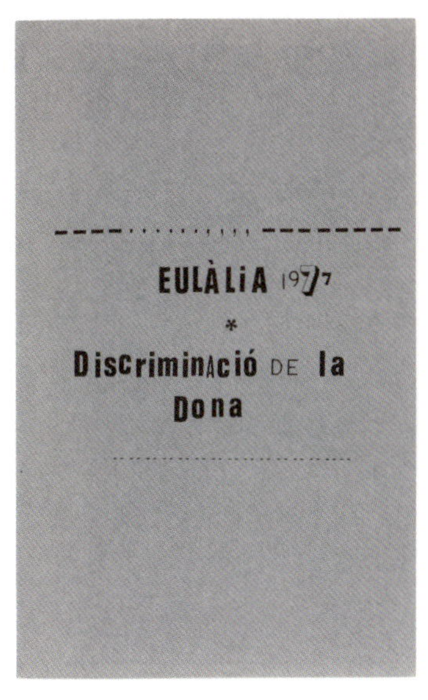

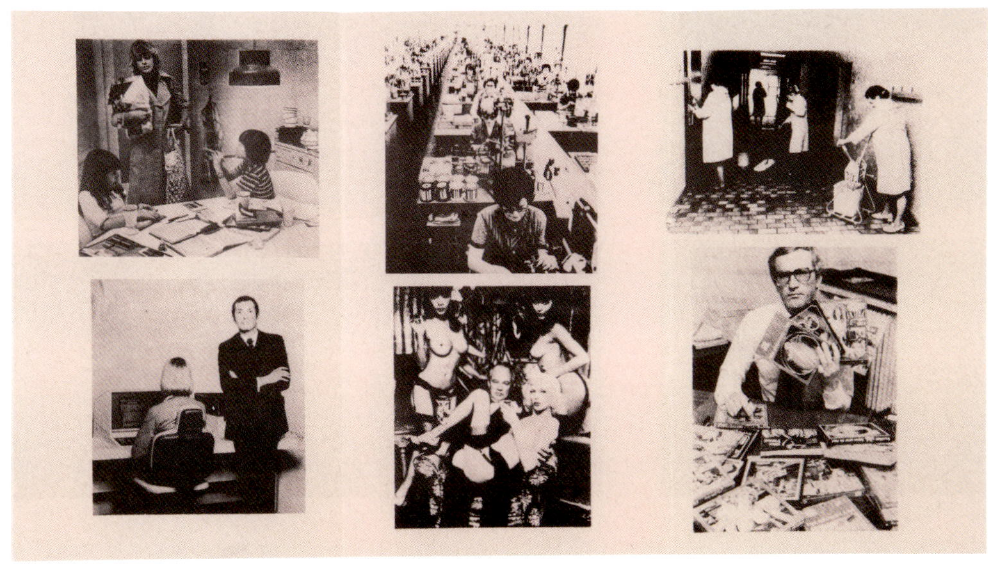

Discriminació de la dona
Booklet. Print on paper
24.7 × 15.5 cm
Barcelona: Proyecto Arte, 1977

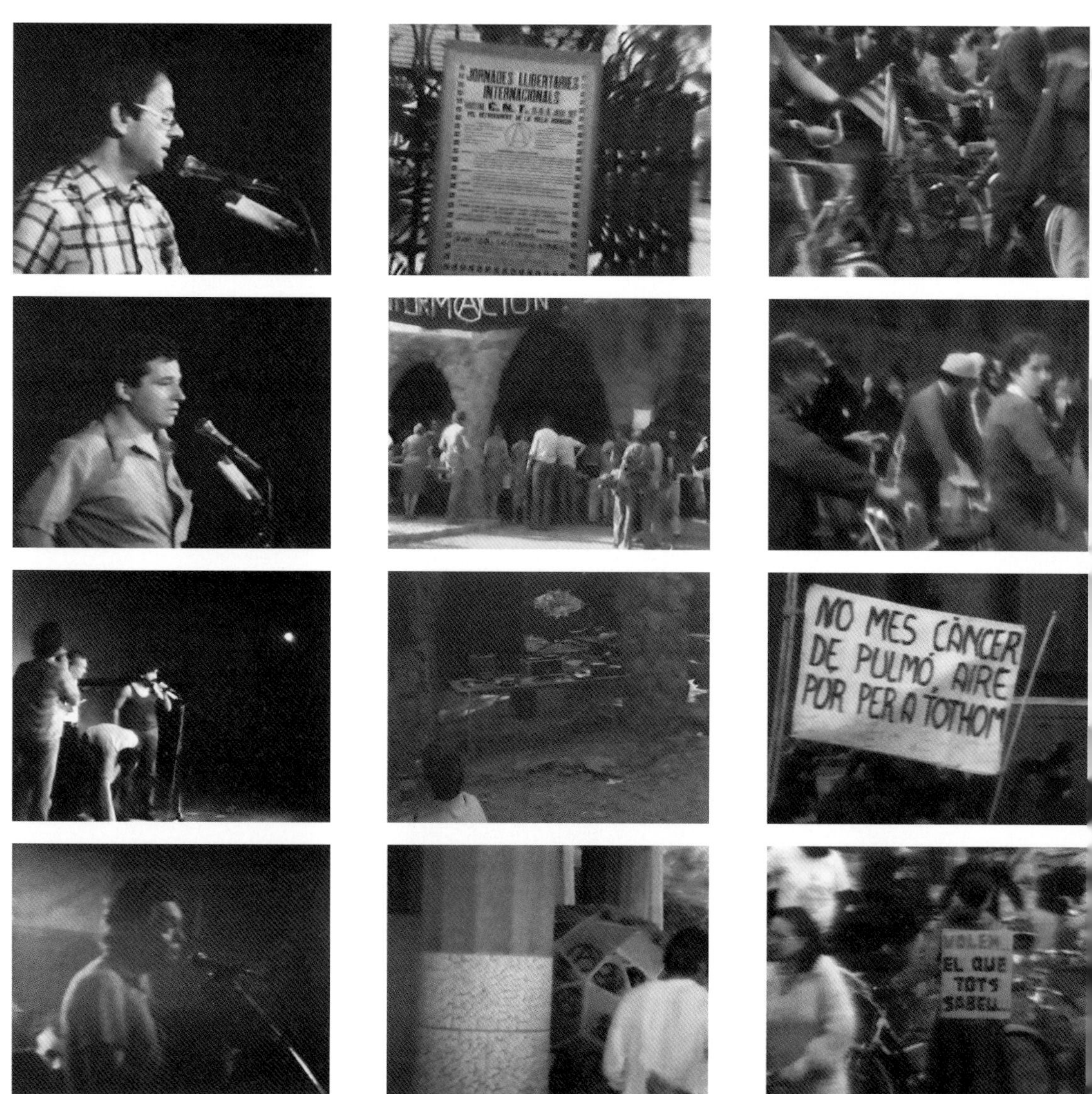

Vídeo-Nou

Jornades Llibertàries Internacionals. Debats al Saló Diana, 1977
Single-channel video, b/w, sound, 120 min 56 s

Jornades Llibertàries Internacionals. Parc Güell, 1977
Single-channel video, b/w, sound, 28 min

Contracultures: Manifestació de bicicletes, 1977
Single-channel video, b/w, sound, 12 min 20 s

Vídeo-Nou 1977-78
Book
25 × 14 cm
[s. l.: s. n.], 1979

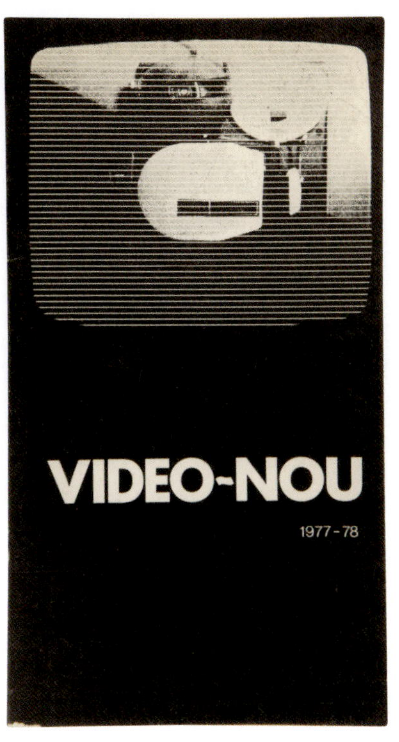

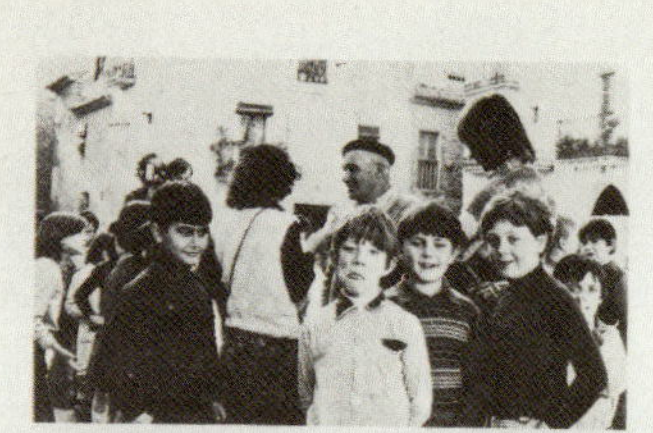

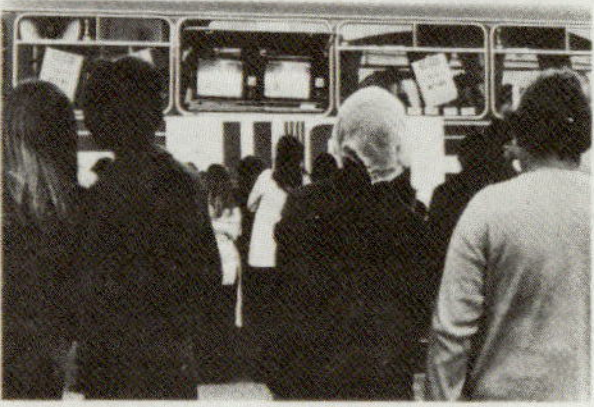

2.1. CAMPANYA POLITICA PER A LA LLIGA DE CATALUNYA
(Abril-maig 77)

La campanya estava centrada en la utilització d'un video-bus (autobús equipat per a realitzar programes de video complets: gravació, montatge, visionat) (vegi's gràfic); basant-se en l'experiència realitzada pel Partit Socialista Francès l'any 76. L'àmbit en què es realitzava era la província de Girona, en el període d'un mes.

L'esquema de treball era el següent:

Després d'una informació sòcio-econòmica prèvia de cada una de les comarques, recollida abans d'iniciar-se la campanya pròpiament dita, es visitaven cada dia un o dos pobles. Al llarg del dia es realitzava una cinta-reportatge sobre les característiques físiques i sòcio-polítiques del poble en qüestió, a base d'entrevistes directes al carrer, llocs de treball, escoles, etc.

Aquest material es reconvertia, mitjançant un muntatge realitzat al propi video-bus, en una cinta acabada, que era objecte del visionat per part dels mateixos protagonistes i resta de veïns del poble, el mateix dia al vespre.

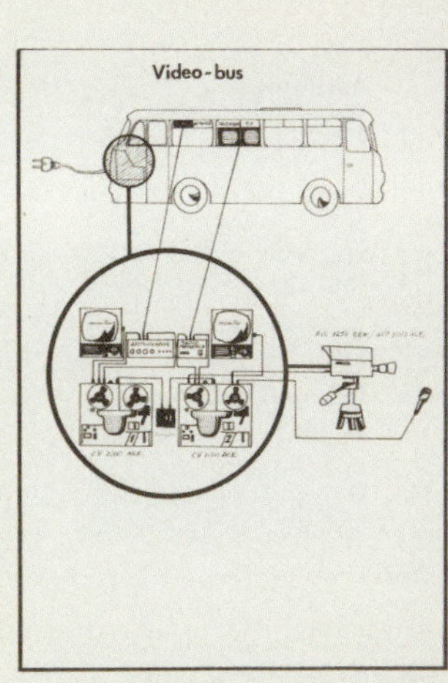

A aquest muntatge s'hi afegia una de les "cunyes polítiques" (propaganda política del partit en qüestió), gravades prèviament. El visionat es realitzava en algun lloc cèntric del poble (plaça, etc.), des dels monitors-televisor instal·lats al propi autobús. En general, el visionat de la cinta es convertia en una ocasió de forta concentració de veïns, que suscitava discussions, comentaris, etc. entre la gent, que desbordava àmpliament el marc de la propaganda política d'un partit concret, per a centrar-se al voltant de temes més lligats a la vida del poble.

En algunes ocasions es va realitzar també una gravació del moment del visionat, per a captar les reaccions del públic respecte a la seva pròpia imatge – la dels protagonistes directes –, respecte a la problemàtica del poble i la propaganda política.

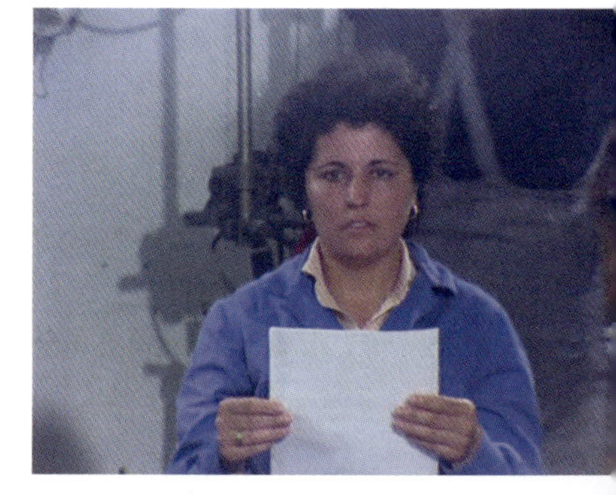

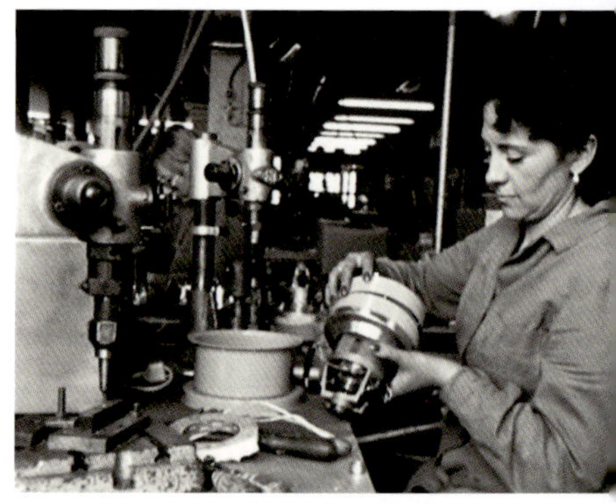

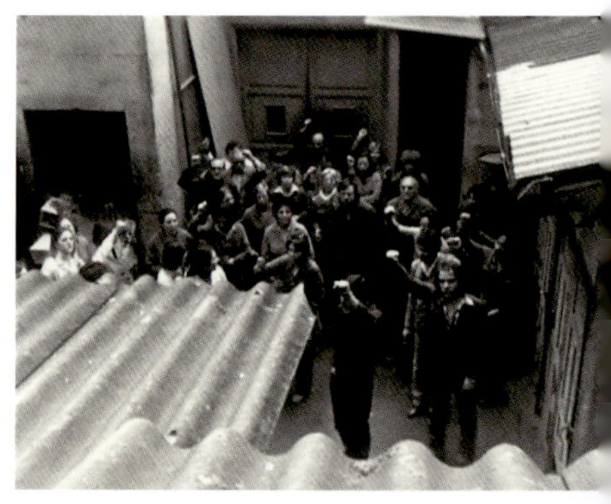

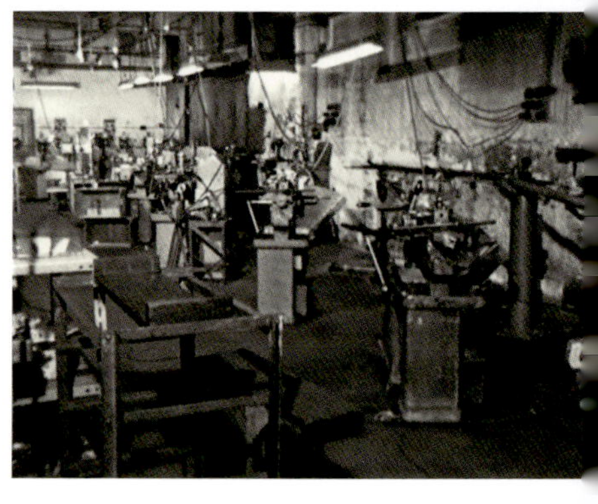

Joaquim Jordà
Numax Presenta..., 1980
Single-channel video, b/w and colour, sound, 105 min

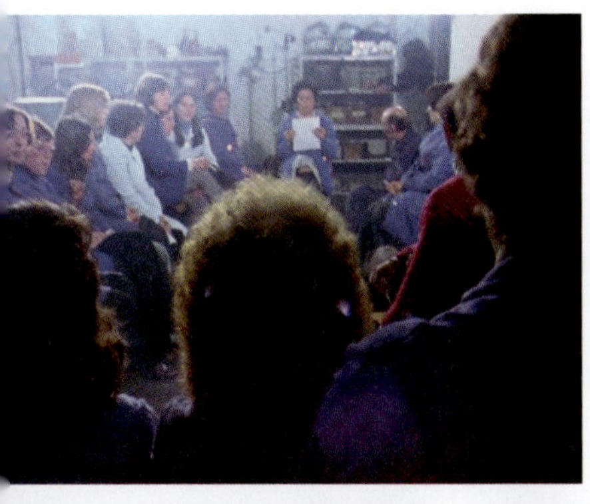
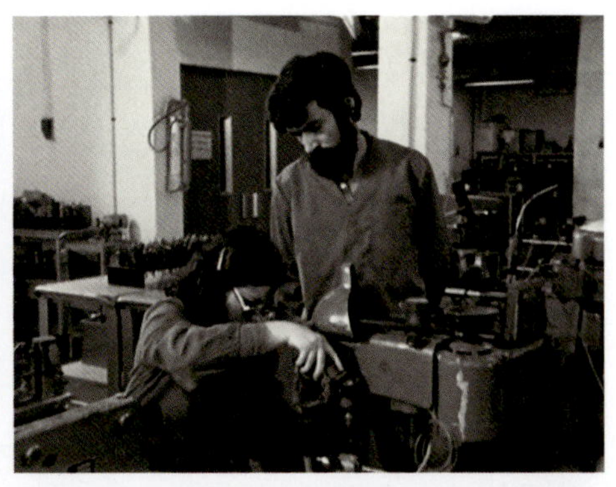
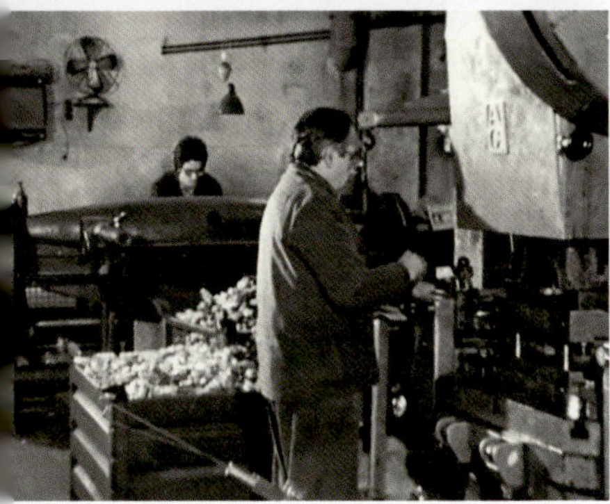
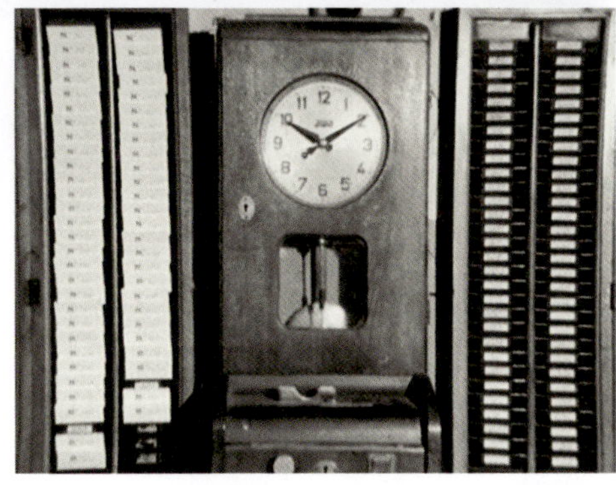
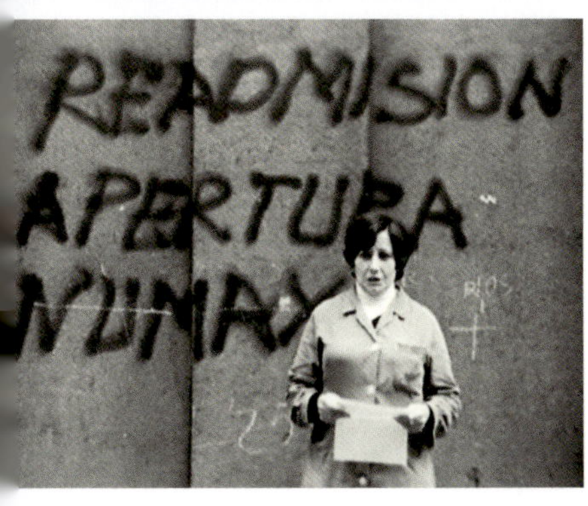

READMISION
APERTURA
NUMAX

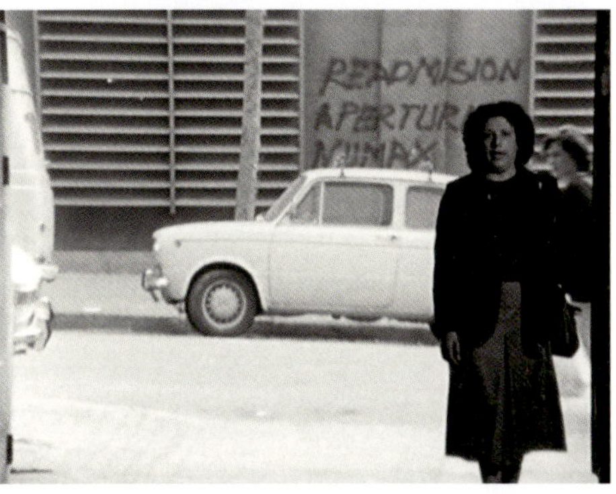

READMISION
APERTURA
NUMAX

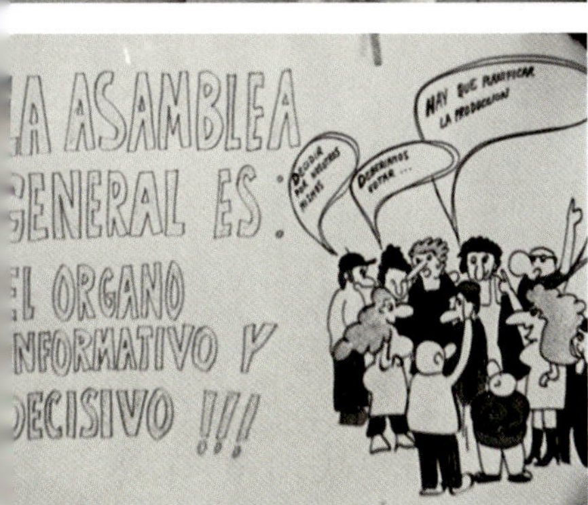

A ASAMBLEA
GENERAL ES:
EL ORGANO
NFORMATIVO Y
DECISIVO !!!
HAY QUE PLANIFICAR LA PRODUCCION
DECIDIR POR NOSOTROS MISMOS
DEBERIAMOS VOTAR...

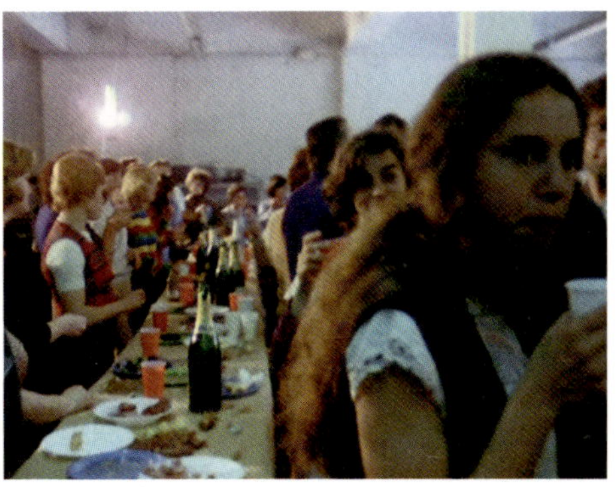

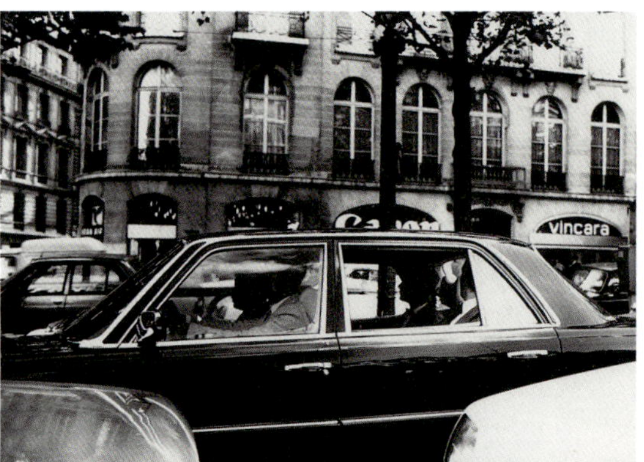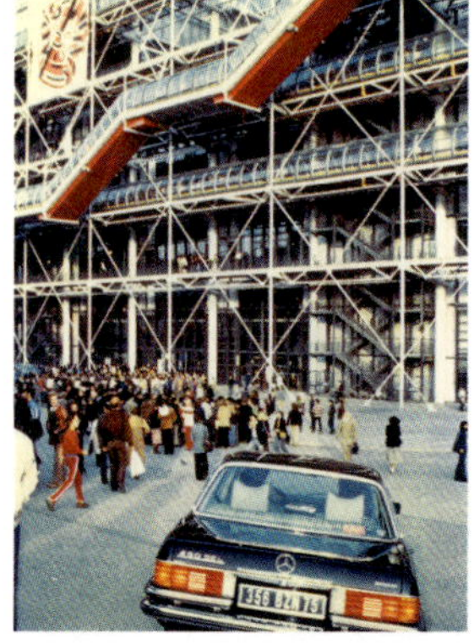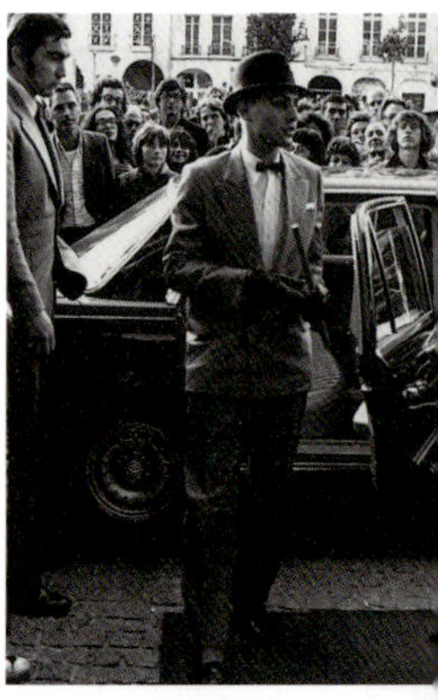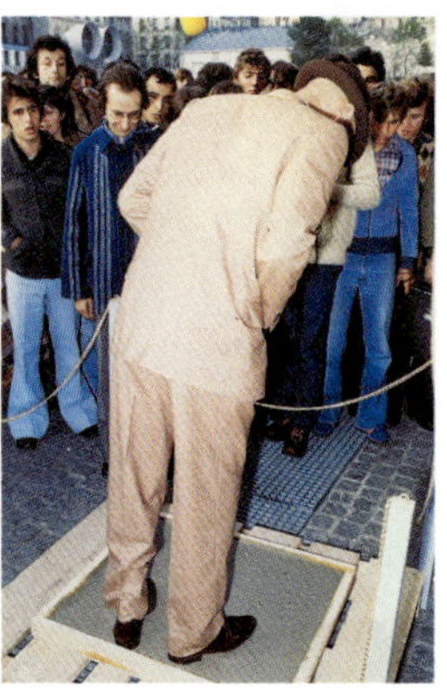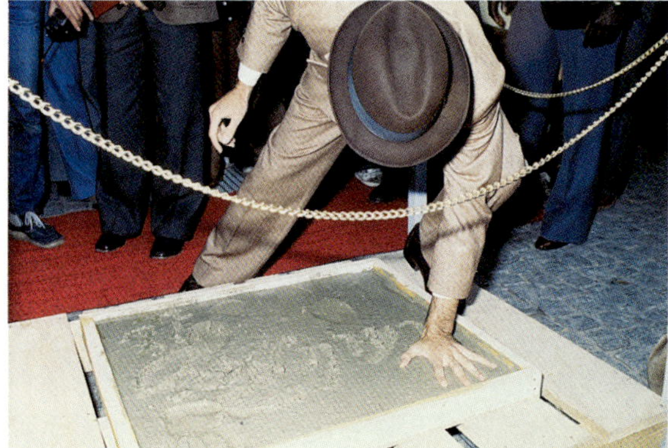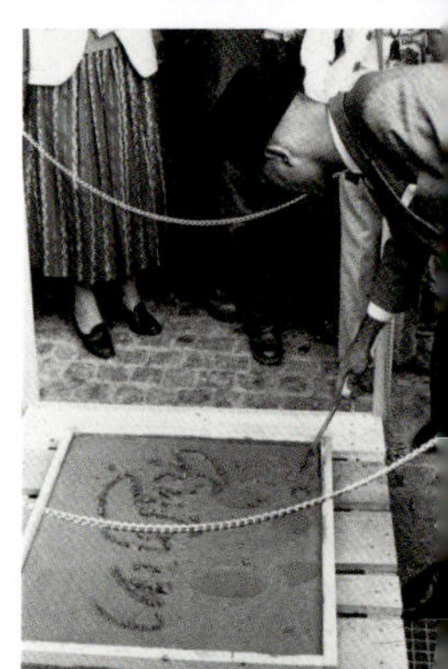

Carlos Pazos
The Floor of Fame, 1978
Single-channel video, b/w and colour, silent, 3 min 31 s
Editing made from black and white documentary photos
and colour slides of the action carried out at the
Centre Pompidou, Paris

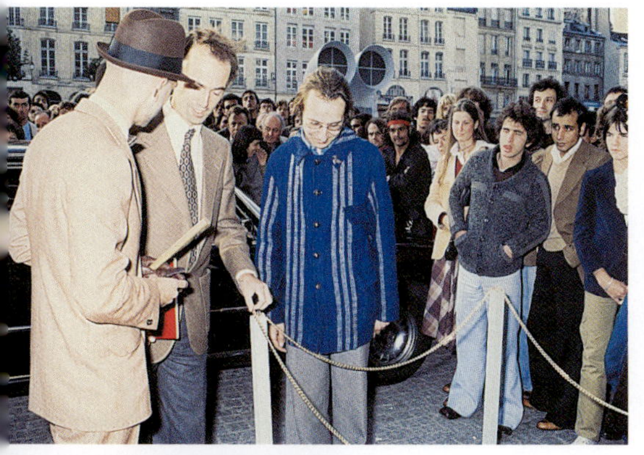
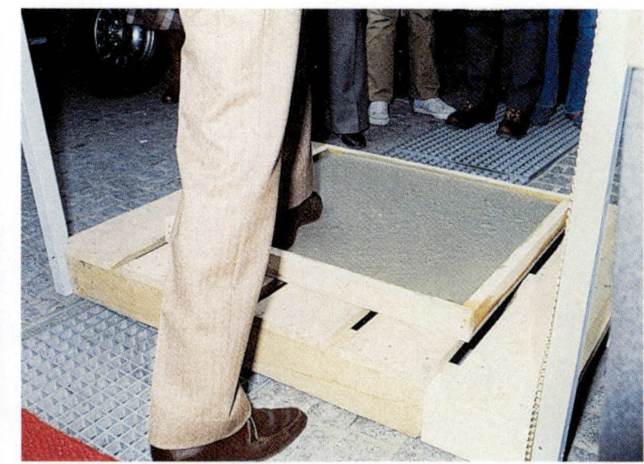
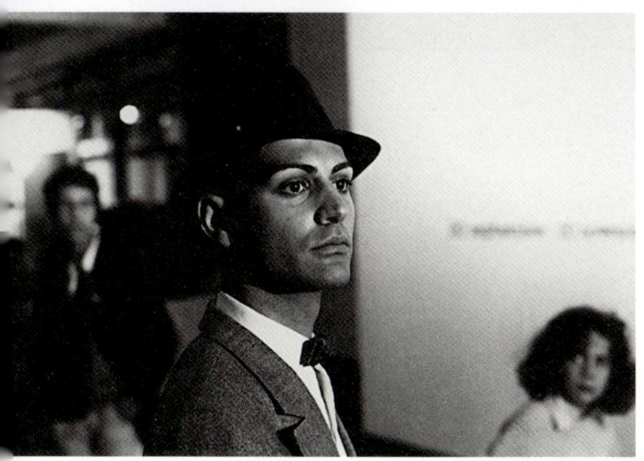
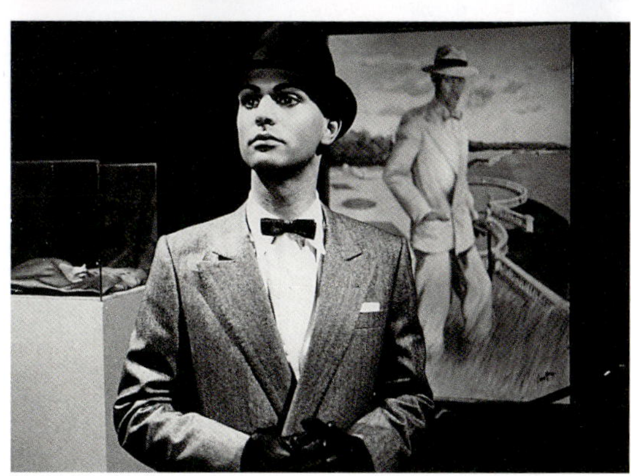

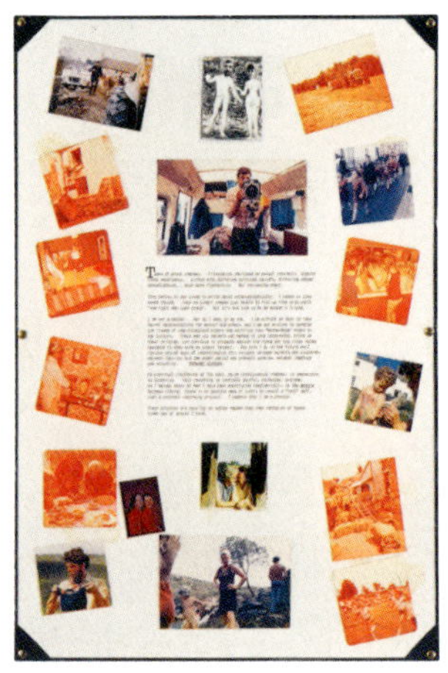
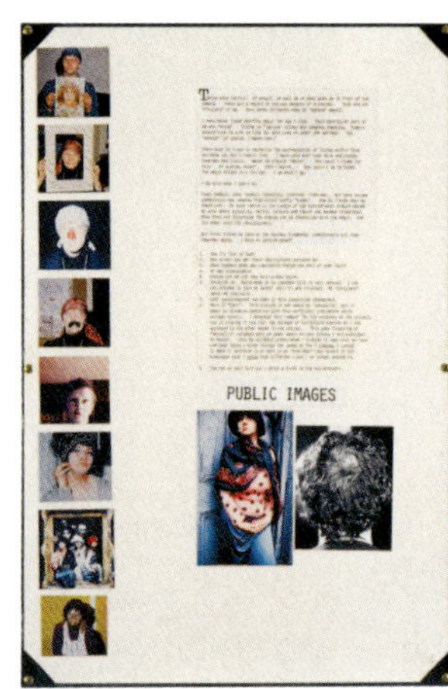
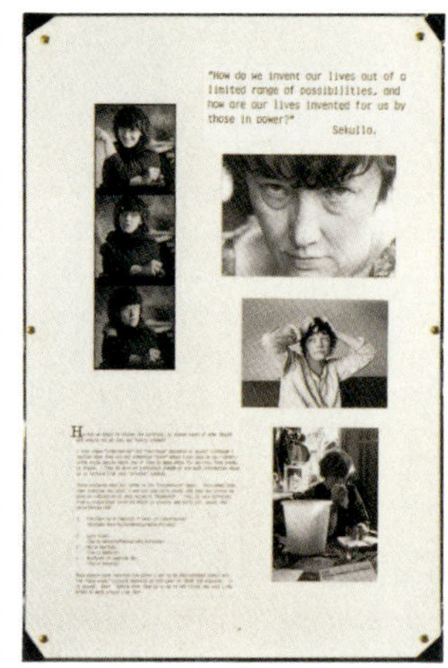

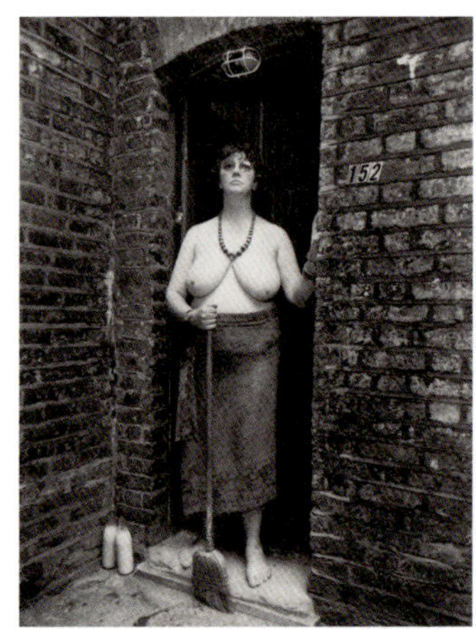
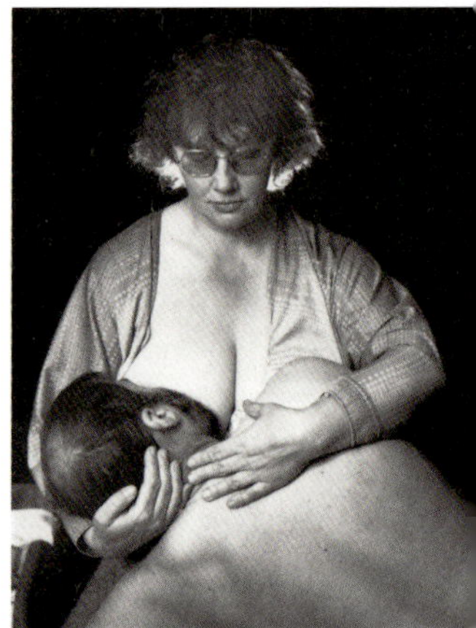

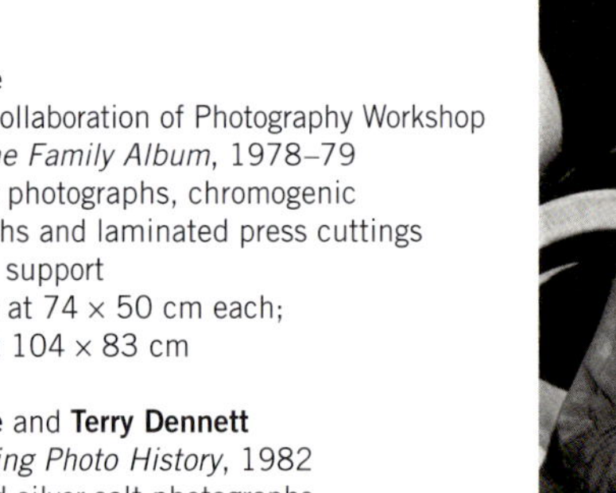
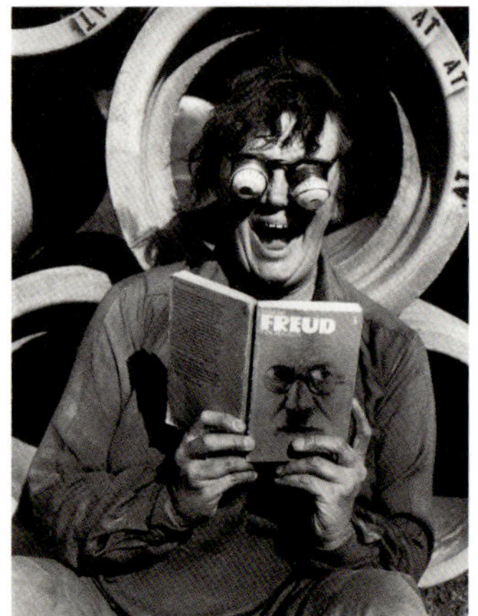
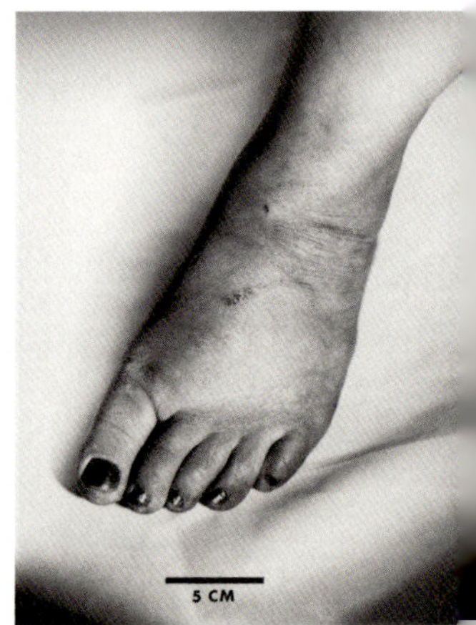

Jo Spence
With the collaboration of Photography Workshop
Beyond the Family Album, 1978–79
Silver-salt photographs, chromogenic
photographs and laminated press cuttings
on plastic support
21 pieces at 74 × 50 cm each;
1 piece at 104 × 83 cm

Jo Spence and **Terry Dennett**
Remodelling Photo History, 1982
Laminated silver-salt photographs
on plastic support
7 pieces at 66.5 × 46.5 cm each

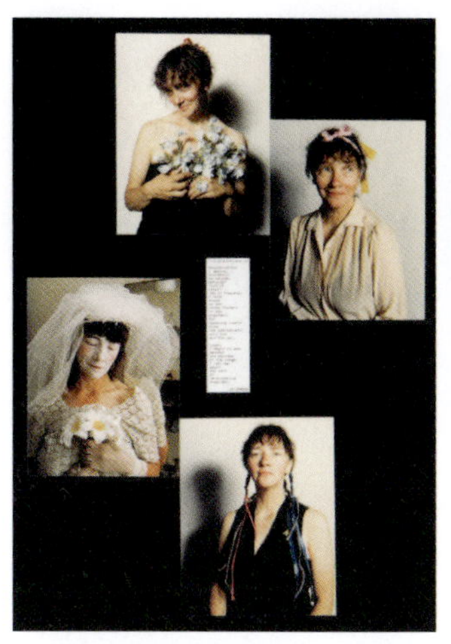
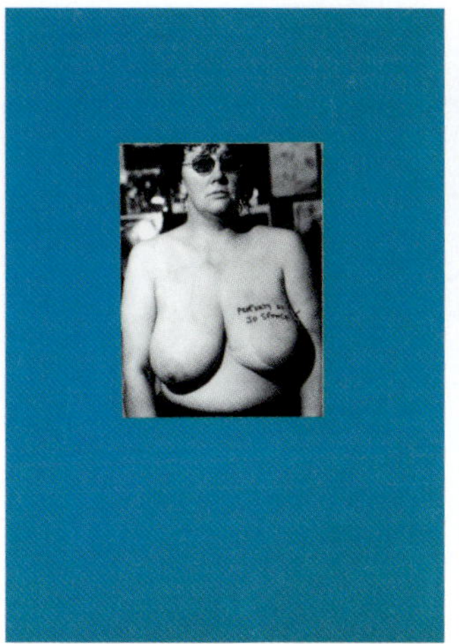
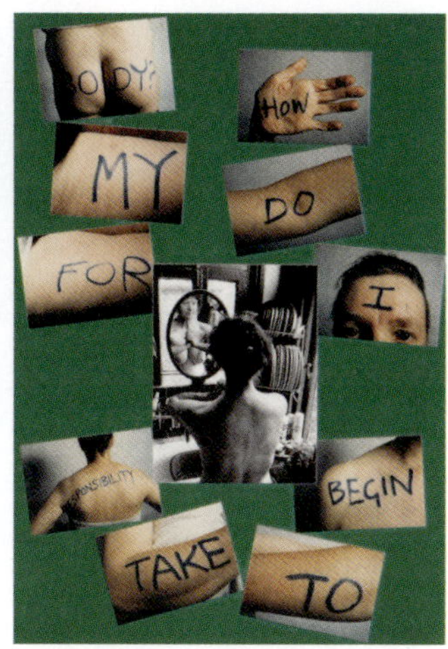

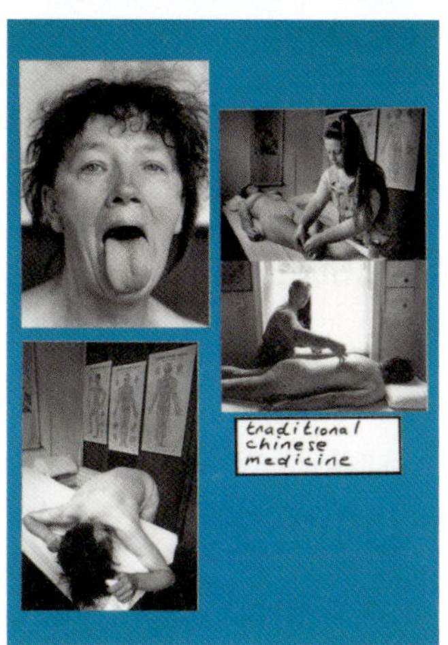

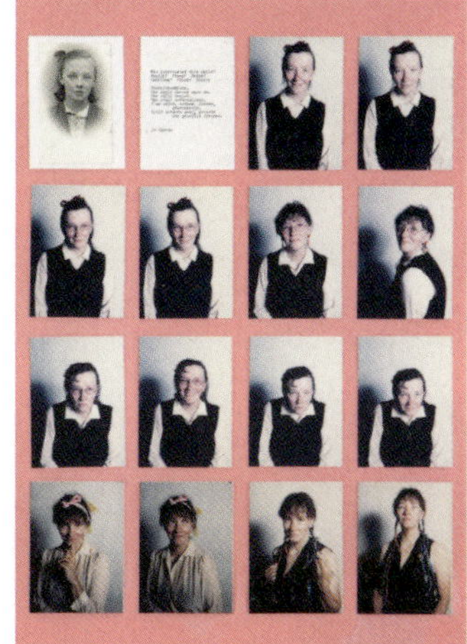
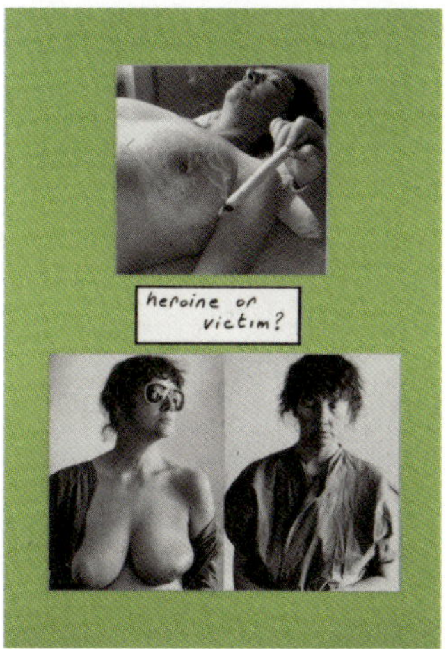

Jo Spence
With the collaboration of Rosy Martin, Maggie Murray and Terry Dennett
The Picture of Health, 1982
Silver-salt photographs, chromogenic photographs
and laminated press cuttings on plastic support
52 elements in various dimensions

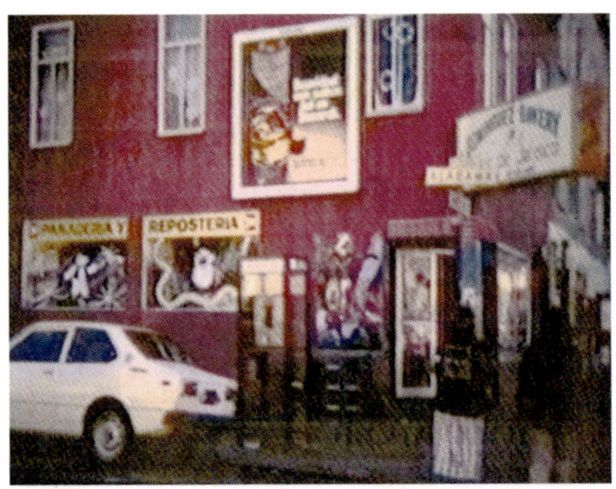

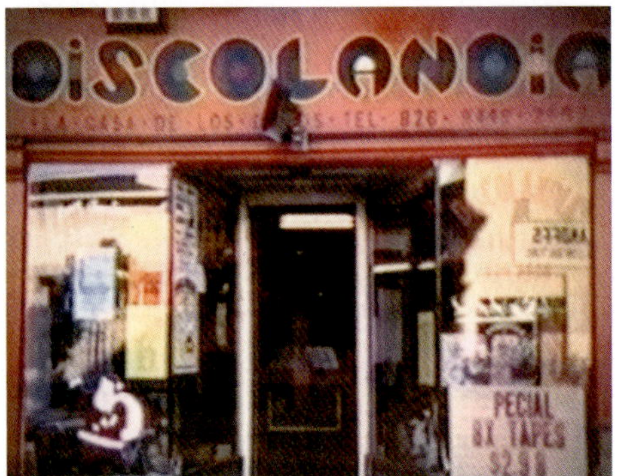

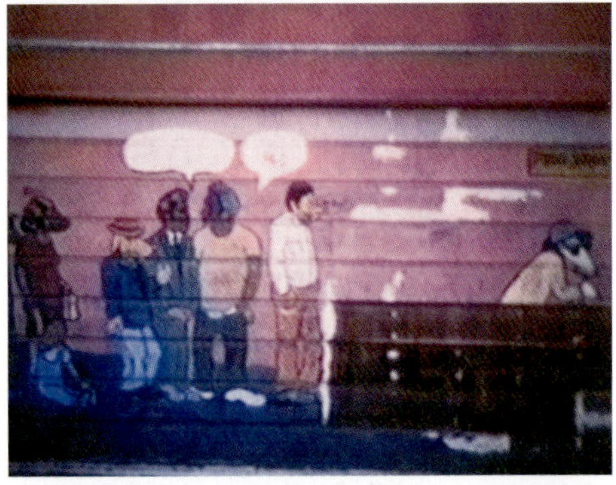

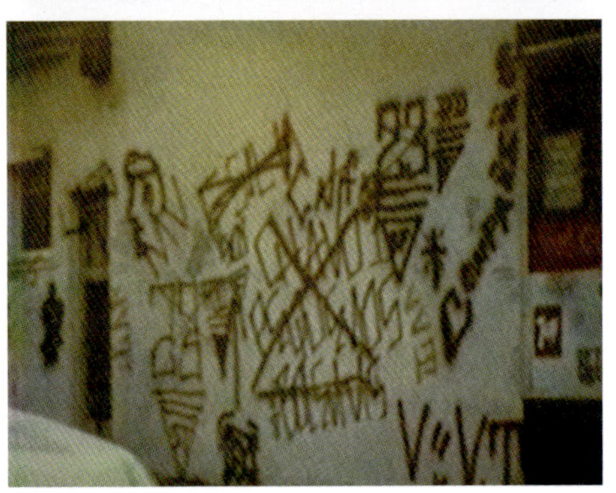

Martha Rosler
Secrets from the Street: No Disclosure, 1980
Single-channel video, colour, sound, 12 min 20 s

*Born to Be Sold: Martha Rosler Reads
the Strange Case of Baby S.M.*, 1988
Single-channel video, colour, sound, 35 min 20 s

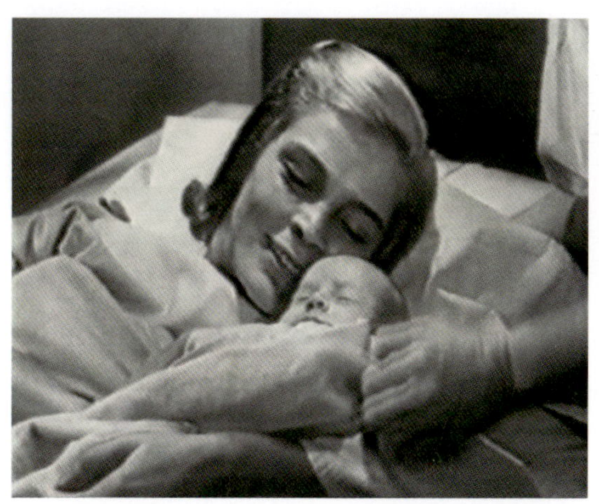
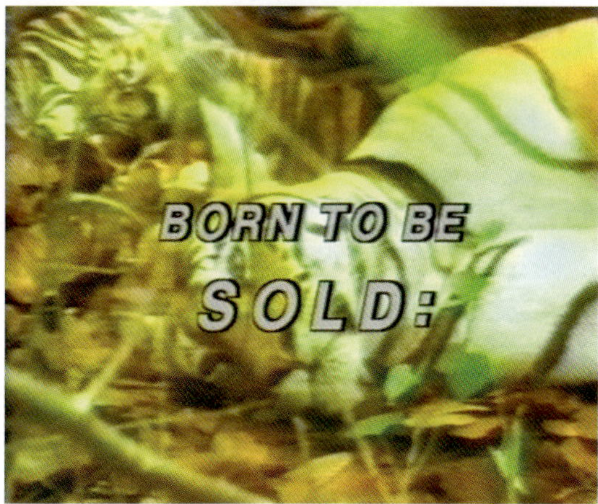

BORN TO BE
SOLD:

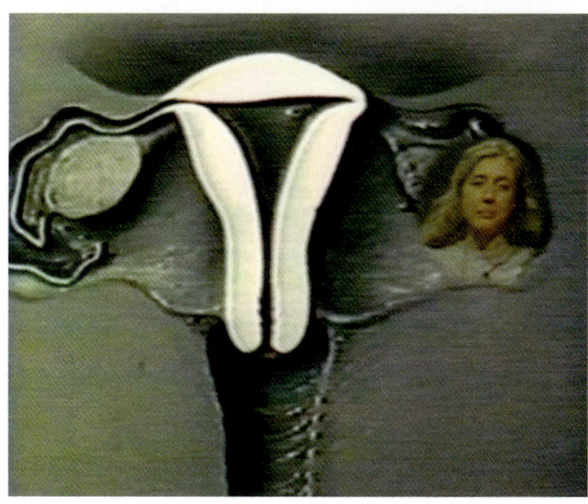
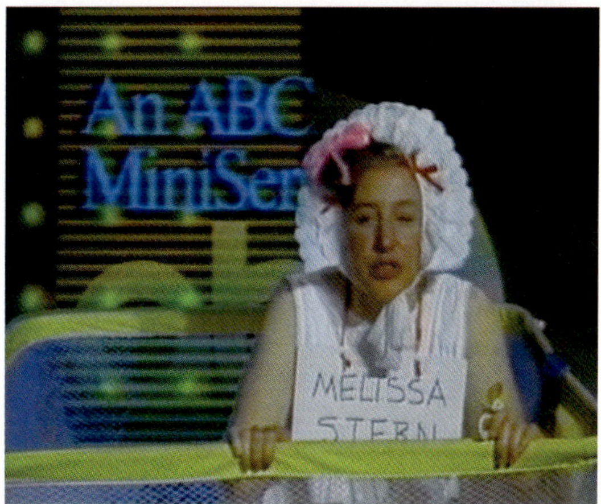

An ABC
MiniSer
MELISSA
STERN

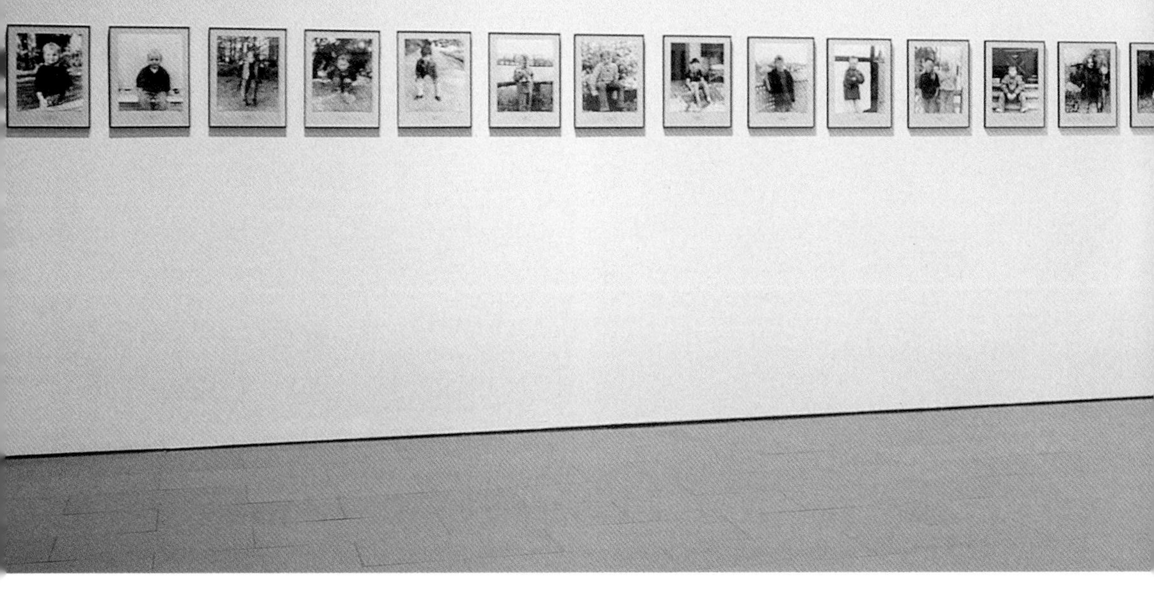

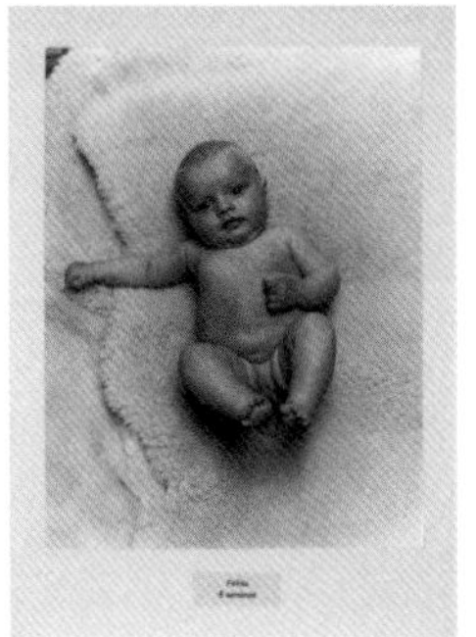 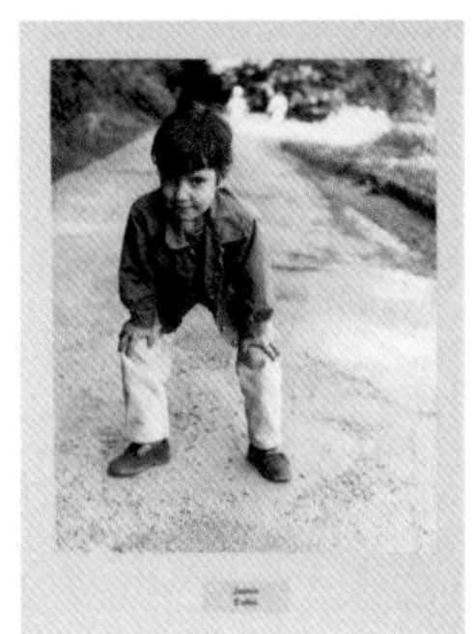 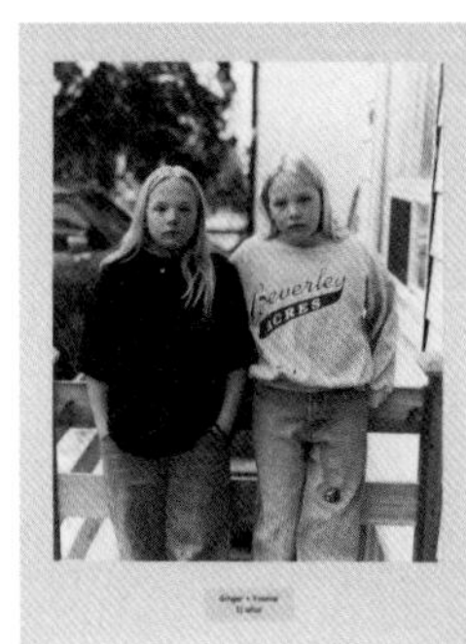 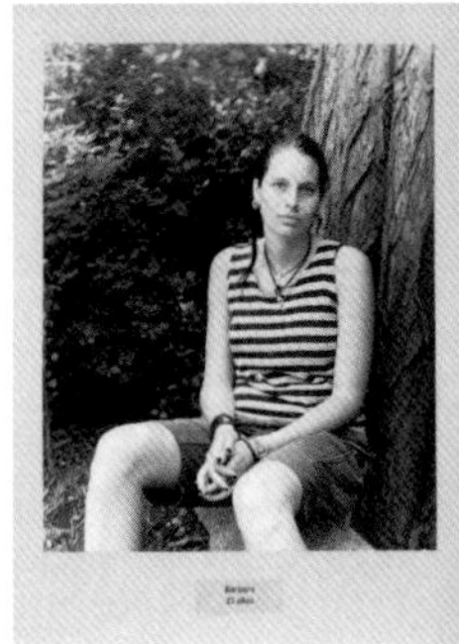

Hans-Peter Feldmann
100 Jahre, 2001
Silver-salt photograph
101 photographs at 30.5 × 24.3 cm each

Installation view, presentation of the MACBA Collection, 2003

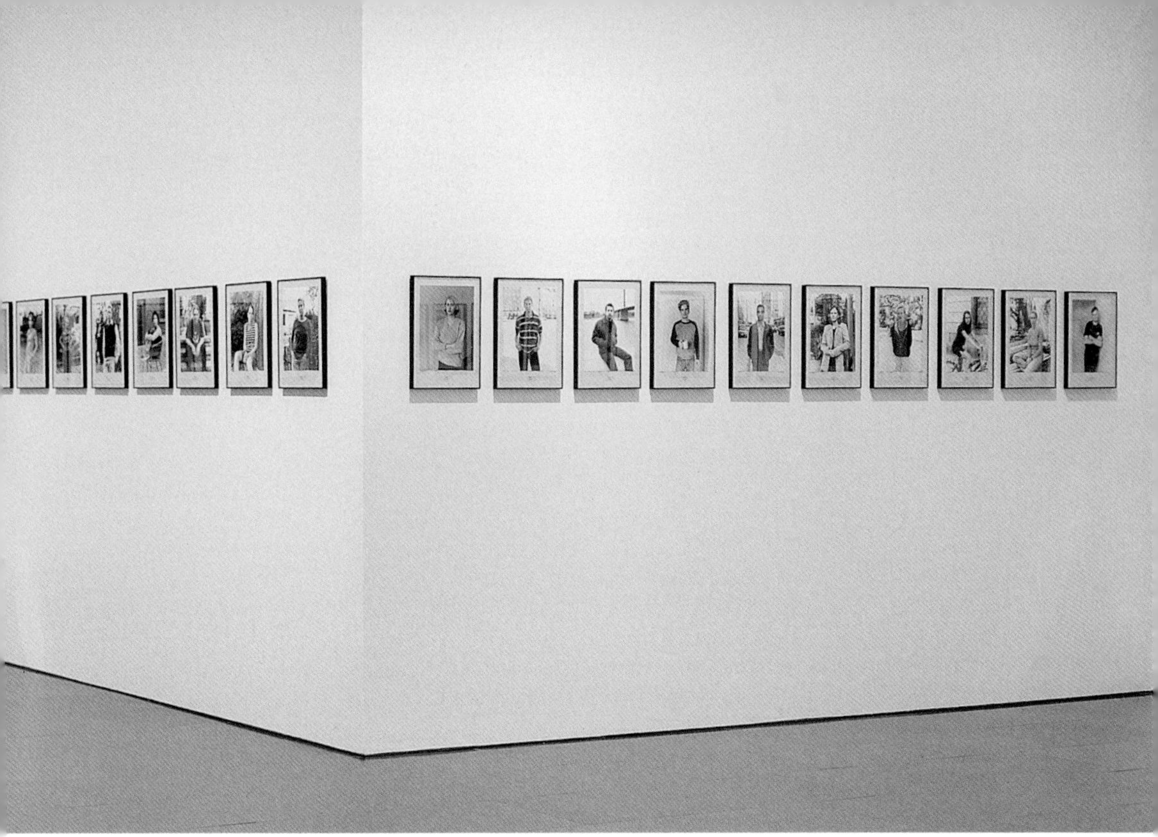

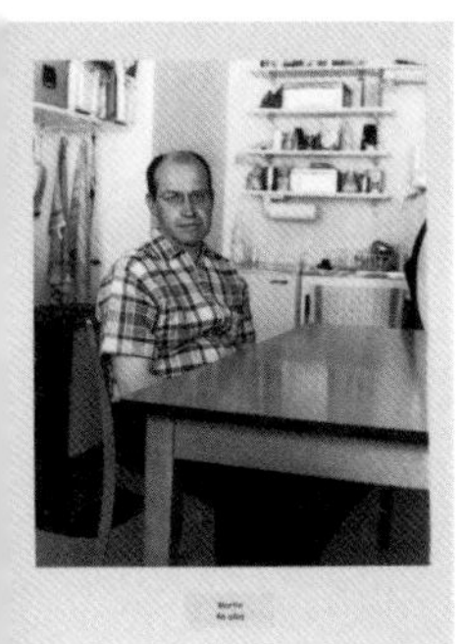

Martha
46 años

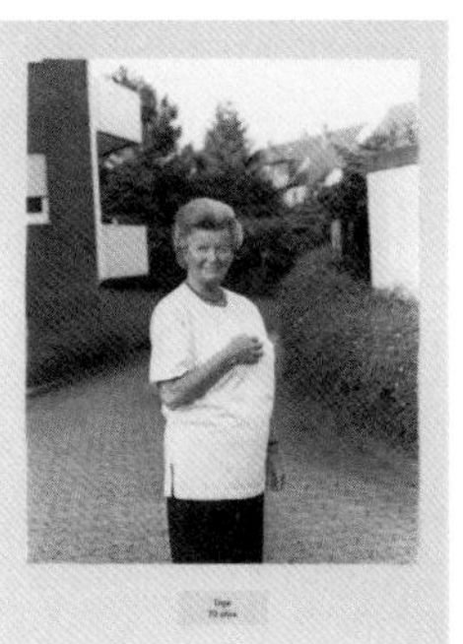

Inge
70 años

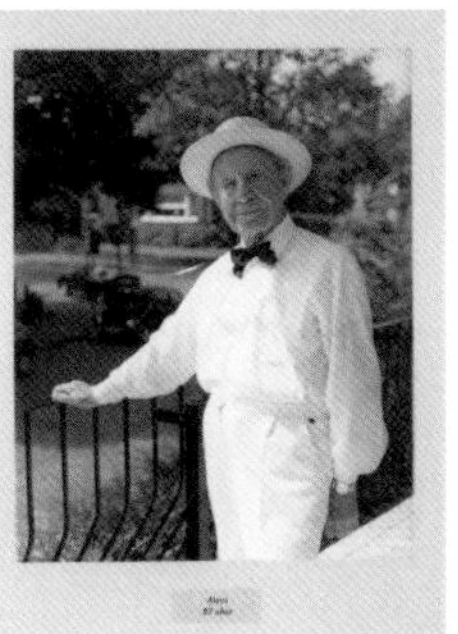

Alexis
87 años

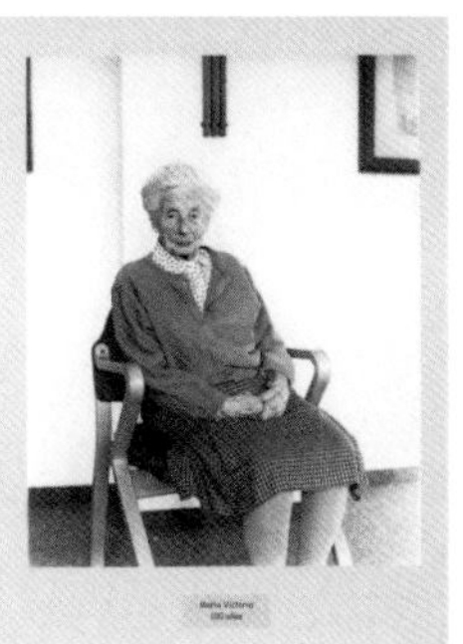

Maria Victoria
100 años

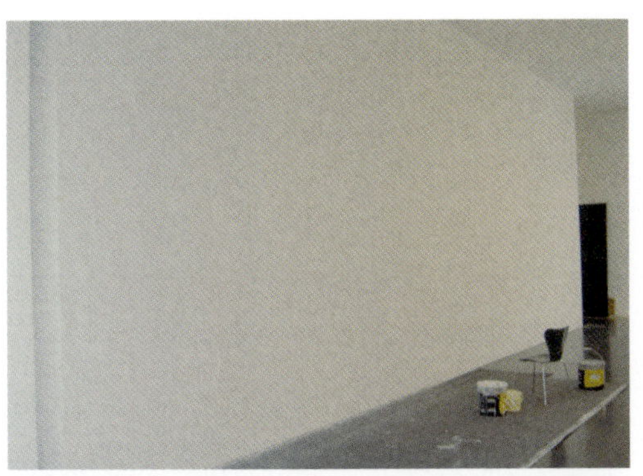

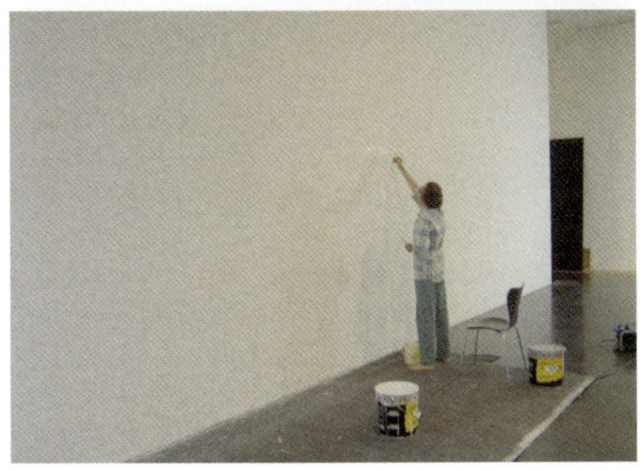
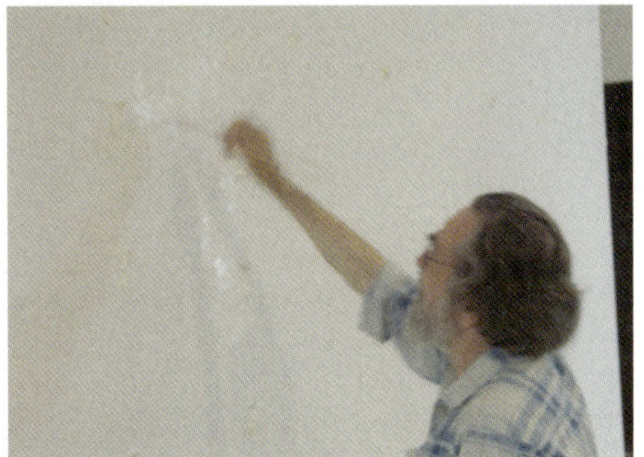
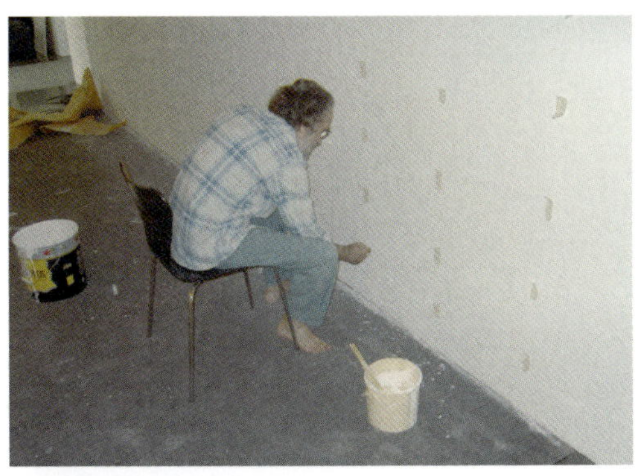
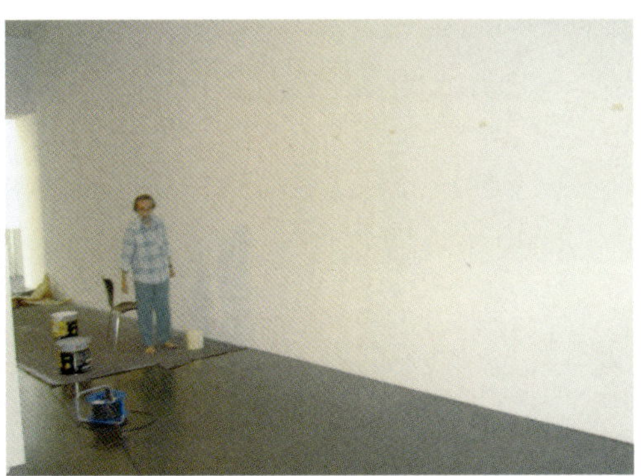

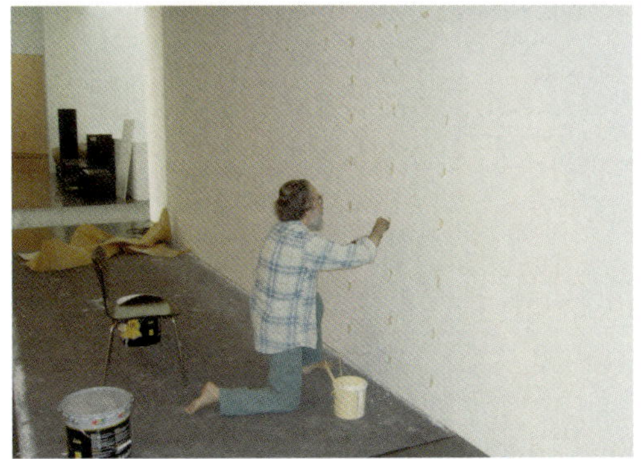

Spatial Order and Disorder: Architecture, Photography, Popular Culture. The Late Seventies and Eighties

In Europe and the United States, the eighties were defined by returns to figural and Neo-Expressionist painting, coinciding with an ever more pervasive multinational market economy. Framed as a reaction against the Minimal and Conceptual art that had emerged in the sixties and seventies, this 'new' aesthetic was known in Germany as *Neue Wilden*, in Italy as *Transavanguardia* and in France as *Figuration libre*. All variously participated in what Hal Foster described at the time as 'the expressive fallacy'.[32] These various Neo-Expressionist tendencies reclaimed a painterly aesthetic that, through its repetition of a historical style (i.e., Expressionism), also suggested the extent to which this style had been 'appropriated by the very forces that it had [originally] set out to oppose'.[33] That is, these painters simulated direct expression as a means to counter the reproduction and standardisation of subjectivity in advanced capitalism; at the same time, their naive claim to painterly authenticity participated in the elaboration of a national style and an exportable national product.

The various artists represented in the MACBA Collection pertaining to this period challenge this 'return to order'. In the realm of photography, Manolo Laguillo presented work at odds with the advertising images of Barcelona that coincided with the new urban planning spurred by the 1992 Olympic Games. Other international artists like Jeff Wall turned to painting not to revive expression but rather to probe traditional notions of genre, while Juan Muñoz engaged in sculptural work that, as he explains, was meant to 'express without being expressionistic'.[34] Other artists at this time, such as Dan Graham and James Coleman, more specifically explored the processes of perception as these inform the spaces of architecture and the meaning of images respectively. Finally, United States West Coast artists, through their injection of popular culture into the realm of high art, challenged both the contemplative mode of museum perception as well as the spectacular consumption of late capitalism.

32 Hal Foster, 'The Expressive Fallacy', in *Recodings*. New York: The New Press, 1985, pp. 59–77.
33 See Benjamin H. D. Buchloh's critique of this return to figuration in relation to Germany and Italy more specifically in 'Figures of Authority, Ciphers of Regression: Notes on the Return of Representation in European Painting', in Brian Wallis (ed.), *Art After Modernism: Rethinking Representation*. New York: The New Museum of Contemporary Art, 1984, p. 131.
34 Juan Muñoz, as cited by Louise Neri, in 'Art of the Fugue: Louise Neri on Juan Muñoz', *Artforum* 40, no. 8, April 2002, p. 44.

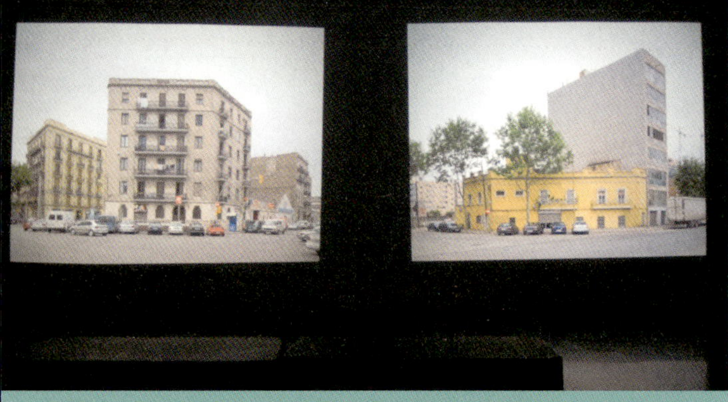

The subject of a 2007 exhibition at the MACBA, Manolo Laguillo's work provides a photographic record of Barcelona's urban transformation in preparation for the 1992 Olympic Games. Numerous photographic works that focus on urbanism from an exclusively celebratory perspective appeared in the decade preceding the Games. In this context, Laguillo's photographs from *Diagonal/Aragó* (1978) to *Frente a la Sagrada Familia* (1981) construct more critical and complex images of the city, making other realities visible. Laguillo's photographs challenge the predominance of the propagandistic image of the city as well as the concurrent ascendance of non-documentary practices in the local art market at that time.

Juan Muñoz came to international prominence in the mid-eighties with sculptural installations that place figures in architectural environments, creating works that evoke a sense of narrative and refer to the history of Western culture. His empty balconies and banisters leading nowhere often harbour sinister connotations, while his illusionistic floors, reminiscent of the Baroque-era masterpieces, theatrically frame the audience as they walk across it. Muñoz's figures – from solitary puppets to laughing Chinese men – present human forms subtended by physical and psychological estrangement. In *The Nature of Visual Illusion* (1994) three figures (Chinese men) are grouped together, while another similar figure is placed at a physical remove. Presented in front of a stagy curtain, the installation creates a tension between the illusory and the real at the same time that we, as viewers, are not quite privy to the joke that makes the figures smile.

    While Muñoz mined the history of art, often making references to the Baroque,
Jeff Wall's precise staging of models in his photographs mimics the deliberation
of painting, referencing nineteenth-century artists from Van Gogh to Manet and their
repeated images of modernity. His large tableaux photographs rethink conventional
painterly typologies through the production of constructed realities. With the new
advances in digital technology, Wall took advantage of the opportunity to suture
distinct realities and presents, as art historian Thomas Crow observes, an 'inscription
of allegorical meaning into a screen of apparently seamless naturalism'.[35] Jeff Wall's
photographic production has been complemented in the MACBA Collection through
the acquisition of the video *Dan Graham's Kammerspiel* (1987). In this work, Chris
Dercon interviews Wall about his eponymous essay of 1982. Framed behind Herman
Daled's version of Graham's *Alteration of a Suburban House* (see below), Wall
discusses Graham's work in relation to what he terms 'vampiric discourse'.[36]

Dan Graham's simultaneous activity on multiple artistic fronts characterises many
of the creative practices of the seventies and eighties, whereby art extended
into real space and time in order to engage in contemporary social issues. His first
work, the photo-essay 'Homes for America', published in *Arts Magazine* in 1966,
analyses and graphically represents the standardisation of suburban housing in
New Jersey; it presents a critical examination of the logic of uniformity behind
'free choice' while locating the magazine as both a site and socio-economic support
for the reception of art. Dan Graham's interest in urbanism and architecture
continues in *Alteration of a Suburban House* (1978–87) in the MACBA Collection.
In these architectural models, a wall of transparent glass substitutes the façade
of a suburban house. A mirror is placed parallel to this façade, dividing the interior
into two realms: the public and the private. The transparent glass allows the interior
to be viewed as if it were a shop window, leaving the bedrooms and the bathrooms
mysteriously hidden. At the same time, the mirror reflects the house's environs
(the other façades and lawn, archetypical signs of a suburban context) and the position
of the spectator. For Jeff Wall, Graham's work is crucial in so far as it presents a
series of mediations in which the suburban house, glass (modernist) house and
skyscraper come together, provoking an 'abstract drama' between the architectural
figurations for the subjected and those in power.

35 Thomas Crow, 'Profane Illuminations:
The Social History of Jeff Wall', in *Modern
Art in the Common Culture*. New Haven
and London: Yale University Press, 1996,
p. 167.
36 As discussed by Jeff Wall in
conversation with Chris Dercon in the video
Dan Graham's Kammerspiel (1987).

James Coleman's *Slide Piece* (1972–73) is a continuous projection of slides with a synchronised narration. Each of the images represents the same photographic picture of a seemingly banal location (a square in the city of Milan), while the authoritative male voiceover carefully analyses the projected scene. The description of the image concludes when the slide changes to show a picture that is completely identical to the previous one, thus frustrating the expectations of the viewer. In this case, the image remains the same but the voiceover analyses the scene from a different point of view. The criticality of *Slide Piece* depends on the accumulation of information it presents. After successive viewings, one's interpretation of the object changes, and a tension ensues between the desire to know the image and the unknown voice that determines how and what we see.

A group of artists working on the West Coast of the United States consistently probe how popular culture images operate, honing in on the contradictions of capitalism and consumerism in the West and at times addressing 'America' more specifically through an exploration of the socio-pathology of everyday life. Mike Kelley's artistic practice, profoundly influenced by his working class, suburban upbringing in Detroit, encompasses a variety of media such as drawing, painting, performance, sculpture, video and installation. Rejecting Minimalism and triumphant Abstract Expressionist painting, Kelley is often aligned with Conceptual art practices, yet his art injects Conceptual art with marginal references from popular culture such as psychedelic posters, left-wing graphics, rock music and underground comics. In *Fresh Acconci* (1995) Kelley together with artist Paul McCarthy re-stage classic seventies performance pieces by Vito Acconci with a decidedly ironic Southern California sensibility. To this end, McCarthy explains: '[*Fresh Acconci*] is a reference to art now, to a resurgence of the seventies and an interest in youth in the art world. There are also references to Hollywood 8 movies and soft porn made in the Hollywood hills… In *Fresh Acconci*, the New York art scene is sandwiched with Hollywood.'[37]

Raymond Pettibon's works are characterised by a frenetic style of drawing with texts that impart a strong critical element related to his works' subjects: sex, violence, religion, relationships and art. Pettibon's work draws on many different sources, including Goya's black paintings, Daumier's cartoons, Hopper's realism and German Expressionism; while in his texts we find quotations and references to

37 See Paul McCarthy's statement as cited on
www.macba.cat/controller.php?p_action=
show_page&pagina_id=29&inst_id=19320
(accessed December 2009).

works by Ruskin, Joyce and Henry James. According to Benjamin H. D. Buchloh, Pettibon's work 'imbues the ruins of figuration and the records of literary memory with their former promises at precisely those social sites where the resistance against techno-scientistic rule and the results of its most advanced devastation are most evident'.[38] Indeed, the strong critical overtone that emanates from his art remind one of the work of fellow West Coast artists like Mike Kelley and Paul McCarthy.

[38] Benjamin H. D. Buchloh, 'Raymond Pettibon: Return to Disorder and Disfiguration', *October*, no. 92, Spring 2000, p. 51.

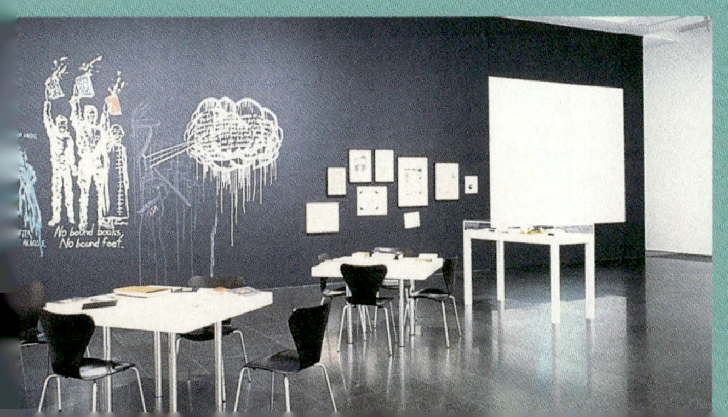

<
Raymond Pettibon, 2002

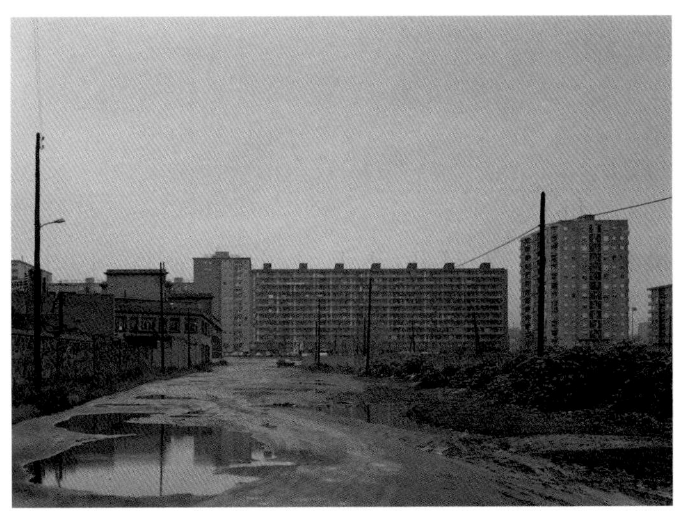

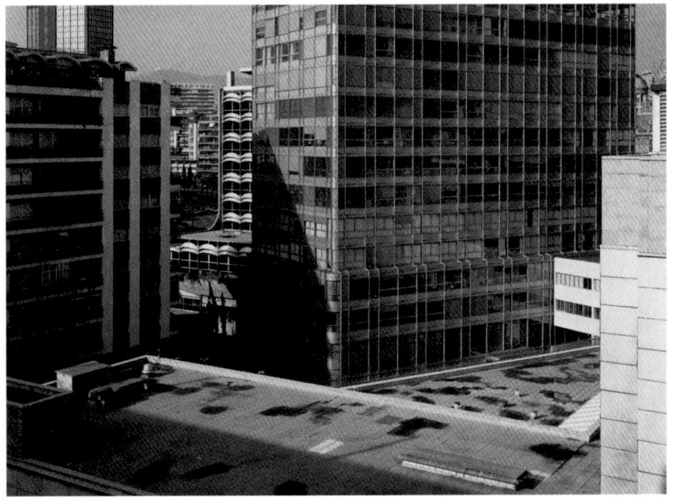

Manolo Laguillo

Nacimiento de la Diagonal, 1979
Platinum palladium photograph
35.5 × 61.5 cm

La trasera de la Plaça de Francesc Macià, 1980
Platinum palladium photograph
24.5 × 33 cm

Frente a la Sagrada Familia, 1981
Platinum palladium photograph
51.3 × 61.3 cm

Vall d'Hebron, 1992
Silver-salt photograph
50.5 × 75.5 cm

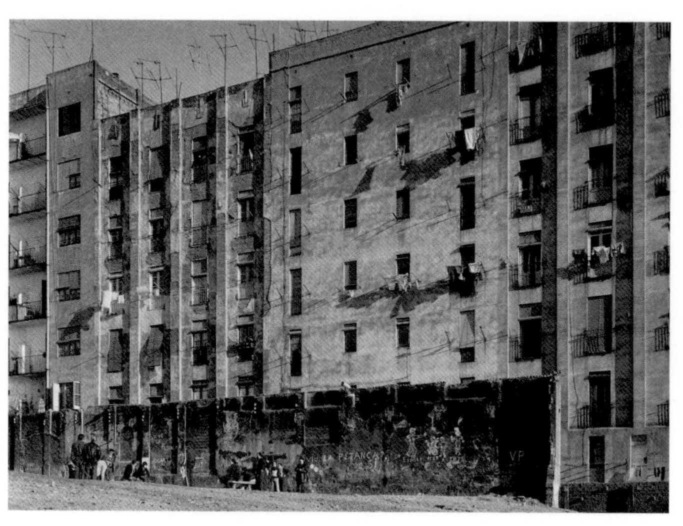

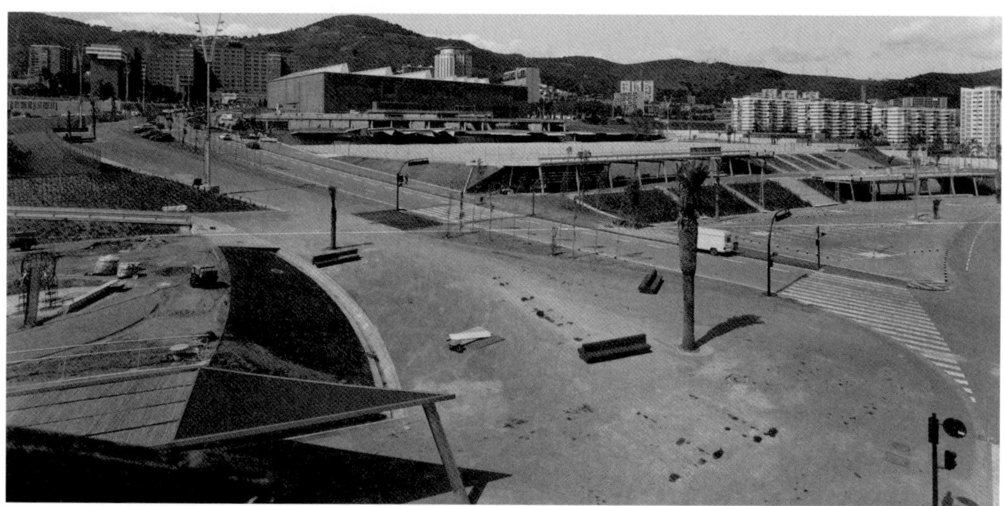

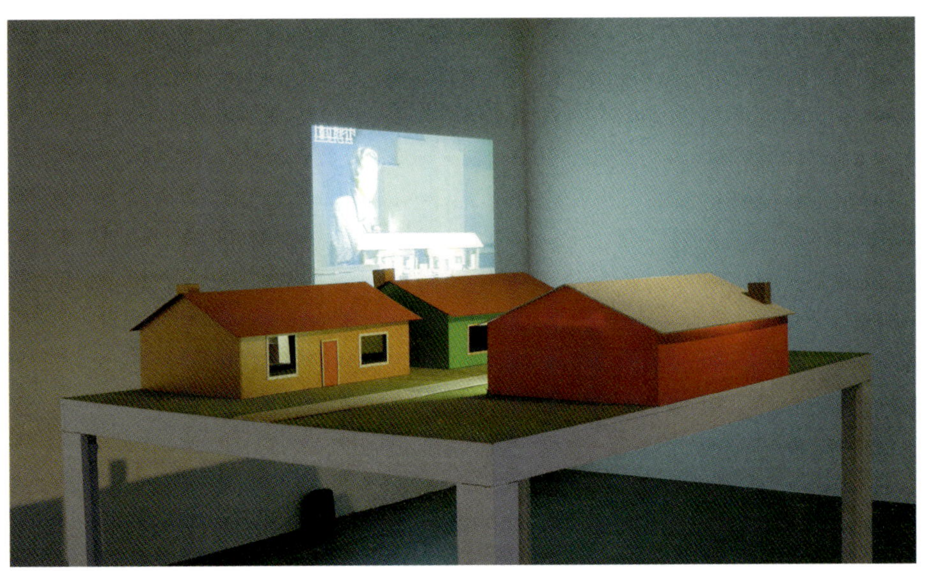

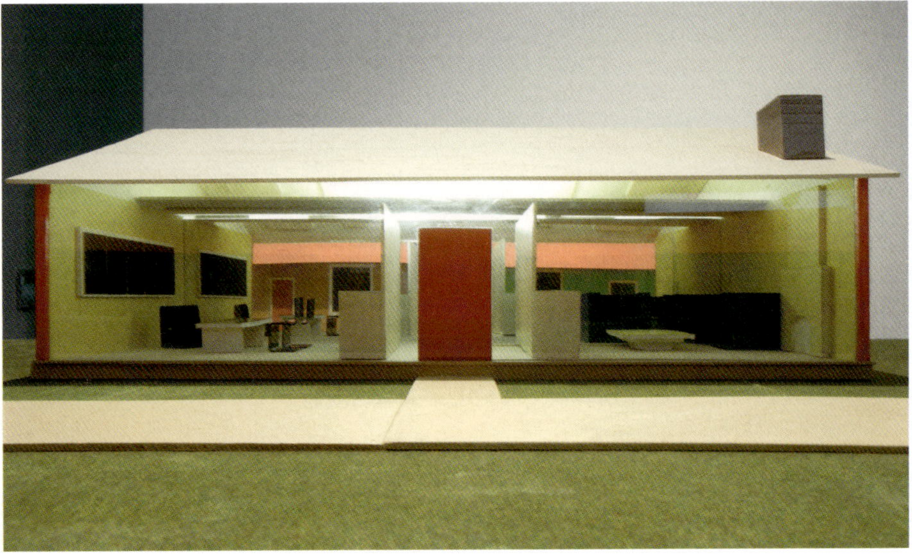

Dan Graham
Alteration of a Suburban House, 1978–87
Plywood, fitted carpet, lightweight cardboard,
balsa wood, mirror, card and methacrylate
184 × 267 × 120 cm

Installation view, *MACBA im Frankfurter Kunstverein*, Frankfurt, 2007

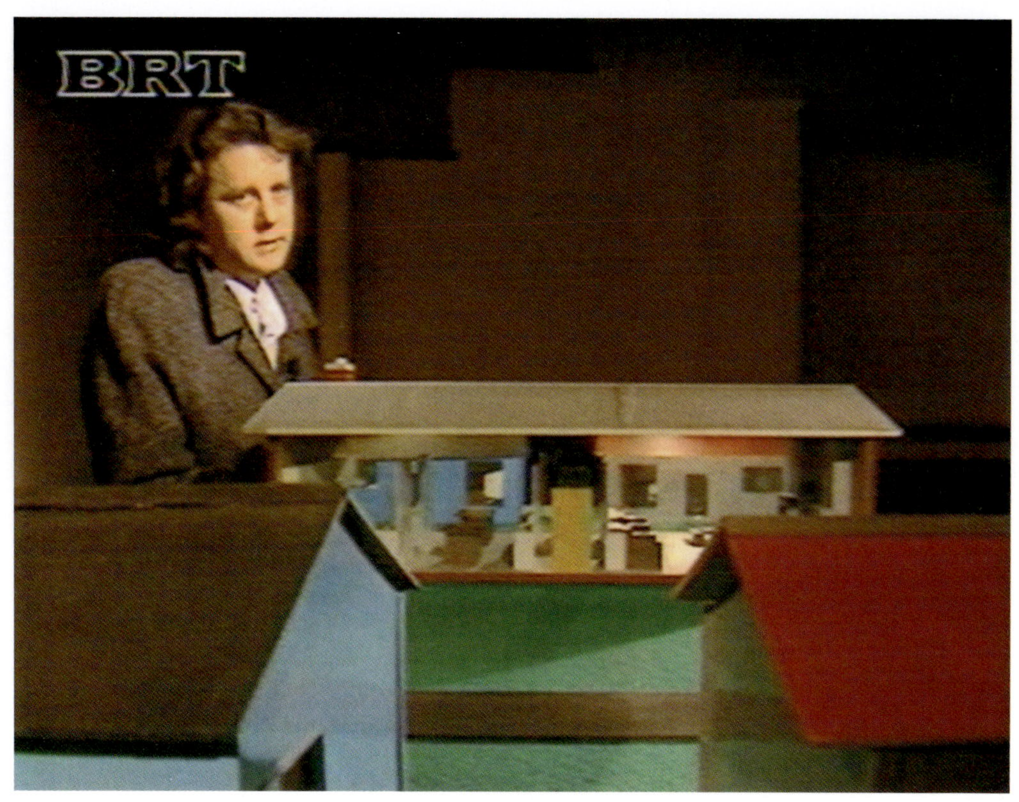

Jeff Wall
Dan Graham's Kammerspiel. Interview (Chris Dercon).
Recorded at the house of Herman Daled in Brussels.
Herman Daled's version of Suburban House, 1987
Single-channel video, colour, sound, 55 min

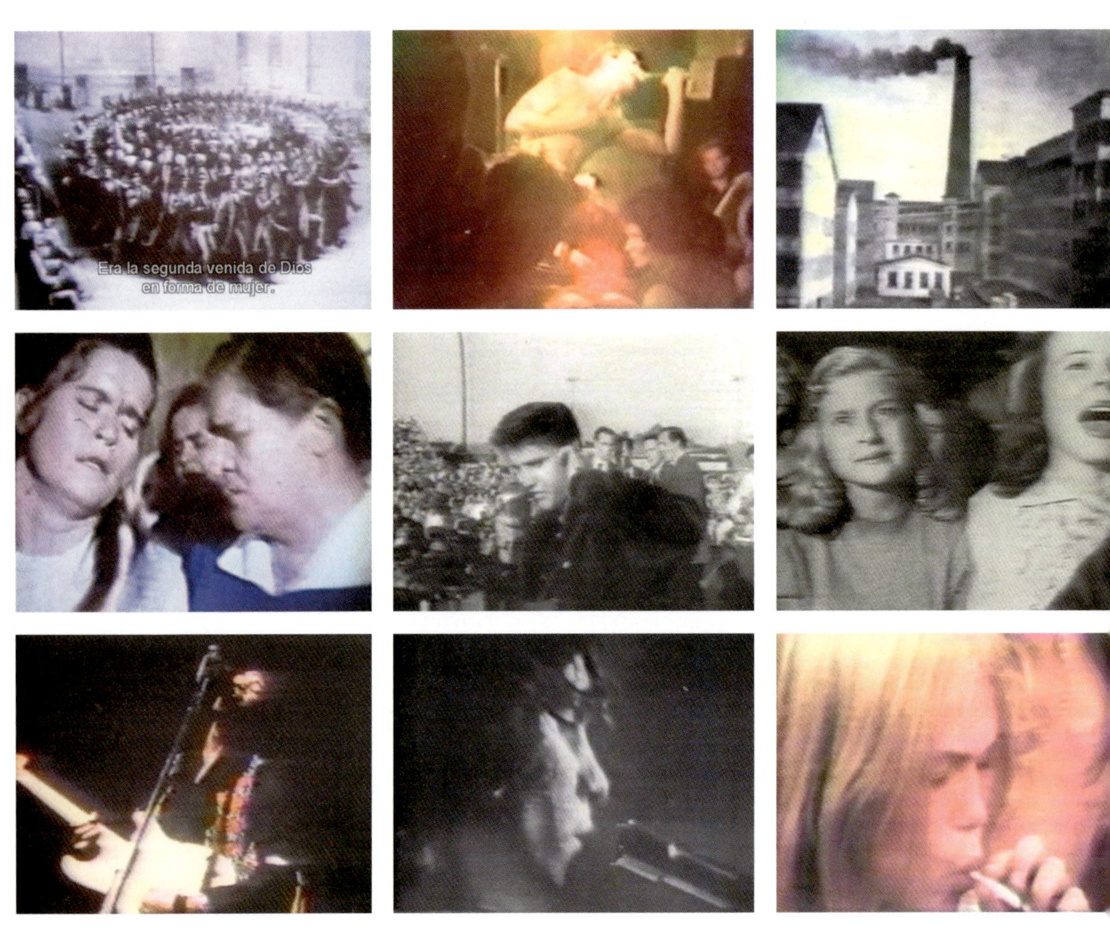

Dan Graham
Rock my Religion, 1984
Single-channel video, b/w and colour, sound, 55 min 27 s

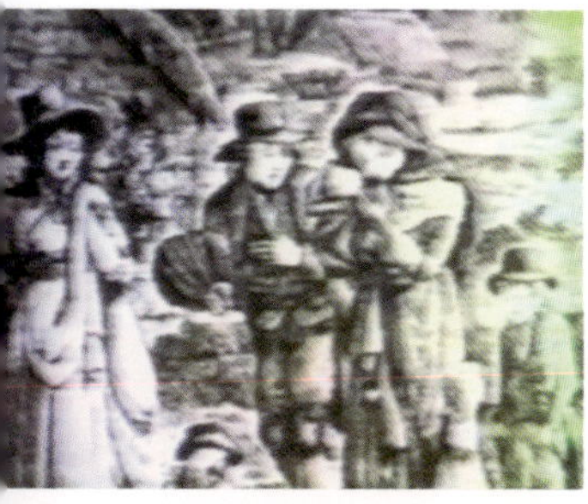

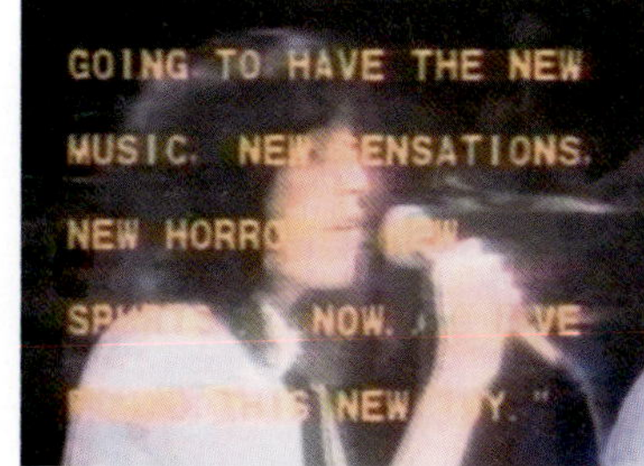
GOING TO HAVE THE NEW
MUSIC. NEW SENSATIONS.
NEW HORRORS. NEW
SPIRITS. NOW. WE HAVE
TO DO THIS NEW WAY."

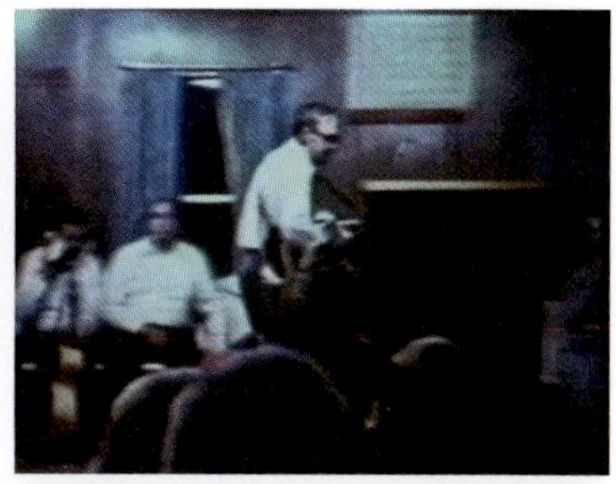

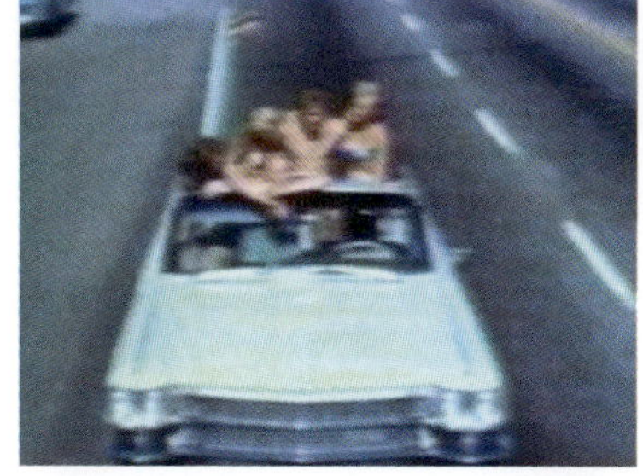

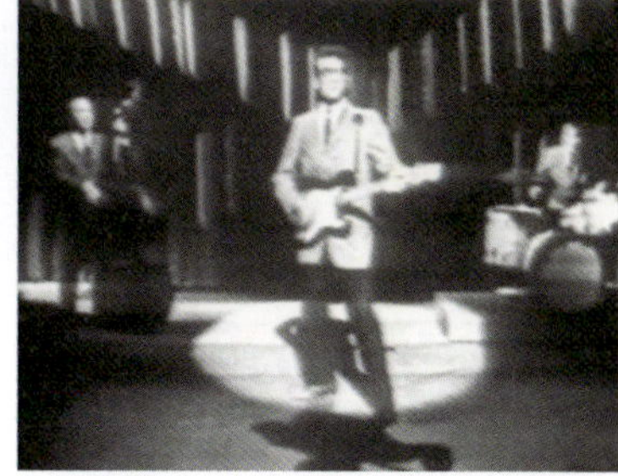

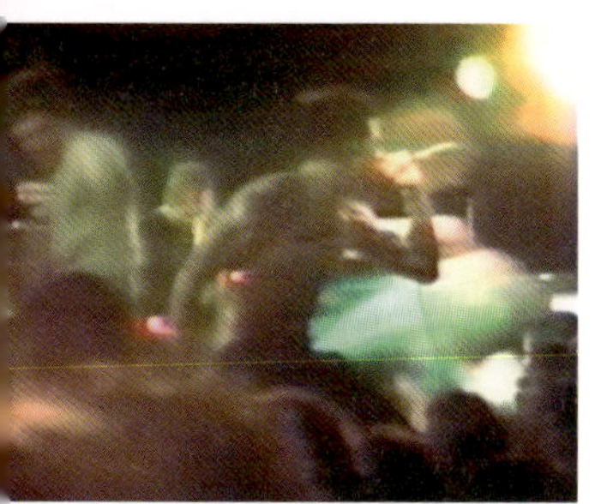
"Fun. fun. fun.
Maybe it won't last
but what do we care
my baby and I just
want a good time

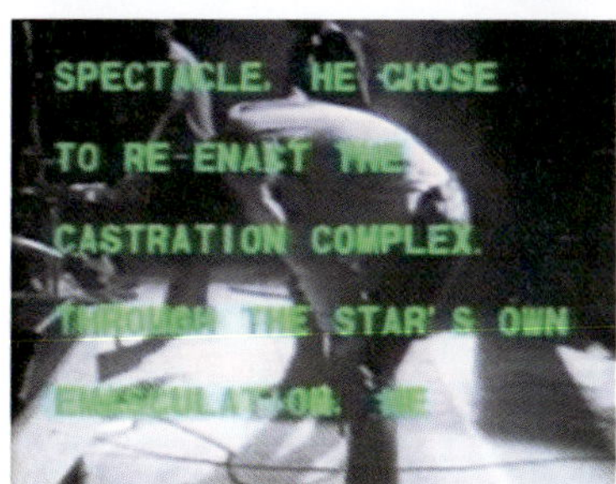
SPECTACLE. HE CHOSE
TO RE-ENACT THE
CASTRATION COMPLEX.
THROUGH THE STAR'S OWN
EMASCULATION. HE

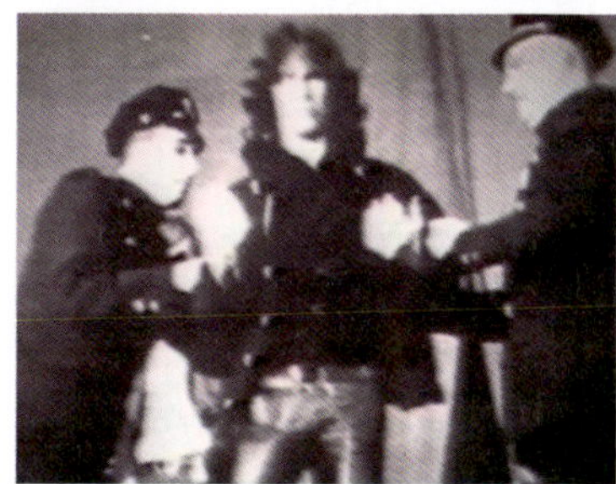

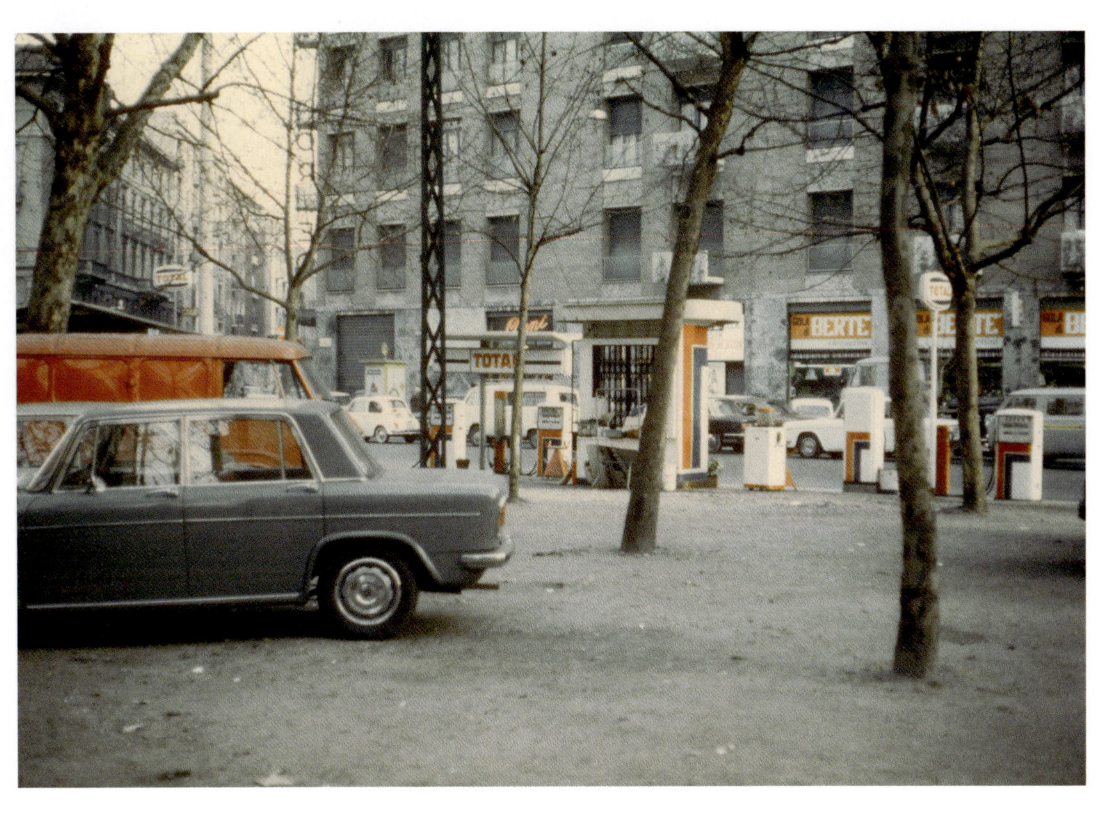

James Coleman
Slide Piece, 1972–73
Projected images and synchronised audio narration

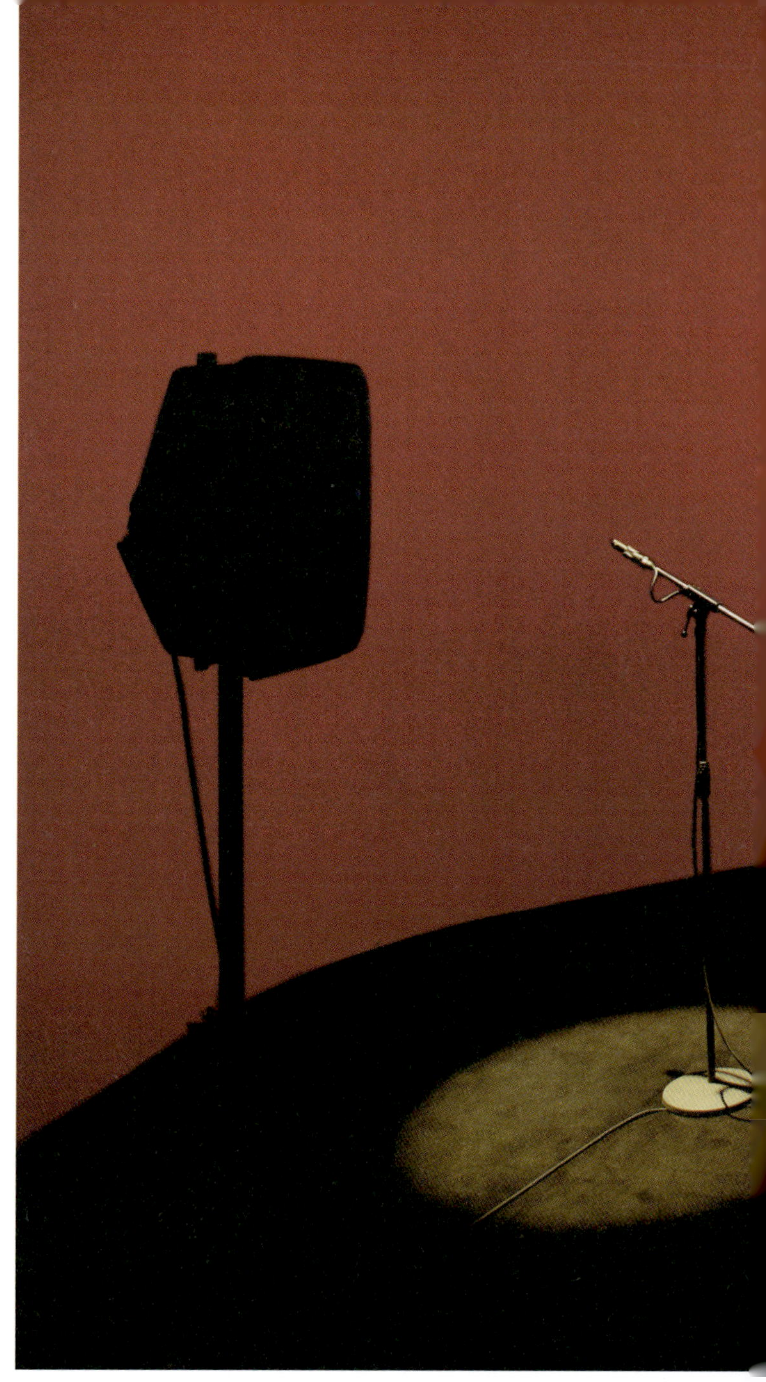

James Coleman
So Different... and Yet, 1980
Videoinstallation. Single-channel video, colour, sound, 54 min
Performance by Olwen Fouéré and Roger Doyle

Installation view, *A Theater without Theater*, MACBA, 2007

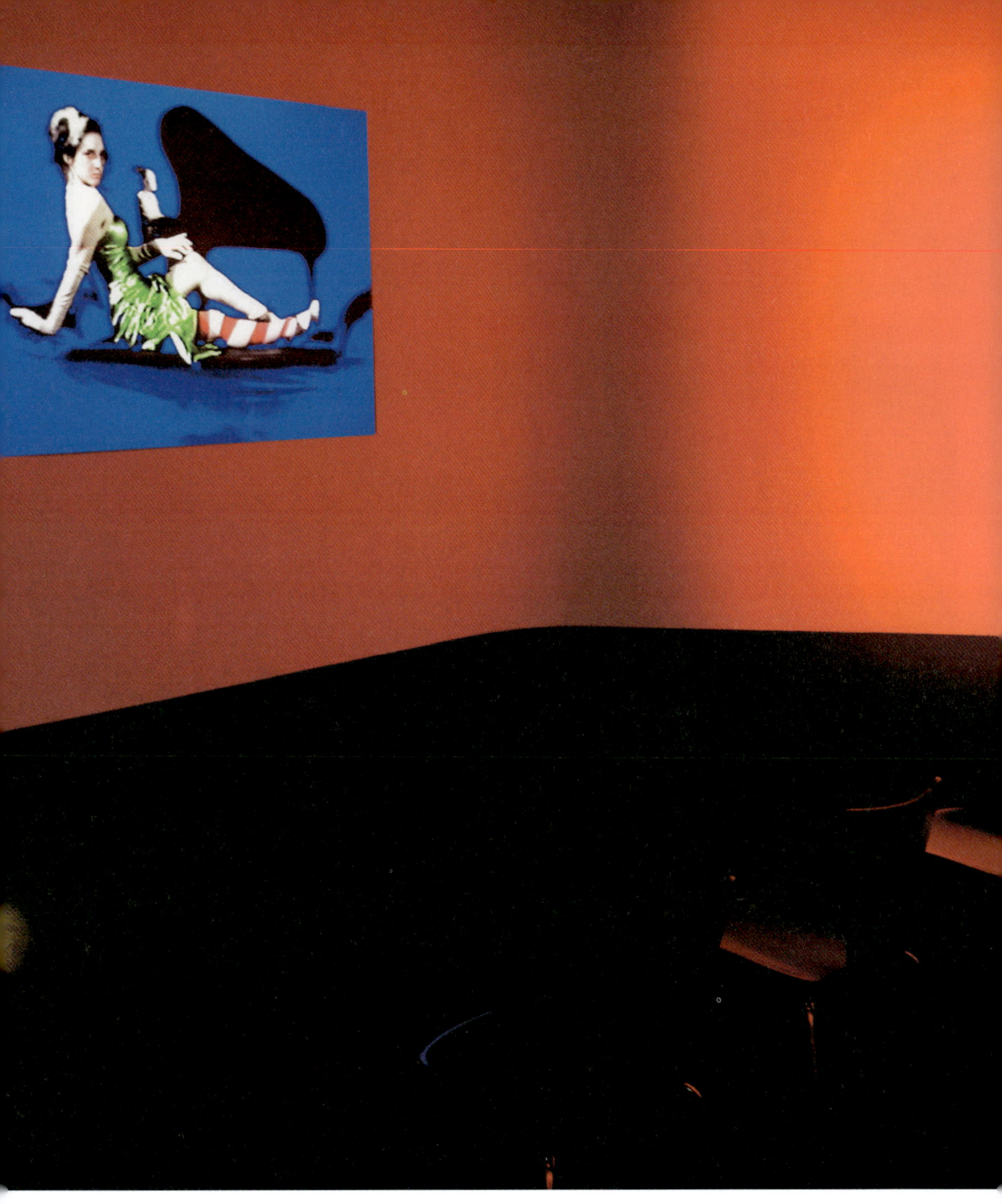

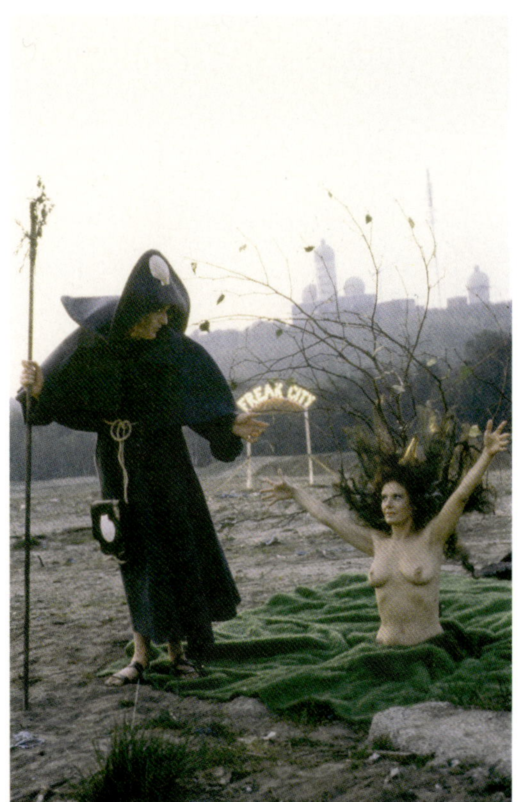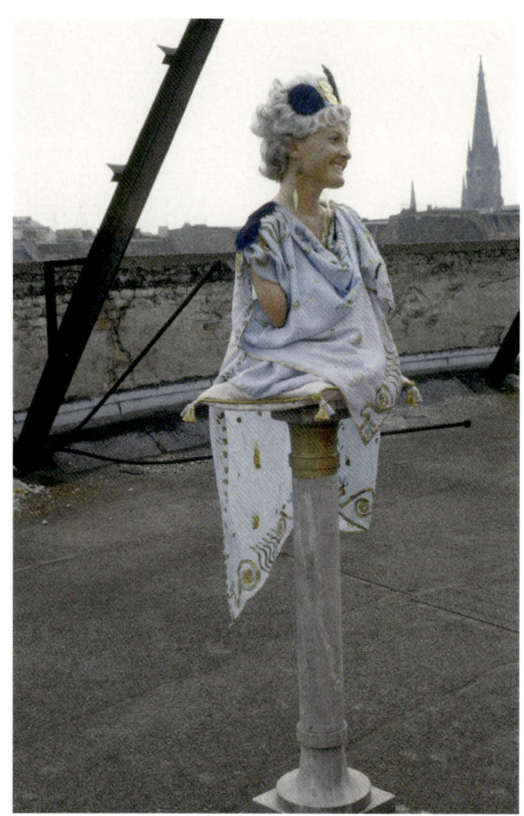

Ulrike Ottinger
Jacobs Pilger; *Torso*; *Narzisstischer Hermaphrodit*
in Beleitung eines Zwerges und einer Bartfrau;
Fräulein Maussi und Paulchen, 1981
Colour photographs of the film *Freak Orlando*
35 mm film transferred to video, colour, sound, 126 min

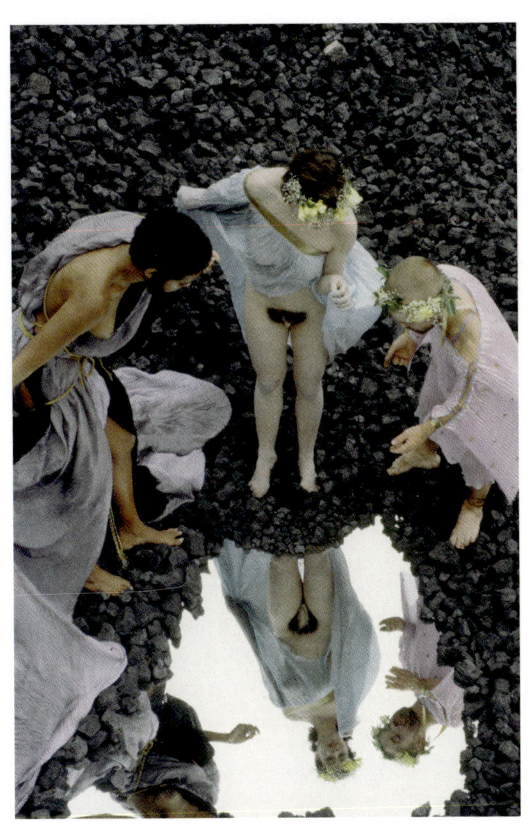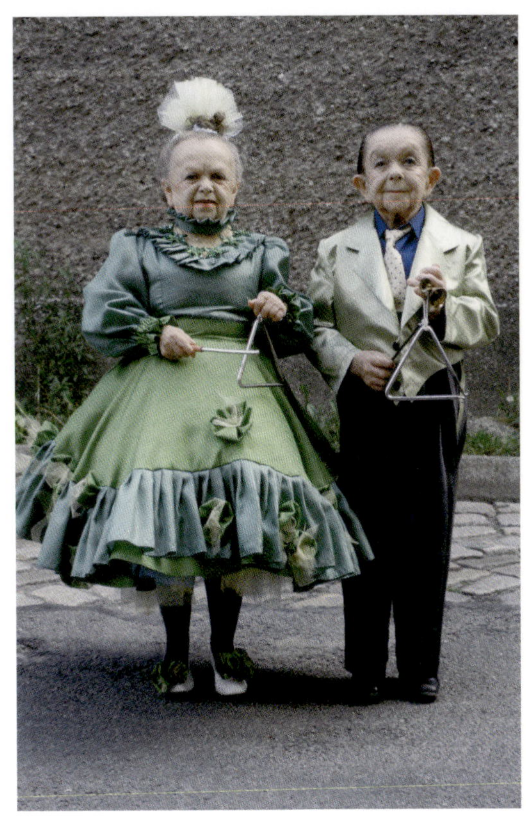

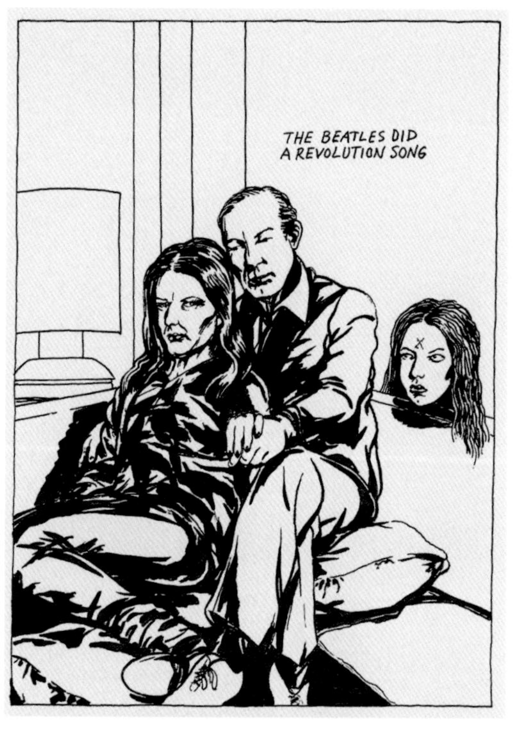

THE BEATLES DID
A REVOLUTION SONG

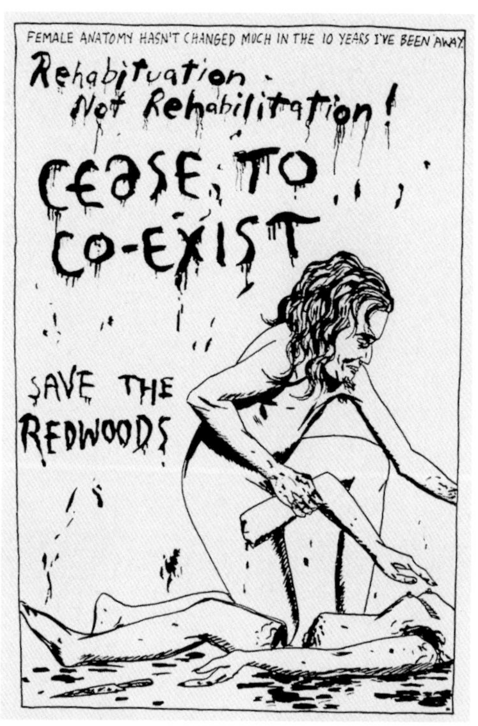

FEMALE ANATOMY HASN'T CHANGED MUCH IN THE 10 YEARS I'VE BEEN AWAY
Rehabituation -
Not Rehabilitation!
CEASE, TO
CO-EXIST
SAVE THE
REDWOODS

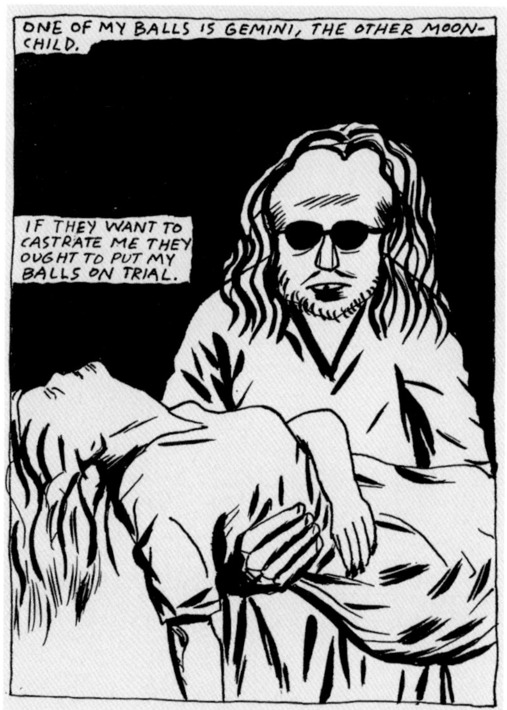

ONE OF MY BALLS IS GEMINI, THE OTHER MOON-CHILD.
IF THEY WANT TO CASTRATE ME THEY OUGHT TO PUT MY BALLS ON TRIAL.

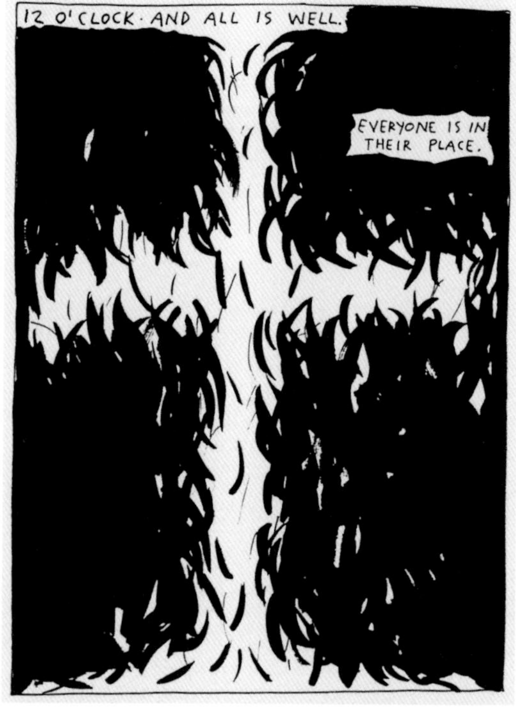

12 O'CLOCK · AND ALL IS WELL.
EVERYONE IS IN THEIR PLACE.

174

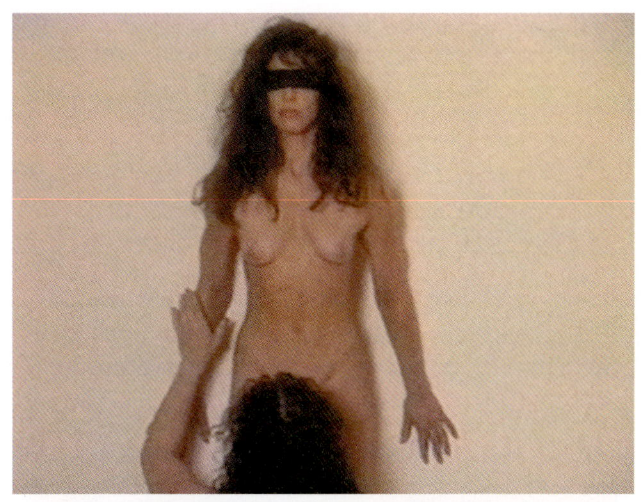

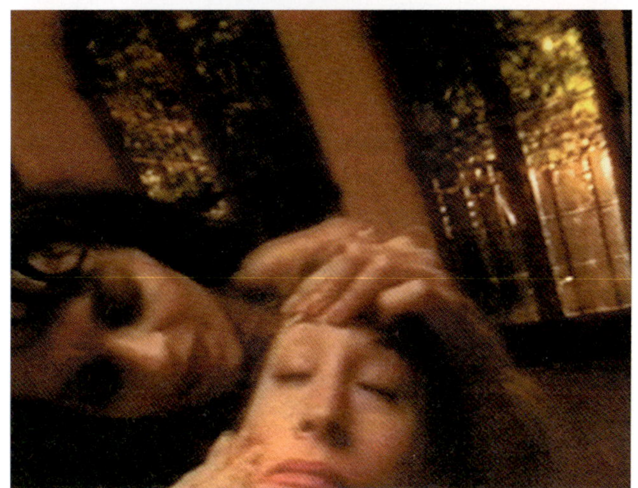

Raymond Pettibon
The Beatles Did a Revolution Song, 1981
Ink on paper
29.2 × 22.9 cm

Female Anatomy Hasn't..., 1985
Ink on paper
36 × 26.3 cm

One of My Balls Is Gemini..., 1985
Ink on paper
26.8 × 21.2 cm

12 O'clock and All Is Well, 1986
Ink on paper
35.5 × 28 cm

Mike Kelley, Paul Mc Carthy
Fresh Acconci, 1995
Single-channel video, colour, sound, 45 min

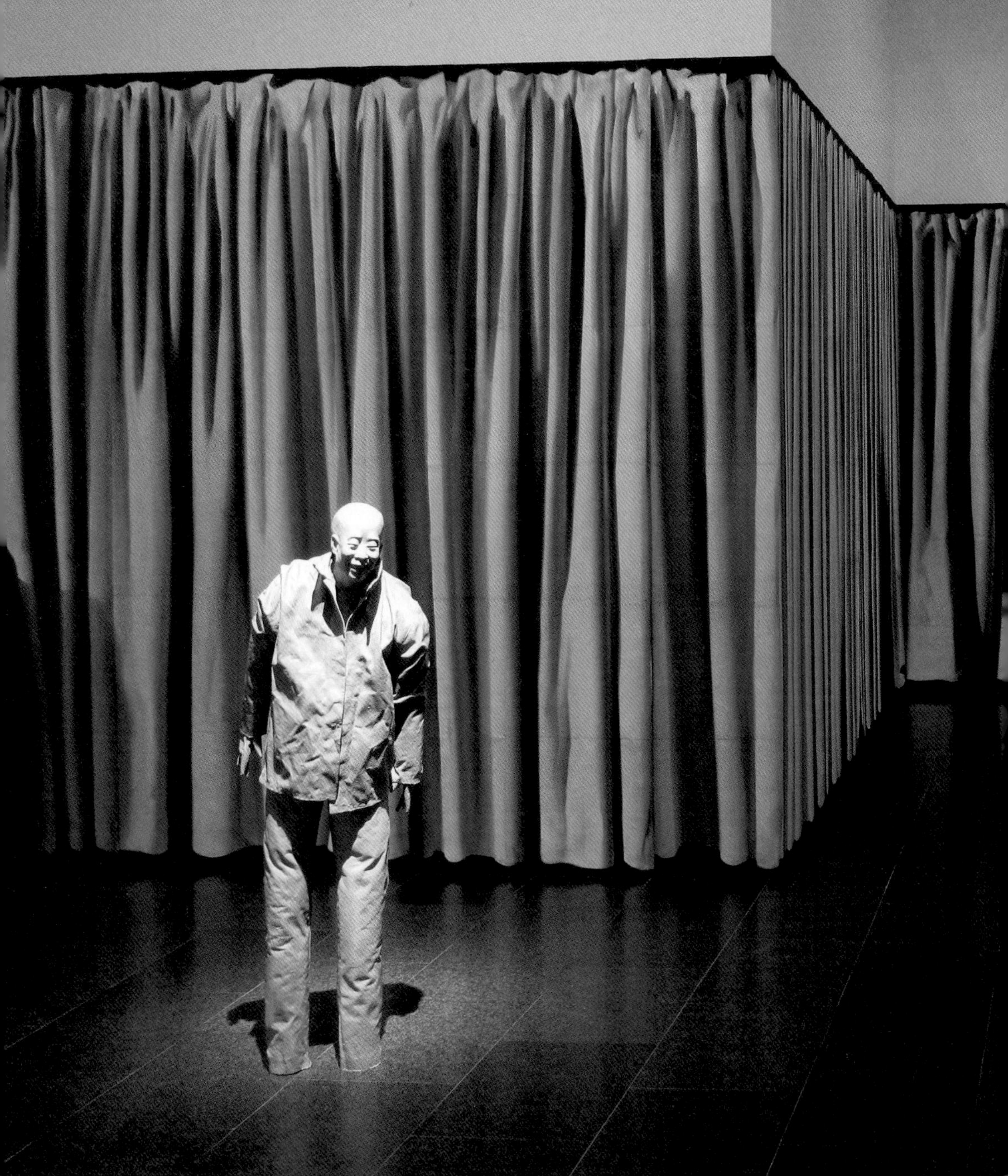

Juan Muñoz
The Nature of Visual Illusion, 1994
Acrylic on canvas and 4 figurines in polyester resin
Dimensions variable

Installation view, presentation of the MACBA Collection, 2006

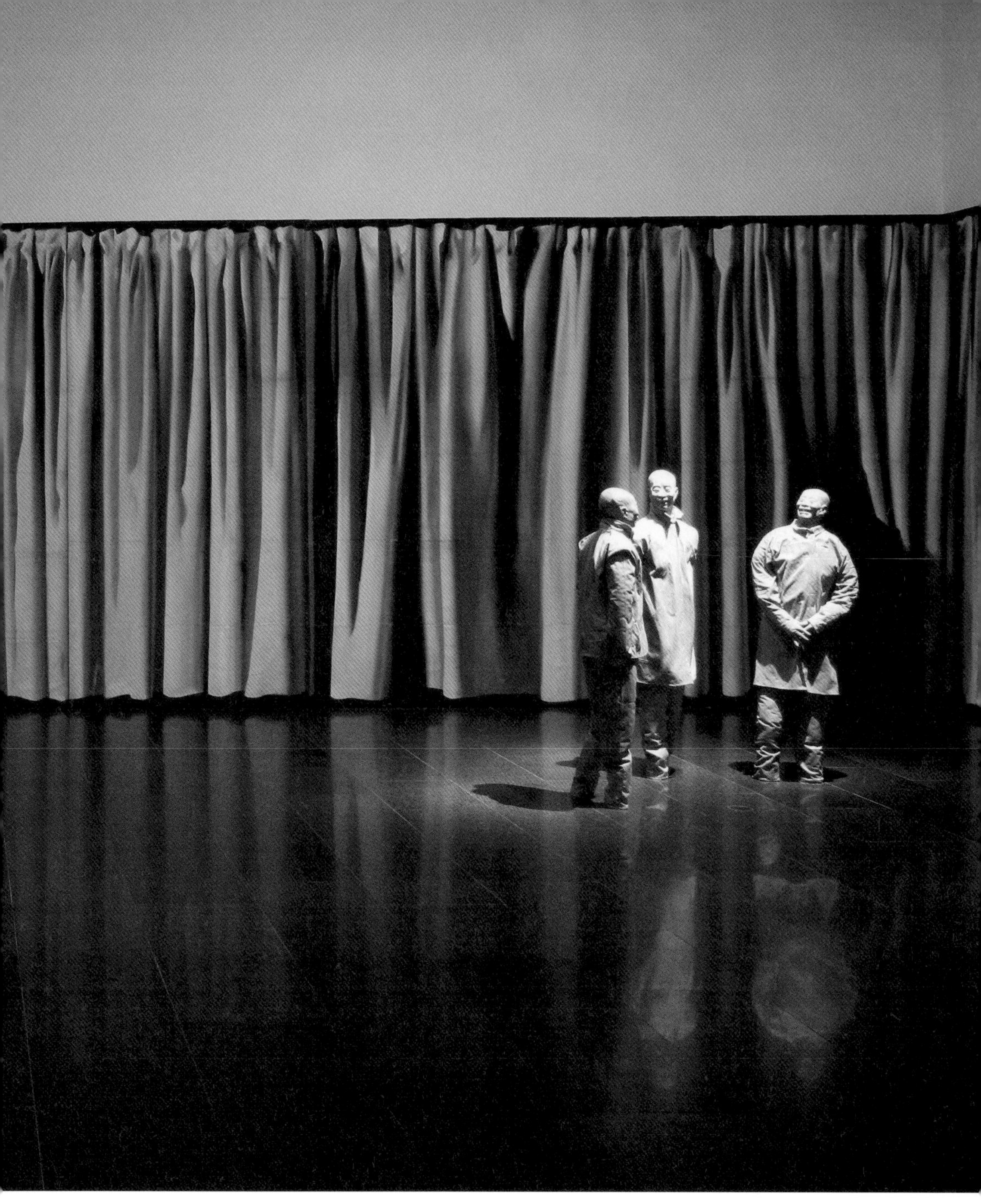

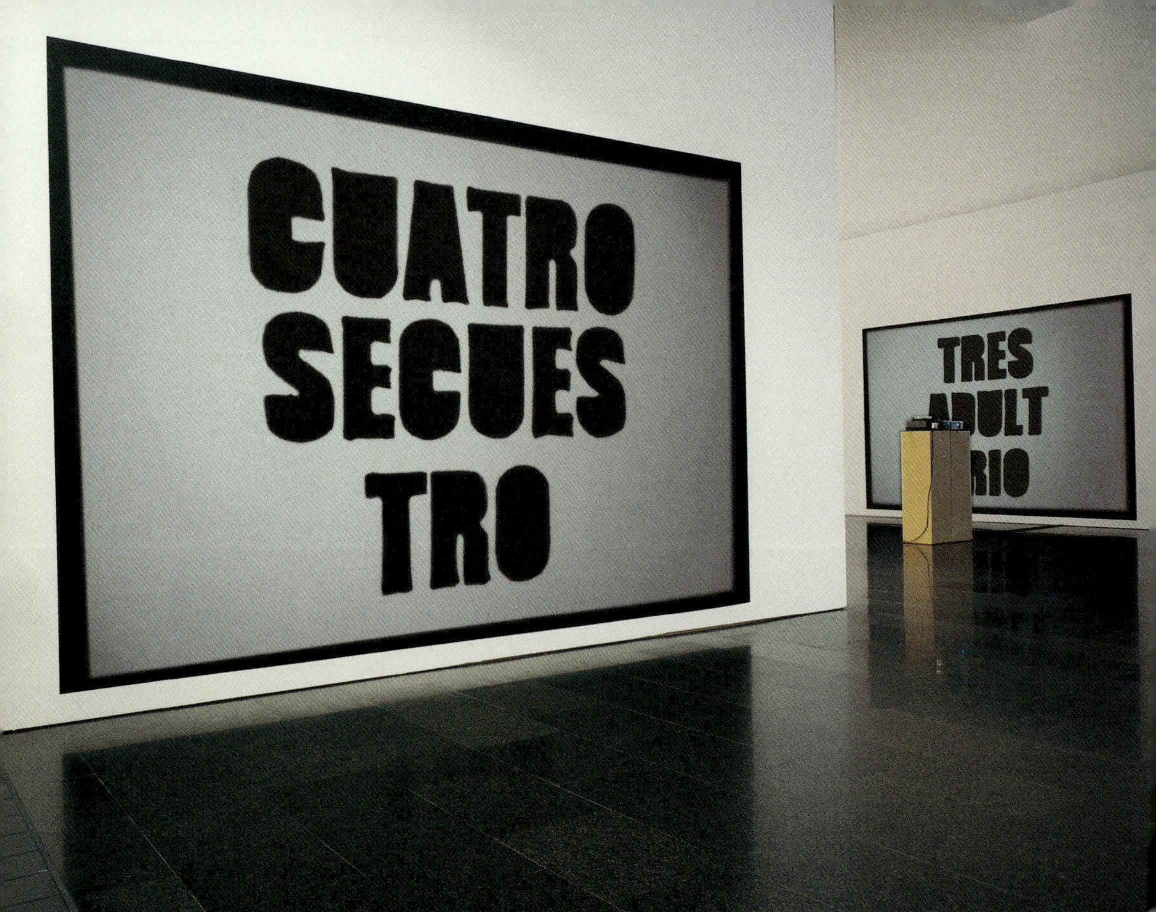

Jon Mikel Euba
Fiesta 4 puertas, 2001
5 simultaneous slide projections

Installation view, presentation of the MACBA Collection, 2003

178

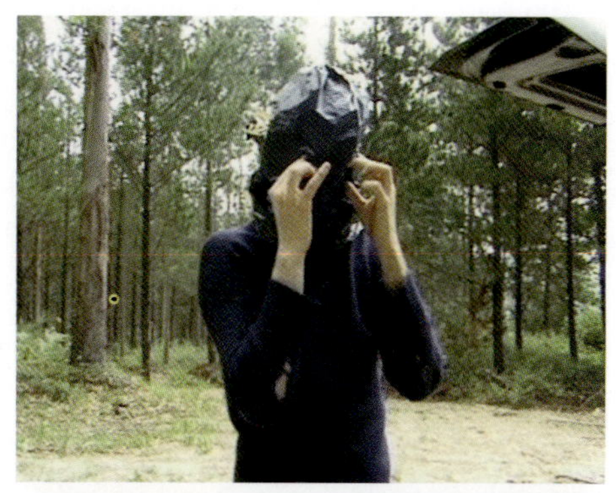

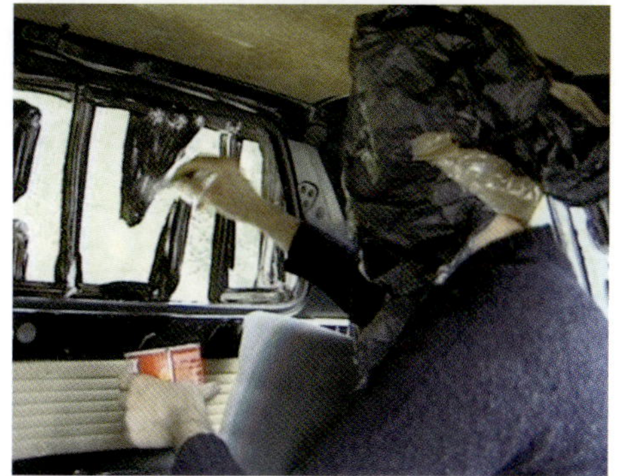

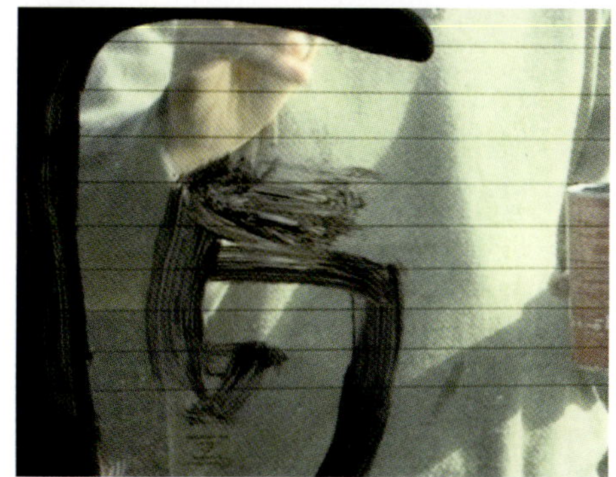

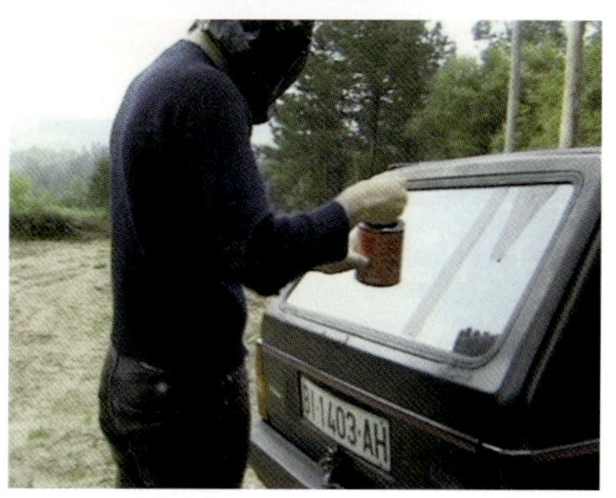

Gatika doble final, 2001
Single-channel video, colour, sound, 11 min

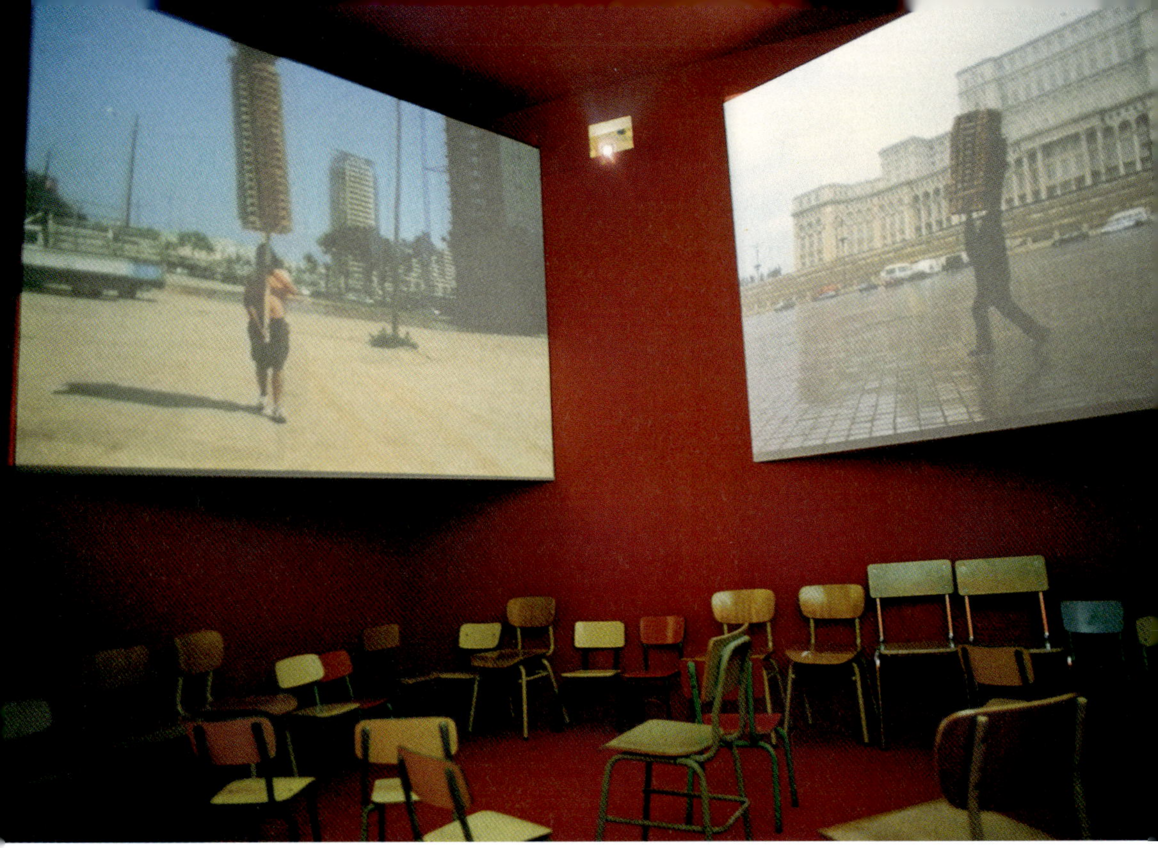

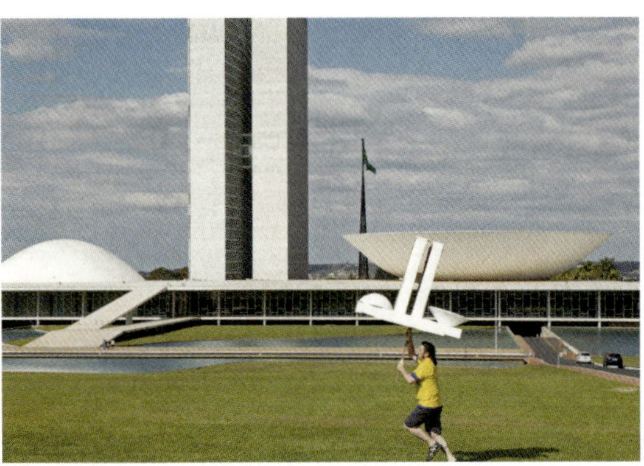

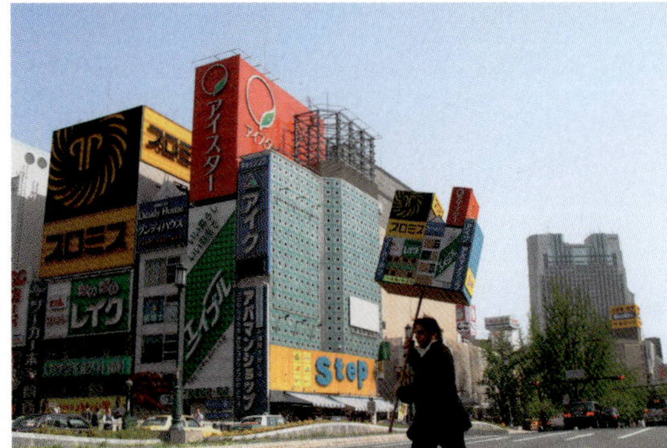

Jordi Colomer
Anarchitekton (Barcelona, Bucarest, Brasilia, Osaka), 2002–04
Video, colour, silent, looped projection; 4 screens; chairs and fitted carpet
Performed by Idroj Sanicne. Photography: Marc Viaplana / Jordi Colomer
Production: Maravills, Spanish Embassy in Brasilia, Generalitat de Catalunya
(Departament de Cultura) and Fundación Marcelino Botín

Installation view, *Jordi Colomer*, Jeu de Paume, Paris, 2008

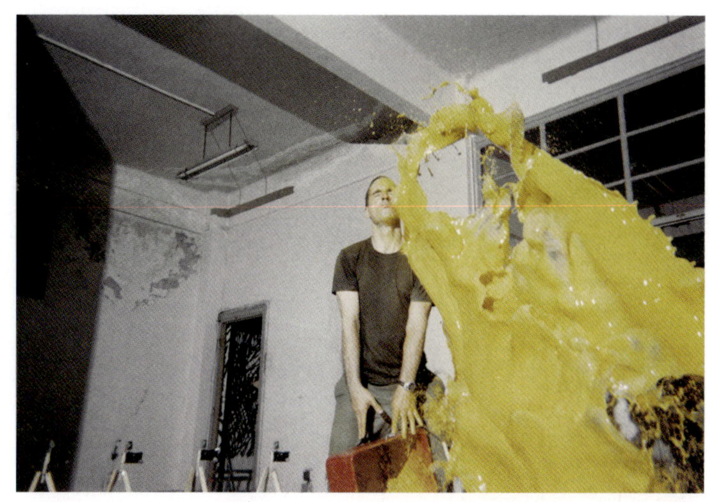

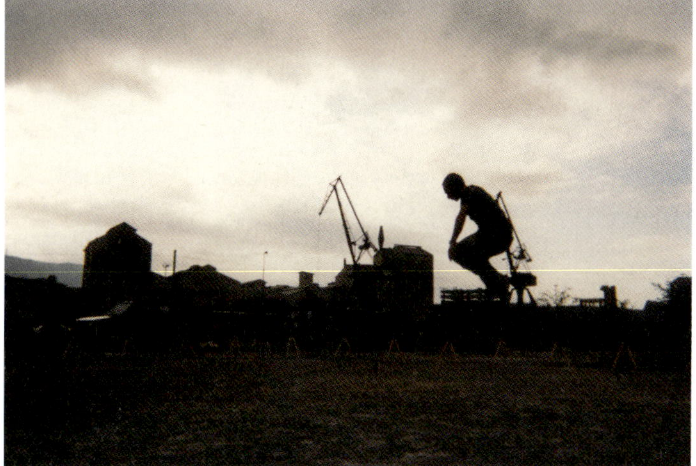

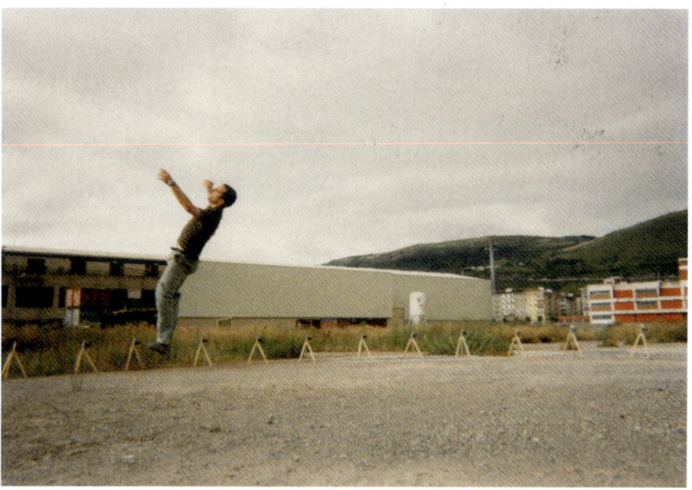

Sergio Prego
Tetsuo, Bound to Fail, 1998
Single-channel video, colour,
sound, 17 min 30 s

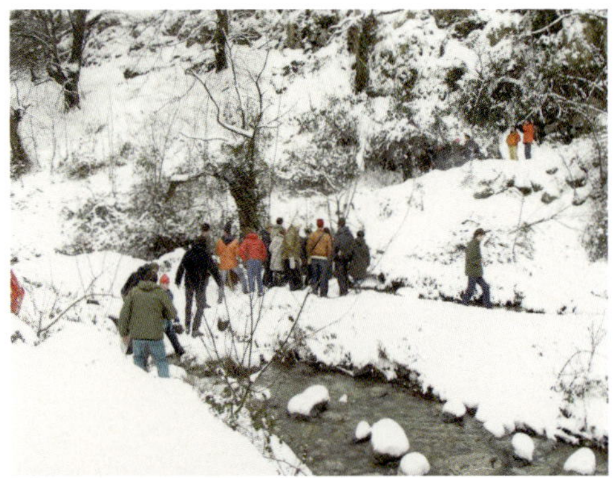

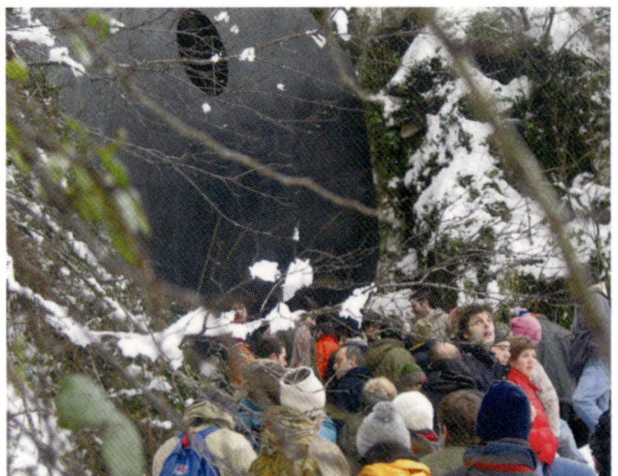

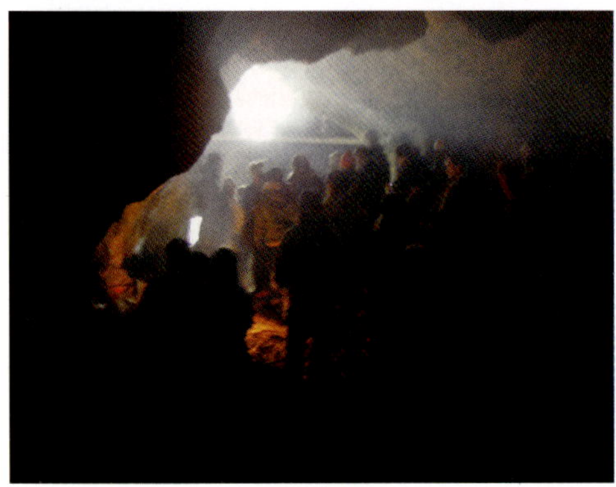

Ibon Aranberri
(Ir. T. nº 513) zuloa, 2003
Single-channel video, colour, sound, 8 min

(IR. T. Nº 513) ZULOA

Far removed from urban areas, the cave of Iritegi is located near the Aitzgorri mountain range, at the far end of a narrow valley that belongs to the town of Oñati (in Guipuzkoa). It sits in the middle of an area of exceptional natural beauty that is not easily accessible by car. Ir. T. nº 513 is its scientific code. The cave has several subterranean passages that extend over many kilometres, and one of them, which is approximately five-metres wide, is the main entrance. It has been excavated several times and archeological remains have been found around the entrance. These archeological remains have been collected and archived by the Aranzadi Scientific Society. The site is now thoroughly catalogued, and there are no plans to undertake further digging in the next few years. However, the cave of Iritegi is extremely interesting in biological terms. It is the permanent home of a large colony of bats of the Rhinolophus ferrumequinum Schreiber species, and seasonal refuge to a smaller colony of the Miniopterus schreibersii Kuhl species. Both species are protected. The cave is periodically visited by scientists and pedagogical excursions are often organized by members of the local nature club. Less frequently, the cave is used by speleologists and as a shelter for animals and people.

Following the directions of archaeological guides, I walked through many locations in the nearby area that are full of rocky caverns. This searching and familiarising process gave me some basic knowledge in the area. The idea of sealing a cave arose as a reaction to this experience. However, this act is not merely meant as a protective measure. On the contrary, its motivation is purely personal. In the course of my fieldwork, I gathered plenty of documentary evidence. I automatically singled out the images I favoured, and erased all signs of my visit as I left each site. Afterwards, I decided to apply the same graphic effect to a life-size setting and measure its effect on society. Among all the caves I visited, the one in Iritegi came closest to my original scheme. In terms of its physical dimensions, its location and so on, it had all the characteristics I had sought. But it could equally have been another cave, another site in a different place.

This project has been approved by all the relevant authorities and has been given all the necessary legal and building permits.

The cave has been physically sealed off. Its original features have been transformed. To achieve this I built a flat, opaque structure that covers the space at the mouth of the cave. I used a modular system of high-resistance metal panels that when joined together seal the entirety of the surface. The silhouette of the structure reproduces the shape of the opening in the rock. Every panel has received a long-lasting anti-corrosive treatment. However, the whole structure can be easily dismantled and removed if necessary.

Taking account of the specific needs of the place, I undertook the following adaptations: 1. Between the surrounding rock and the silhouette of the structure there is a gap wide enough to allow for ventilation. 2. The structure hangs suspended from its anchorage points, so that its weight will not at any point rest on the sediment. 3. Studies of bats highlight their ability to orient themselves in the dark, mainly by means of their sonar. There is a hole at the top of the structure that allows them to go in and out. This hole gives them freedom of movement. Once the adaptation period is over, the bats' behaviour in relation to this new element will be observed. 4. Furthermore, one of the modules at the bottom of the structure is hinged in order to provide an articulated panel that can act as a door if needed. This panel has a lock, and a key to it has been distributed among all the people and societies involved with the cave. Access to this key is unrestricted, any person wishing to can make use of it.

The development of this alteration of the landscape will depend on its ability to adapt to its environment. It will depend on the responses it provokes in nearby inhabitants, and will have to withstand whatever treatment or aggression befalls it. The installation gains meaning from the place in which it is placed. It connects with the imaginary archetypes of the local culture, where the imbedded romantic tradition still represents pre-history as the great myth of our origins.

The definition of the collective identity rests heavily on the idea of landscape as symbolic scenery. Here, the depth of content is trivialized and thus becomes sign.

Going beyond the well-known dichotomy of nature and artifice, this installation aims to take part in the natural ecosystem. In the information society everything is systematically compartmentalized as a method of assimilating reality. In this reductive way, nature is presented to us as paradise lost. I understand our relationship to nature as an exercise in the reassessment of our primordial environment. Nowadays there is always a form of mediation in the exchange between the outside world and the consumer. Thus the metal panels interfere between the raw material and the field of vision of an image that has been previously processed, an infinite number of times, by our brains. Between natural science and science fiction. This project aims to create a disturbance in nature, an alteration in the relationship between the primordial environment and technology. The sealed cave is designed to be imagined as a closed space from within the darkness of its interior, or to be observed from the outside, as if it were an illusory vision within the landscape (a black hole, a door to unknown universes).

Besides the alteration made to the place, all information about the cave has been reconfigured. The existing maps have been changed, and the installation has been referred to in all archives of the relevant fields of study.

For the opening, we organized a group excursion to the cave.

Ibon Aranberri, 2003

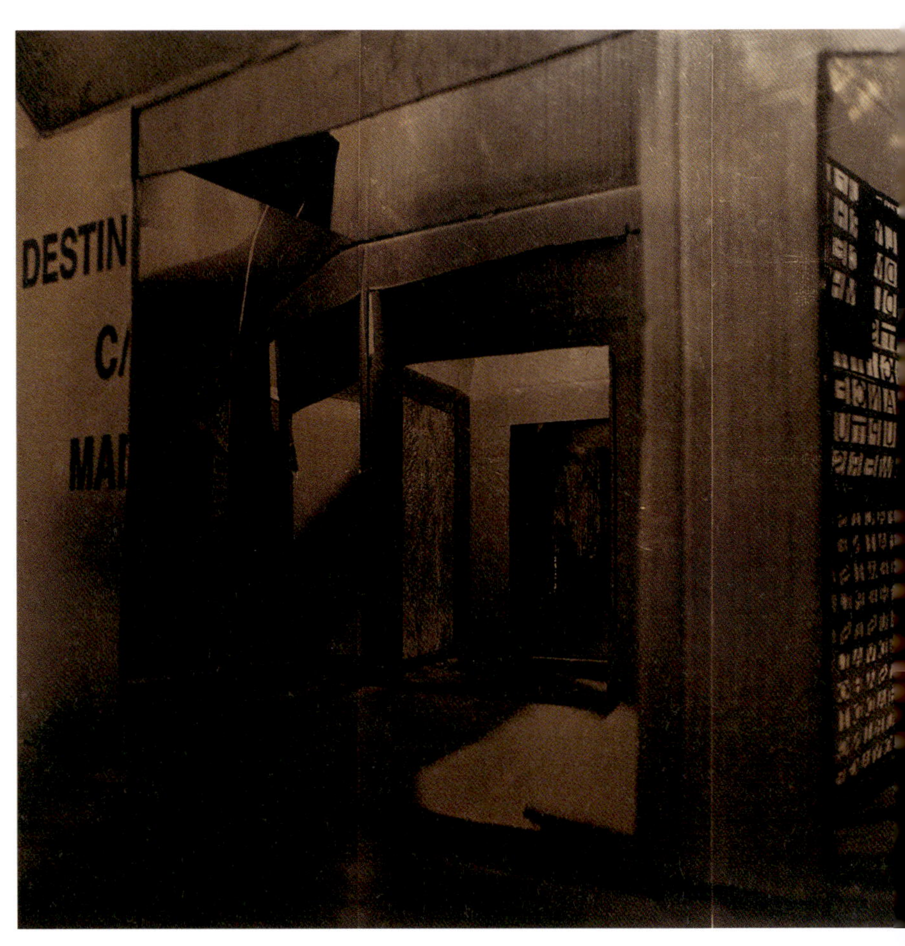

Cristina Iglesias
Políptico VII, 2002
Screen print on copper mounted on iron pannels
6 parts, 250 × 100 × 0.15 cm each

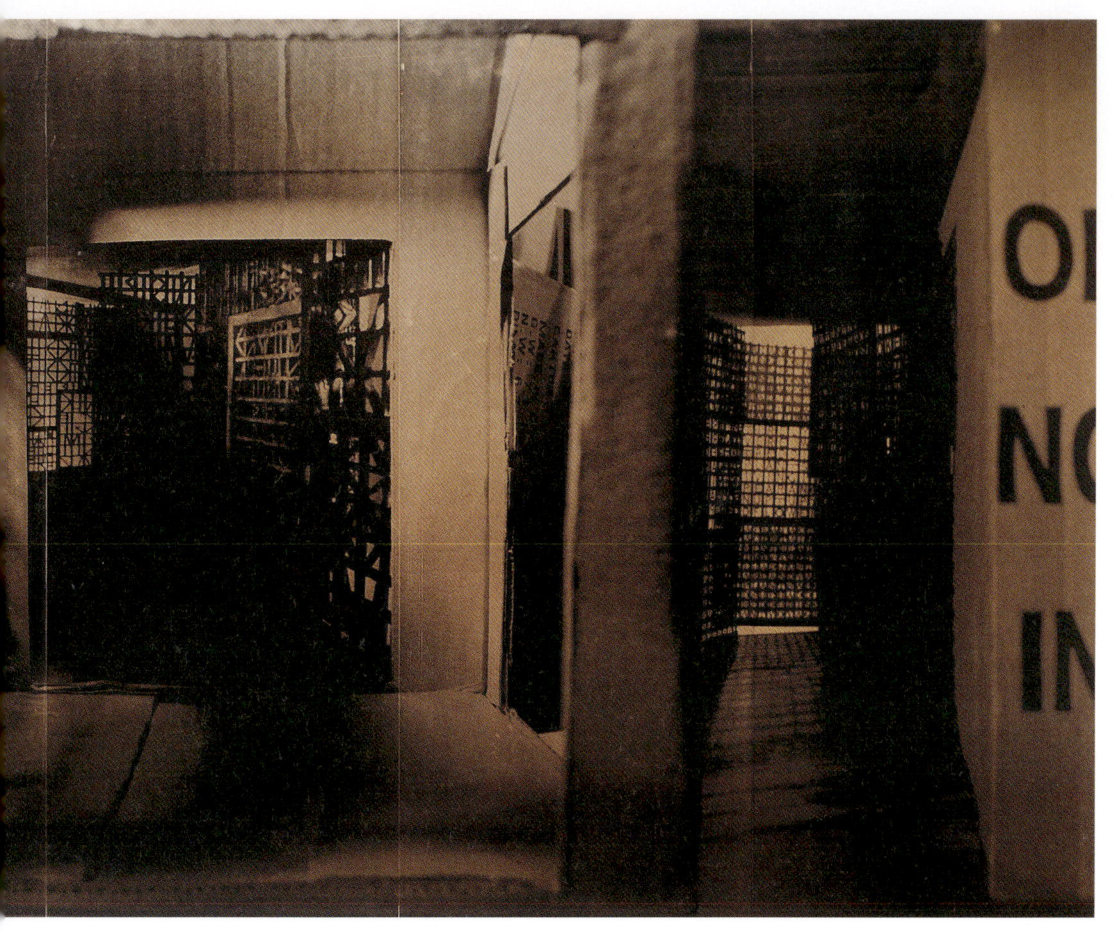
O
NC
IN

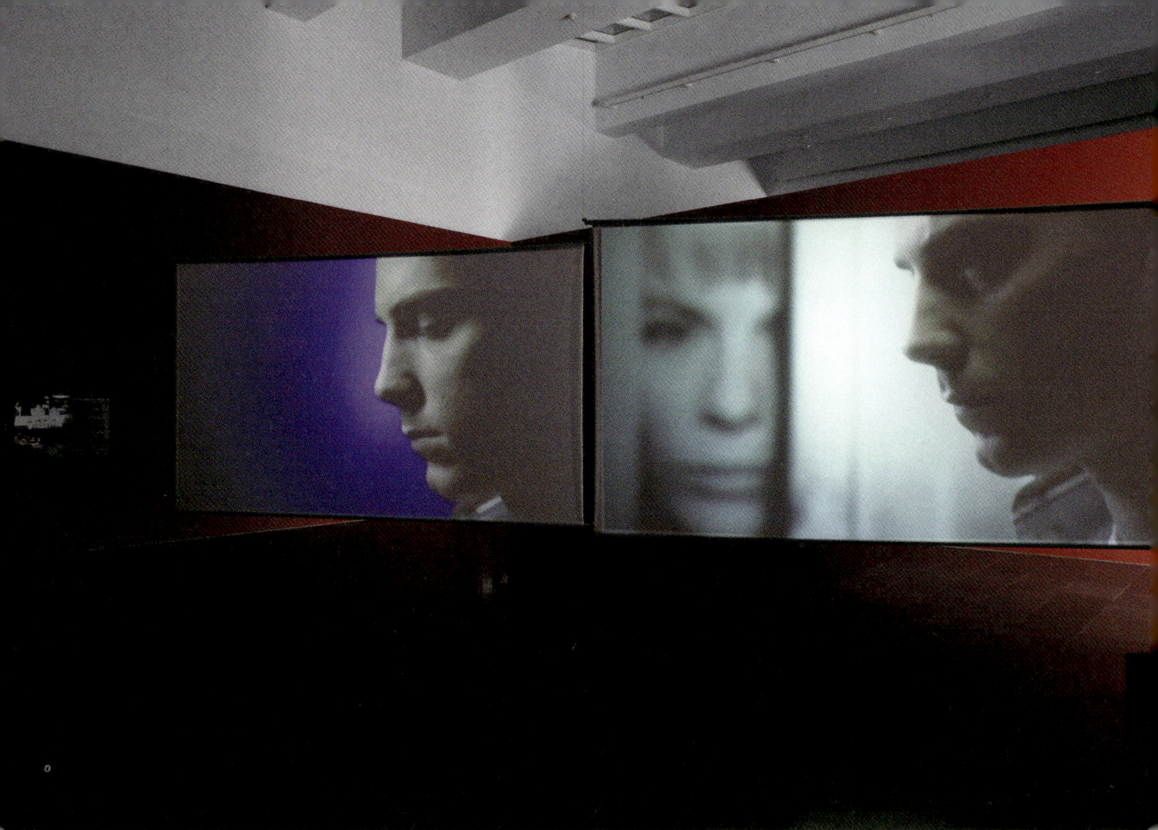

Mabel Palacín
La distancia correcta, 2002–03
Two-channel video, colour, sound, 8 min 30 s

Installation view, presentation of the MACBA Collection, 2006

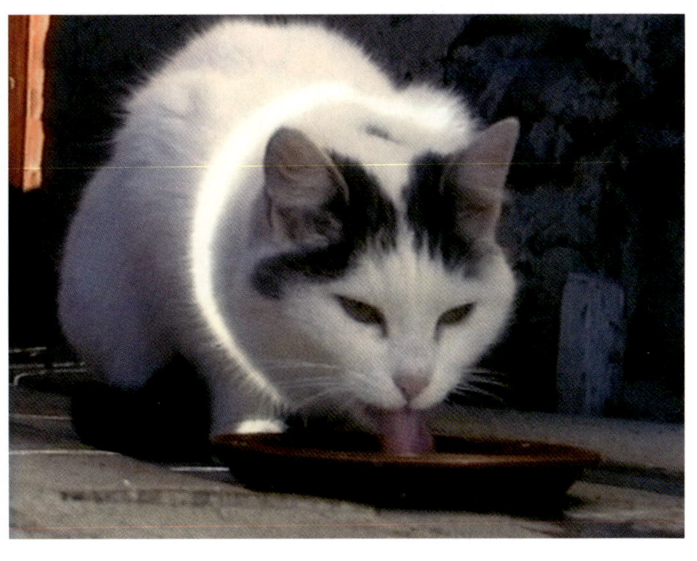

Peter Fischli/David Weiss
Büsi (Kitty), 2001
Single-channel video, colour, silent, 6 min 30 s

Participation: Archives, Documentaries, Relations.
The Nineties and the 2000s decade

From the mid-nineties to the 2000s decade, the MACBA Collection isolates
particular modalities of contemporary artistic practice that speak to the conditions
of globalisation, the production of knowledge and how to engender new relations
with art's publics. At this time, some artists display what Hal Foster terms
an 'archival impulse', while others return more specifically to documentary modes
of production in both film (and video) and photography in order to engage
contemporary social issues and the task of historical representation. Finally, whether
through such concepts as 'relational aesthetics', 'community', 'sensorium', or simply
the command to 'participate', artists today are also taking up the artistic legacy
of the sixties and instantiating new relations with their audiences. In this context of
a broader discussion of what participation means, the MACBA has actively proposed
an alternative to what Nicolas Bourriaud characterises as *l'esthétique relationnelle*
(relational aesthetics) in order to redefine the museum's role and develop new forms
of alliances with the publics its serves, thereby working collectively in the
construction of an alternative public sphere.

Pedro G. Romero has been working on the *Archivo F.X.* project since the late nineties.
Archivo F.X. takes the form of a collection that documents cases of anticlerical
iconoclasm in Spain during the period between the nineteenth-century revolutions
and the Civil War. The materials, some of which belong to the MACBA Collection,
are classified in a Thesaurus whereby each image is related to a concept, an artist
or a category from the history of modern art. In this way, a formal relationship
is established between images of iconoclasm (the result of the destruction of a
pre-existing image) and the visual culture acquired through the avant-gardes
and contemporary art. The archive can be consulted online (www.fxysudoble.org)
at any time.

It is within a contemporary context marked by the redefinition of documentary
practices that one might situate what Catherine Russell describes as an
'experimental ethnography'. She makes a case for experimental ethnography not as
a new category or genre of film, but as a 'methodological incursion of aesthetics
on cultural representation, a collision of social theory and formal experimentation'.[39]
Within these terms, formal experimentation serves to challenge traditional
documentary's (and ethnography's) naturalisation of cinema, a move that typically
serves to buttress the genre's claim to realism – a realism which, within the medium
of film, works to underscore the 'I was there *and I saw*' logic of ethnographic
authority.[40]

Such a framework productively extends to the realm of contemporary art and
installation practices, whereby artists explore documentary forms in the context
of globalisation and an expanding art world. Ursula Biemann's *Performing the Border*
(1999) instantiates this new type of documentary through her use of interviews,
scripted voiceover, as well as text superimposed on the image. Filmed in a US-Mexico
border town, the film investigates the growing feminisation of the global economy
through its impact on the women who live and work in this area. Chantal Akerman's
Une voix dans le désert (2002), part of her original installation of *De l'autre côté*
(2002), also takes up the US-Mexico border as its subject. But in Akerman's film it
is the consistency of her formal vocabulary – i.e., the frontal framing of the interviews
and the extended tracking shots of the border's varied geographic and policed
terrain – that performs the act of description. In regard to her relentless emphasis
on duration, Akerman explains: 'How much time should we take to show this street
[or, in this case, border] so that what's happening is something other than a mere
piece of information? So that we can go from the concrete to the abstract and come
back to the concrete.'[41]

Fiction or the foregrounding of aesthetics in documentary practice is also a
crucial component in the works of Alexander Sokurov and Tacita Dean. Sokurov's
Spiritual voices: From the Diaries of War (1995) develops in the form of a diary,
in which an unbiased narration unravels in poetic intonation. As in Akerman's films,
we are shown real people in their particular situations: Russian border control
guards on the Tadjik-Afghanistan border. Sokurov offers an aesthetic view of the
lives of the people in the film; as he follows the soldiers around, we the spectators

39 Catherine Russell, *Experimental
Ethnography: The Work of Film in the Age
of Video.* Durham, N.C.: Duke University
Press, 1999, p. XI.
40 James Clifford, *The Predicament of
Culture: Twentieth-Century Ethnography,
Literature, and Art.* Cambridge, Mass.;
London, England: Harvard University
Press, 1988, p. 35.
41 Miriam Rosen interviews Chantal
Akerman. 'In Her Own Time', *Artforum* 42,
no. 8, April 2004, pp. 122–27.

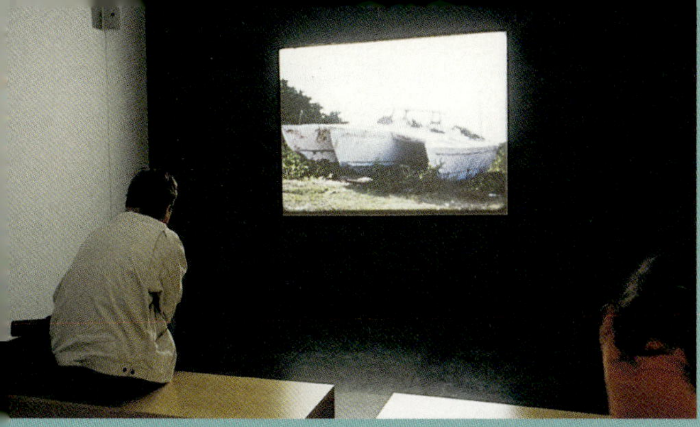

follow Sokurov. Dean, on the other hand, is more specifically fascinated with the fictions underlying truth. Her film *Disappearance at Sea* (1996) was loosely inspired by Donald Crowhurst's failed around-the-world sea voyage and was followed by her sequel *Teignmouth Electron* (2000), which revolves around the transformation of this forgotten tale. Acquired by the MACBA, the second 7-minute film records her trip to the Teignmouth Electron, Crowhurst's boat, to photograph and explore the vessel in its current location on Cayman Brac.

Where Dean works with outmoded technologies and images of obsolete or forgotten spaces, Harun Farocki's two channel video installations *Eye/Machine I, II,* and *III* (2001–03) examine 'intelligent' image processing techniques such as electronic surveillance, mapping and object recognition in order to probe how military technologies infiltrate civilian life. His work charts a genealogy of image production from the Second World War to the present, underscoring the political and ideological function of image making through his combination of newsreel, archival and industrial/technological footage. In their *La tierra de la madre* (1994) Marcelo Expósito and Joseantonio Hergueta similarly combine different types of footage, but not in order to interrogate image technology but rather to make history *present*. In this work, they explore the forced exodus of children to the Soviet Union during the Spanish Civil War, juxtaposing the narration of the central figure, Conchita Eguidazu, with archival news footage.

Such experimentation as to the possibilities of reinventing documentary also extends to the realm of photography in the MACBA Collection. Allan Sekula's slide projection *Waiting for Tear Gas* (1999–2000) offers a compelling and politically

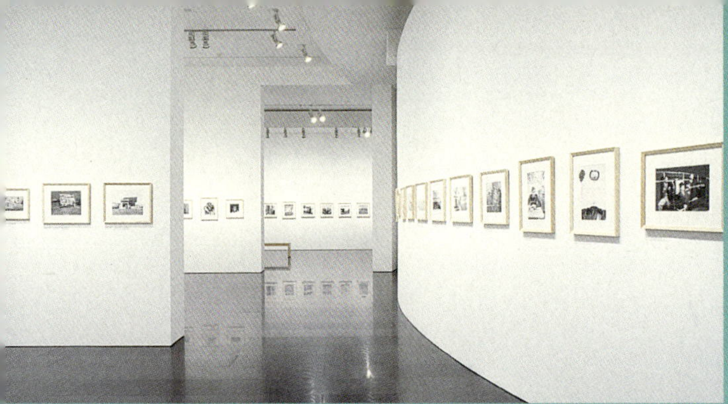

committed chronicle of the Seattle demonstrations against global capitalism in 1999. David Goldblatt's *Dainfern* series (2001–02) explores the geographic proximity of Dainfern, a luxury complex located on the outskirts of Johannesburg, and the squatter's settlement Zewenfontein. Andrea Robbins and Max Becher's series *The Americans of Samaná* (1998–2001) documents the descendants of freed African-American slaves who travelled to the Dominican Republic in 1824 as part of a scheme initiated by President Pierre Boyer of Haiti, with the cooperation of the American Colonization Society.

By way of conclusion, I would like to return to what I briefly touched upon earlier: the MACBA's response to Bourriaud's *l'esthétique relationnelle*. With this term Bourriaud describes an art that takes as 'its theoretical horizon the realm of human interactions and its social context, rather than the assertion of an independent and *private* symbolic space'.[42] With the recent debates about 'relational aesthetics', contemporary artists are celebrated or critiqued based on the degree to which their interactive spaces instantiate entertainment and leisure, or division and antagonism.[43] At stake here is whether in the contemporary context of globalisation, a 'relation' amounts to anything more than an economic transaction.

Krzysztof Wodiczko broaches the status of a 'relation' as it pertains more specifically to immigration in his *Alien Staff* (1992–93), which is at once portable public address equipment and a cultural network for individual immigrants and groups. As he explains: 'It is an instrument that gives the individual immigrant a chance to "address" directly anyone in the city who may be attracted by the symbolic

42 See Nicolas Bourriaud, *Relational Aesthetics*. Paris: Les presses du réel, 2002, p. 14 (original emphasis).
43 For a critical response to Bourriaud, see Claire Bishop, 'Antagonism and Relational Aesthetics', *October*, no. 110, Autumn 2004, pp. 51–79.

form of the equipment and the character of the "broadcast" programme.'[44]
Resembling the biblical shepherd's rod and the eighteenth-century burgher's baton,
Alien Staff is equipped with a high-tech mini-monitor and small loudspeaker. As the
small size of the monitor may attract attention and provoke observers to come very
close to the monitor – and therefore the operator's face – the usual distance between
two subjects will decrease and thus instantiate a new relation outside conventional
spaces.

In addition to acquiring such works that both address and instantiate new
relations, as an institution the MACBA also productively responds to the question
of 'relation' through its extensive public programmes (discussed by Jorge Ribalta
in this volume, pp. 224–65) and also through the production of alternative
exhibition formats, including *How do we want to be governed?* curated by Roger
Buergel in 2004. Presented in various public spaces in the Poblenou-Besòs district
in Barcelona, *How do we want to be governed?* articulated an itinerary throughout
the city and generated a context for public programmes that took place in the
exhibition and other venues. Without a doubt, the project presented a type
of 'expanded' exhibition that included seminars, lectures and film screenings.
The objective was twofold: to reinvent the museum's presence in an industrial
neighbourhood undergoing transformation and to relate the museum's presence
to what has been described as the *mobilisation citoyenne mondiale* – that is, 'to the
creation of a global public opinion that reclaims planetary democracy and the just
distribution of common goods'.[45]

[44] See Wodiczko's statement as
reproduced on the MACBA's website
www.macba.cat/controller.php?p_action=
show_page&pagina_id=29&inst_id=19584
(accessed December 2009).
[45] See the statement about the exhibition
How do we want to be governed? on
www.macba.cat/controller.php?p_action=
show_page&pagina_id=34&inst_id=16818
(accessed December 2009).

POR FABO R ESTAMO S PARADO

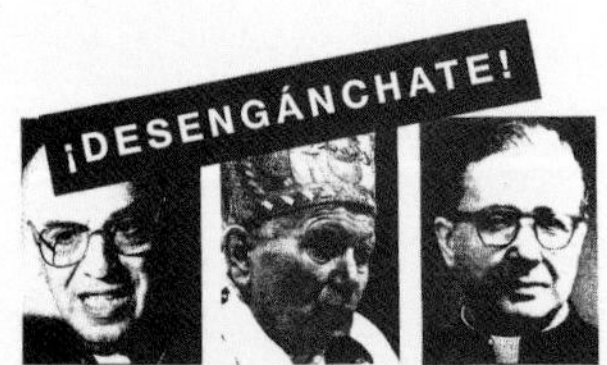

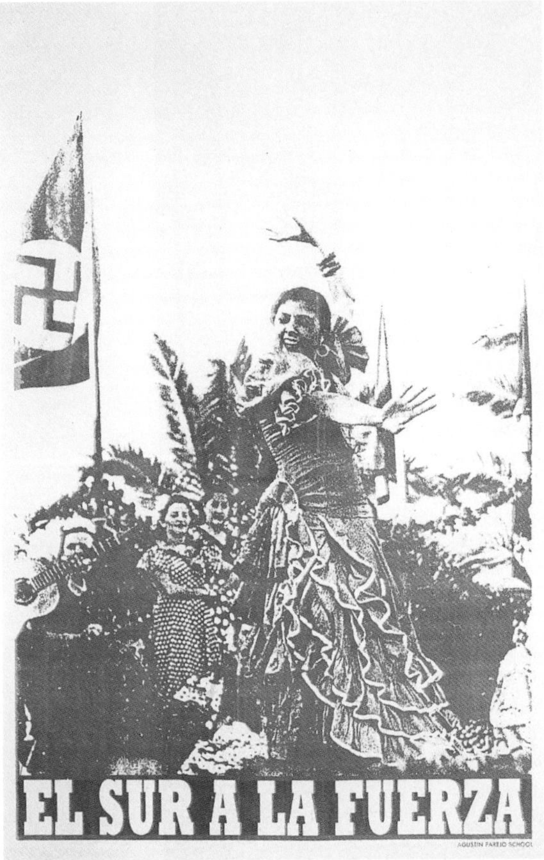

Agustín Parejo School
Por fabor estamos parado, 1987
16 postcards and 1 calendar, ink print on paper
Various dimensions

Postcard, 10.5 × 16 cm

El sur a la fuerza, 1990
6 posters, 8 colour photographs and 3 slides
Various dimensions

Poster, 59.2 × 39.4 cm

Apostata, 1991
7 postcards, 2 stickers and folder with 3 typewritten
documents and 3 collages on paper
Various dimensions

Postcard, 16 × 11 cm

Sin Larios, 1992
Poster, map, postcards, sheets, lighter, ballpoint pen,
t-shirt, single-channel video, colour, sound, 5 min 23 s
Various dimensions

Poster, 70 × 32.5 cm

The intervention on the monument to the Marqués de Larios in Málaga by the local group Agustín Parejo School (APS) was part of the *Plus Ultra* Project, which, in the framework of the events of Expo 92 in Seville, proposed a set of projects in historical spaces in each of the eight provinces of Andalusia.

The project consisted of making a spatial dislocation for ten days on the monument to the Marqués de Larios, a sculpture by Mariano Benlliure, which was inaugurated in 1899. The monument is in the Plaza de la Marina in Málaga, the nerve centre of the city. APS proposed to supplant the sculpture of the Marqués de Larios, which crowns the monument, with the *Allegory of Work*, a sculpture that stands on one of the lower podiums. The Marqués de Larios would be moved, not to the foot of the monument, but to one of the pavements around the Plaza de la Marina, next to a traffic light, thus blending in with the other citizens.

This is a sly historical reference to the riots in Malaga in 1931, under the Republic, when the masses gave vent to their social indignation by dragging the sculpture of the marquis down from his pedestal and replacing it with the so-called the *Allegory of Work* by the sculptor Mariano Benlliure. The symbolic change was evident: from a monument to a rich bourgeois dignitary to a monument to work.

The APS proposal was submitted to Malaga City Council to obtain the necessary permits, but it was turned down with no specific official reasons given. The Malaga College of Architects provided the space for it in July 1992.

Agustín Parejo School

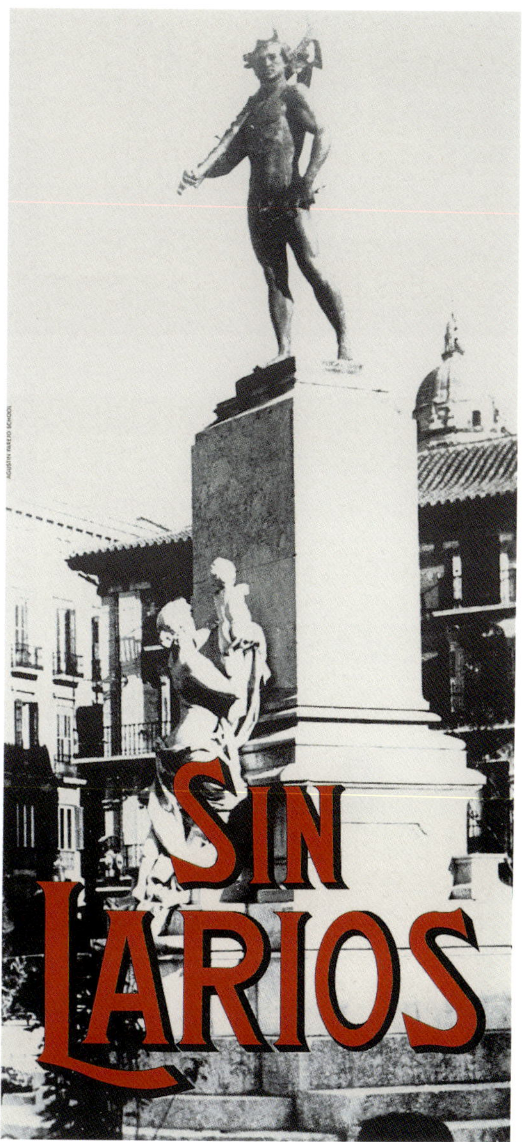

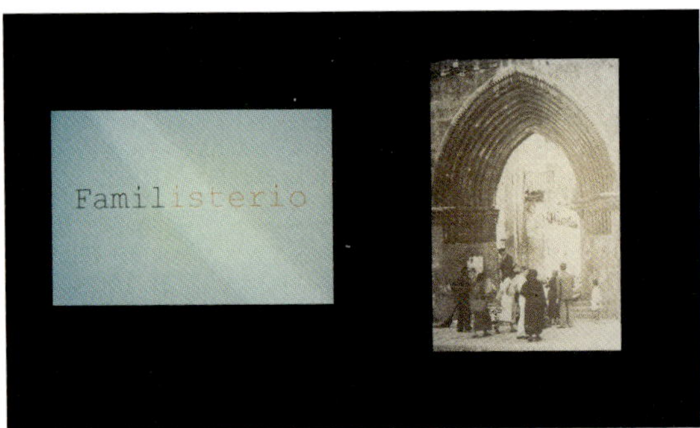

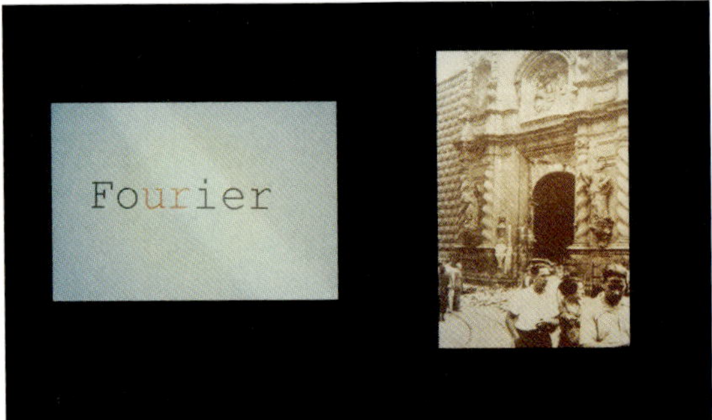

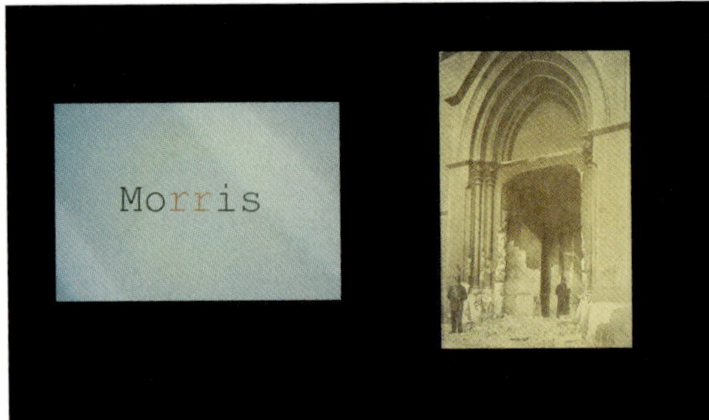

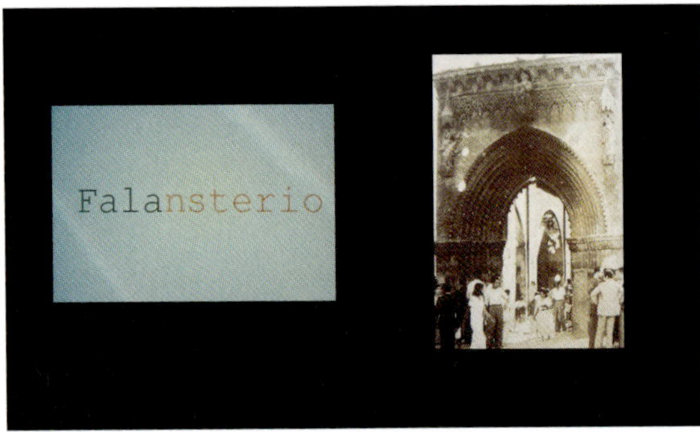

Pedro G. Romero/Archivo F.X.
Tesauro Anarquitectura
Antagonismos, casos de estudio, 2001
Double simultaneous slide projection
Dimensions variable

Pedro G. Romero
Routing slips and various publications,
1989/2007
Series include: *La sección áurea* (1989);
r.a.r.o. (1991); *El tiempo de la bomba* (1993–97);
¿Llegaremos pronto a Sevilla? (1997–99);
and the project Archivo F.X. (1999–2007)
Various dimensions

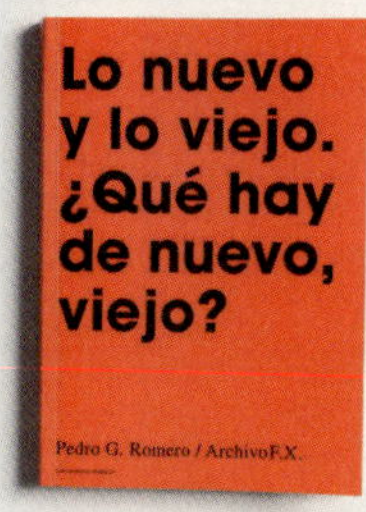

Lo nuevo
y lo viejo.
¿Qué hay
de nuevo,
viejo?
Pedro G. Romero / Archivo F.X.

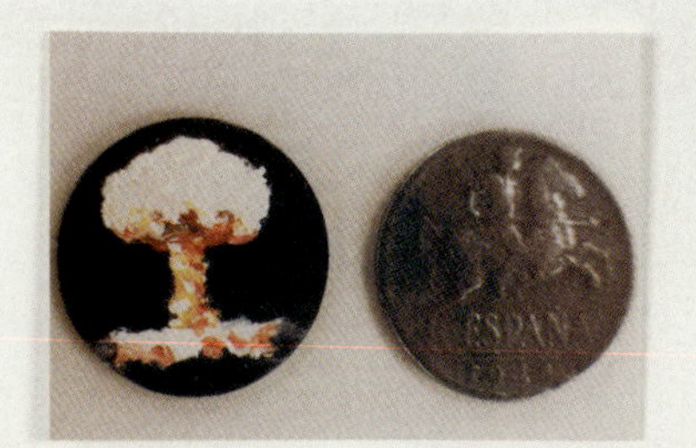

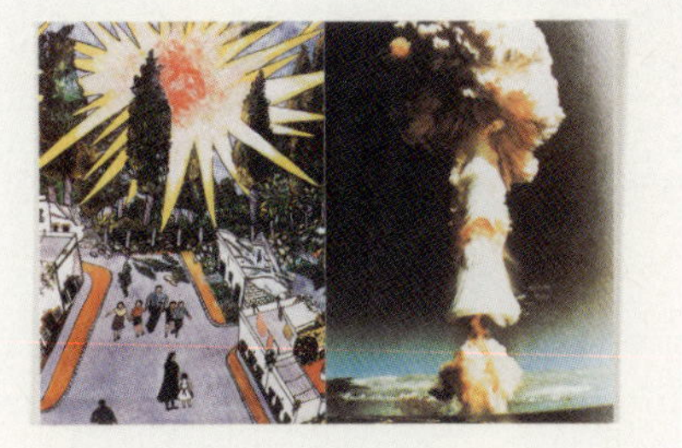

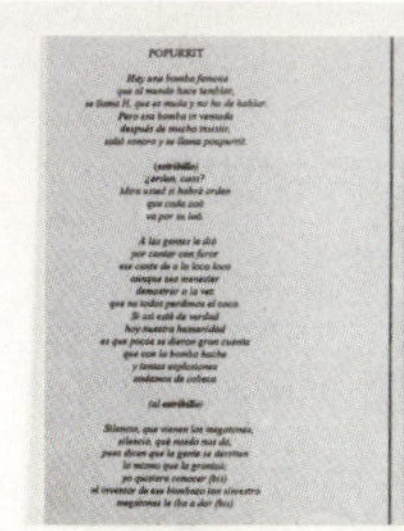

POPURRIT
CARNAVAL 1936
LOS REPRESENTANTES DEL
Hongo Maravilloso
Los Supervivientes
del Japón
Los curtidores de
HONGOS

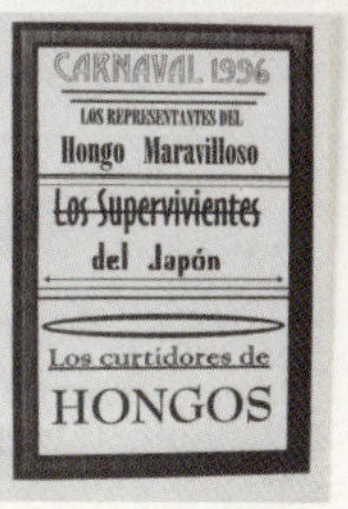

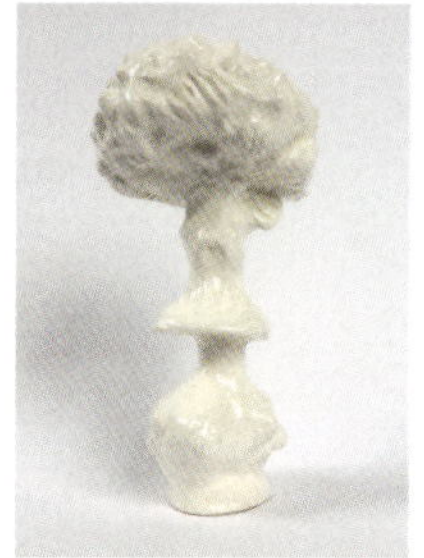

PEDRO G. ROMERO
s/t (B-NAIF) 1995
mixta
de la serie Calle del Infierno
mecanismo recopilación y presentación del parentesco iconológico de imágenes populares
que representan explosiones o implosiones, con otras de diverso carácter, científico,
histórico, artístico, etc.
mechanism the compilation and presentation of the iconological relationship of popular images
representing explosions or implosions with others of different kinds, some scientific, historical or
artistic, etc.
otras solea del portugues

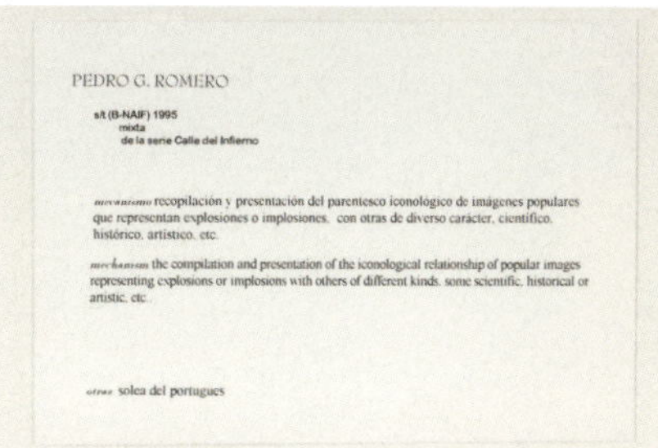

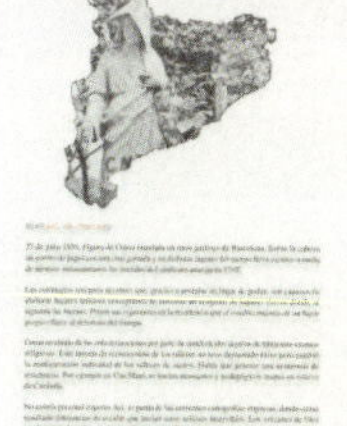

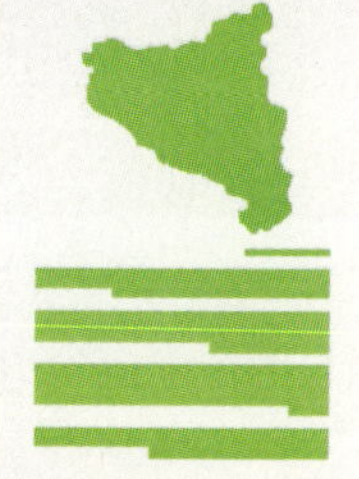

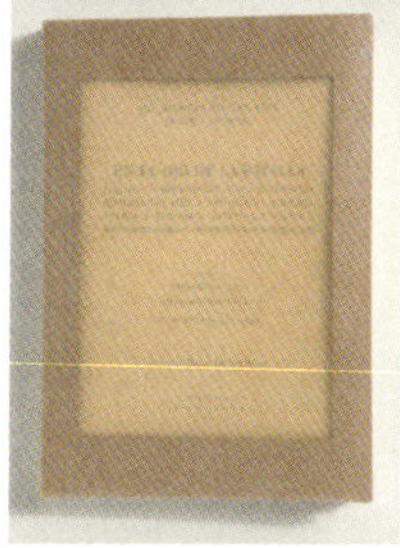

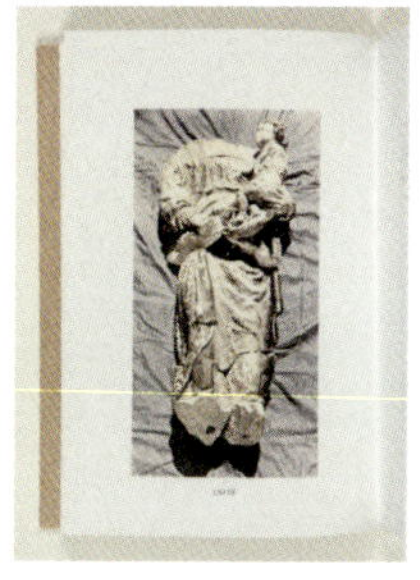

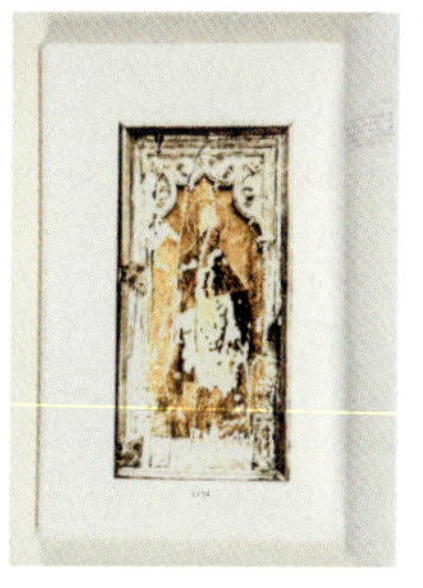

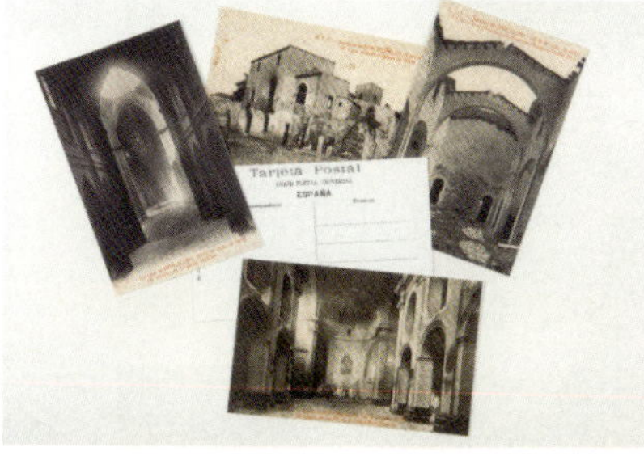

Tarjeta Postal
ESPAÑA

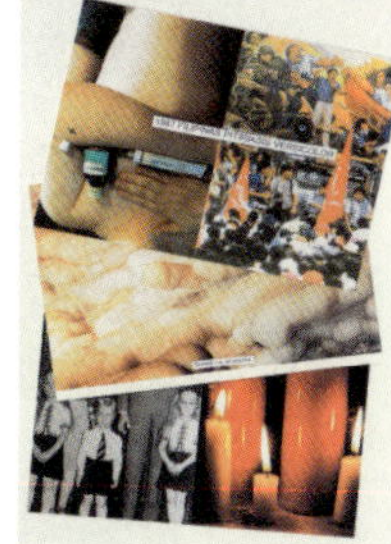

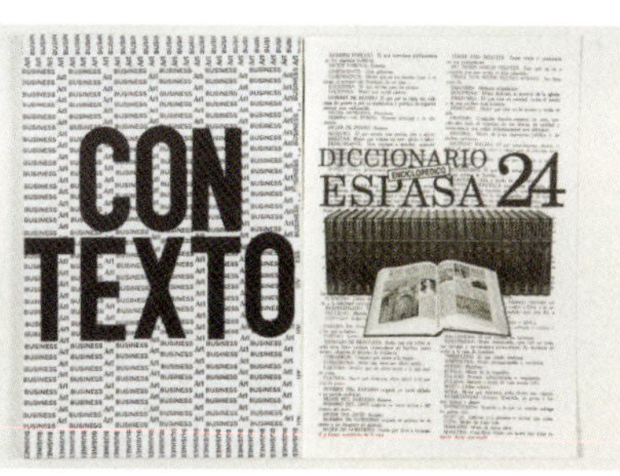

CON
TEXTO
DICCIONARIO
ESPASA 24

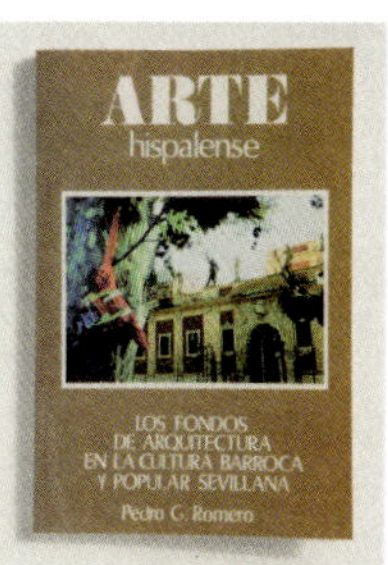

ARTE
hispalense
LOS FONDOS
DE ARQUITECTURA
EN LA CULTURA BARROCA
Y POPULAR SEVILLANA
Pedro G. Romero

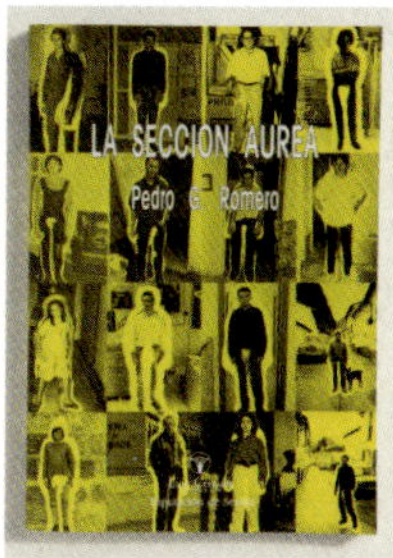

LA SECCIÓN ÁUREA
Pedro G. Romero

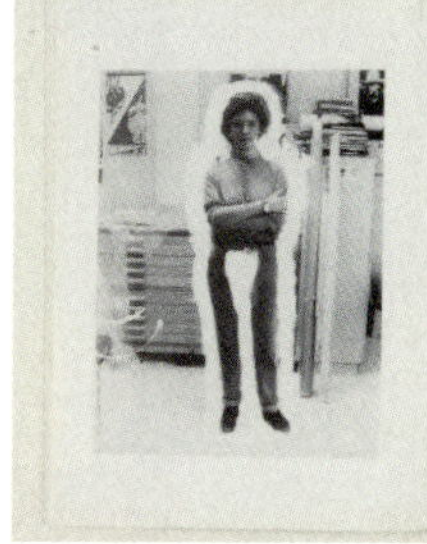

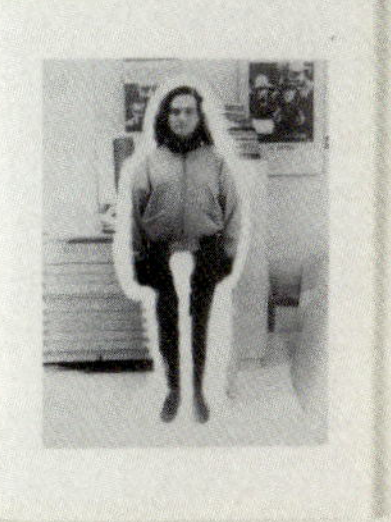

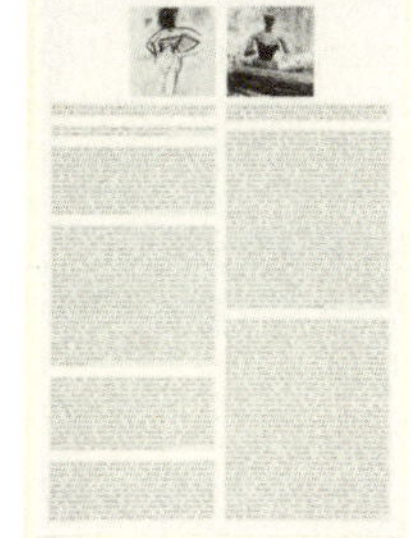

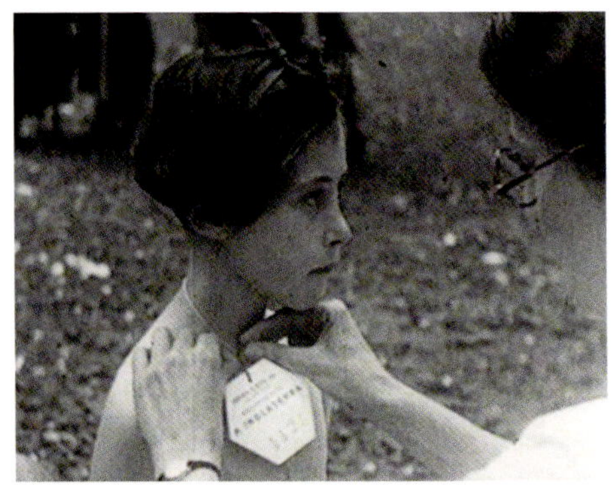

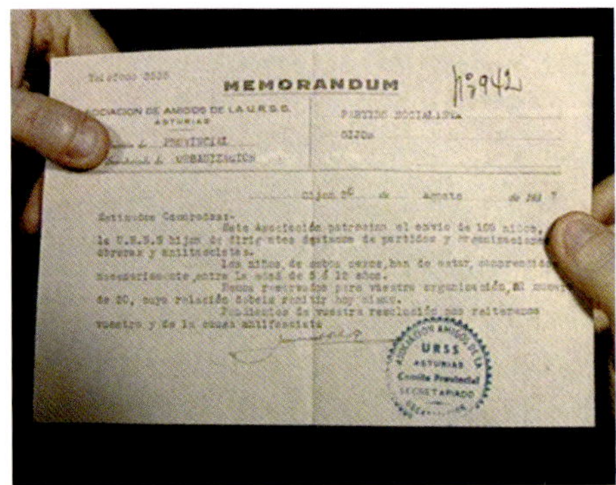

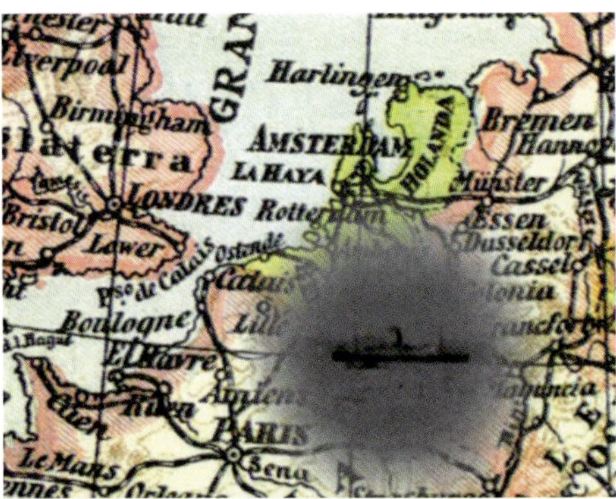

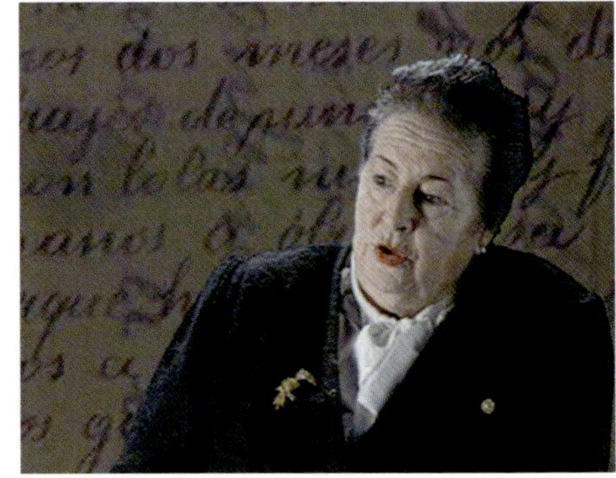

Marcelo Expósito, **Joseantonio Hergueta**
La tierra de la madre, 1994
Single-channel video, b/w and colour, sound, 21 min

Marcelo Expósito
Octubre en el norte: temporal del noroeste, 1995
Single-channel video, b/w and colour, sound, 92 min

Marcelo Expósito, **Arturo-Fito Rodríguez** and **Gabriel Villota**
No haber olvidado nada, 1996–97
Single-channel video, b/w and colour, sound, 54 min

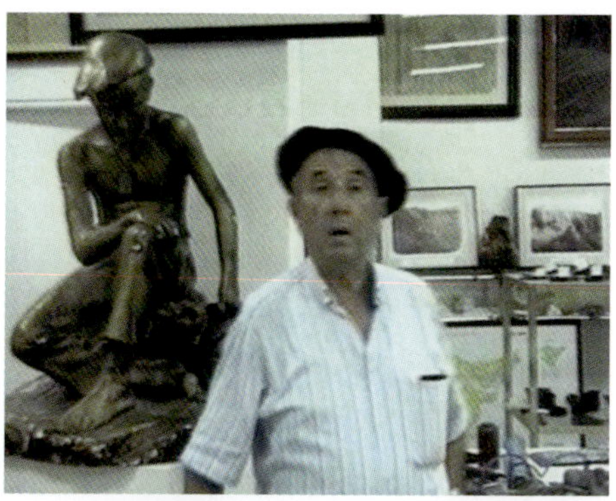

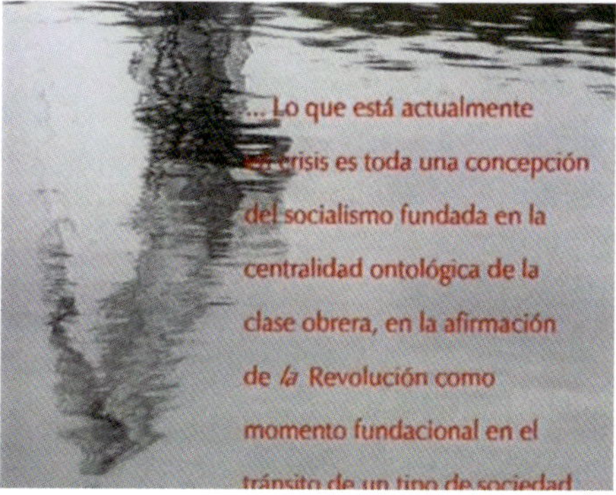
... Lo que está actualmente
en crisis es toda una concepción
del socialismo fundada en la
centralidad ontológica de la
clase obrera, en la afirmación
de la Revolución como
momento fundacional en el
tránsito de un tipo de sociedad

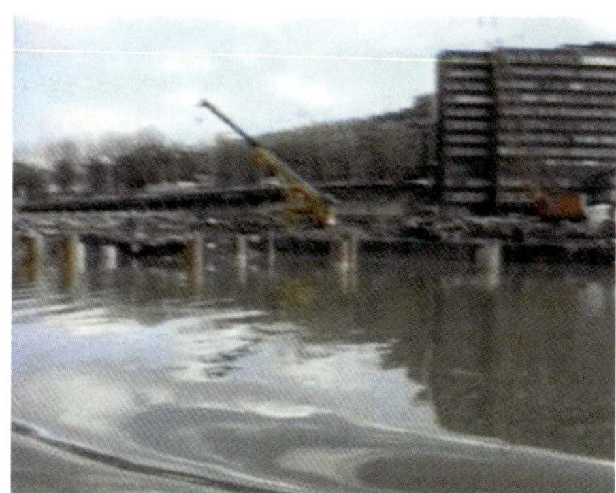

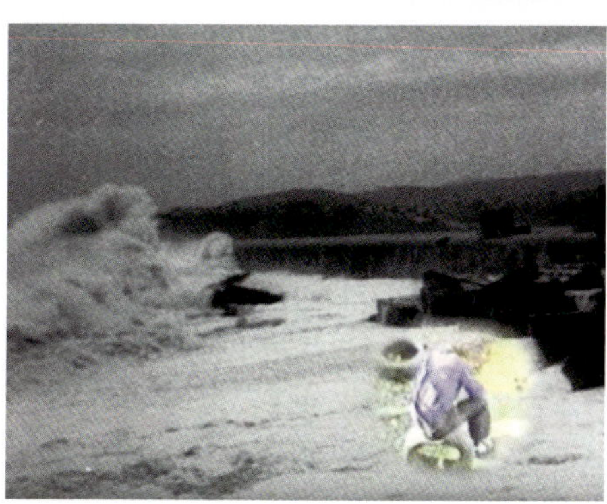

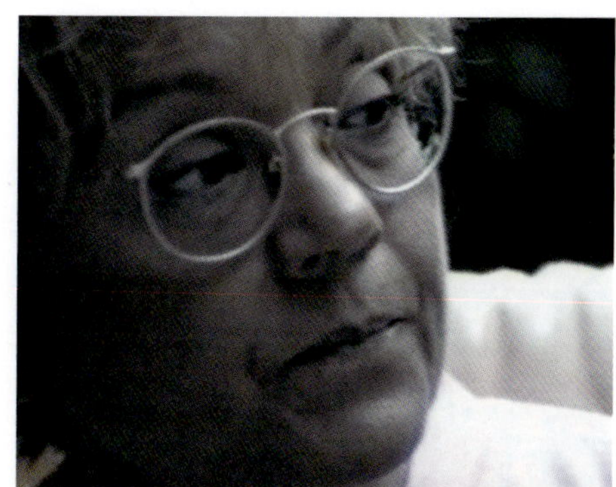

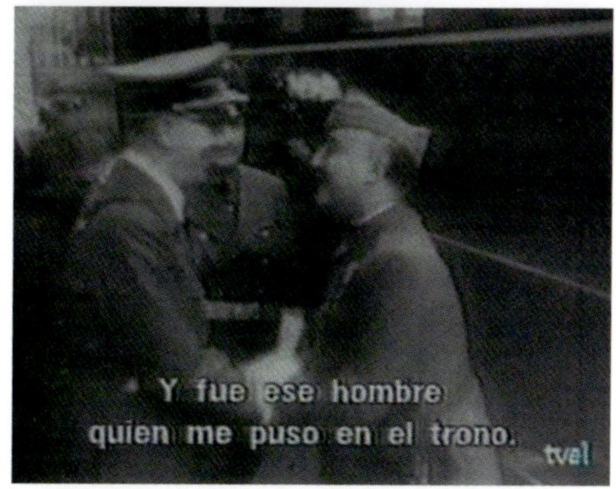
Y fue ese hombre
quien me puso en el trono.
tve1

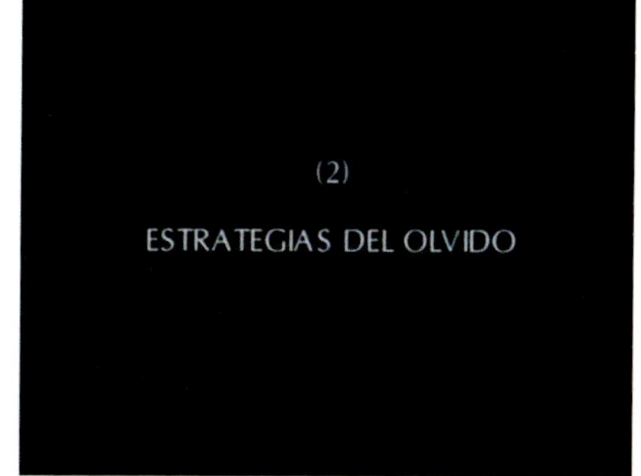
(2)

ESTRATEGIAS DEL OLVIDO

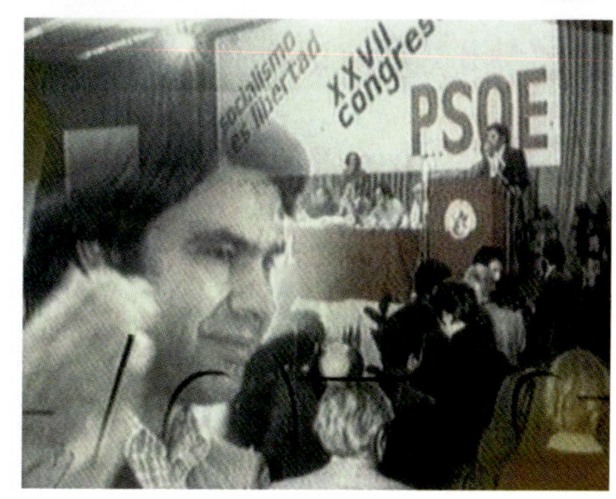
socialismo
es libertad
XXVII
congreso
PSOE

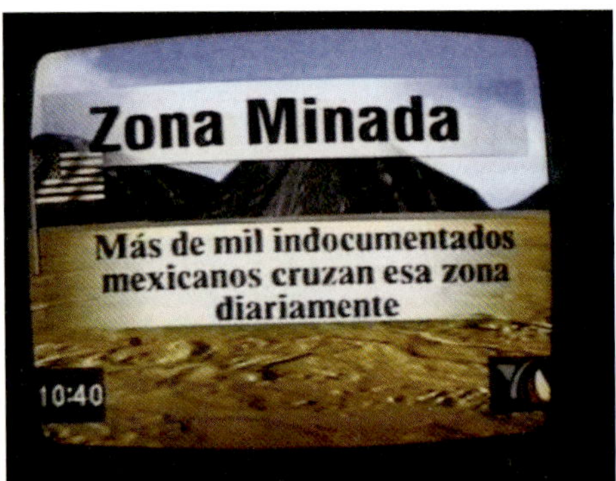

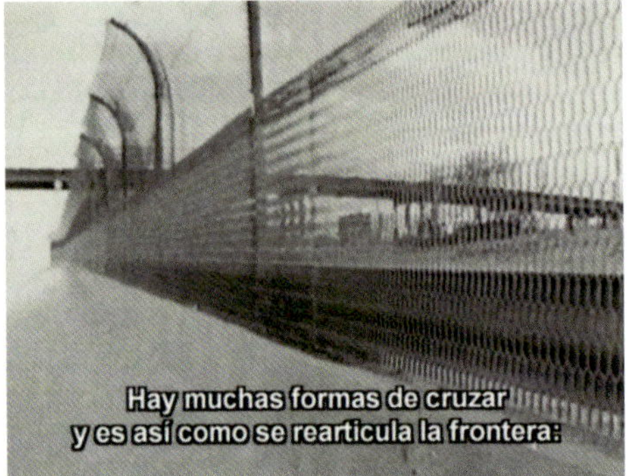

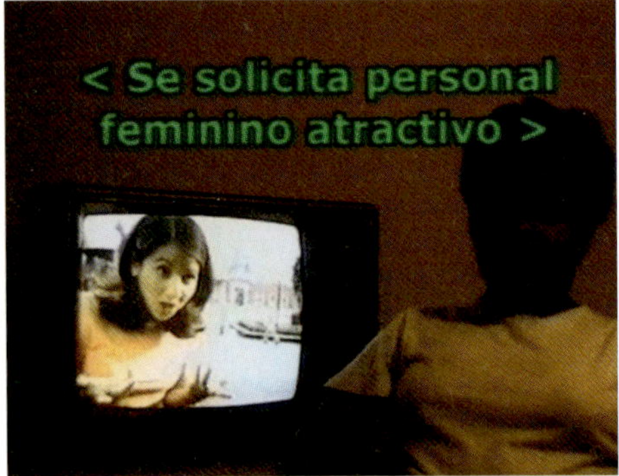

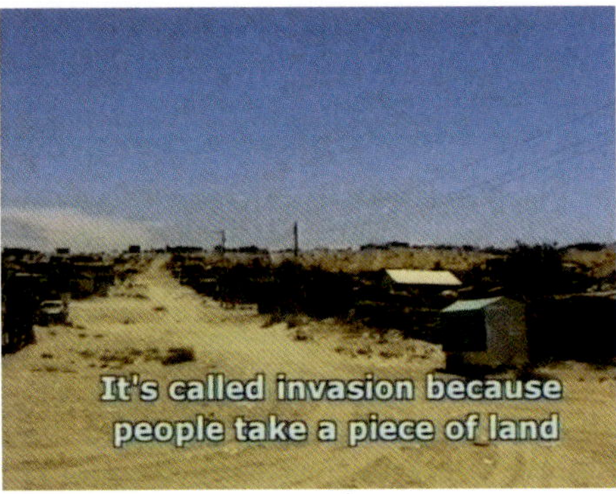

Ursula Biemann
Performing the Border, 1999
Single-channel video, b/w and colour, sound, 42 min

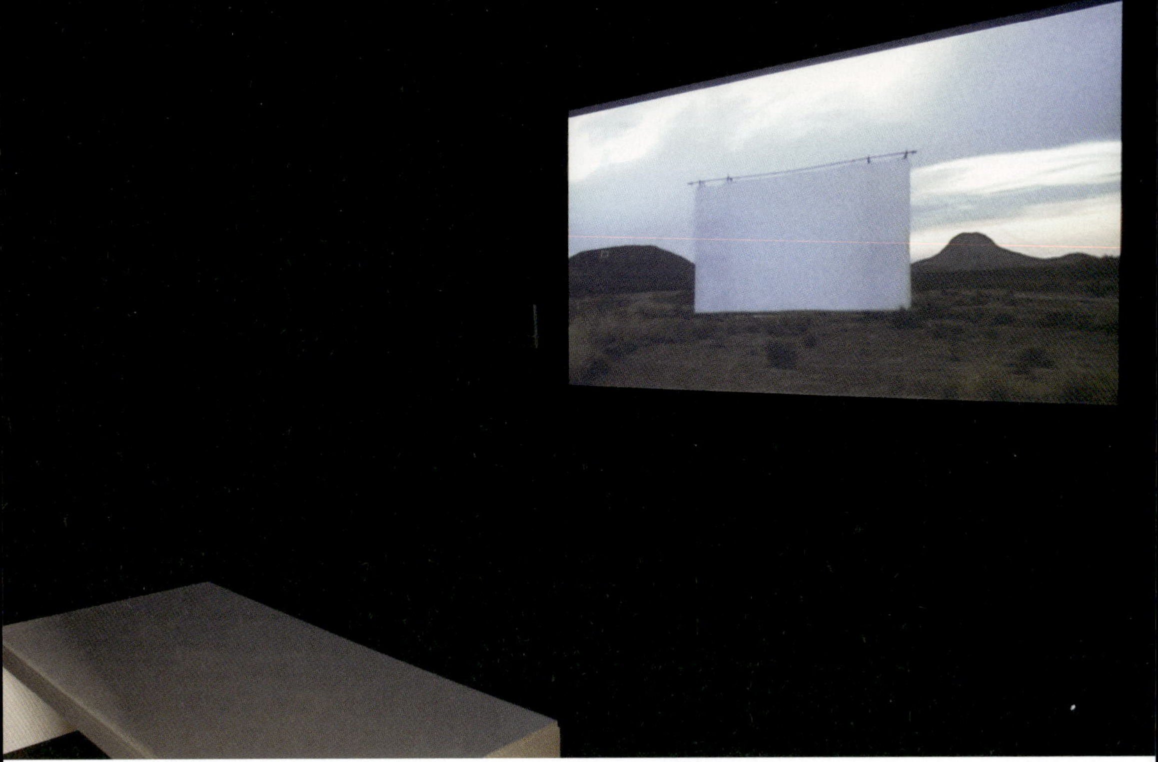

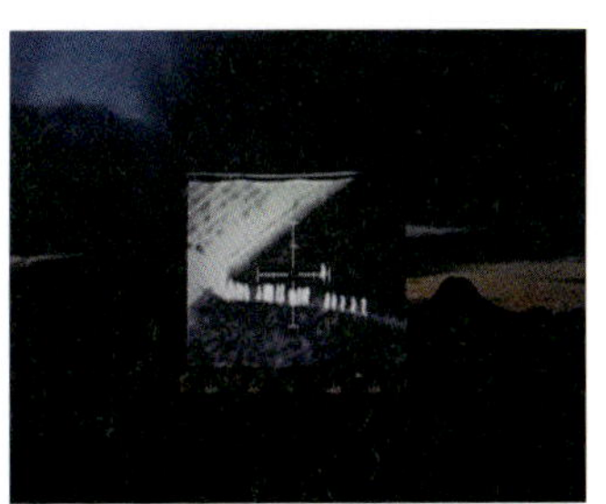 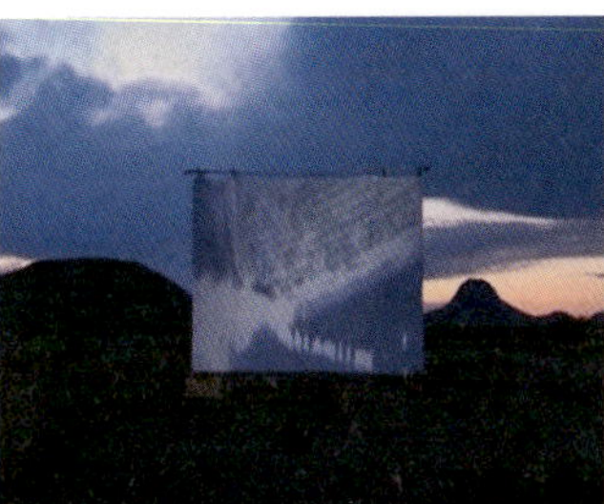 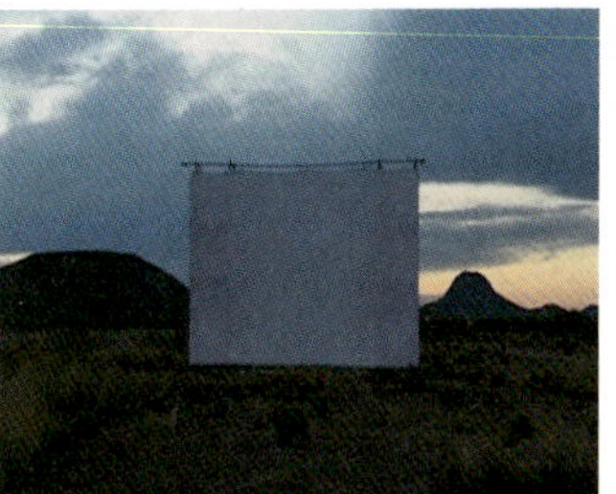

Chantal Akerman
Une voix dans le désert, 2002
Single-channel video, colour, sound, 52 min

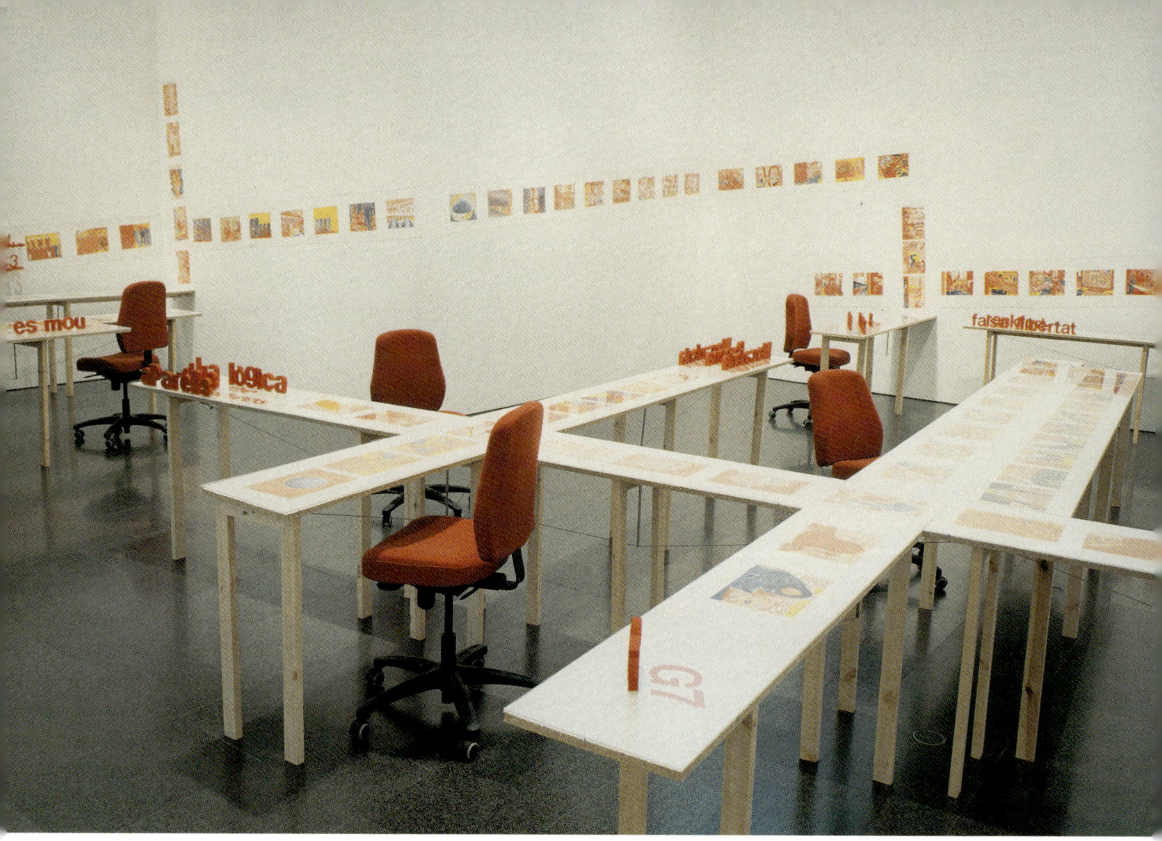

Andreas Siekmann
Aus: Gesellschaft mit beschränkter Haftung, 1996–2002
Tables, chairs, stickers, watercolour and marker on paper,
Plasticine and expanded polyurethane
Dimensions variable

Installation view, presentation ot the MACBA Collection, 2004

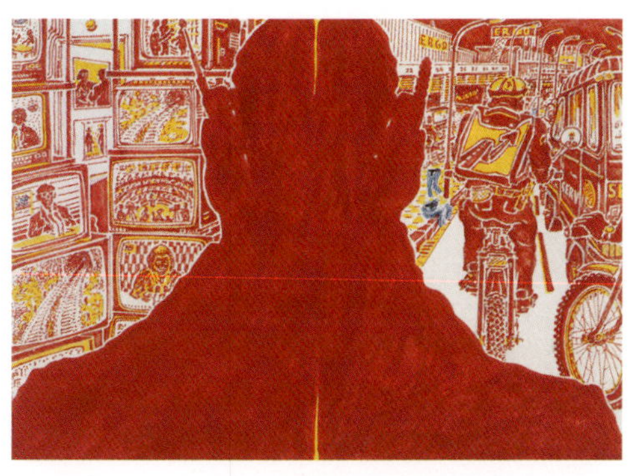
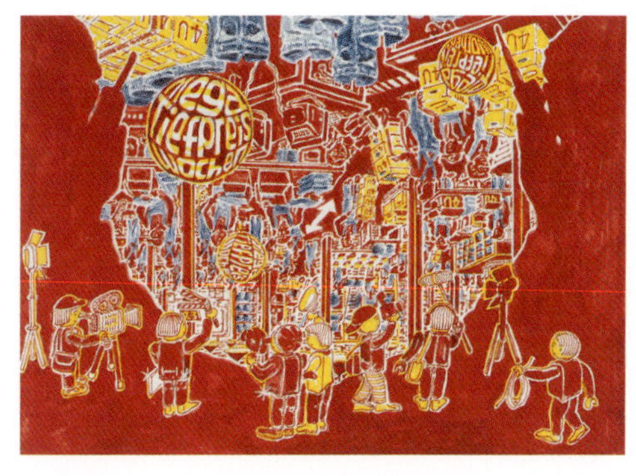

ega
iefpreis
och

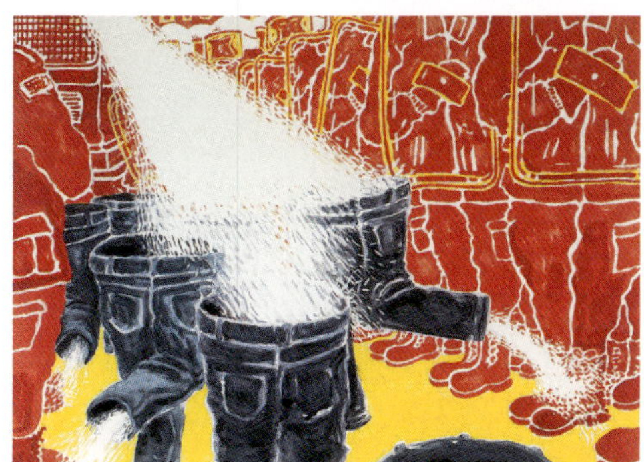
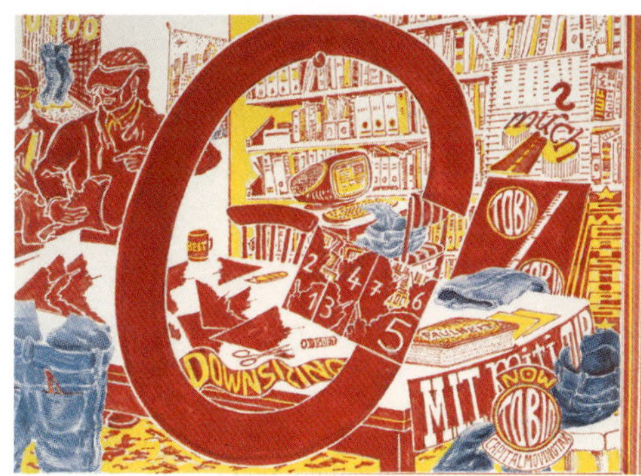

DOWNSIZING
MIT
NOW
TOBI

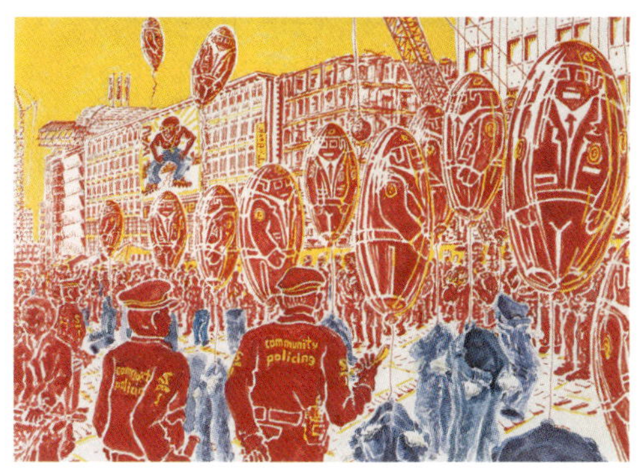

community
policing

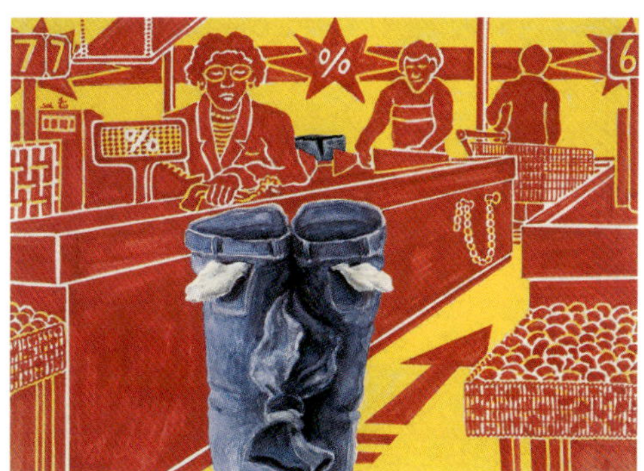

7
%
6

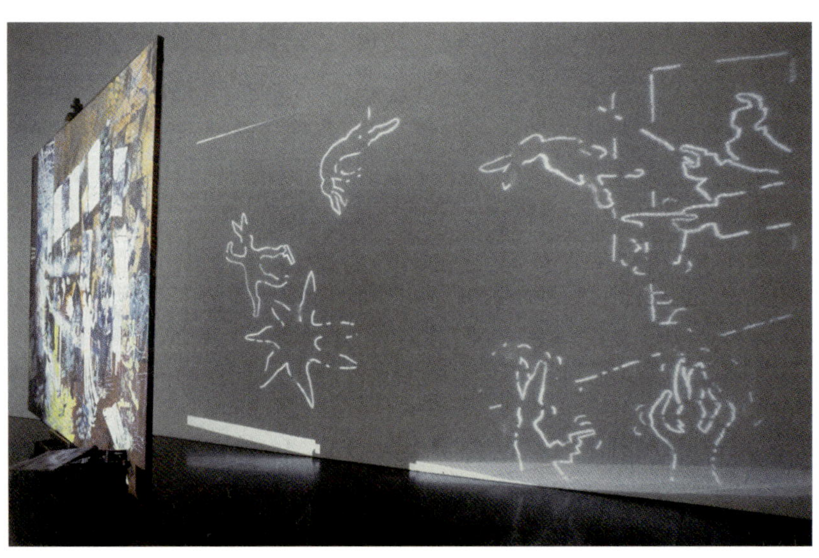

Alice Creischer
*L'atelier de la peintrice. Allégorie réelle déterminant une phase
de sept années de ma vie artistique dans la République de Berlin*, 2000
Acrylic and collage on polyethylene, painter's easel, touch-up table and flashlight
Recto and verso, 232.5 × 367 cm

Installation view, presentation of the MACBA Collection, 2004

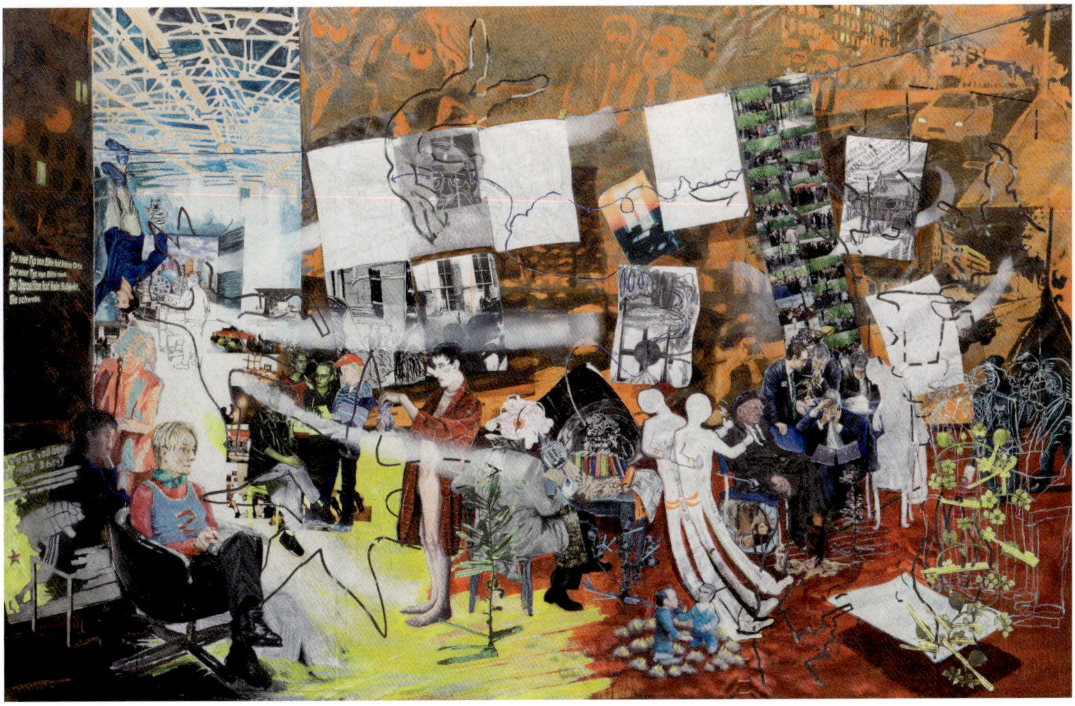

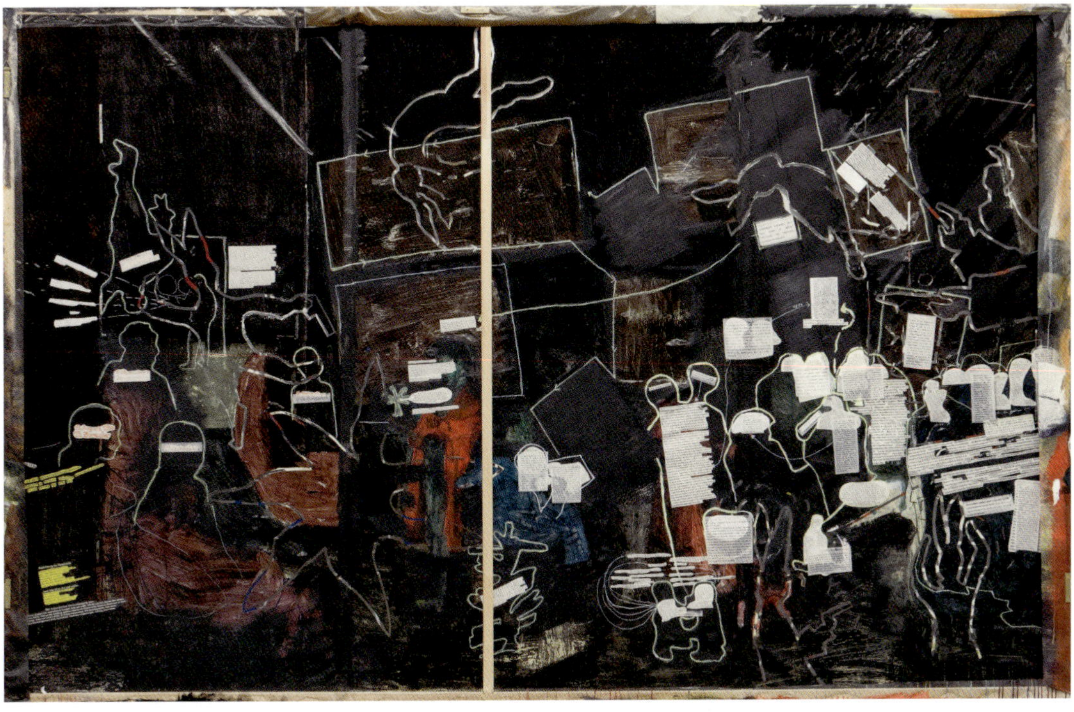

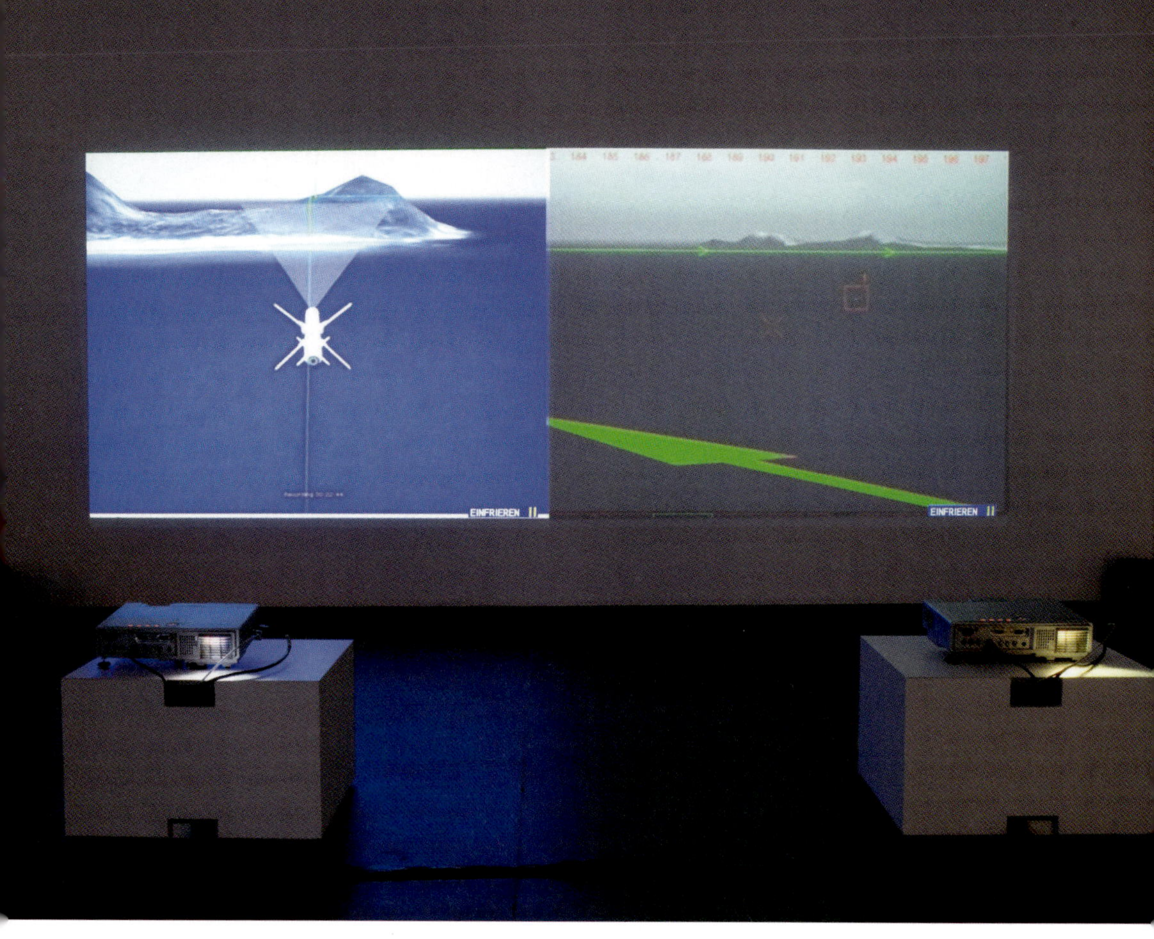

Harun Farocki
Eye/Machine, I, II, III, 2001–03
3 two-channel videos, colour, sound, 25 min each

Installation view, *MACBA im Frankfurter Kunstverein*, Frankfurt, 2007

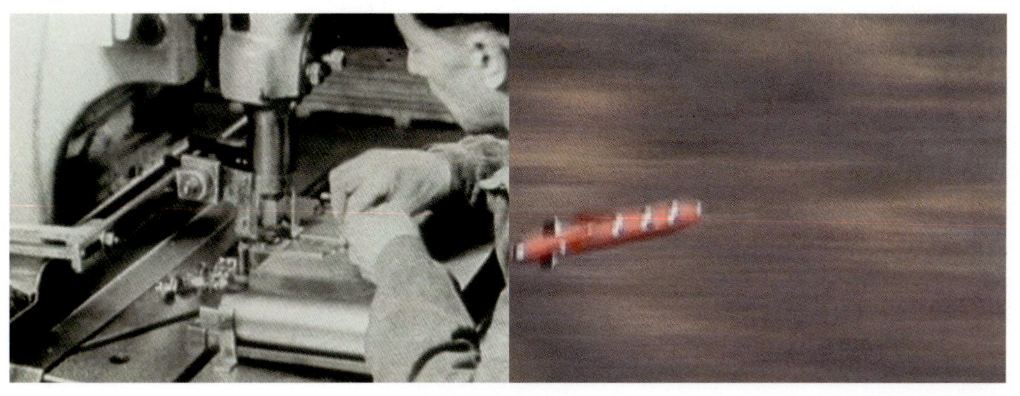

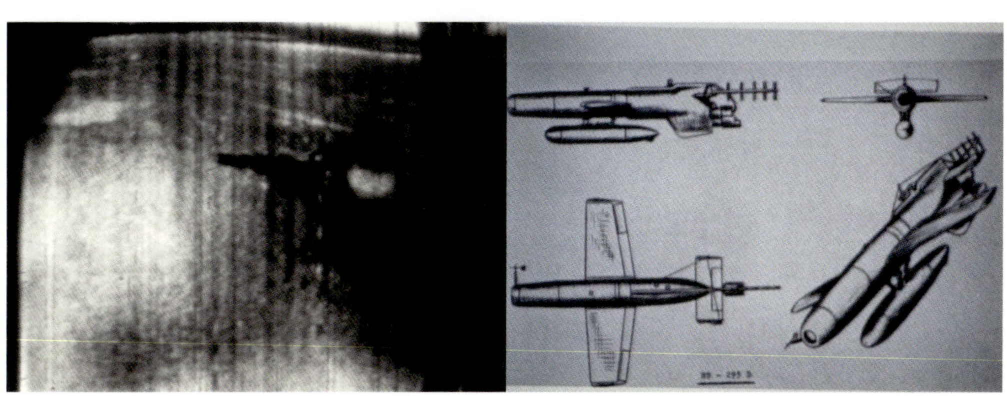
BV - 295 b

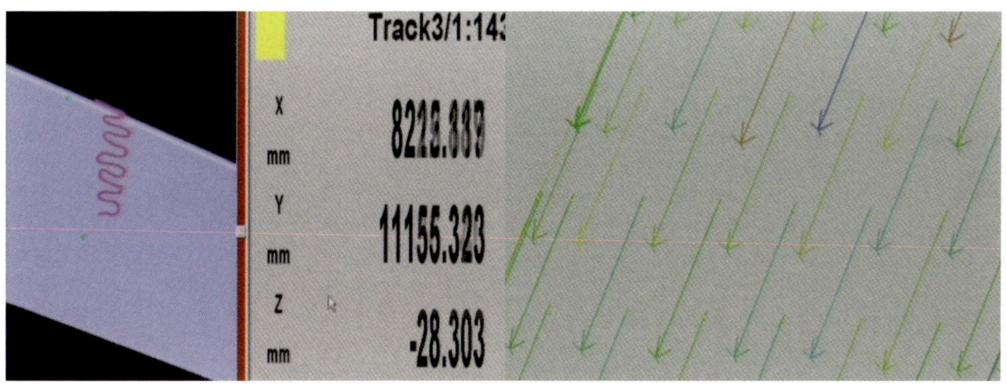
Track3/1:143
X
mm
8212.303
Y
mm
11155.323
Z
mm
-28.303

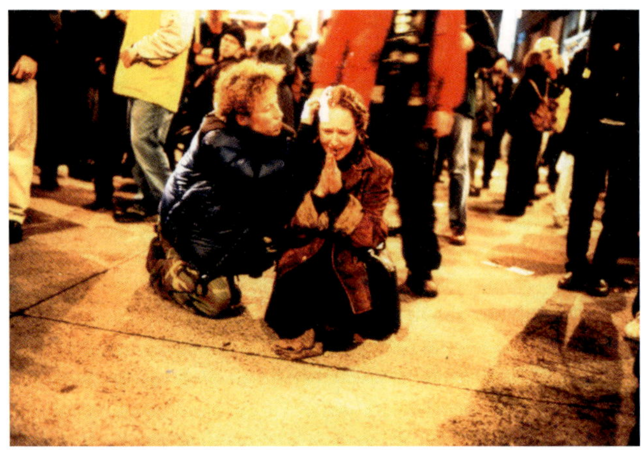

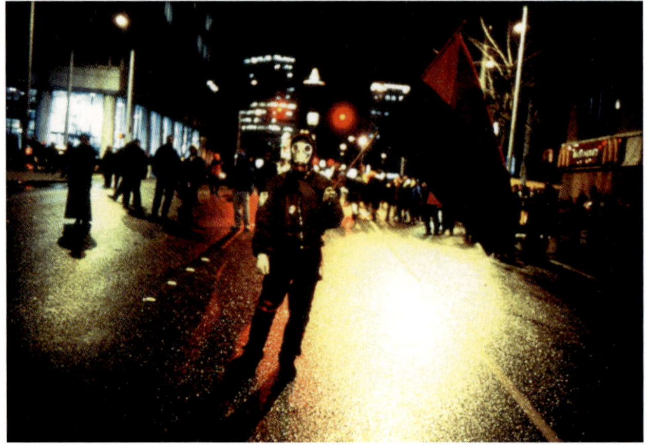

Allan Sekula
Waiting for Tear Gas, 1999–2000
Slide projection and vinyl
Dimensions variable

WAITING FOR TEAR GAS

The working idea was to move with the flow
of protest, from dawn to 3 AM if need be,
taking in the lulls, the waiting and the
margins of events. The rule off thumb for
this sort of anti-photojournalism: no flash,
no telephoto zoom lens, no gas mask, no
auto-focus, no press pass and no pressure
to grab at all cost the one defining image
of dramatic violence.

Later, working at the light table,
and reading the increasingly stereotypical
descriptions of the new face of protest,
realized all the more that a simple descriptive
physiognomy was warranted. The alliance
on the streets was indeed, stranger, more varied
and inspired than could be conveyed by cute
alliterative play with "teamsters" and "turtles".

Describe the attitudes of people waiting,
unarmed, sometimes deliberately naked in
the winter chill, for the gas and the rubber
bullets and the concussion grenades. There
were moments of civic solemnity, of urban
anxiety, and of carnival.

Again, something very simple is missed
by descriptions of this as a movement founded
in cyberspace : the human body asserts
itself in the city streets, against the abstraction
of global capital. There was a strong feminist
dimension to this testimony, and there was
also a dimensions grounded in the experience
of work. It was the men and women who work
on the docks, after all, who shut down
the flow of metal boxes from Asia, relying
on individual knowledge that there is always
another body on the other side of the sea
doing the same work, that all this global trade
is more than a matter of a mouse-click.

One fleeting hallucination could not be
photographed. As the blast of stun grenades
reverberated amidst the downtown skycrapers,
someone with a boom box thoughtfully
provided a musical accompaniment: Jimi
Hendrix's mock-hysterical rendition of the
American national anthem. At that moment,
Hendrix returned to the streets of Seattle,
slyly caricaturing the pumped-up sovereignty
of the world's only superpower.

Allan Sekula

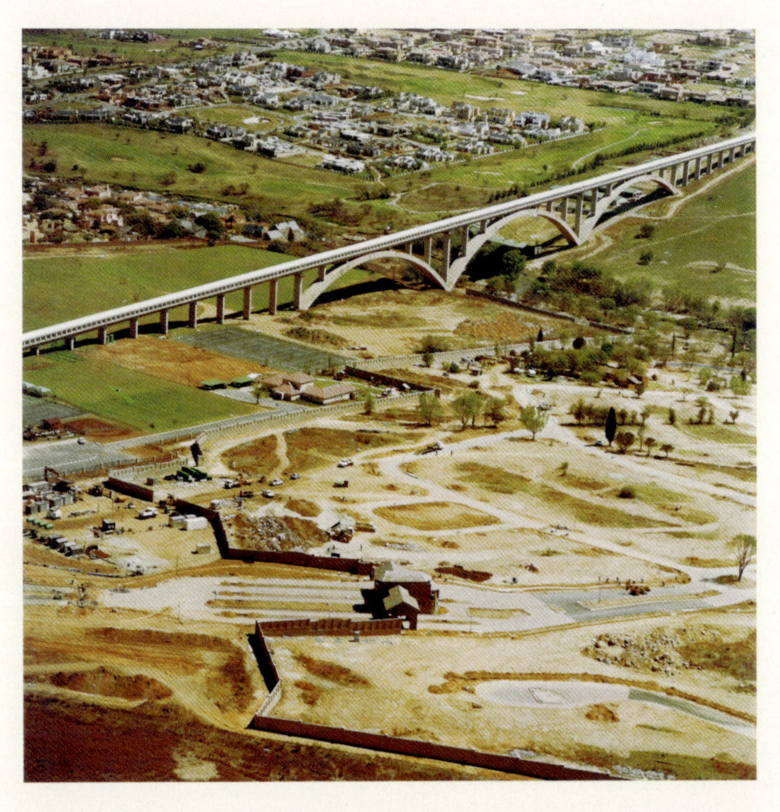

David Goldblatt
*Dainfern Valley, an extension to Dainfern Golf Estate
and Country Club: the security wall and gatehouse are
in place, roadmaking is in progress, and the velds has
been stripped to allow for special grassing. 26 September
2001. 'Dainfern' Series,* 2001
Ink jet print on card
83 × 60 cm

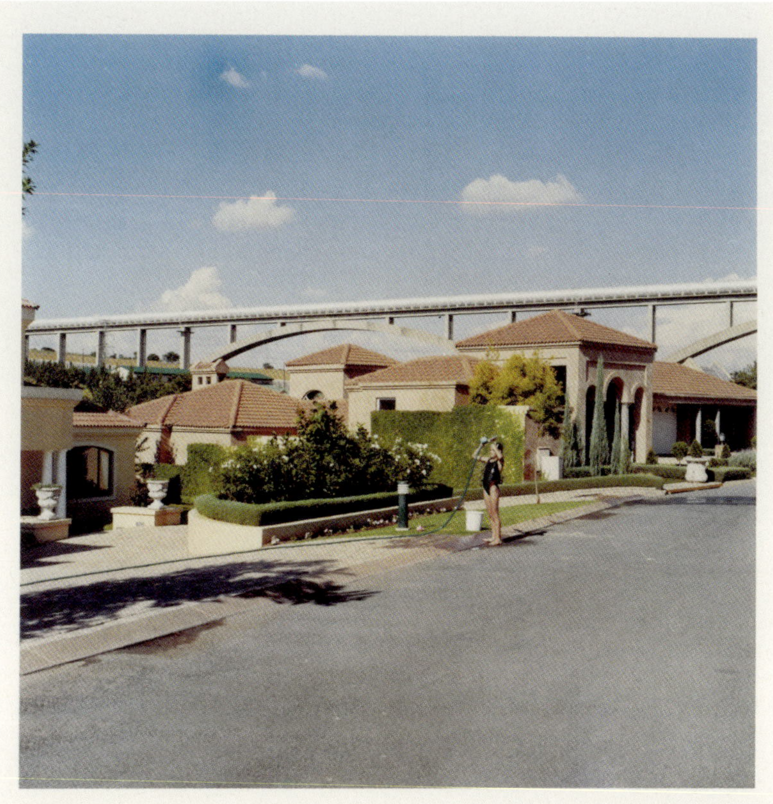

'Tuscan' House and Diepsloot Outfall Sewer,
Dainfern Golf Estate and Country Club.
20 January 2002. 'Dainfern' Series, 2002
Ink jet print on card
83 × 60 cm

Entre/Acte, Imágenes de frontera I is a reworking of eight minutes filmed in Super 8 on the border between La Quiaca, Argentina, and Villazón, Bolivia. The film forms part of the 1997 archives of the *maquettes-sans-qualité* (discontinuous arrangements of photographs and captions, texts, film documents, video for consultation and accounts of practices, started in 1995). The 1997 archives were revisited in 2004 by Alejandra Riera and Fulvia Carnevale as a contribution to the project *Ex-Argentina. Pasos para huir del trabajo al hacer* (Ex-Argentina. Steps for flight from labour to doing) by Alice Creischer, Andreas Siekmann and Gabriela Massuh. A publication printed in Argentina by the Cooperativa Chilavert Artes Gráficas print shop, a factory taken over and managed during the crisis by its workers, represented the first showing of this work, which was picked up once again for the exhibition project *How do we want to be governed?*, undertaken by Roger Buergel and Ruth Noack in 2004 and presented at the MACBA. *Entre/Acte* also formed part of the exhibition *maquettes-sans-qualité. Travail en grève/Work on strike* that took place at Barcelona's Fundació Antoni Tàpies in 2005, curated by Nuria Enguita Mayo.

For the artists, the significance of a return to this work in the context of the project undertaken by Buergel and Noack lay most of all in focusing the question of governmentality on the modalities of production and appearance or withdrawal applicable to certain endeavours in artistic experimentation. By 'artistic experimentation', the artists understand not 'the output of isolated contemporary artists', but 'the works that continue, after a struggle for survival, to safeguard a degree of autonomy from mediating authorities. Such autonomy is evidently conflictive in a world where the emergence of countless mediating authorities transforms the rate of evolution of that which governs us, everything that is created or presented with multiple re-retakes or ultimately overlooks or distorts the meaning of anything that does not adapt to the necessary speed.'

'It is true that *Entre/Acte, Imágenes de frontera I* offers eight minutes of poor quality images of women and men, mostly indigenous people, on the border between Argentina and Bolivia, bowed under the unacceptable logic of the *machin-machine*, as revealed in Godard's *Number two*, where he appears onscreen in his editing suite as a worker in his own factory of images and sounds. This *machin-machine*, a social body in which we are all involved in one way or another, in the place where we each find ourselves (increasingly so, since no place and

no human group seems to be in a position to govern itself), invites us to reflect on the risk involved in infinitely reconstructing the History of everything we fight against (a risk facing all documentary work). This is why careful attention must be paid to the choice of acceptable forms of transmission to ensure the operational nature of the criticism of existing representation policies inherent in work and to include the procedures of self-presentation.'

The acquisition of *Entre/Acte, Imágenes de frontera I* as part of a contemporary art collection raises the following issue: For the artists 'any re-presentation of *Entre/Acte* requires an "updating" according to a context and a given present'. This updating, one of the driving forces that endows the *maquettes-sans-qualité* with meaning, 'should be taken up by a working collective reconstituted in relation to a historical circumstance of our present, so that both the work, the images and their problems, and even their relative necessity, are once again challenged. Each updating constitutes the deep-seated meaning of the work. The attempt to adapt to a present does not signify precipitation, a relation to the current situation; on the contrary, it implies attacking the most immediate image of our time. To be more precise, we might refer to taking into account a series of "non/topical considerations". This means accepting the need to undo as a way of starting over. And it is in this movement that it is occasionally possible to draw existences that are running away. Recovering the force of a work in the process of challenging it does not mean that this "vital movement" cannot be encountered in the form of a pause, of a moment's stoppage, of a sudden need to stand still, thereby distancing the untiring interchangeability that makes each and every one of us obsolete.'

This updating is not possible in the framework of an art collection that fixes a moment of the 'work under way' as definitive. We should, then, regard *Entre/Acte, Imágenes de frontera I* as an archive, considering it not as a finished work but as a work that has had part of its most significant potential amputated; either that, or be alert to the right moment for its reappearance (which cannot be simply the annual presentation of an art collection) and recreate the context of collective dialogue that the work requires for its re-presentation.

14

ENTRE/ACTE, Imágenes de frontera I
Fragment of the *maquettes-sans-qualité* archives of 1997
updated in 2004 by Alejandra Riera and Fulvia Carnevale

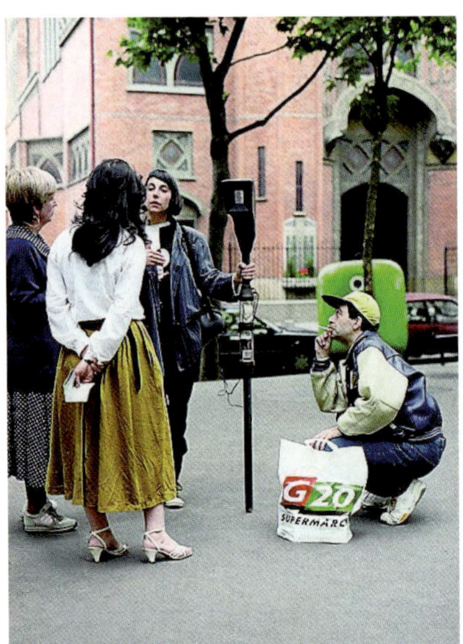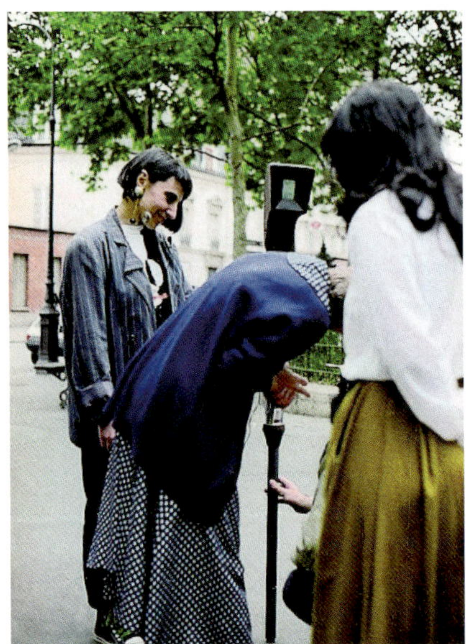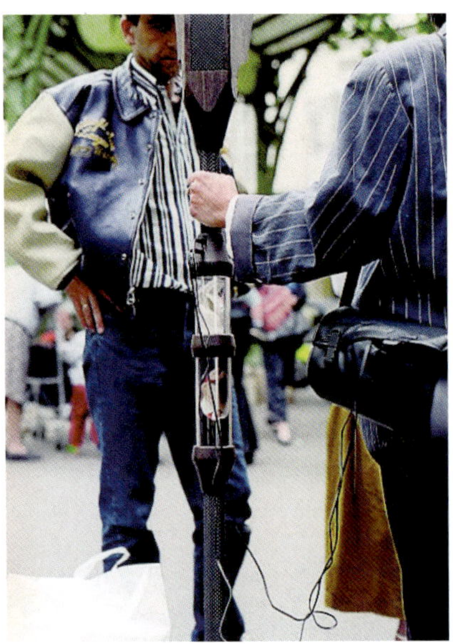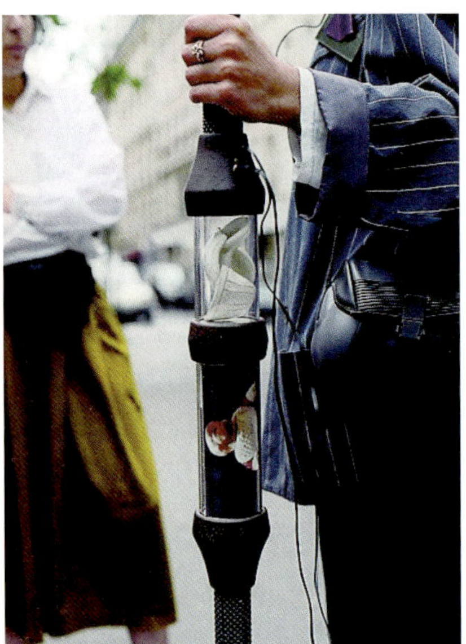

Krzysztof Wodiczko
Alien Staff, 1992–93
Crozier with video, colour, sound, 15 min 20 s
and single-channel video, colour, sound, 33 min 25 s
Dimensions variable

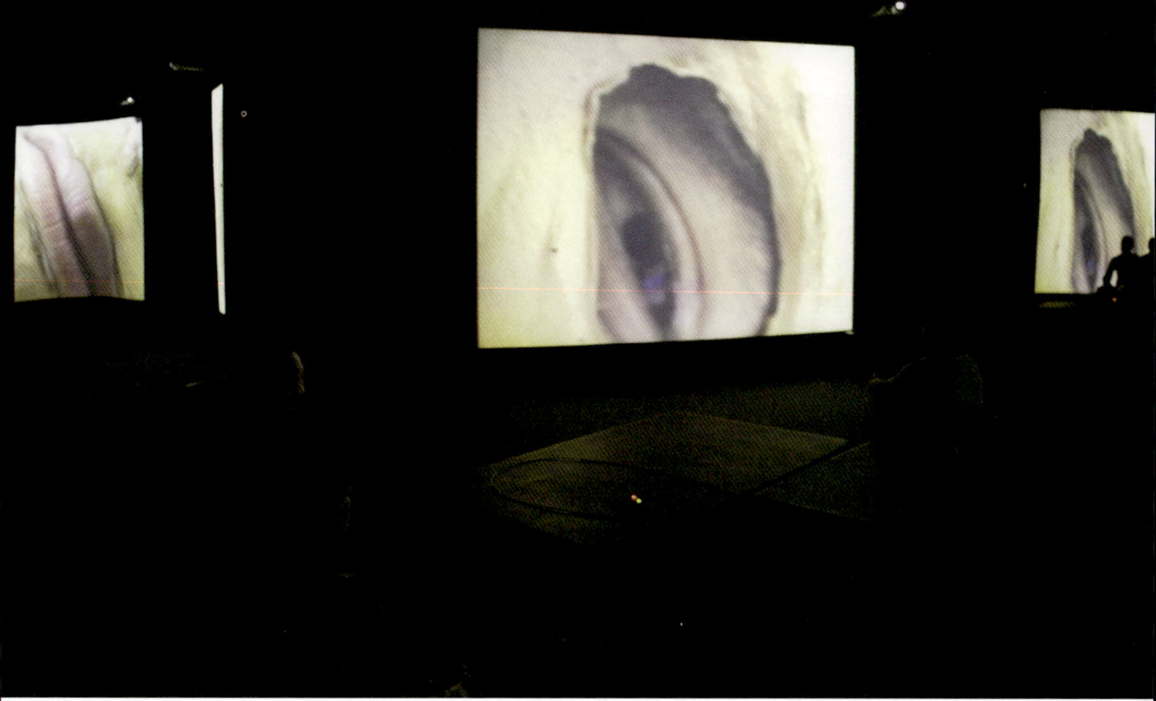

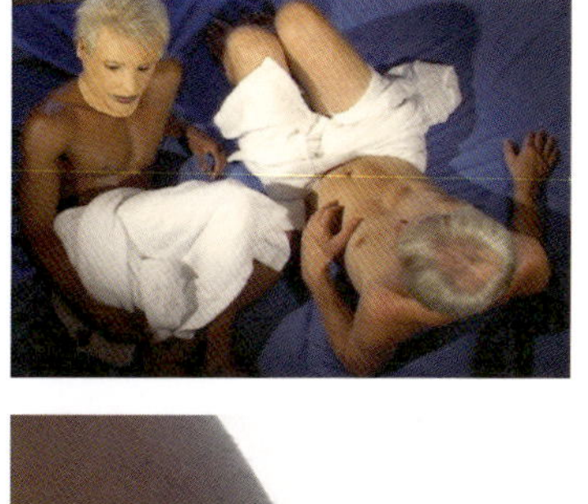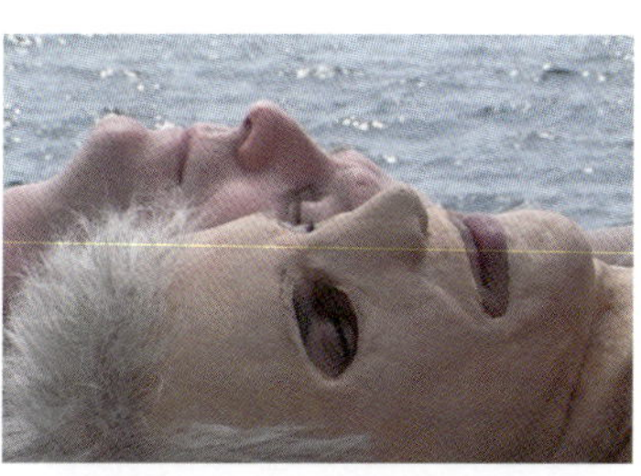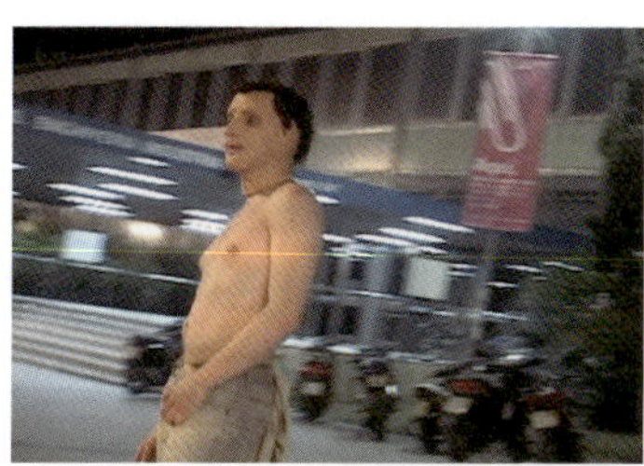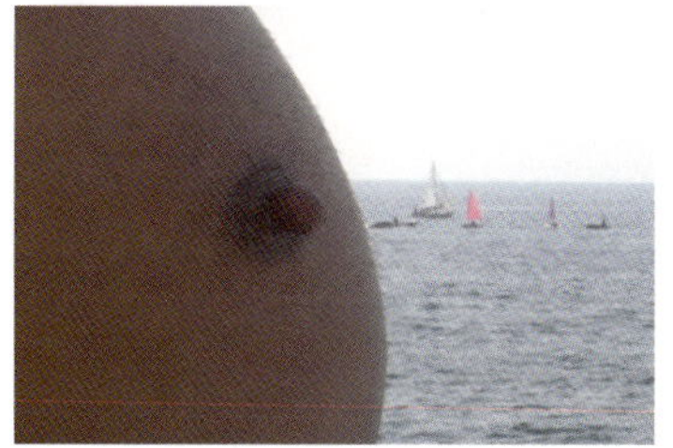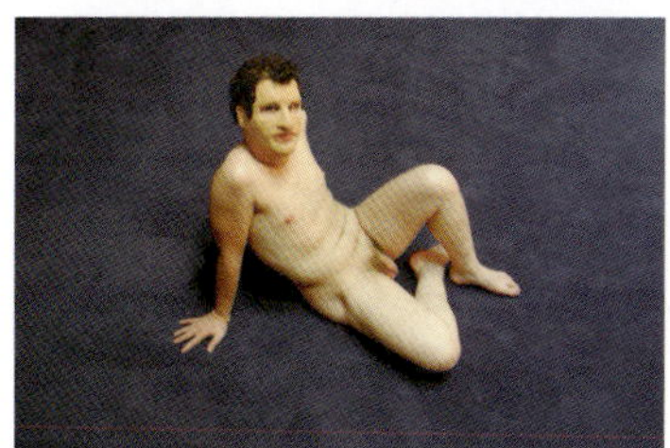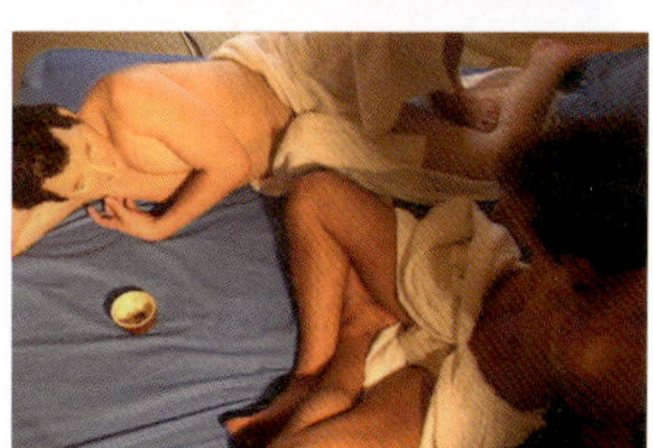

Dias & Riedweg
Voracidad Máxima, 2003
Two-channel video installation, colour, sound,
71 min 14 s, 4 mirrors, seats and control

Installation view, *Dias & Riedweg. Possibly Talking About the Same*, MACBA, 2003

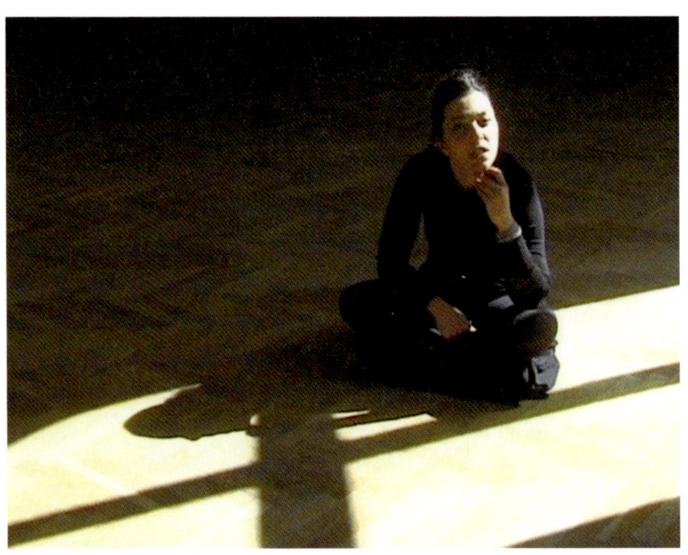

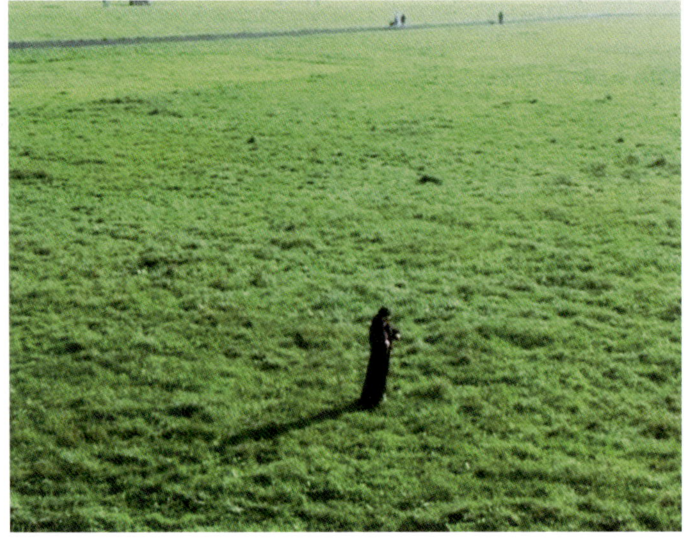

Maja Bajevic
Double Bubble, 2001
Single-channel video, colour, sound, 3 min 40 s

Maja Bajevic, **Emanuel Licha**
Green Green Grass of Home, 2002
Single-channel video, colour, sound, 17 min 53 s
and sound recording

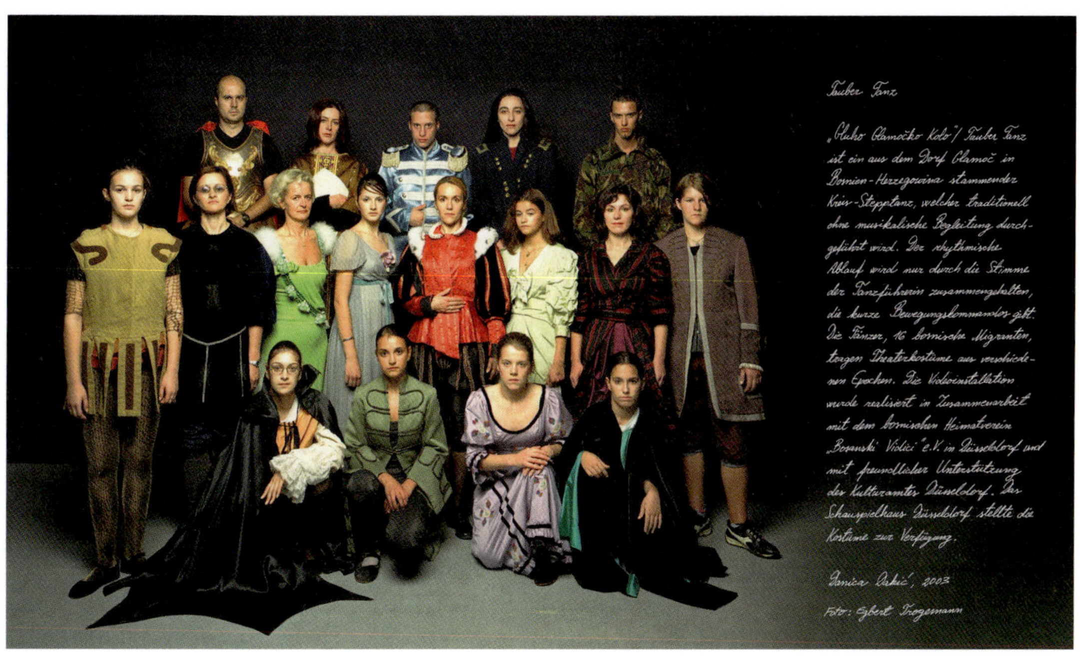

Danica Dakic
Tauber Tanz / Deaf Dance, 2003
Single-channel video, colour, sound,
3 min 40 s and Cibachrome slide in
an aluminium box and fluorescent light

Light box, 30 × 50 × 10 cm

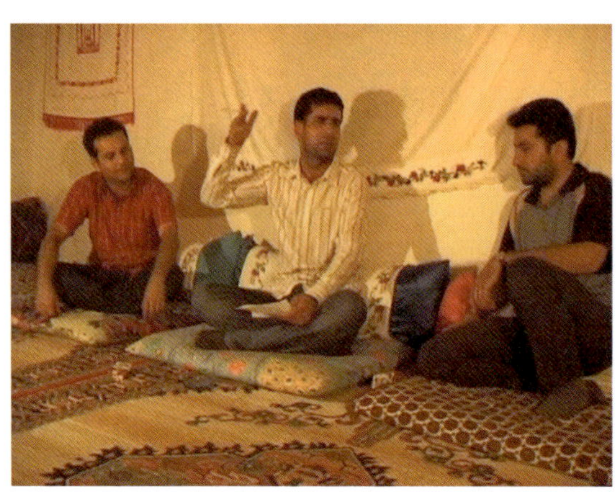 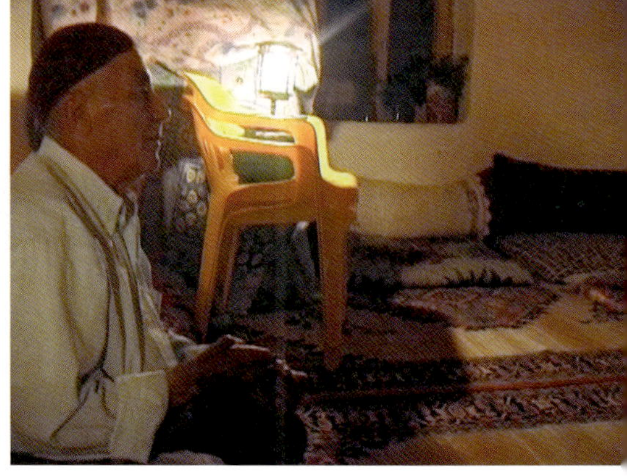

Fikret Atay
Lalo's Story, 2004
Single-channel video, colour, sound, 4 min 55 s

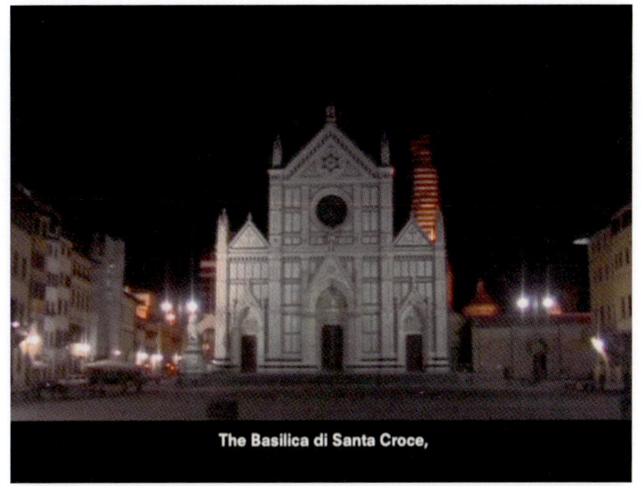

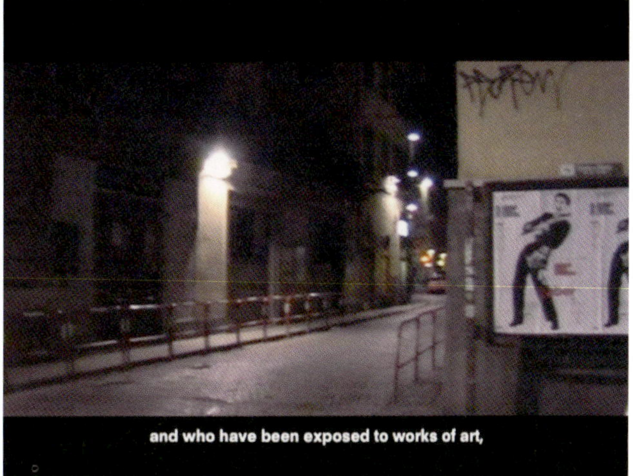

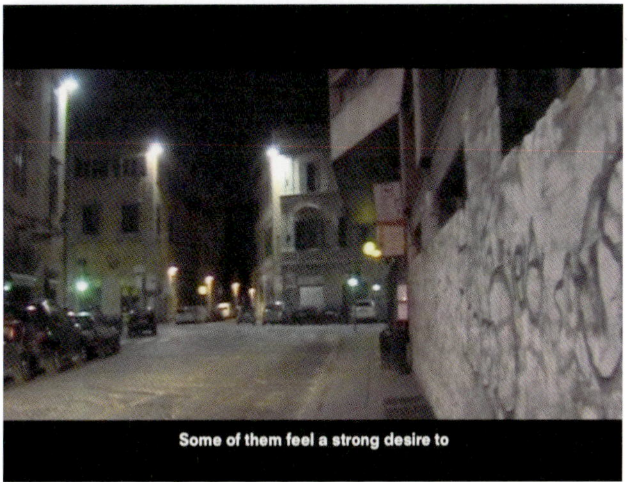

Frank Hesse
*Florence: From St. Croce to
the Institute of Art History*, 2006
Single-channel video, colour, sound,
11 min 50 s

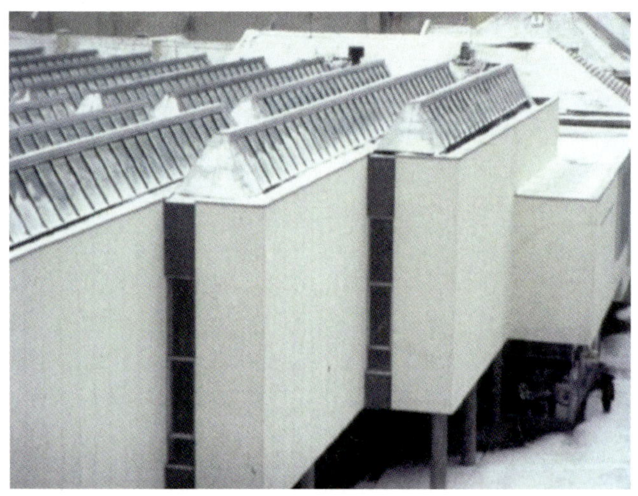

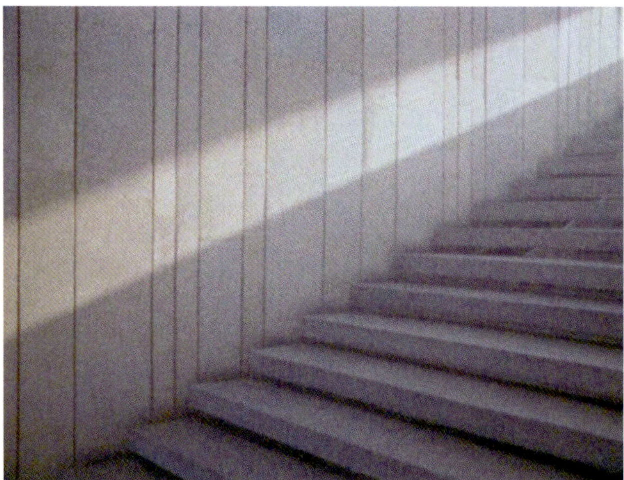

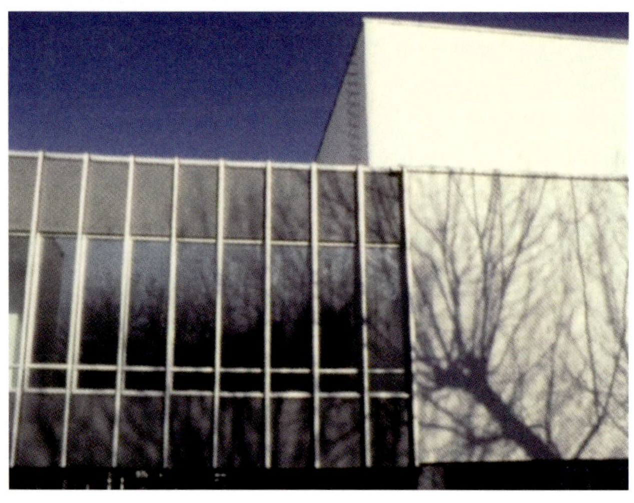

Deimantas Narkevicius
Scena, 2003
Super 8 mm film transferred to video,
colour, sound, 9 min 30 s

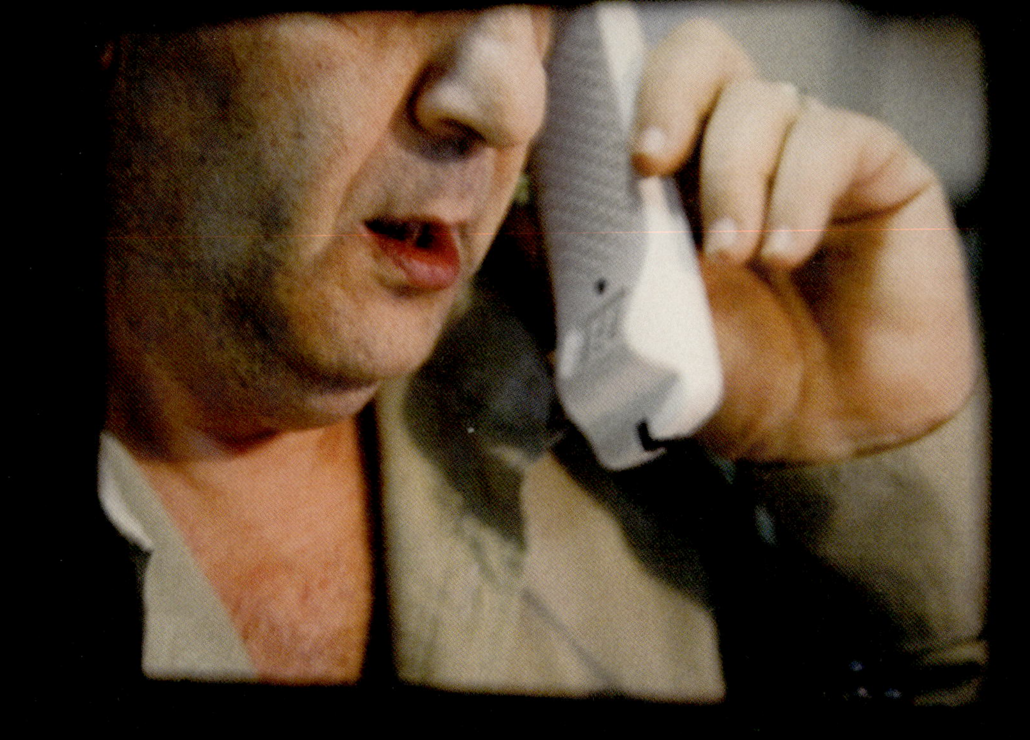

Rosalind Nashashibi
Bachelor Machines Part I, 2007
16 mm film, colour, sound, 31 min

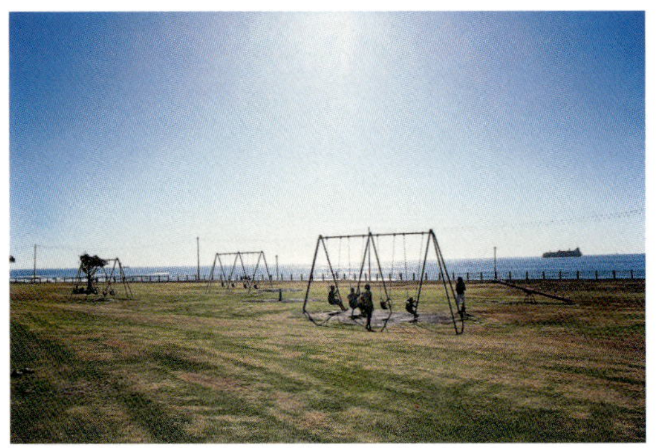
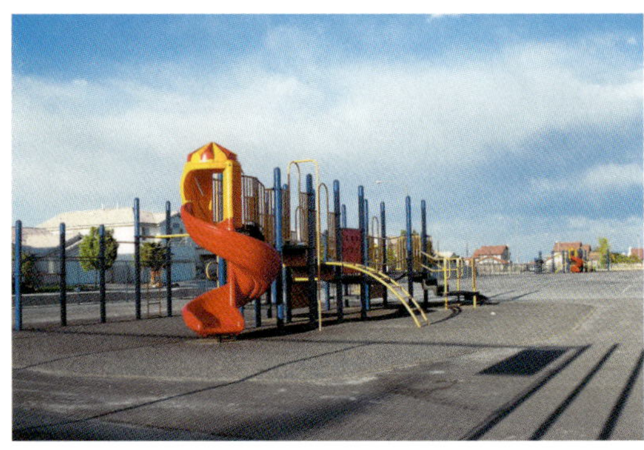
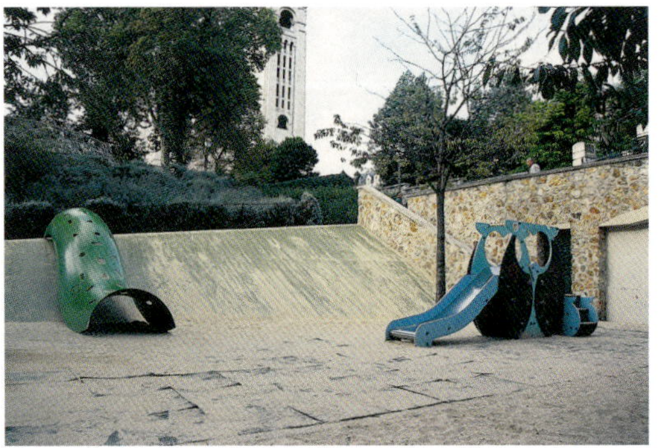
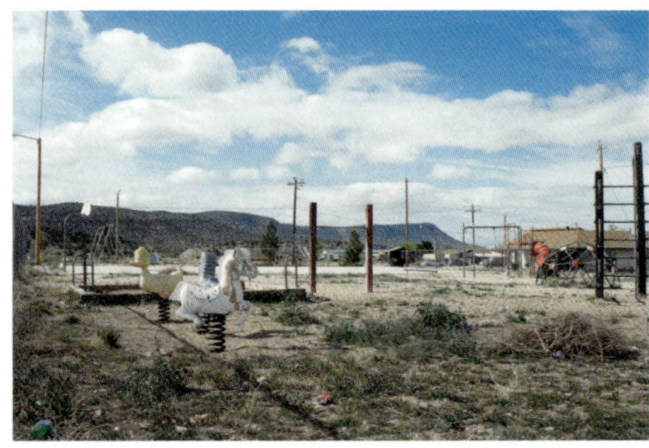
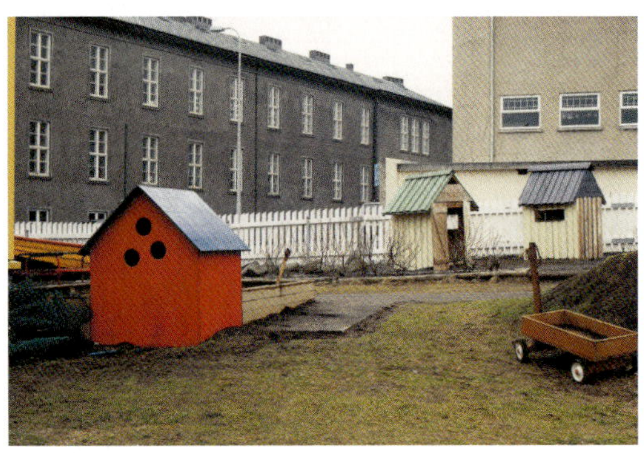
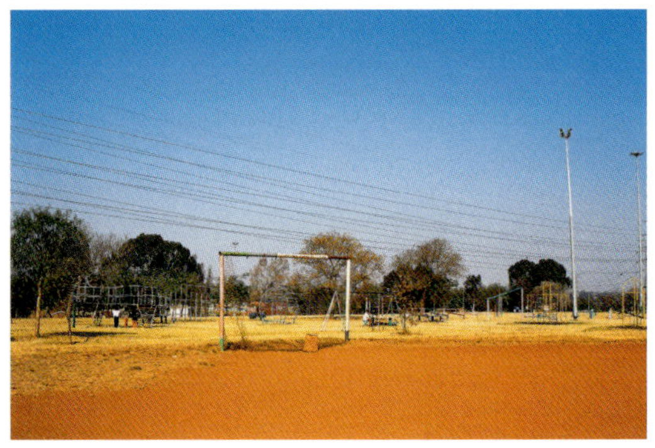

Peter Friedl
Playgrounds, 1995–2004
5 simultaneous slide projections
transferred to digital archives and vinyl
Dimensions variable

Aarle-Rixtel, Lange Akker, 1999 I Acoma, 2001 I Albuquerque, Kit Carson Park, 2001 I Albuquerque, Lomas Boulevard, 2001 I Alexandra, Johannesburg, East Bank Park, 2003 I Alexandra, Johannesburg, Lapas Park, 2003 I Alto Paraíso de Goiás, Rua de 12 de Dezembre, 2001 I Amsterdam, Vondelpark, 1999 I Antwerpen, Regenboogpark, 2002 I Arcata, Stewart Park, 2000 I Athlone, Cape Town, Lower Klipfontein Road, 2001 I Balik Pulan, 2000 I Barahona, Avenida Enriquillo, 1999 I Barcelona, Carrer de Bilbao, 2003 I Barcelona, Jardins del Doctor Fleming, 2003 I Barcelona, Parc de Carles I, 2003 I Barcelona, Parc de la Ciutadella, 2002 I Barcelona, Plaça de la Sagrada Familia, 2002 I Barcelona, Plaça de les Caramelles, 2003 I Barcelona, Plaça de Pablo Neruda, 2002 I Basel, Claramatte, 1999 I Basel, Riehenstraße, 1999 I Basel, Schützenmattpark, 2000 I Berlin, Alte Schönhauser Straße, 2000 I Berlin, Blücherstraße, 1999 I Berlin, Ernst-Thälmann-Park, 2000 I Berlin, Heinrich-Zille-Park, 2003 I Berlin, Helmholtzplatz, 2004 I Berlin, Hohenstauferplatz, 1996 I Berlin, Humboldthain, 2000 I Berlin, Kollwitzplatz, 2004 I Berlin, Marheinekeplatz, 1999 I Berlin, Mariannenplatz, 1999 I Berlin, Monbijoupark, 2004 I Berlin, Schlosspark Bellevue, 2001 I Berlin, Teutoburger Platz, 2000 I Bilbao, Paseo Campo Volantin, 2002 I Bloemfontein, Kudu Road, 2002 I Blouberg, Cape Town, Marine Drive, 2003 I Braga, Praça Conde de Agrolongo, 2000 I Brandvlei, Meulstraat, 2003 I Brasília, Parque da ciudade, 2002 I Brasília, Praça do Compromiso, 2002 I Brasília, Supersquadra Sul 310, 2002 I Bremen, Bürgerpark, 2002 I Bremen, Papestraße, 2002 I Brooklyn, Prospect Park, 2002 I Brooklyn, Vincent V. Abate Playground, 2002 I Calvinia, Stasieweg, 2003 I Cap-Haïtien, Parc Vincent, 2000 I Cape Town, Beach Road, 2002 I Cape Town, De Waal Park, 2003 I Cape Town, Kloof Street, 2001 I Cape Town, Station Road, 2003 I Cape Town, Tamboerskloof Road, 2003 I Cape Town, Tuin Plein, 2003 I Cape Town, Yusuf Drive, 2001 I Chinle, Chinle Kindergarten Center, 2001 I Crescent City, Taylor Street, 2002 I Cuba, Guadelupe Plaza, 2001 I Den Haag, Bezemstraat, 1999 I Diepkloof, Soweto, Immint Road Park, 2002 I Dube Village, Soweto, Mahalefela Road, 2001 I Dubrovnik, Gruska Obala, 2003 I Durango, Main Avenue, 2001 I East London, Fitzpatrick Road, 2001 I Eureka, Hammond Park, 2002 I Fort Bragg, Harold O. Bainbridge Park, 2002 I Frankfurt am Main, Mainkai, 1 2004 I Frankfurt am Main, Obermainanlage, 2000 I Frankfurt am Main, Oppenheimer Platz, 2004 I Frankfurt am Main, Taunusanlage, 2000 I Frankfurt am Main, Untermainkai, 2000 I Genève, Parc La Grange, 2000 I Genève, Plaine de Plainpalais, 1998 I Georgetown, Lebuh Armenia, 2000 I Gugulethu, Cape Town, NY 134 Playground, 2002 I Hamburg, Gertrudenkirchhof, 2000 I Hamburg, Lohmühlenpark, 2000 I Hamburg, Rostocker Straße, 2000 I Hannover, Maschpark, 2003 I Hannover, Welfengarten, 2003 I Henties Bay, Dr Libertina Amathila Street, 2003 I Henties Bay, Omdel Park, 2003 I Hout Bay, Hout Bay Park, 2003 I Jalama Beach, 2001 I Jeffrey's Bay, Diaz Road, 2001 I Jendouba, Route nationale 17, 2002 I Johannesburg, Fuel Street, 2002 I Johannesburg, George Lea Park, 2001 I Johannesburg, Hyde Park, 2001 I Johannesburg, Joubert Park, 2001 I Johannesburg, Jukskei Park, 2003 I Johannesburg, Olivedale Community Centre, 2003 I Johannesburg, Pieter Roos Park, 2002 I Johannesburg, Triomf Park, 2001 I Johannesburg, Weiner Park, 2001 I Johannesburg, Zoo Lake, 2001 I Kairouan, Rue de la Grande Mosquée, 2002 I Katutura, Windhoek, Sukhot Family Park, 2003 I Katutura, Windhoek, UN Plaza, 2003 I Keetmanshoop, TransNamib Sports Club, 2003 I Khomas, Windhoek, Anemone Street Family Park, 2003 I Kimberley, Queens Park, 2002 I Kingman, Hualapai Mountain Road, 2001 I Las Vegas, Mardon Avenue, 2001 I Las Vegas, Rue de Parc, 2001 I Le Kef, Avenue Habib Bourguiba, 2002 I Leipzig, Johanna-Park, 2002 I Leipzig, Rudolphstraße, 2002 I Lekeitio, Santa Elena Etorbidea, 2002 I Linz, Blumauerplatz, 2001 I Linz, Nussbaumstraße, 1998 I London, Kensington Gardens, 2001 I London, Shoot up Hill, 2001 I London, St. Cuthbert's Road, 2001 I Los Angeles, La Cienega Boulevard, 2001 I Los Angeles, Yucca Street, 1999 I Los Angeles, Yukon Avenue, 2001 I Lüderitz, Lüderitz Playground, 2003 I Lüneburg, Im Timpen, 2003 I Luxembourg, Parc Municipal, 2000 I Lyon, Place Edgar Quinet, 2002 I Lyon, Place Moncey, 2002 I Lyon, Place Bellecour, 2002 I Lyon, Place Raspail, 2002 I Lyon, Rue des Estrées, 2002 I Mafikeng, Jan Viljoen Avenue, 2003 I Maniago, Parco Pubblico, 2000 I Marfa, 1999 I Middelburg, Henrik Potgieter Street, 2001 I Minneapolis, Spruce Place, 2000 I Modesto, Gracaeda Park, 2002 I Mondesa, Swakopmund, Independence Street, 2003 I Monterey, Dennis the Menace Playground, 2002 I München, Akademiestraße, 2002 I München, Alter Botanischer Garten, 2002 I München, Luisenstraße, 2002 I Muizenberg, Cape Town, Long Beach Road, 2003 I New Horizons, Bunny Cairns Park, 2001 I New York City, ABC Playground, 2003 I New York City, Augustus Saint-Gaudens Playground, 1999 I New York City, Bleecker Playground, 1999 I New York City, Chelsea Park, 1999 I New York City, Clement Clarke Moore Park, 2002 I New York City, Columbus Park, 2003 I New York City, De Salvio Playground, 1999 I New York City, Diana Ross Playground, 2002 I New York City, First Park, 1999 I New York City, Heckscher Playground, 1999 I New York City, Madison Square Park, 2000 I New York City, McKinley Playground, 2003 I New York City, Sara D. Roosevelt Park, 2000 I New York City, St. Vartan Park, 2000 I New York City, Stuyvesant Town, 2000 I New York City, Tompkins Square, 2000 I New York City, Union Square, 2000 I New York City, Washington Square, 1999 I Nice, Jardin Jean Moreno, 2000 I Nice, Jardin Roland Dorgeles, 2000 I Nice, Parc Vigier, 2000 I Orick, Head Start Playground, 2002 I Paris, Bibliothèque Nationale, 1999 I Paris, Jardin Albert Schweitzer, 2000 I Paris, Jardin des Tuileries, 2003 I Paris, Jardin du Luxembourg, 2000 I Paris, Rue du dessous des Berges, 2000 I Paris, Square Armand Trousseau, 2000 I Paris, Square Montholon, 2000 I Paris, Square Villemin, 2003 I Peach Springs, Hualapai Indian Reservation, 2001 I Point Arena, Main Street, 2002 I Pretoria, Arcadia Park, 2003 I Pretoria, Burgers Park, 2003 I Pretoria, Jubilee Square, 2003 I Queens, Murray Playground, 1998 I Reykjavík, Bergþórugata, 1999 I Rio de Janeiro, Largo do Machado, 2002 I Rio de Janeiro, Largo Paulo Cândido, 2002 I Rio de Janeiro, Praça da República, 2002 I Rio de Janeiro, Parque do Museu da República, 2002 I Rio de Janeiro, Parque do Flamengo, 2002 I Rio de Janeiro, Parque do Ibirapuera, 2002 I Rio de Janeiro, Rua Marquês de Abrantes, 2002 I Rio de Janeiro, Rua São Salvador, 2002 I Rotterdam, Bospolderplein, 2000 I Rotterdam, Heemraadspark, 2000 I Rotterdam, Lelyboskade, 2000 I Rotterdam, Schiedamsesingel, 2000 I Sacramento, John C. Fremont Park, 2002 I Sacramento, South Side Park, 2002 I Salinas, Mission Park, 2002 I Samedan, Muottas Muragl, 2002 I San Francisco, Golden Gate Park, 2002 I San Francisco, Margret S. Hayward Playground, 2002 I San Franciso, Mission Playground, 2002 I San Francisco, North Beach Playground, 2002 I San Francisco, Walter U. Lum Place, 2002 I San Sebastian, Parque de Araba, 2002 I San Sebastian, Plaza del Padre Clavet, 2002 I San Sebastian, Plaza Zuberoa, 2002 I Santa Cruz, Lorenzo Park, 2002 I Santa Rosa, Hendley Street, 2002 I São Paulo, Avenida Sumare, 2002 I São Paulo, Parque do Trianon, 2001 I São Paulo, Praça Pévola Byington, 2002 I São Paulo, Praça Princesa Isabel, 2002 I Singapur, Clementi Avenue, 2000 I Singapur, Serangoon Road, 2000 I Sipan, Sipanska Luka, 2003 I Solothurn, Chantier, 2001 I Soweto, Five Roses Park, 2001 I Swakopmund, Strand Straße, 2003 I Toulouse, Prairie des Filtres, 2002 I Tunis, Cité el Khadra, 2002 I Umtata, Sisson Street, 2002 I Upington, Quarry Street, 2003 I Venezia, Giardini Pubblici, 2000 I Venezia, Giardino Papadopoli, 2001 I Venice, Ocean Front Walk, 2001 I Villeurbanne, Square des anciens combattants d'Afrique du Nord, 2002 I Visalia, Recreation Park, 2002 I Vryburg, Livingstone Street, 2003 I Walvis Bay, Lagoon Park, 2003 I Walvis Bay, The Esplanade, 2003 I Wien, Esterházypark, 1999 I Wien, Josef-Strauss-Park, 2002 I Wien, Kühnplatz, 1999 I Wien, Mexiko Platz, 2003 I Wien, Stadtpark 2003 I Windhoek, Zoo Park, 2003

These notes, written on February 2009, are a reworking of several previous
'texts-in-progress'. My aim here is to give an account of the collective
evolution of the institutional production and experimentation under way at
the MACBA in the last decade. Specifically, apart from the many articles
in the Museum's various publications and supports, the existing texts are:
'On Public Service in the Age of Cultural Consumption', in *Parachute*,
no. 111 (July–September 2003), pp. 144–55; 'Mediation and
Construction of Publics. The MACBA Experience', at http://republicart.net/
disc/institution/ribalta01_en.htm (also available in Spanish, French and
German); 'Contrapúblicos. Mediación y construcción de públicos',
in *Ramona. Revista de artes visuales*, no. 55 (October 2005), pp. 24–38;
and 'Patrimoni comú, modernitat perifèrica, educació política, crítica
institucional. Notes sobre la pràctica del MACBA', in *Papers d'Art*, no. 90
(2006), pp. 28–31. I would like to stress the collective nature of the
activity described in this article. In addition to the MACBA's team, various
other individuals and groups have formed part of this process, including
Xavier Antich, Manuel Asensi, Enric Berenguer, Miren Etxezarreta, Joan
Roca, Marcelo Expósito, Carlos Prieto, Beatriz Preciado, Jordi Claramonte,
Madeinbarcelona, Suely Rolnik, Roger Buergel, Raúl Sánchez, Jesús
Carrillo, Pedro G. Romero, Ana Longoni, Allan Sekula, Marc Pataut,
Krzysztof Wodiczko, Brian Holmes, Mercè Tatjer, Salvador Clarós, Noemí
Cohen, Perla Zusman, the Fòrum de la Ribera del Besòs, Paco Marín
and Jean-François Chevrier among others.

EXPERIMENTS IN
A NEW INSTITUTIONALITY
Jorge Ribalta

1. Memories of the future

Between 2000 and 2008, we at the MACBA have carried out various projects seeking to re-establish the relation between the museum and the city. A cycle of institutional experimentation extends from The Agencies (2001) and the photographic project about Barcelona and the exhibition *Universal Archive. The Condition of the Document and the Modern Photographic Utopia* (late 2008), to the exhibitions *How do we want to be governed?* (2004) and *Desacuerdos* (2005), paralleling the city's social dynamics. These projects, set in the tradition of the museum practice of institutional critique, sought to outline a model of metropolitan art policy for present-day and future geopolitical conditions.

The work of the Museum during this period constituted a project of institutional regeneration with the objective of offering a credible model of the art institution in a country like Spain, where these institutions had not evolved at an international pace and still today share the public discredit of a state with endemic democratic shortcomings. It is important to remember that under Franco's dictatorship, which dominated the central period of the twentieth century, Spain stood on the sidelines of the development of modern art institutions, which was happening internationally according to the model that the MoMA, New York, had implanted in the thirties, and which became generalised in Europe after the Second World War. It was only in the late eighties that Spain joined the process of modernising art institutions, once democracy had been restored but at a time when modern museums had given way to the new 'postmodern' art institutions, dominated by the tourism-related and economic imperatives of the growth model of post-industrial, neoliberal capitalism. In Spain, the development of these institutions has been determined by the paradigm of the culture industry, which overlooks the educational role of the museum and its role as a constituent part of the public sphere. As opposed to the spectacularised, instrumentalised, trivial conception (governed by a soft model of participation based on statistics and consumption) that dominated the emergence of museums in Spain throughout the

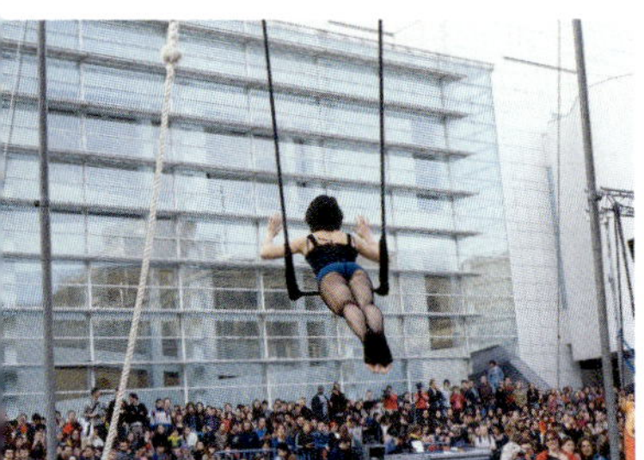

Circus versus Global Empire, campaign against a Europe for Capital and War, Plaça dels Àngels, Barcelona, 15 March 2002

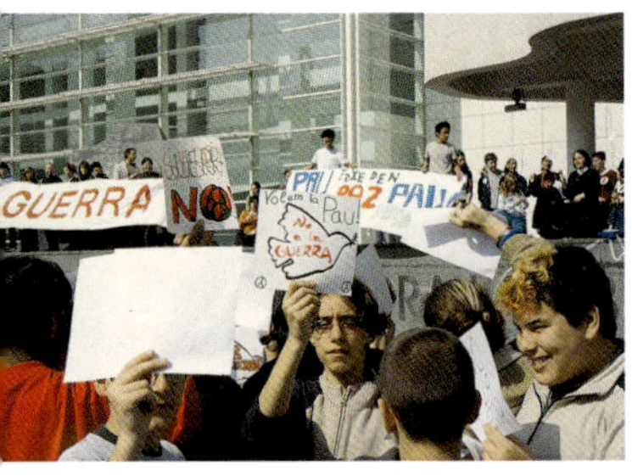

Demonstrations against the Iraq War, Plaça dels Àngels, Barcelona, spring 2003

eighties and nineties, and still continues today, the MACBA's experience in the last decade has represented a counter-model, characterised by a search for a critical anchorage in the tradition of modern art institutions and by the determination to grant centrality to the educational dimension of the museum and its public.

However, the significance of the MACBA's experience in the last decade is not limited to the national scale; it must be seen in the international context of the debate about art and the museum. The so-called 'MACBA model' constitutes a singular understanding of the museum as a space for debate and conflict, and a critical re-reading of the modern tradition that brings together artistic methods, social knowledge and action in the public sphere as a way of reinventing the field of art and according it a new significance and social legitimacy. This has been a fundamental aspect of the MACBA during this period: its capacity for institutional experimentation. The Museum has moved forward in this respect with no institutional interlocutor of the same characteristics at the international scale. By means of a particular reading of the debates and experiences of institutional critique since the sixties, the Museum has tackled a series of projects drawing on the institution's anchorage in the city and has been able to reinvent itself and suggest hypotheses for a new kind of institution.

Historiography, post-colonialism and common heritage

In addition to rethinking the role of the museum in the public sphere, the MACBA's activities (visibly materialised in the construction of a collection, a programme of temporary exhibitions and a programme of activities) have sought to promote a different narration of the art of the second half of the twentieth century. They also aim to table the relation between modern art and modernity by establishing Barcelona's peripheral role in the configuration of the dominant discourses about modern art. Inspired by feminist and post-colonial studies, this line of work was based on the recognition of the fact that forms of knowledge and power structures are totally inseparable.

The concept of periphery is semantically inverted here; rather than what might be considered a culturally subordinate position, it adopts a process of self-recognition and the construction of a viewpoint that challenges the central power/knowledge structures, in opposition to which it is defined. In this way, it seeks to identify and understand the specific cultural processes that make Barcelona a peripheral centre of modernity (and I stress the contradiction of 'peripheral centre'). It also seeks to make the processes involved in the construction of these prevailing relations of knowledge/power relatively transparent and open to debate.

This process has involved challenging a dominant conception of culture based on discourses of identity rooted in Romantic concepts, on the one hand, and in the cultural industry, on the other. This conception makes culture an ideological instrument for the construction and legitimisation of local and national myths of identity, which simultaneously serves to market its foremost figures in today's global market of programmed differences. Its hegemony is detrimental to other possible policies in which culture and education constitute a guiding nucleus. We will only be able to rework the project of a popular form of education inherited from modernity when we overcome this division between art and culture. It is important to stress the perverse effects of this dominant situation in which culture moves away from the production of discourse, debate and public life, and becomes a celebration of identity and localist myth-making and the economic driving force of a model of extrovert city.[1]

In this context, we see the local in a sense that is neither identitary nor essentialist. Rather than localist (that is, according to an ahistorical logic of reproduction of a metaphysical, immutable identity), it is a singular concretion in a territory of global conditions and historical forces. The local is the specific production of the various historical options with which we are presented and from which we have to choose, removed from any notion of identity. The question is not to celebrate what we are, but to ask ourselves why we are as we are or, even, what we can be. In this sense, there is no identity because there is no stable subject, but a multiplicity of relations producing various positions of subject. Defending this complex, relational, anti-Romantic understanding of the local therefore means promoting a self-critical relation with the forms of production of knowledge. It translates not into the logic of reproduction of what already exists, but into an incipient opening and readjustment of global relations of sovereignty over historical options, as expounded by Immanuel Wallerstein with relation to utopistics, seen as 'an alternative, credibly better and historically possible (but far from certain) future'.[2]

Nor is the local that which is close at hand. Today, notions of proximity are used to manage social conflict by means of an anti-modern neo-communitarianism that serves to override the antagonism and conflict that is constitutive of the social, thereby seeking to construct homogeneity and cancel out differences. Cultural management emerges as an instrument for new, soft, 'biopolitical' forms of governability, culture is used as a supposedly depoliticised agent for the construction of consensus

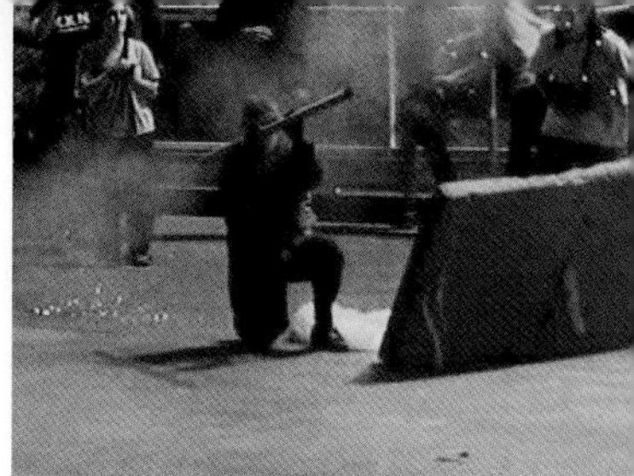
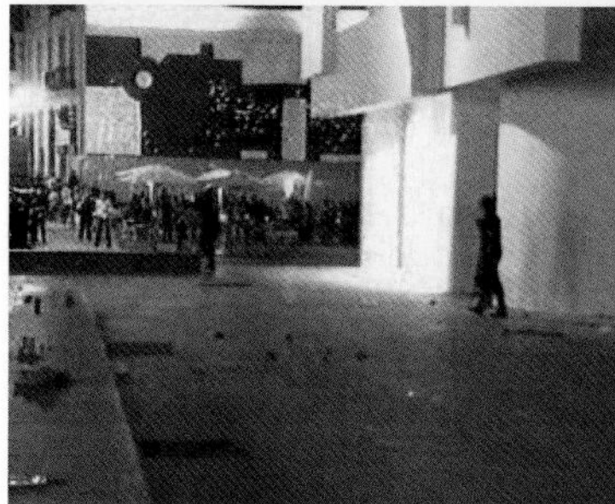
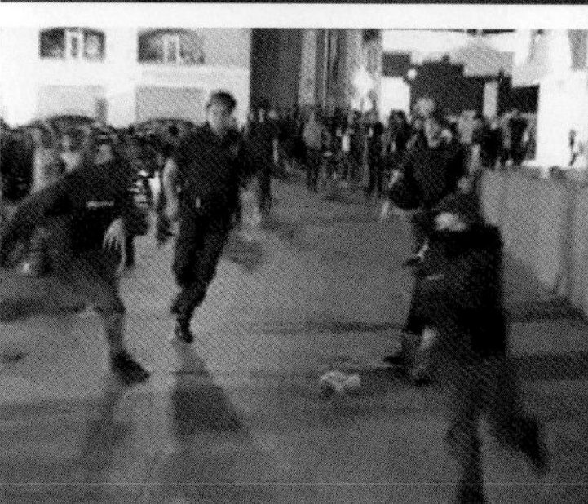

Plaça dels Àngels, Barcelona, 23 October 2006. Images recorded by Informativos Telecinco

1 Miren Etxezarreta, Albert Recio and Lourdes Viladomiu, 'Barcelona: una ciudad extravertida', in Manuel J. Borja-Villel, Jean-François Chevrier and Craigie Horsfield, *La ciutat de la gent*. Barcelona: Fundació Antoni Tàpies, 1997, pp. 221–55.
2 Immanuel Wallerstein, *Utopistics*. New York: The New Press, 1998.

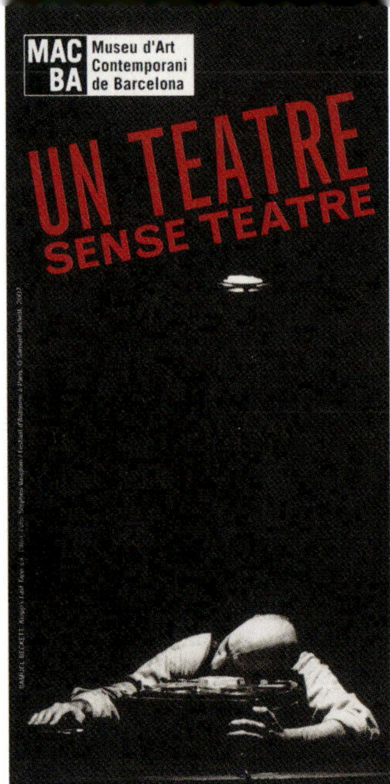

Flyer of the exhibition *A Theater without Theater*, MACBA, 2007

3 Alberto Cardín, *Lo próximo y lo ajeno. Tientos etnológicos II*. Barcelona: Icaria Editorial, 1990.

and social discipline, which is manifested in Barcelona, for example, in new policies to promote civic-mindedness. In the face of this, we defend an understanding of the artistic space as a space of debate, difference and radical alterity.

The local is, then, a specific way of being open to others and transformed by them. As anthropologist Alberto Cardín articulated, years ago,[3] the local is not just the close at hand, the identical, it is also the alien. The local is a process of reinvention in which we must be able to look beyond the identitary and localist baggage that ties us to ancestral myths and the perpetuation of the prevailing order, naturalised by nationalist and essentialist ideologies. This baggage, *de facto*, prevents us accepting our historical conditions and options with all their consequences – that is, accepting them so that we are able to decide about them, change them and contribute to a new geography of centres and fringes.

How does this discourse materialise in the Museum? One way is an interest on the part of the Collection and the temporary exhibitions programme in artists and art scenes (such as Latin America or Eastern Europe), which have not occupied dominant positions in the discourses on modern art promoted by the central legitimising institutions of the twentieth century. Another is through thematic exhibitions that suggest hypotheses for other possible narrations of artistic modernity, taking as a departure point and interpretative axis some of the aspects repressed or pushed out by accepted formalist modernity.

Recent examples are exhibitions such as *Art and Utopia. Restricted Action* (summer 2004), which proposed an alternative reading of modern art after Mallarmé and the relations between art and poetry, or in the presentation of the Collection entitled *Relational Poetics* (autumn 2004). The latter was based on references to Édouard Glissant, suggesting a notion of relationality involving not just an anti-fetishist reading of the artistic object but also a peculiar version of the postcolonial theories of hybridisation and interculturality, an alternative to the nationalist identitarian discourse. Another example is *A Theatre without Theatre* (spring 2007), an exploration of theatricality as the repressed side of dominant artistic visuality since the second half of the twentieth century, determined by Michael Fried's classic condemnation of the theatre. More recently, *Be-Bomb* (autumn 2007), curated by Serge Guilbaut, presented his known theses on the fight for cultural hegemony on the post-war geopolitical scene. The most recent attempt to this end was the exhibition *Universal Archive. The Condition of the Document and the Modern Photographic Utopia* (late 2008), which looked at artistic modernity in terms of the photographic document, a genre historically subordinated to the arts, and the structure of testimony (that is, an alliance between elites and subordinate groups) as the central issue of artistic and political representation in modernity.

This process is also self-critical in terms of the dominant mechanisms of representation and exhibition in the museographic field, and highlights the perhaps inevitable reification and monumentalisation represented by the expository complex. The exhibition tends to be a device at the service of the identitarian myth of authors who address neither the structural and social dimension of the construction of the public artistic sphere nor everyday collective forms of creativity that are hard to define. How can we break with this logic? Attention to the artists and scenes that are considered 'minor', alternative forms of distribution or a relative use of archive resources in the exhibition (including documentation and ways of appropriating the exhibition space that grant a use value and relativise the purely expository value) are attempts to explain not just a history of the works and their authors, but primarily a history of the collective social processes of the construction of artistic debates, a history of public artistic spheres. This historiography calls for self-critical museum mechanisms and methods that focus on repressed and elusive aspects in the epistemological model of the exhibition. This type of mechanism is also a way of introducing into the exhibition format a 'perverted' conception of the publics and the education I will go on to address.

Publics and counterpublics

The Museum's contribution to a radically democratic public sphere is, initially, to be self-critical and open to debate. Discursive activity plays a central part at the MACBA. It serves to help counteract the hegemony of the exhibition device and the representational paradigm as the museum's principal method or public discursive space. Our starting point is an understanding of social life as being constituted by different publics, with differing interests. According to this logic, the museum has to accommodate different and equal uses for these different publics, which are neither limited to the exhibition space nor excessively determined by the imperative of visibility. We also attempt to research methods of discourse circulation by means of the website and other forms of publication and publicity. Further, we question the prevailing privilege of author's rights over the rights of the public,[4] with the emphasis on understanding processes of construction of publics and the social mechanisms of discourse circulation.

Public is a concept in which several meanings coexist simultaneously and which are defined self-reflectively. The concept of public has to do with that which is common, with the state,

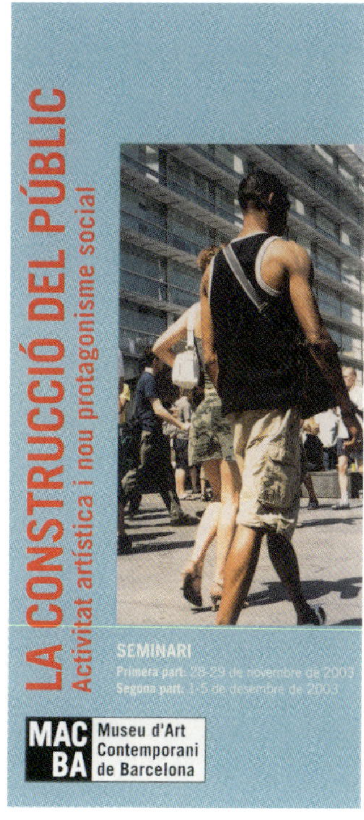

Leaflet of the seminar *Constructing the Public*, MACBA, 2003

4 See in particular the editorial to the *Agenda informativa del MACBA*: 'Patrimonio común e institución pública: del derecho del autor al derecho del público', reproduced in *Ag 2004–2006. Selección de textos de la Agenda informativa del MACBA, Quaderns portàtils*, no. 05 (2006) at www.macba.cat.

with shared interest, that which is accessible. There is a historic mobility in the public-private opposition that lies precisely in the mobility of publics and their forms of self-organisation. The public has a twofold meaning of social totality and specific audience.

Michael Warner describes the ambiguity and multiplicity of meanings of the notion of public in his book *Publics and Counterpublics*.[5] Publics are elusive forms of social groupings that form reflexively around specific discourses. Public is one of the recurrent terms in the culture debate, which does not mean that it is a simple term or one with an obvious meaning.

Art is a public activity, directed at debate and confrontation with others. Today we are seeing how art institutions and policies have gradually replaced the discourses of universal access to culture with a new discourse that places the cultural experience on a similar footing to processes of consumption. Unlike the abstract, homogenising conception of the spectator that characterises modern art and its institutions, the new discourse of the culture industry, which identifies public with consumption, tends to recognise differences, though it does so according to the criteria of marketing and generates populist cultural policies. From this viewpoint, working for the public means giving them what the public expects, presuming a pre-existence of such publics, which are supposedly comprehensible, measurable and controllable by statistical processes. This cultural policy follows the pattern of television consumption and therefore shares its consequences: a progressive trivialisation and impoverishment of experience, in which the critical, emancipatory dimension of cultural experience is eliminated in favour of false participation.

This consensual discourse has demobilising consequences in civil society, and for this reason we propose another approach. The public does not exist as a predefined entity to be attracted and manipulated; the public forms in open, unpredictable ways in the very process of construction of discourses, by means of their various means of circulation. Consequently, the public is not someone there to be reached, who are there passively awaiting cultural merchandise; the public is formed by the actual discursive process and by the act of being convened. The public is in a state of constant mobility. The consequences of this way of seeing in terms of cultural policies and practices means challenging dominant conceptions of the production and consumption of culture, according to which these roles are immovable, like closed processes, and therefore merely reproduce what already exists, and give way to a range of new possibilities for action, in which the public acquires the active role of

5 Michael Warner, *Publics and Counterpublics*. New York: Zone Books, 2005.

producer with the potential for organisation and other forms of sociability. In this way, the public can seem like a project, like the potential for constructing something that does not yet exist and may push back current limitations. It is precisely this non-pre-existence of the public (what we might term its fantasmatic dimension) that suggests the possibility of reconstructing a critical cultural public sphere. It is precisely this potential and this openness that guarantee the existence of a democratic public sphere, a space that does not have to be unitary to be democratic, as Chantal Mouffe has theorised.[6]

A multiplicity of publics is preferable to a single public sphere. Nancy Fraser speaks of the need to explore hybrid forms of public spheres and of the organisation of weak and strong publics, in which opinion and decision-making can find ways of negotiating and recombining relations. Fraser introduces the concept of 'subaltern counterpublics' to refer to the 'parallel discursive arenas where members of subordinated social groups invent and circulate counterdiscourses to formulate oppositional interpretations of their identities, interests and needs', and adds: 'In stratified societies, subaltern counterpublics have a dual character. On the one hand, they function as spaces of withdrawal and regroupment; on the other hand, they also function as spaces and training grounds for agitational activities directed towards wider publics. It is precisely in the dialectic between these two functions that their emancipatory potential lies.'[7] Ultimately, this exploration of counterpublics leads to a post-bourgeois public sphere, which should not necessarily be identified with the state.

This rejection of a consensual conception of publics gives rise to a pedagogical model for art and culture, directed at experimentation with forms of self-organisation and self-learning. The objective of this method is to produce new structures that can generate new forms (a non-hierarchical, decentralised, delocalised network, etc.) bringing together artistic and social processes. The idea is to give publics 'agency', to foster their capacity for action and look beyond the limitations of traditional divisions between actor and spectator, and between producer and consumer.

At the MACBA, we aim to rethink the dominant conceptions of the public and experiment with other methods of cultural work based on other possible forms of mediation. This means rethinking and redefining the public in terms of the contributions of feminism, subaltern studies, queer theory and the experiences of new social movements. It also involves seeing publics as agents of transformation rather than of reproduction, thereby reaching beyond the present-day limitations of

6 See for example her introduction to *The Return of the Political*. London-New York: Verso, 1993.
7 Nancy Fraser, *Justice Interruptus: Critical Reflections on the "Postsocialist" Condition*. London-New York: Routledge, 1997.

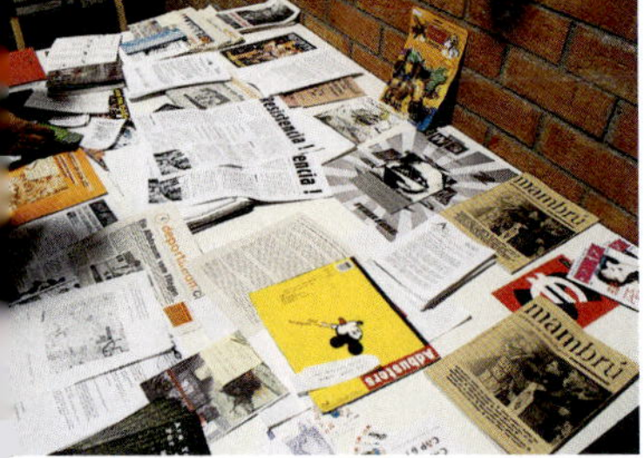

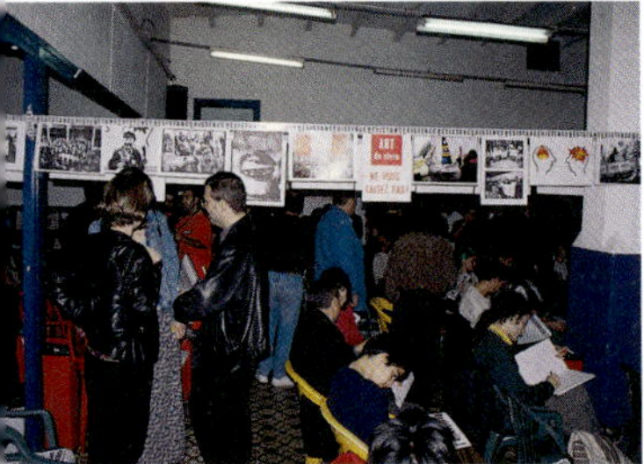

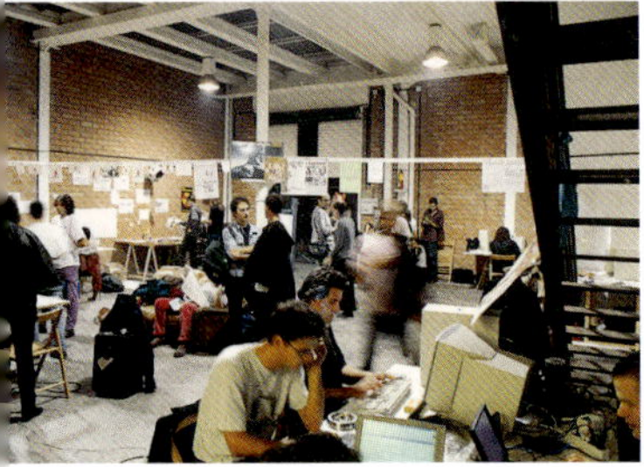

The Direct Action as one of the Fine Arts workshop, Barcelona, 2000

traditional political representation, based on a bourgeois conception of the public sphere.

The MACBA's experiments presented here are from the 2000–08 cycle. The central issue they all address is how to reinvent the artistic field as where social knowledge and action come together in the public sphere, using specific projects and constructing legitimacy as part of the process. These projects seek to develop a working method that has interiorised the demands of a democratic radicalisation inherent in the practices of institutional critique, and attempt to encourage the dissemination of spaces of criticism, freedom, play and experimentation in other institutional areas (schools or hospitals, for example), thereby extending the symbolic privilege of the artistic to other fields. These are contributions to an experimental public sphere with a deterritorialised conception of the museum, which is formed temporarily and provisionally by means of practice. To use the terms of Deleuze and Guattari, we could say that the idea is to introduce molecular spaces into molar structures. The experimental hypothesis is the possibility of constructing a new institutionality that is more in keeping with the conditions of forms of subjectivisation and the social experiences of our times and open to the future.

2. Agencements (2000–02)

The Direct Action as one of the Fine Arts workshops, which took place in autumn 2000, was the first attempt on the part of the Museum to set artist collectives and social movements to work together. It is important to grasp the singularity of the situation of social movements in Barcelona at this time and the way in which, since then, the MACBA's cycle of institutional experimentation has developed parallel to and inseparably from the cycle of social experimentation in the same period in the city. In addition to the long tradition of an active civil society in Barcelona (one of the singular features being the central role of the neighbourhood movement in the city's urban processes after democracy was restored in the late seventies), this moment coincided with the emergence of the movement for a civil society and global justice that broke out in Seattle in 1999. The movement triggered the series of mobilisations, which, in the following two or three years, gave way to the global resistance movement or anti-globalisation, a very broad-based, heterogeneous movement that came together at that time under the umbrella of debate about the negative effects of neoliberalism and the state of systemic chaos that capitalism had entered in the nineties.[8] This state

8 The notion of systemic chaos is taken from work by Immanuel Wallerstein and Giovanni Arrighi. See for example the works by Immanuel Wallerstein, *Historical Capitalism*. London: Verso, 1983; *Antisystemic Movements*. London: Verso, 1989; and the book by Giovanni Arrighi and Beverley J. Silver, *Chaos and Governance in the Modern World System*. Minneapolis: University of Minnesota Press, 1999.

reached its climax with the crisis in Argentina in 2001–02, which became the test ground for the future of neoliberal capitalism.

Discussion about direct action brought up to date by the global movement and its relation with politically involved artistic traditions (such as Situationism and its more directly antagonistic derivations) obviously formed the core of the project. As Ernesto Laclau suggests, political forms of self-organisation and direct action are a postmodern reaction to the limitations of traditional modern liberal bourgeois forms of political representation and a symptom of the structural dislocation of post-Fordist capitalism. Laclau refers to a 'spatialisation' of events as an alternative to the paradigm of modern temporality, based on a political programme projected into a permanently deferred future. This dislocation creates the potential for radical democracy by means of new policies of immediate intervention.[9]

The workshop was organised into five areas of work:

– New forms of underemployment and precarious labour. Here we were joined by groups such as Ne Pas Plier from Paris, which worked on starting up a new publication with local pro-basic income groups. Ne Pas Plier were known for the application of their designs to communication supports and intervention in public spaces, always in collaboration with groups of unemployed and underemployed people in the Paris region.

– Borders and migrations. Together with members of the Kein Mensch ist Illegal (No one is illegal) network, promoted by Florian Schneider, we worked with organisations for the rights of illegal immigrants on developing a criticism of the injustices derived from the dominant neoliberal ideology that favours mobility of the market and capital but restricts the social mobility of the working classes and accentuates social inequality. This debate gave rise to various Border Camps the following summer in the south of Spain.

– Property speculation and gentrification, with the participation of the Fiambrera Obrera group, based in Madrid and Seville, who also coordinated the workshop. They worked with Reclaim the Streets, famed for their imaginative strategies in environmental protests and carnival-type interventions in public spaces in England.

– The media was a theme running right through the workshop. The central idea was how to help generate new independent autonomous communication networks. This debate in the workshop produced the Indymedia network in Barcelona, the network that emerged from the Seattle protests and soon became a global figurehead for the movement. Here, we were joined by RTMark (later The Yes Men), which brought its experiences of

9 Ernesto Laclau, *Nuevas reflexiones sobre la revolución de nuestro tiempo*. Buenos Aires: Nueva Visión, 1993.

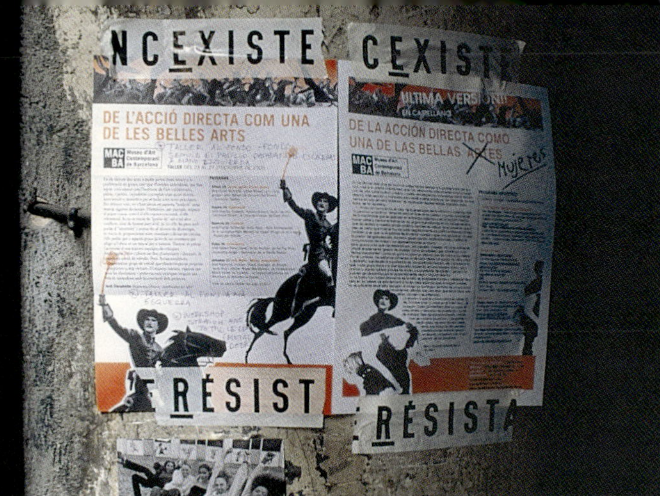

The Direct Action as one of the Fine Arts leaflet, 2000

tactical appropriation and distortion of corporate communication strategies, which had a great influence on subsequent local campaigns.

– Finally, another across-the-board theme were policies of direct action and the question of 'agency' or 'empowerment' as ways of reinventing emancipatory or revolutionary policies.

The aim of the workshop was to initiate processes to bring together local political struggles with artistic methods in order to create a continuum and constitute an institutional meeting point with the movements. It was successful in bringing together a broad spectrum of Barcelona's social movements at a very special moment for political dynamics. After a long period of relative standstill, new political experiences were emerging in the city, such as MRG (Movimiento de Resistencia Global), which was very active between 2001 and 2002, and which, despite soon breaking up, was the germ of a multiplicity of later initiatives.

The Direct Action as one of the Fine Arts workshop was the starting point for a more complex project that followed on immediately as a logical consequence: The Agencies, a project carried out in the first half of 2001.

The Agencies

The concept of agency was a recurrent theme at the Museum in those early years. We understood the concept of agency in two senses. One was to do with the idea of 'empowerment' – that is, giving publics power and autonomy, in keeping with the idea of plurality of productive forms of appropriation of the museum. The other meaning was that of micro-institution, a body that mediates between the museum and publics. The agency structure sought to create a molecular organisation of the museum with the aim of multiplying public spaces and processes of self-training by the various collectives involved in these agencies.

At the time, we defined The Agencies project as 'an element of mediation between narrative and public practices and subjects: that is, between the museum and the city' and as 'an activist project that uses the following methods: a) action or activity, related to certain social movements, which may materialise in events such as a party, the programming of activities or direct action, with the objective of generating democratic public space, of recovering the public sphere; b) workshops and debate as means of producing cultural resistance and c) the dimension of production rather than consumption'.

An understanding of the significance and impact of The Agencies requires a familiarity with the context of Barcelona in the months leading up to the World Bank Summit, planned for June 2001, but finally cancelled due to the organisers' fears of a violent reaction in the city. This was after the anti-globalisation protests in different cities such as Prague or Gothenburg, when protests were reaching a moment of maximum visibility and influence, which came to a head (and began its decline) in Genoa, also in July 2001. Genoa marked a turning point in the cycle of protests that began in Seattle in 1999, though we did not realise this at the time. Among other reasons, the effects of the New York attacks of 11 September 2001 had a decisive impact on the political pressure brought to bear on the movement as a result of an increasing criminalisation by the police and in the media, which ultimately determined its dynamic. That moment in 2001 was perhaps the movement's moment of greatest dynamism in Barcelona. Despite the cancellation of the Barcelona Summit, the counter-summit organised by the movements went ahead and The Agencies played a central role in the process, particularly in the design of communication and public profile strategies that transformed traditional methods of intervention on the part of anti-capitalist movements in the city.

The Agencies was an ongoing workshop, an experiment in self-education and also a proposed pedagogical method based on the assumption that learning is derived from immediate needs and takes place in a context of direct confrontation with real problems and protests. Learning is the result of the empirical need for effective solutions to specific problems.

There were five agencies:

– A graphic agency, which produced posters and printed matter for the counter-summit, like the 'Dinero Gratis' (Free Money) campaigns and posters against the World Bank that parodied official municipal campaigns.

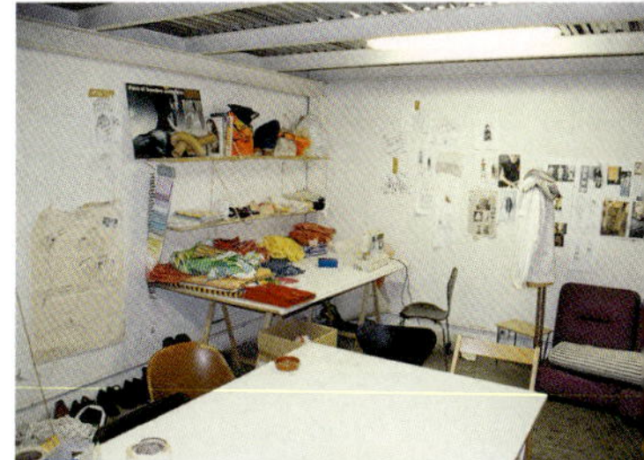

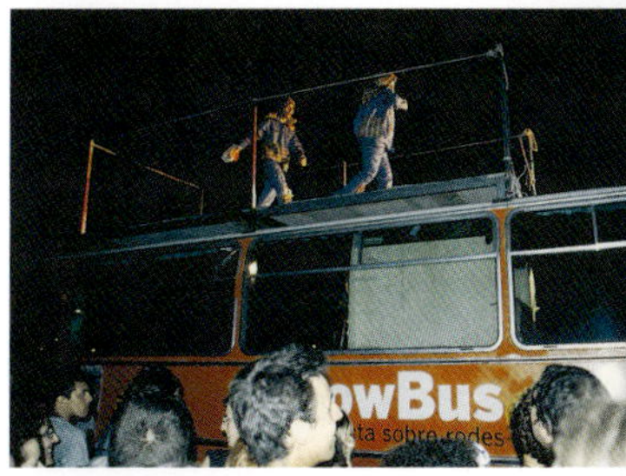

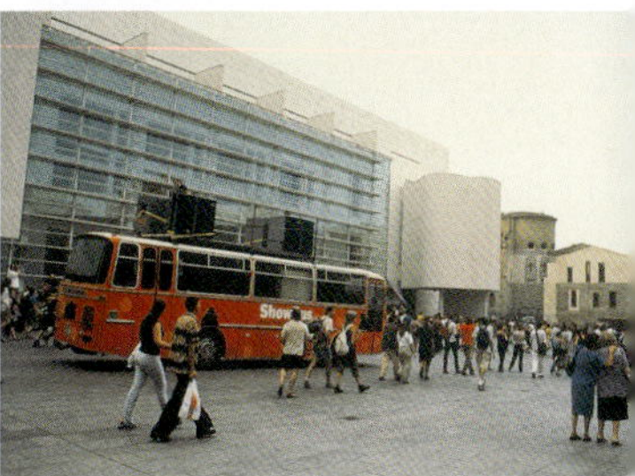

Workshop and Show Bus of The Agencies during the campaign against the meeting of the World Bank, Plaça dels Àngels, Barcelona, June 2001

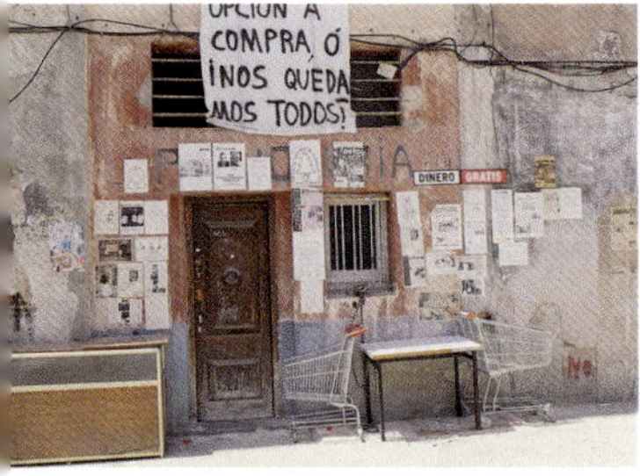

Poster of the 'Dinero Gratis' campaign, Forat de la Vergonya, Barcelona, June 2001

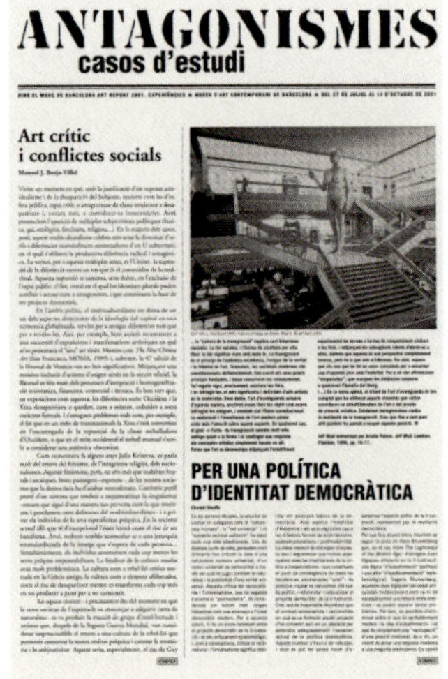

Neswspaper of the exhibition *Antagonisms. Case Studies*, MACBA, 2001

– A photography agency, which produced images and an archive for the various campaigns.

– A media agency, which was instrumental in the development of Indymedia Barcelona, and the magazine *Està Tot Fatal*, a communication and opinion-making instrument for the counter-summit.

– Another agency designed and produced tools for intervention in public space in protest situations. Inspired by the designs of Ne Pas Plier and Krzysztof Wodiczko, it developed projects such as *Prêt à révolter*, fashion for safety and visibility during demonstrations in the street, and *Art Mani*, a kind of photo-shield for protection against police charges designed to act as a photomontage in the illustrated pages of newspapers when photographed by reporters. There was also the Show Bus, a bus specially equipped with a sound system and video projection screens, which could be used as a mobile exhibition space for a variety of uses in public demonstrations or actions. All of these projects were visible and played their part during the events of June 2001 in the streets of Barcelona.

– Finally, another agency took over the running of the Museum's bar, which became a relational space, a place to eat and drink, but also a social space for events with groups, video programming and Internet access.

In addition to these projects, The Agencies involved the organisation of workshops with artists such as Marc Pataut (of Ne Pas Plier), Krzysztof Wodiczko and Allan Sekula. The workshops were organised to meet the needs of the groups involved in producing images and instruments throughout the various campaigns.

The Agencies took place at the Museum alongside two exhibitions, *Antagonisms. Case Studies* and *Documentary Processes. Testimonial Image, Subalternity and the Public Sphere. Antagonisms* was a major historical exhibition, presenting a series of case studies of moments of confluence of artistic practice, social movements and political activity in the second half of the twentieth century. For example, parts of the exhibition included a political reinterpretation of Minimalism from the radical materialist viewpoint of Carl Andre and a selection of the multiplicity of graphic work produced in the context of the AIDS protests of the eighties, involving collectives such as Act Up and Gran Fury; and the more recent work of Andrea Fraser, *Services*, which looks at the transformation of the productive status of artists in the context of a 'biennialisation' of the art scene, just to mention a few examples.

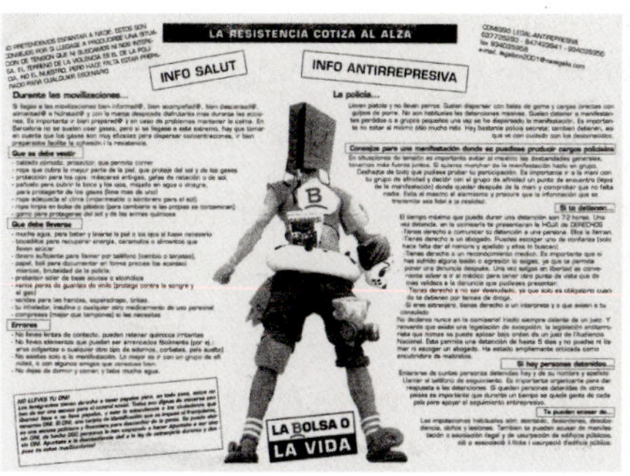

Leaflet of the campaign against the World Bank, June 2001

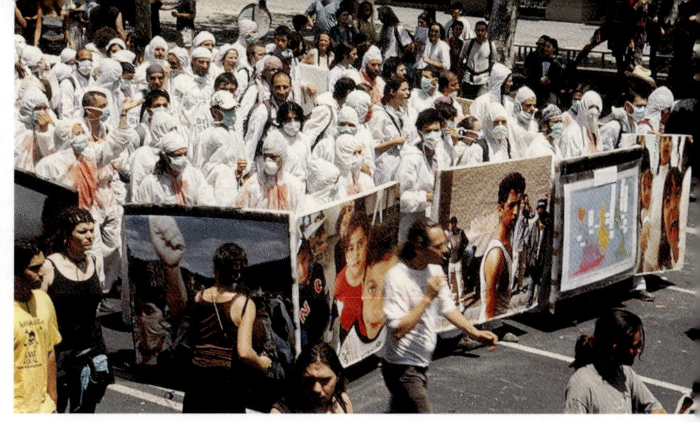

Tutti Bianchi's demonstration against the World Bank, Barcelona, 24 June 2001

Documentary Processes

The third element in this constellation was the exhibition *Documentary Processes*. The idea was to organise the exhibition as a form of direct action and therefore as an instrument for the counter-summit and the needs of anti-capitalist groups. Images were used to construct a criticism of the social consequences of neoliberal monetarist policies as a contribution to a different critical imaginary to the consensual images promoted by the institution, which served to render all conflict invisible or neutral. The exhibition was a reflection on the documentary as an artistic genre that has been historically constructed as a political genre, and sought to generate opinion and debate (with the potential for real political change), centring on the representation of subordinate classes and a denunciation of their precarious living conditions. It also set out to situate this historical debate in the contemporary context of the status of photographic and audiovisual representation in the digital age. The hypothesis underlying the exhibition was that in order to have a real political effect, the documentary required more complex processes of mediation, a task in which the method and theory of testimony could be instrumental.[10]

The exhibition presented a selection of photographic and audiovisual works as a basis for examining the transformation of the documentary genre by means of hybridisation with forms of narrative and mediation derived from the concept of testimony. Testimony is a narrative genre that serves to make the voice of subaltern classes accessible to other social groups, including the elites, by means of the figure of a mediator. As John Beverley explains, 'the problem of testimony is also that of representation and representativeness'; it can represent the possibility of a democratising alliance between the intelligentsia and the popular classes without subordinating the heterogeneity of groups to official representation. Testimony emerges in

10 *Documentary Processes. Testimonial Image, Subalternity and the Public Sphere*, MACBA-La Capella, Barcelona (summer 2001). This exhibition is documented in the publication *Institut de Cultura: La Capella, Temporada 2001* (Barcelona: Ajuntament de Barcelona, 2002) and at www.macba.cat (with the participation of Roy Arden, Ursula Biemann, Marcelo Expósito, Patrick Faigenbaum and Joan Roca, Harun Farocki, Marc Pataut, Andrea Robbins and Max Becher, Allan Sekula, Frederick Wiseman).

a context of crisis of representativeness among old political parties and is inseparable from the emergence of postmodern forms of constructing political identities by means of 'new social movements'.[11]

In the context of the crisis of photographic and audiovisual representation in the digital age, the documentary has to come up with other strategies of resistance to legitimise a form of realism or 'representativeness' in order to preserve the critical, transforming potential of the image, which is the genre's precondition. In this sense, the notion of testimony is vital in that it involves a different working process that establishes negotiation between subaltern and dominant cultural positions, giving rise to a new relation of collaboration between an author and social subjects. This process involves a transformation of the figure of the author and his/her position and function. The collaborative dimension establishes an alliance between subjects

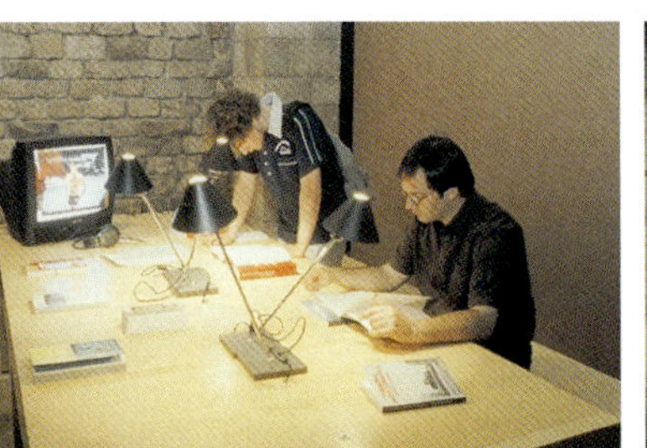
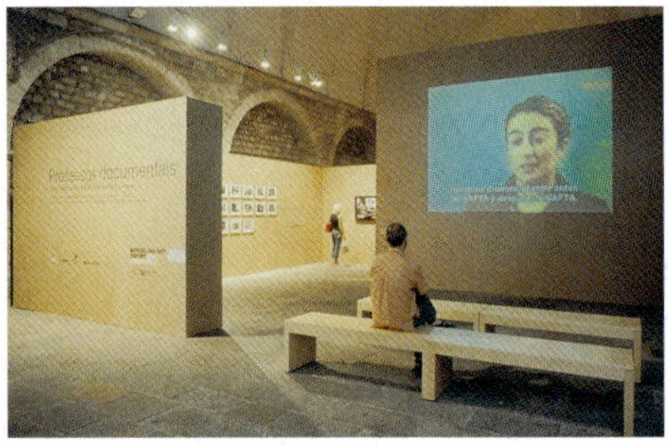
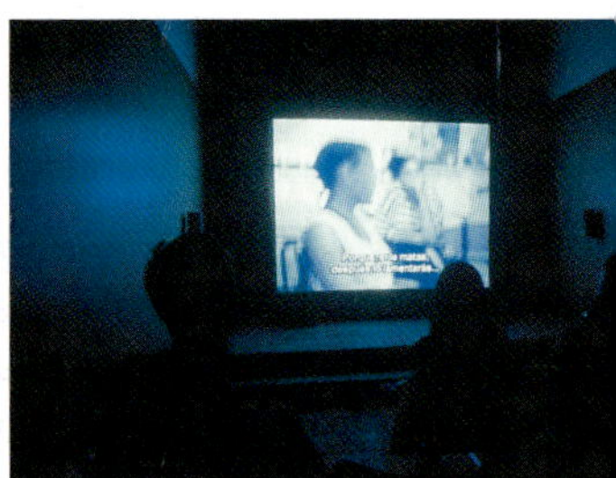

Documentary Processes exhibition, La Capella, 2001

that breaks with the implicit hierarchy of forms of pious, victimistic representation that characterise the paternalistic humanism of the classic documentary.

In the exhibition, the works were the product of a will to construct images that present historic and geopolitical conditions in which some subaltern groups are living today. It is evident that economic and cultural globalisation and financial capitalism have legible effects on some transformations of cities and the public sphere. These include the growing privatisation of public services and the crisis in public welfare policies, the speculative remodelling of urban space, new forms of exploitation and precariousness at work, and the rise of the service and tourism economy affecting the way cities represent their histories, supplanting singular identitary features with a simulacrum of history and an indistinguishable blur. At a time like this, it seems absolutely vital for the image to maintain a representative value and a realist ethic, so that it can stand up to the trivialisation of the real into mere effect and preserve all its potential by narrating the experience of historic processes.

11 John Beverley, 'Introduction', in John Beverley and Hugo Achugar (eds.), *La voz del otro: testimonio, subalternidad y verdad narrativa.* Lima-Pittsburgh: Latinoamericana Editores, 1992, pp. 7–18.

The theme of the document and the historic project of realism in this institutional process at the MACBA will be recurrent and reappear later on, at the end of this itinerary.

Relational spaces

What were the effects of these projects?

Evidently, they generated a public perception of the Museum as a space of debate and criticism. Anti-capitalist groups saw in the Museum an antagonistic space in the institutional framework, as shown by the spontaneous organisation in the Plaça dels Àngels, outside the Museum, of a circus against the European Community Summit, in March 2002, with which the Museum itself had nothing to do.

There were also effects at other levels. Indymedia Barcelona became a permanent structure contributing to a transformation of the discourses and communication methods of social movements. The year 2001 was also a watershed for the graphic campaigns of the city's movements. Most importantly, however, these projects contributed to a new political imaginary in the institutional field, which was then still resisting theorisation. It was possible to see an incipient new institutional space that broke with the traditional geometries of the social contract by means of new forms of alliance and asymmetrical collaboration between anti-institutional movements and the Museum. Rather than social processes being given an aesthetic makeover or deactivated, this generated a newly created collaborative space in which the Museum began to form part of social struggles. This took institutional critique to a new dimension.

What were the implications of this experimentation inside the Museum?

At this same time, a project that explored the redefinition of the protocols of use of the expository space and its hybridisation with non-traditional visibility mechanisms was the exhibition about the work of Pere Portabella, *Plotless Stories. The Films of Pere Portabella*, which ran at the Museum in early 2001. The exhibition combined the exhibition device with those of a self-service consultation audiovisual and bibliographic archive, a cinema and a programme of activities including an audiovisual cycle, a seminar and a series of lectures. While providing a discursive structure for a historic narration of the relevance of Portabella's work as a filmmaker in the context of the new cinemas of the sixties and seventies, the device left room for other possible constructions or readings of the same body of work and period. For this it used both the programme of lectures (during which guest speakers suggested these other constructions) and

Leaflet for the campaign against a Europe for Capital and War, 2003

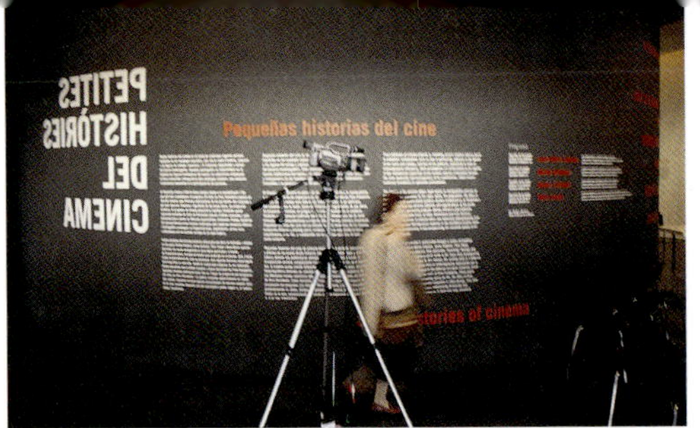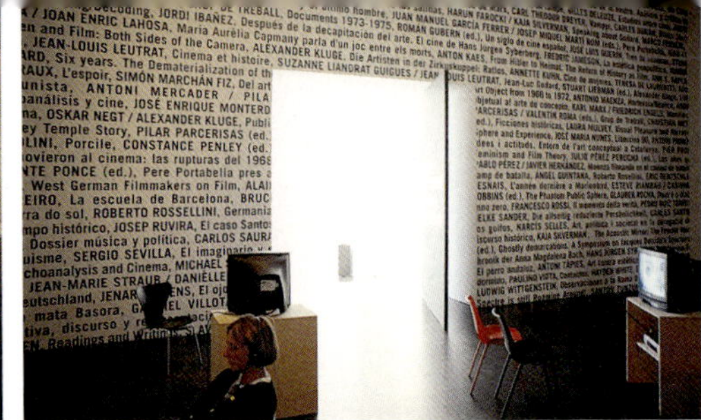
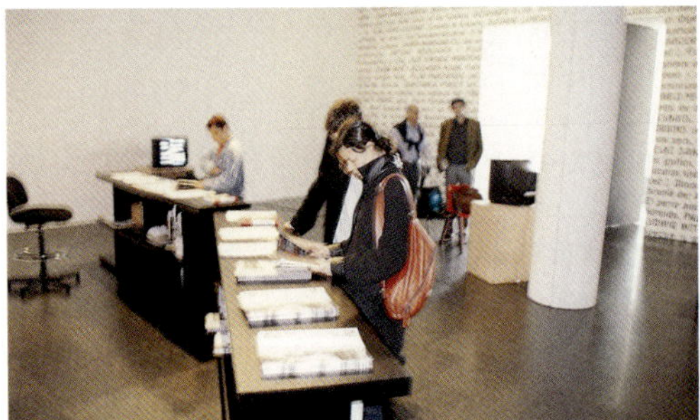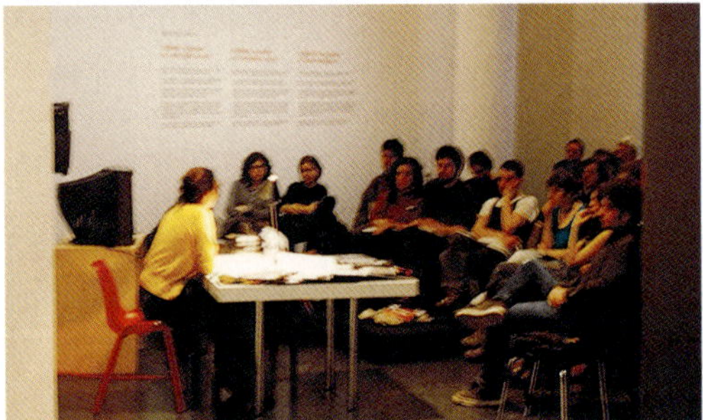

*Plotless Stories. The Films of
Pere Portabella* exhibition, MACBA,
2001

the self-consultation materials, allowing users to construct their own narrative. The device thereby avoided fetishising and mythifying the figure of the artist, and freezing his historic role by means of the logic of tribute; instead, it encouraged reinterpretation by leaving it open to other workings, present and future. This project could be seen as an example of how the museum can learn from criticism, in this case the practices of institutional critique (those of Michael Asher, Hans Haacke or Marcel Broodthaers, among others), and transform itself in a rather more transparent context that is open to interaction. In a sense, it also 'demuseumises' itself, or frees itself of some of the more rigid, authoritarian historic legacies that resist change.[12]

This experience gave rise to the video and film programme *Good Vibes. The Politics of Resistance and Music Cultures*, which ran from February to July 2002. It was the result of a literal interpretation of the phrase 'They came to dance, but ended up getting an education', which was used to promote the film *Thank God it's Friday*.[13] The programme was organised as a look at some of the movements or styles of popular or consumption music over the last three decades, with particular emphasis on social and political aspects in the formation of these styles. *Good Vibes* was presented in two formats, offering different forms of use: a programme of screenings and a self-service consultation unit.

It is no coincidence that the subject of *Good Vibes* was the subcultures surrounding different musical styles, which constitute a material setting for some of the social practices theorised in the radical democracy project and at the Birmingham School

12 For more information see the publication coordinated by Marcelo Expósito, *Historias sin argumento. El cine de Pere Portabella.* Valencia-Barcelona: Ediciones de la Mirada-MACBA, 2001.
13 Quoted in Jeremy Gilbert and Ewan Pearson, *Discographies. Dance Music, Culture and the Politics of Sound.* London: Routledge, 1999, p. 1.

of Cultural Studies.[14] This interest in popular or consumption music formed part of the redefinition of borders between popular and elite cultures. This does not mean that the differences no longer exist; rather that we cannot explain them by taking for granted the traditional elitist function of high culture, seen in an ideal, universalist sense. Here, we can learn from practices such as punk, which bring together strategies of avant-garde art (Artaud, Fluxus, actionism and extreme uses of the body associated with the most radical performance tradition), commercial culture (the record industry and its star system) and, as witnessed in the early eighties, political activism (the expression of rebellion by a generation of youths who suffered the first cutbacks in the welfare state with the advent of the neoliberal hegemony of the Reagan-Thatcher governments in the English-speaking world). This condition of an artistic practice that, depending on the context, functions alternatively as high or low culture involves a new, non-essentialist understanding of contemporary art and culture.

The different styles become attempts to create relatively autonomous public counterspheres in response to given contexts using the material culture available. As far back as the seventies, punk expressions such as 'no future' or 'do it yourself' heralded what Laclau was to define as the 'specialisation' of politics, referred to earlier.[15] We also see how the practice of raves that emerged in Thatcher's neoliberal England led to new carnival-style practices of political protest and public expression, now the habitual tools of anti-globalisation movements. Furthermore, music subcultures have been a breeding ground for the networks of communication and distribution outside the established circuits of commercial culture. They are also a favourable medium for the formalisation and expression of practices of transgression of identity by means of mechanisms and corporal habits that subvert the dominant codes of gender identity, in the form of clothes, tattoos and drugs, alongside new theorisation about the performative and socially constructed nature of gender identities.

Finally, music subcultures are also a prime opportunity to reflect on the ambivalences and contradictions of culture as a counter-hegemonic space of resistance and transgression in the face of the neutralising capacity of commercial culture. The idea, then, is not to idealise the space of consumption music as an advanced utopian social laboratory, but to understand this musical area as a singularly eloquent setting for the ambiguities and contradictions inherent in culture in global multicultural capitalism, where the supply/demand of instant gratification and the ideal of individual freedom promote permanent transgression. However, this endless transgression is balanced out

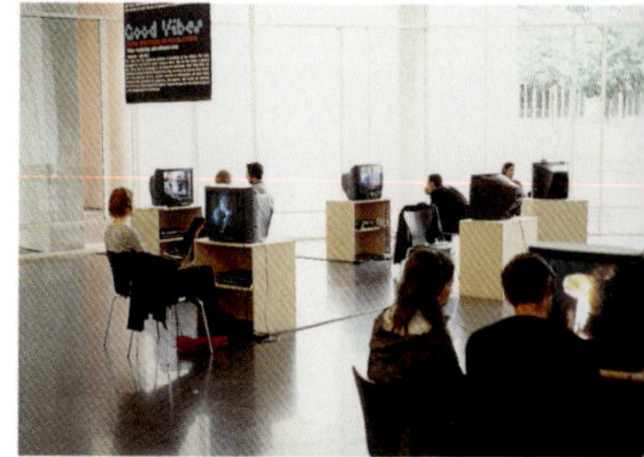
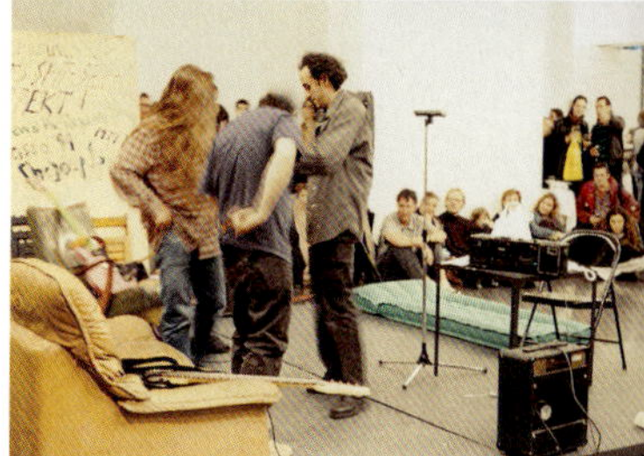
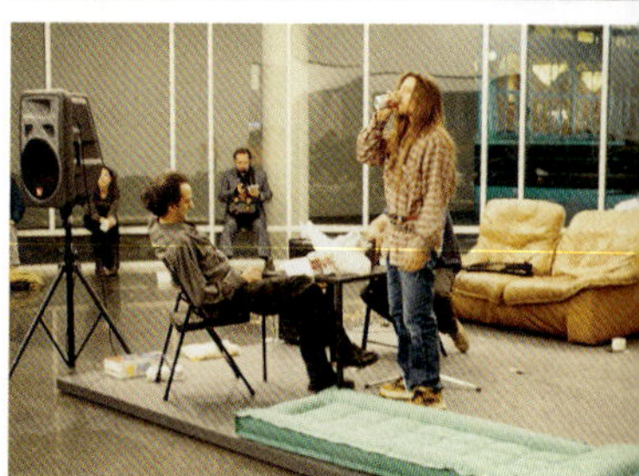

Good Vibes, 2002 and Sir Drone's performance, opening of *Raymond Pettibon*, MACBA, 7 February 2002

14 The canonical study is the work of Stuart Hall and Tony Jefferson (eds.), *Resistance through Rituals. Youth Subcultures in Post-War Britain*. London: Routledge, 1993.
15 Laclau, op. cit.

by the permanent assimilation and neutralisation undergone by an equally endless demand, a kind of mercantilisation and consumption of subversion. This constant demand for something different leads to its opposite: homogenisation. This complex tension between resistance and reproduction has to be the basis for thinking of new ways of working in the field of culture.

3. Another relationality (2003–06)

The Barcelona 2004 Universal Forum of Cultures was an event promoted by the City Council to draw together the economic, political and media resources needed for a major urban renewal of the city (in this case centring on the Besòs seafront, thereby finishing the process begun with the 1992 Olympic Games), with culture as an alibi. It took place in the summer and, in itself, the event signified new forms of interpenetration of culture, politics and economics in the post-industrial age and, more specifically, of the exploitation of culture to legitimatise neoliberal policies for international promotion of the city. The City Council's choice of this event formed part of a strategy of urban growth based on big events, given the city's condition of capital without a state. The Forum represented a change of scale for the city, expansion beyond metropolitan limits, and was the biggest urban transformation since 1992, in a city whose modern urban history has been marked by the celebration of major international events since the 1888 Universal Exposition.

Forum 2004 was part of a global phenomenon of the transformation of Western urban economies to the tertiary sector that began in the late seventies with the first industrial crisis, when tourism became one of the principal economic objectives. In this process of capitalist restructuring, the new urban economies in the post-industrial or post-Fordist age have granted culture a major new role as a production sector. Various theorists have charted the process, from Fredric Jameson in the early eighties, with his well-known writings on postmodernity, to David Harvey or Antonio Negri and Michael Hardt more recently, to mention just a few. Jameson describes the process as a transformation in which 'everything... can be said to have become cultural'.[16] The concept of 'cognitive capitalism' has emerged to denote this process of coming together of new information and communication technologies with immaterial, creative, relational and affective labour, which is acquiring new centrality in the cultural industries and breaking the traditional opposition between leisure and work. Capitalism 'sets subjectivity to work', as Paolo Virno says in his paradigmatic analysis.[17]

16 Fredric Jameson, *Postmodernism or, The Cultural Logic of Late Capitalism*. Durham, N.C.: Duke University Press, 1991. See also David Harvey, *The Condition of Postmodernity*. Cambridge, Mass.: Blackwell, 1990; Antonio Negri and Michael Hardt, *Empire*. Cambridge, Mass.: Harvard University Press, 2000.

17 See his books *Virtuosity and Revolution: The Political Theory of Exodus*. Minneapolis: University of Minnesota Press, 1996; and *A Grammar of the Multitude: For an Analysis of Contemporary Forms of Life*. New York: Semiotext, 2004.

The economic model outlined for twentieth-century Barcelona was that of a tertiarised, creative city based on design industries, what the municipal government called 'the city of knowledge'. A great deal of municipal institutional propaganda went into creating a high profile idealisation of this economy of knowledge and 'immaterial labour', involving new forms of self-employment in the cultural industries and the emergence of a new self-employed working class that was highly qualified but also over-exploited and impoverished in precarious conditions: the cognitariat.

Forum 2004 brought with it a massive new deployment of the institutional propaganda machine, continuing in a more radical vein the logic instigated in the run-up to the Olympics in the late eighties. The technique of managing consensus using idealised images of the city also seemed to respond to growing social pressure from the middle and working classes, who were having difficulty maintaining the material conditions they had acquired in the latter half of the twentieth century.

In this context, with the idea of offering a countermodel to the Forum of Cultures, in autumn 2004 the exhibition *How do we want to be governed?*[18] ran successively in changing formats in various sites in the Poblenou-Besòs area, on the outskirts of the Forum 2004 site. It was an exhibition in process, involving a museum method based on a combination of artistic work and social dynamics. The task of the curator was to dialogue with city collectives, in this case the neighbourhood movement in the area around the Besòs, the Fòrum de la Ribera del Besòs.

The exhibition process began formally in January 2003 with a series of debates at the Museum entitled *From Les Glòries to the Besòs. Urban change and public space in the metropolis of Barcelona*,[19] organised in the context of the Muntadas exhibition, *On Translation*. Muntadas's project involved a debate about the cultural translation that could be extrapolated to the transformations under way in the city, the privatisation of public space and the loss of density and historic memory in the neoliberal metropolis. The series of debates was an attempt to analyse and publicly debate the situation in Barcelona immediately prior to the Forum 2004, with the participation of its principal institutional and social agents. This programme of debates was the visible beginning of a process of collaboration with local groups and neighbourhood movements in the Poblenou-Besòs area, particularly the Fòrum de la Ribera del Besòs, an umbrella for many social movements in the area that accommodated the Forum.

The social flipside to the advertising campaigns promoted by the City Council on the occasion of Forum 2004 perhaps

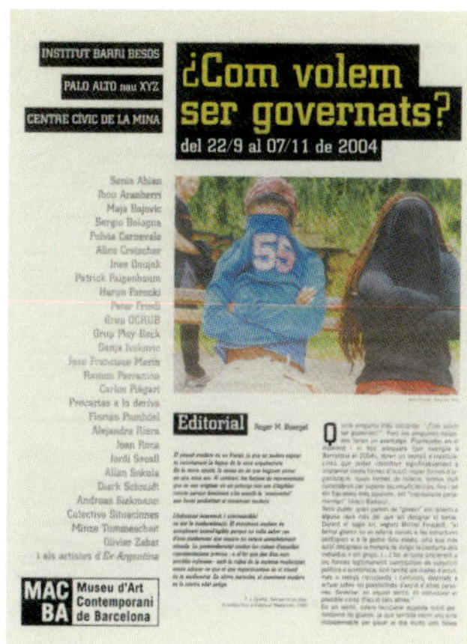

Newspaper of the exhibition *How do we want to be governed?*, MACBA, 2004

18 *How do we want to be governed?*, IES Barri Besòs, Palo Alto, Centre Cívic La Mina, 22 September– 7 November 2004. With the participation of Sonia Abian, Ibon Aranberri, Maja Bajevic, Sergio Bologna, Salvador Clarós, Alice Creischer, Ines Doujak, Miren Etxezarreta, Patrick Faigenbaum, Harun Farocki, Grup Taifa, Sanja Iveković, Paco Marín, Ramon Parramon, Carlos Piegari, Precarias a la deriva, Florian Pumhösl, Alejandra Riera, Joan Roca, Dierk Schmidt, Jordi Secall, Andreas Siekmann, Colectivo Situaciones, Mercè Tatjer and Minze Tummescheit. 19 *From Les Glòries to the Besòs. Urban change and public space in the metropolis of Barcelona*, public debates from 13 January to 13 March 2003, with the participation of Jordi Borja, Paco Marín, Salvador Clarós, Rafael González-Tormo, Mercè Tatjer, Eugenio Madueño, Oriol Bohigas, Josep Maria Montaner, Eduard Bru, Llàtzer Moix, Rafael Encinas, Eugeni Forradellas, Emili García, Ferran Sagarra, Marcelo Expósito, Josep Lluís Mateo, Muntadas, Ramon Parramon, Jaume Pagès, Josep Ramoneda, Joaquim Espanyol and Joan Roca.

reached its peak in the new forms of communication that emerged with the reactivation of social protest in Barcelona between 2000 and 2004, a process that has yet to be sufficiently explored. The movement took form around three major successive campaigns: in June 2001 against the meeting of the World Bank, in March 2002 against the European Summit, and the campaign against Forum 2004. At local level, these campaigns saw a radical transformation in the forms of communication and public intervention of the new social movements, and generated a wealth of experimental complexity in the field of intervention in a context that was strongly mediatised by institutional advertising. Social movements gained a new awareness of the centrality of the image and the symbolic in social conflicts in post-industrial capitalism.[20]

How do we want to be governed? was set in this climate of mobilisation as part of the critique of the logic of the big event, such as Forum 2004, as cultural policy and presented itself as a countermodel. In similar fashion to The Agencies, though in a very different metropolitan and global context, the project sought to foster collaboration between the institution and new social movements. Here, it is important to understand the widespread popular rejection of the Forum by the city itself, both by the more classic neighbourhood and social movement and new anti-globalisation or anti-capitalist trends, and by broad sectors of unorganised civil society. Such a broad-based rejection was not directed solely at the falsely participative populist rhetoric that the Council tried to use to create a soft discourse on multiculturality; it also corresponded to a widely shared social need to create a breach in the image of consensus and point out the deficiencies, contradictions and myths inherent in the neoliberal tertiary model. This was symptomatic of civil society's demands for open debate about the urbanistic and economic model of tertiary, extrovert city adopted by local authorities, and of a mistrust of the model's social consequences. This social mistrust was corroborated in late 2004 by the failure of the Forum not just as a convincing, significant cultural event (which it never was), but also, to use its own terms, as a driving force of economic and social revitalisation for the city.

In autumn 2003, we had set up a collaboration network with anti-Forum movements, based on the experience gained in previous years, principally in The Agencies, and drawn up a strategy for programming public events in the city that would highlight the activity of the movements and their organisational capacity. The idea was to constitute a temporary public countersphere in the context of a city subject to an all-pervading insti-

20 There are publications that document this cycle of new social movements in Barcelona between 2000 and 2004. Special mention should be made of: Unión Temporal de Escribas (UTE), *Barcelona marca registrada. Un model per desarmar.* Barcelona: Virus Editorial, 2004; Various authors, *La otra cara del Fòrum de les Cultures S.A.* Barcelona: Edicions Bellaterra, 2004; and Enrique Leiva, Ivan Miró and Xavier Urbano, *De la protesta al contrapoder. Nous protagonismes socials en la Barcelona metropolitana.* Barcelona: Virus Editorial, 2007.

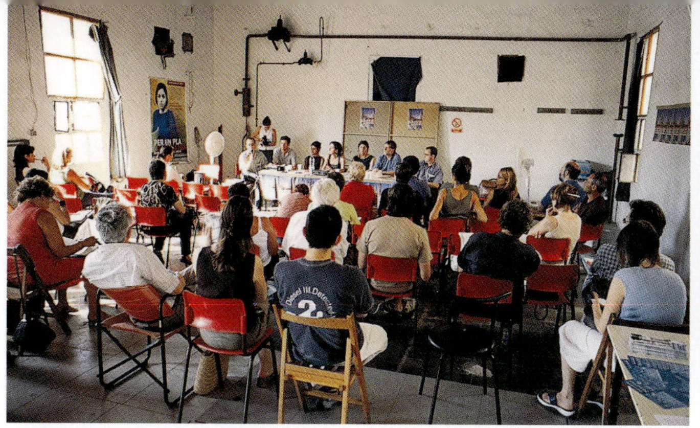

I Jornada llegat industrial i innovació,
La Escocesa, Barcelona, 30 June 2003

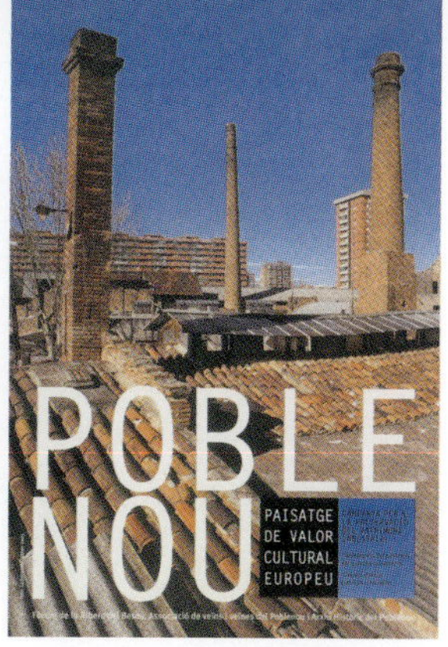

Poster of the campaign for the
conservation of the Poblenou industrial
heritage, Grup de patrimoni del Fòrum
de la Ribera del Besòs, 2003

tutional propaganda machine. In November, we presented a
seminar called *Constructing the Public. Artistic Activity and
New Social Protagonism.*[21] Taking part, among others, were
members of the Argentine collective Situaciones, whose theory
had had a major influence on the experiences of popular mobilisation and self-organisation during the Argentine crisis, followed with close attention by social movements in Barcelona.[22]
The seminar also involved Paolo Virno, whose intervention took
the form of an itinerant programme in various institutions and
spaces of the new social movements in the city. In March 2004,
we presented a seminar with Immanuel Wallerstein and, in April,
another with Antonio Negri, once again travelling to various venues in the city. This cycle culminated in a seminar on decentralised communication and activism in late April,[23] coinciding
with the celebration of EuroMayDay and with the keynote participation of Naomi Klein. Klein's participation was strategic to
the movement because she had received an invitation to take
part in Forum 2004. Her refusal of that invitation and her agree-
ment to take part in the EuroMayDay seminar helped to dele-
gitimise the Forum and denounce its incapacity to connect with
the social movement.

How do we want to be governed?

How do we want to be governed? was curated by Roger Buergel
and founded on notions of governability presented by him and
based on readings of Giorgio Agamben and Michel Foucault. It
came together in an exhibition from September to November in
various spaces in the Poblenou-Besòs area, presented as an
alternative, deterritorialised model of the museum, constituted
in activity rather than as a prelegitimised, predetermined space.
Its metropolitan setting sought to highlight local histories that
had been forgotten or crushed by hegemonic versions of the
city's history. The project's work with local collectives in the Fòrum

21 *Constructing the Public.
Artistic Activity and New Social
Protagonism*, 28 and 29 November
2003, with the participation of
Roger Buergel, Alice Creischer
and Andreas Siekmann, Colectivo
Situaciones, Alejandra Riera,
Catherine David, Michael Warner,
Marina Garcés, César de Vicente,
Brian Holmes and Georg
Schoellhammer. The seminar
with Paolo Virno took place from
1–5 December.
22 As shown in the book by Colectivo
Situaciones, *Argentina. Apuntes
para el nuevo protagonismo social.*
Barcelona: Virus Editorial, 2003.
23 *The Revolution (will not be)
Televised. Conference on the
Decentralised Communication
of Activism*, 30 April 2004. With
the participation of Carles Ameller,
Franco Berardi 'Bifo', Amador
Fernández-Savater, DeeDee Halleck,
Naomi Klein, Avi Lewis and
José Pérez de Lama. Coordinated
by Marcelo Expósito.

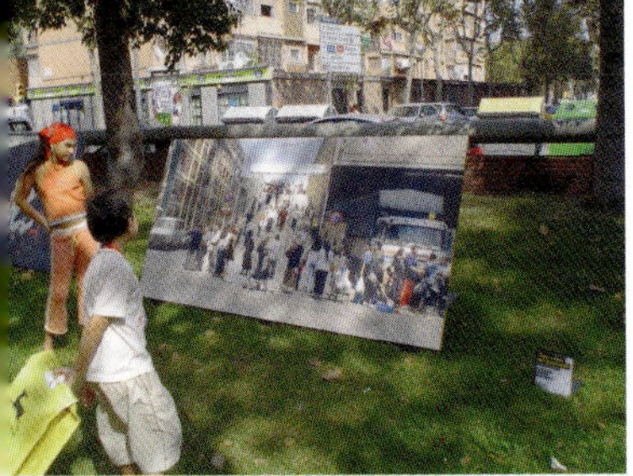

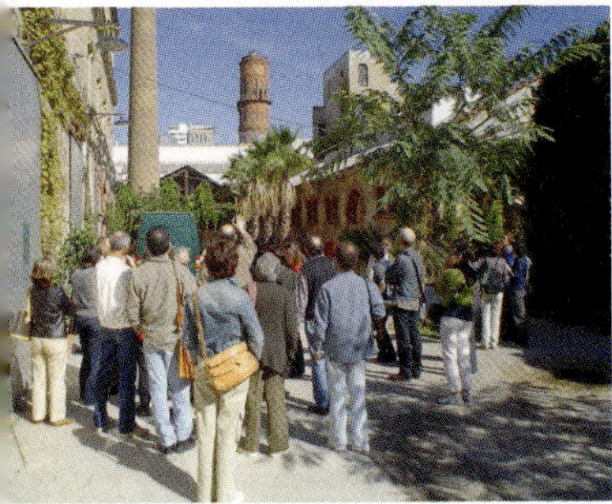

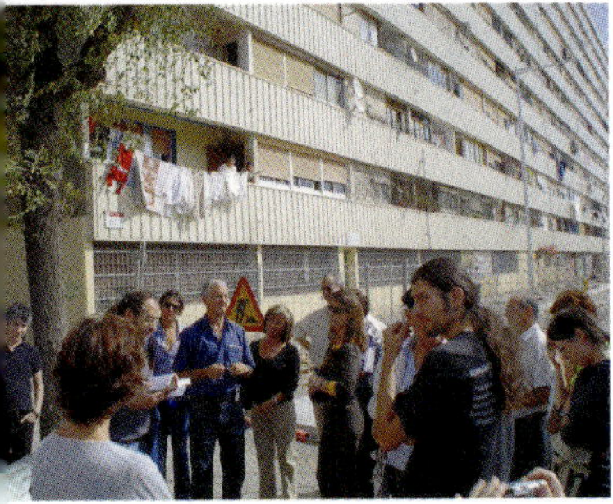

Photographs by Patrick Faigenbaum in Rambla Prim and urban routes around Poblenou and La Mina, as part of the exhibition *How do we want to be governed?*, autumn 2004

de la Ribera del Besòs was organised as a 'bottom-up board of trustees' that reproduced the organisational structure of the museum, redirecting it towards the participation of sectors of civil society that are politically active but do not constitute the political and economic elite that tend to form a museum's board of trustees. The working process took the form of meetings and discussions with the curator and local collectives to outline the exhibition and particularly the commissioned projects involving the local 'anchorage' of the exhibition and, therefore, critical reinterpretations of dominant urban histories and imaginaries. The commissioned projects (undertaken by Patrick Faigenbaum and Joan Roca in the Besòs, Sonia Abian and Carlos Piegari in Poblenou, and Ramon Parramon and Paco Marín in La Mina) aimed to showcase historic struggles for the memory of labour and industrial heritage, public services and facilities, precarious labour and the reconstruction of modern local political utopias associated with the political activity of the various social and historical union movements, among others. The recovery of the city's invisible popular memory resisted the potential homogenising, amnesiac effect of Forum 2004.

The exhibition was staged in various public spaces in the Poblenou-Besòs area and organised as a route through the city. This route took place in both space and time. The different spaces that hosted the exhibition opened and closed successively, like a constantly changing stage set. The exhibition layout generated a context for a programme of public activities (debates and lectures, performances, screenings) that took place in expository spaces and other places in the area.

The route began in a school, the Institut d'Educació Secundària (IES) Barri Besòs, which had played a major role in providing public services for the district and a meeting place for social movements. It continued to a historic industrial space that is now in use for tertiary production (Palo Alto, in the important Carrer Pellaires complex) and the Centre Cívic La Mina, a cultural centre that is characteristic of the social democratic urban planning of the eighties in Barcelona, in a neighbourhood that historically embodies the shortcomings and inequalities of public policies in the metropolitan area. The route ended at a shopping mall that is emblematic of both the privatisation of new public spaces and unforeseen forms of social appropriation: Diagonal Mar. This itinerary, with its discontinuities and tensions, represented a reading of the city's history that formed a counterpoint to the dominant imaginary and aimed to draw out other images and reconstruct subaltern histories that have been cast by the wayside by the hegemonic construction of the modern metropolis.

The content of the exhibition was organised according to three themes:

Firstly, modernity seen as a category that is not exclusively universal, but that incorporates specificities or anomalies in the way it takes place in different parts of the world: industrialisation, urbanisation, secularisation, individualisation, bureaucratic administration, and so on.

Secondly, neoliberal immanence and the passage from Fordism to post-Fordism. What kind of post-Fordist mentalities do we find in different parts of the world? What lessons can we learn from the local in a transnational dialogue? The revival of pre-modern phenomena such as radical regionalism was of particular interest here, though rather than ethnic districts within multicultural metropolises, the focus was on the relations between diasporas and origins.

Thirdly, the state of exception as a norm (the total mobilisation of subjectivity in post-Fordism, or 'subjectivity set to work') and the discourse of the radical subject, theorised by Agamben and Virno.

The themes were monographically developed with relative independence in the three respective venues.

The exhibition at the IES Barri Besòs centred on the issue of good government, using the reproduction of an allegorical mural by Lorenzetti, and staged the device of the art exhibition as a means of political intervention. It did so using documentation of a historic cycle of art exhibitions presented in non-artistic spaces. These included the 1968 Latin American Art Biennial at the headquarters of the Confederación General de Trabajo de Rosario, in the context of the Conceptualist experiences of the *Tucumán Arde* cycle, and Alice Creischer and Andreas Siekmann's *ExArgentina* project, about the 2001–02 crisis in Argentina, presented some months previously at the Ludwig Museum in Cologne[24] as institutional therapy right after a G-8 summit held in the same venue. Another was an artistic experience that had taken place at the IES Barri Besòs itself in 1989, in the context of a conference about the future of city peripheries, marking the foundation of the area's neighbourhood movement and the formation of the Fòrum de la Ribera del Besòs.[25] While telling this micro-history, the exhibition was presented in the school as part of this tradition of constructing spaces of confluence between art and the social movement, at the same time centring on the issue of the exhibition as a medium and a public space.

Set in a former Poblenou factory, Nave XYZ in Palo Alto, the exhibition staged the movement towards post-Fordism and neoliberal immanence using the metaphor of workers leaving

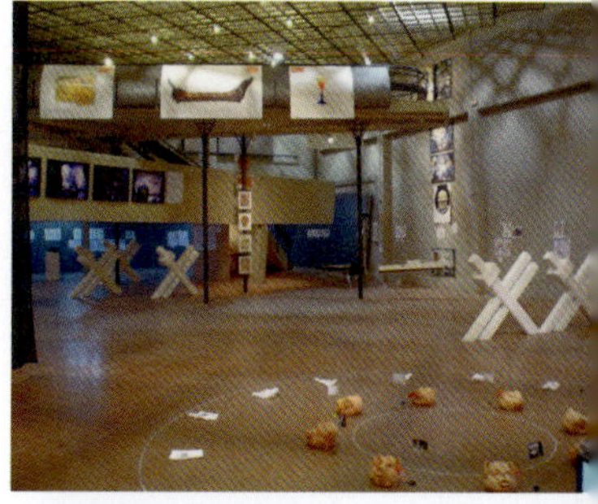

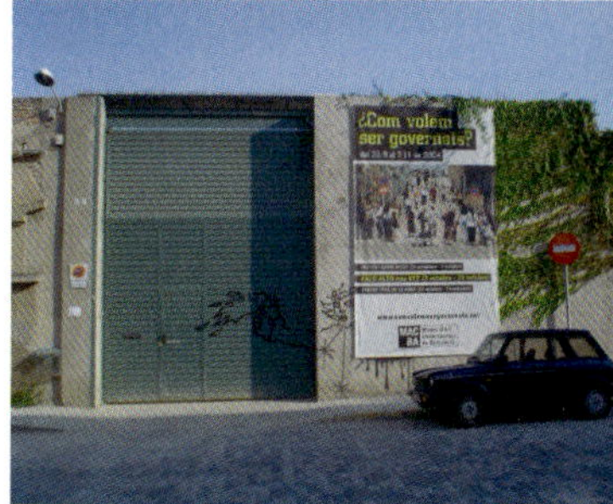

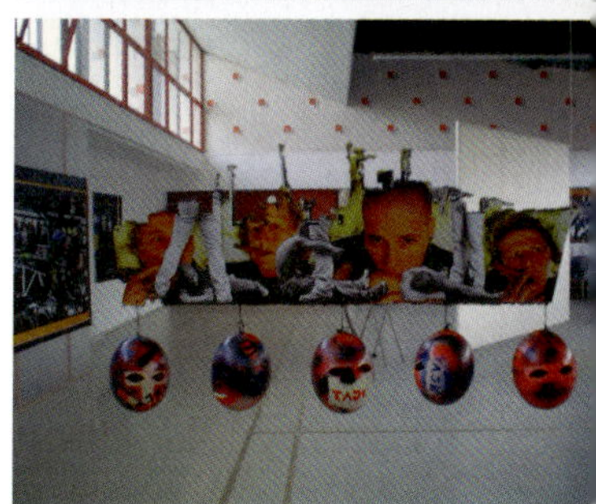

How do we want to be governed?, IES Barri Besòs, Palo Alto Nave XYZ and Centre Cívic La Mina, 2004

24 See www.exargentina.org.
25 See the publication produced as a result of this experience, Joan Roca (ed.), *El futur de les perifèries urbanes. Canvi econòmic i crisi social a les metròpolis contemporànies*. Barcelona: Institut de Batxillerat Barri Besòs, 1994. The conference and exhibition took place 10–13 May 1989.

the factory, one of the images marking the birth of the cinema and the subject of a work of the same name by Harun Farocki (also archive research into the memory of this foundational moment in the cinema in the twentieth century). The image of workers leaving the factory brought together various meanings. The first was the documentary tradition as an artistic and political genre historically involved in the representation of new subjects of the masses and social movements. Then it was a metaphor of the change to post-industrial economy and post-Fordist production and sociability, of the change from proletariat struggles to the new protests of self-employed, cognitariat workers. It was also an allusion to social life after work, to the 'night of the proletarian', to the time for culture and political education, for self-organisation, pointing to the inseparable confluence of education and politics in movements for emancipation. In this case, it was also an allusion to the memory of the worker movement and, by extension, to the present-day struggle for Barcelona's industrial heritage.

Finally, the exhibition at the Centre Cívic La Mina presented the idea of the state of exception as a norm, in the form of a monographic presentation of the *ExArgentina* project, by Creischer and Siekmann.

At the metropolitan scale, this exhibition was determinant to the organisation of citywide debate about industrial heritage (which was the catalyst after Forum 2004 for debate about the city's model of growth, centring on the Can Ricart campaign). At the scale of the Museum's work, meanwhile, its consequences were determinant to the revision of education programmes. The experience at IES Barri Besòs pointed out the need to form a more complex, organic part of the field of education, transposing the spaces of experimentation from the field of cultural institutions to the field of education institutions. The Museum had to go into the school curricula. This was also a way of radicalising the premises of institutional critique, opening up to other institutional spaces than the museum.

The reorganisation of education programmes also involved the Museum offering training at all education levels, including the university, and thereby contributing to the training of professionals in the field of culture. This was the origin of the Independent Studies Programme.

Political education

In his lecture as part of the *How do we want to be governed?* programme, Sergio Bologna judiciously raised the key question in this age of flexible accumulation, self-employment and tertiary economies: where and how does political education take place?[26]

26 'How do We Want to be Self-employed Workers?', a lecture given on 30 September 2004 at the IES Barri Besòs.

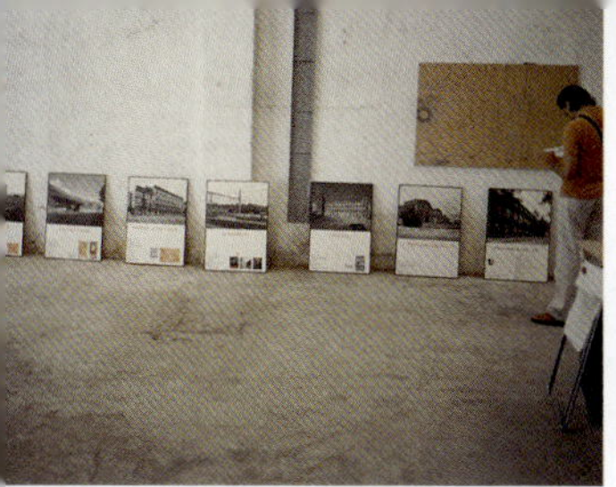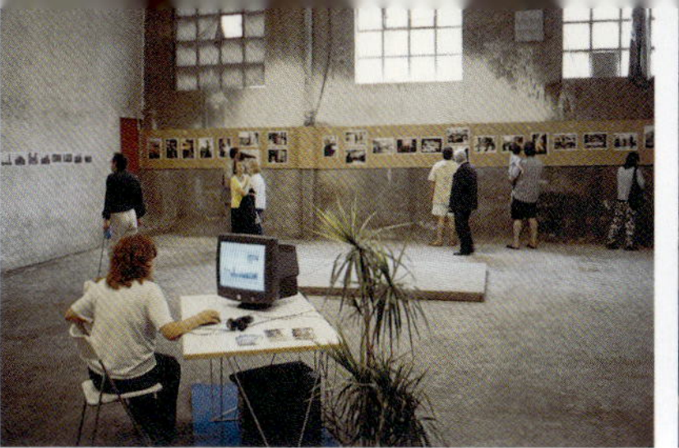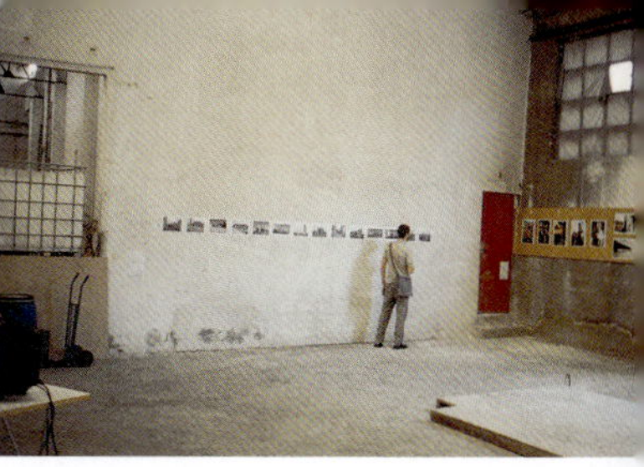

Photography exhibition at Can Ricart
as part of Open-doors Day, 11 June 1005

In Fordist capitalism, the factory, as well as being the place of production, was the space for political education. Conflict was inseparable from innovation; historical knowledge and social agitation were the two sides of the coin. With the new centrality of self-employment in post-industrial capitalist production, an entire political culture generated in the factory disappeared. Post-Fordist flexibility demands processes of self-training and continuing education, but leaves a question mark hanging over the venues for political education. Nonetheless, the education imaginary is still modelled by the culture of full-time factory work, no longer the dominant form of employment: 'we are no longer in a situation in which 'emancipating thought' can be disseminated by a laborious task of training', and therefore, as Bologna concludes, the construction of new spaces for political education is now the fundamental task. The will to take on this task was the starting point of the MACBA's Independent Study Programme (PEI), which started in January 2006.

How can a discussion about the museum as producer of historiographic narratives be linked to the aspirations and responsibilities of a political education, of a 'perverted pedagogy' inspired by René Schérer and Jacques Rancière?[27] Though very different, the two cases are attempts to denaturalise the area of institutional education and manifest some of its premises, particularly the way in which the education framework constructs its own subjects and reproduces existing conditions of inequality by means of rigid divisions. Drawing together these two debates makes a critical understanding of the historic task of the museum inseparable from a likewise critical pedagogy that is capable of challenging the existing framework and restoring the links between the fields of science, education, art and culture. This means contributing to the conditions needed for the emergence of other subjects – other publics.

The confluence of historiography, collecting and education has another sense. Education is patently one of the most basic, fundamental forms of heritage and was crucial to the progress of the popular classes in the twentieth century. In this sense, the debate about heritage is linked to the potential of

27 René Schérer, *La pedagogía pervertida*. Barcelona: Editorial Laertes, 1983; Jacques Rancière, *The Ignorant Schoolmaster. Five Lessons in Intellectual Emancipation*. Stanford: Stanford University Press, 1991.

a museum's collections to transform, not merely reproduce. The challenge lies in exploring new ways of managing common heritage in a dialogue with social subjects and, in the process, bring down the existing administrative and social borders. At that point, it seemed necessary to insist that the often condemned distance between contemporary arts and society is a breach constructed by the administrative organisation of the various state competencies into culture on the one hand, and primary and secondary education on the other and, on yet another, further education and research. This division of competencies between three different administrations has decisive consequences for the insertion of the artistic in the everyday lives of people and reproduces a separation that effectively deprives citizens of a fundamental potentiality in their personal training, which will affect them for the rest of their lives. While these structures remain administratively separate, it will be difficult for art to escape from the ghetto of the market and the culture industries, and to formulate itself socially in a different way to how it does today.

The Museum had seen the consolidation of various discursive lines that have emerged from previous years' work in different workshops and programmes. In 2005, we undertook a new organisation of these programmes (critique of discourse, gender studies, new social movements, economy, critique of therapies, urban studies, artistic historiography, etc.), with the intention of consolidating a unitary organisation that would shape a Study Programme. However, rather than reproducing the academic structure, the idea was to create another type of complex model that would respond to a coming together of academic training, theoretical research and practice, social interaction and cultural intervention. The aim was to develop a completely new way of bringing together intellectual and academic practice with social practice and the public sphere, beyond the established disciplinary fields of art and theory.

In this sense, the PEI sought to incentivise the capacity for action in the field of professional activity based on a critical approach to art and culture. Taking as its basis a conception of the artistic field as production, drawing together different social systems and individual knowledge, it aspired to produce activity that could question the framework established by neoliberal technocracy. We realised the necessity of reconsidering the significance and importance of the museum as an institution that emerged historically from the enlightened project of popular education. The field of museum studies therefore became inseparable from criticism of the processes of construction of knowledge and their politics.

Another relationality

In autumn 2004, coinciding with *How do we want to be governed?*, a new presentation of the collection opened at the Museum with the generic title *Relational Poetics*, prompting reflection on the texts by Édouard Glissant about the poetics of relation as a criticism of or alternative to an essentialist conception of cultural identity. The exploration of relationality continued with the exhibition *A Theatre without Theatre,* which extended the debate to the issue of theatricality as the repressed side of post-war artistic modernity, according to the dictum of the great formalist critics such as Clement Greenberg and, in particular, Michael Fried, whose canonical essay *Art and Objecthood*[28] constitutes the purest late-modern formulation of the radical opposition between modern visuality and the theatre.

This line of work on relationality and theatricality explored the hypothesis of a possible relational paradigm as a criticism of the representational model of the museum's work, which submits its public activity to a visual paradigm, the central device of which is the exhibition. In this respect, and as an attempt to go beyond the limitations of representation and promote spaces of experimentation that further processes, activity and debate rather than their objectification in works of art, the relational model could be a useful theoretical and practical framework.

The concept of relationality formed part of the working method of *How do we want to be governed?* and later took the form of a two-part seminar entitled *Another Relationality*, which took place in November 2005 and March 2006.[29] Relationality was a concept that allowed us to make an openly controversial intervention in the debate about art institutions and their publics, restoring the political density to a concept that was used to defend a soft pseudo-organisation of artistic and social phenomena and create a simulacrum of participation based on the trivialisation and spectacularisation of the concept of antagonism as a constituent part of the social space. We, conversely, saw the relational as a space for the art that questions a hyper-legitimised institutional autonomy, investigating new forms of interaction with the social, though without seeking to over-stage them.

We had to rescue the relational debate from the aristocratic ghetto of 'relational aesthetics' of Nicolas Bourriaud and his Palais de Tokyo, which seemed to us to be a perverse objectification of both political activism and the new forms of immaterial, affective, communicative and relational production of post-Fordism. Capitalism penetrates into subjectivity and sets it to work, and, in this way, the traditional modern idea of culture

28 Michael Fried, 'Art and Objecthood', *Artforum*, no. 5, June 1967, pp. 12–23.
29 *Another Relationality. Rethinking Art as Experience*, with the participation of Alexander Alberro, Leo Bersani, Claire Bishop, Bernard Blistène, Jesús Carrillo, Helmut Draxler, Kaja Silverman, Beatrice Von Bismark and WHW, 25 and 26 November 2005; and *Another Relationality (part 2). On the Cure in Times Devoid of Poetry / On Poetry in an Age that has no Cure*, with the participation of John Beverley, Antonella Corsani, Marcelo Expósito, Brian Holmes, kpD, Maurizio Lazzarato and Suely Rolnik, on 17 and 18 March 2006.

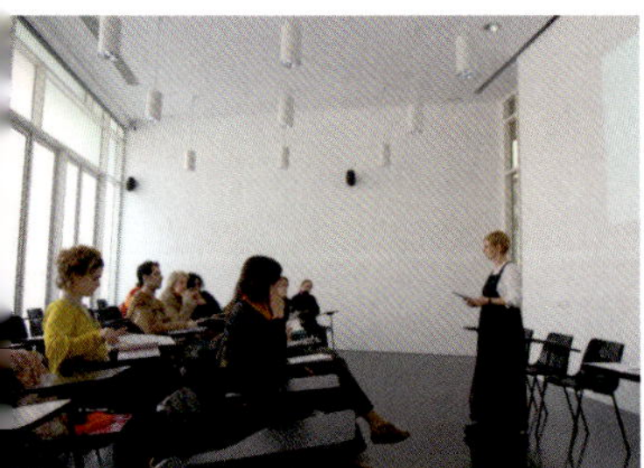

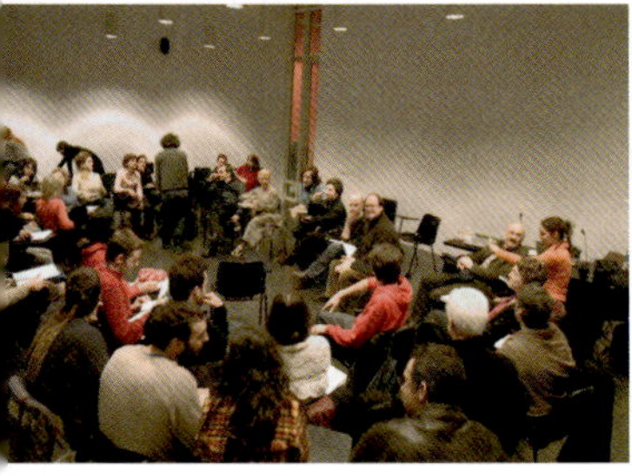

Seminar *Another Relationality (part 2)*, MACBA, March 2006

and art as an independent sphere, set apart from instrumental reason, is plunged into an irreversible crisis. The crucial issue tabled by the debate about relational art seemed to be precisely this: how to reinvent artistic autonomy in a context where this autonomy appears to be unthinkable. As we saw it, Nicolas Bourriaud's relational aesthetics corresponds to a superficial, soft and falsely consensual conception of artistic experimentation, which is actually immobilist and regressive in that it 'aestheticises' the immaterial communicative paradigm and its implicit social and creative processes, imposing an expository regime that interrupts their mobility, and freezes and makes fetishes of practices. Hence the search for 'another relationality', a search that is inseparable from the search for 'another artistic autonomy'.

However, relationality was not just a debate about the social space in museums: as a fundamental epistemological question it is inseparable from discourses that are critical of the various forms of essentialism. As Leo Bersani explains, 'notions of social relationality have, at least since Descartes, been determined by the privileging of epistemological concerns over questions about the nature of being. Following Heidegger and his critique of Cartesian epistemology, we would reverse this priority, although by being we of course do not mean an ontological essence or entity, but rather something like a principle of universal connectedness. A modern reflection on being must be aware of itself not as an approximation of metaphysical truth; rather, the ontology most congenial to an age of information is one that identifies being as relationality, as the principle of connectedness assumed by all technologies of transmission, as well as by the social imaginary that can refract or violate it.'[30]

Bersani defines the relational subject as being constituted by and as positions of subject, stripping of meaning the opposition between subject and object. Art, Bersani continues, 'illuminates relationality by provisionally, and heuristically immobilising relations'.[31] From the viewpoint of the Museum, we saw the relational as a space for art that temporarily suspends preconstituted institutional autonomy and investigates new forms of interaction with the social, though without seeking to overstage this process. We saw the museum as a space for this experimentation, not solely or principally to exhibit it. We tried to find ways in which art could make a significant contribution, based on its specificity, to a multiplication of public spheres.

Having reached this point, from the perspective of work done, we also considered that some caution was needed with regard to the relational paradigm in order to avoid a determin-

30 Interview with Leo Bersani, at www.macba.cat/uploads/ 20051107/ bersani_eng.pdf (accessed December 2009).
31 Leo Bersani and Ulysse Dutoit, *Caravaggio's secrets*. Cambridge, Mass.: The MIT Press, 1998, p. 72.

istic logic or a teleological view of relational art as the historical superseding of artistic autonomy and liberal forms of aesthetic and political representation. After several years of institutional experimentation, we could see how radical practices (which we had attempted to theorise under the umbrella of 'another relationality') can pave the way for the emergence of regressive new forms of populist, communitarian cultural policy, which have to be shown up and criticised. We found that governments of social democratic descent (though actually neoliberal) appropriate to themselves the language of radical experimentation and promote communitarian forms of socio-cultural management, the effects of which are highly perverse and destructive for public life. This context gives rise to pseudo-artistic proposals that tend to replace political forms of organisation and representation of civil society with new forms of cultural management and marketing. This process turns political, juridical and social questions into cultural questions, consequently proposing their management by strategies of socio-cultural facilitation. In this way, the cultural appears as a synonym of consensual space, of false social homogeneity, with universalist, pre-political connotations. An example at the large scale of this process in Barcelona was Forum 2004. But this logic also operates on the small scale, and possibly much more perversely. In short (and this concerns those of us who think that this experimentation is fundamental to the construction of civil society and democratic public space), radical experimentation in combining the aesthetic and the social movement can pave the way for the reappropriation and consensual, aesthetic resignification of these experiments by the new pseudo-progressive neoliberal technocracy, thereby leading to their annulment. We have to be aware of this risk, and our immediate challenge would seem to be to find ways of avoiding it without, evidently, relinquishing radical experimentation.

In our promotion of debate about relationality, evidently we do not aim to reproduce that which we were criticising – that is, consensual communitarian logic – without restoring political density to artistic activity, and not just in its 'relational' forms. It is therefore necessary to warn of the dangers of the relational discourse. Avoiding communitarianism means promoting positions of differentiation and the visualisation of antagonism. The idea was to conceive of a relationality that annulled neither the conflict nor the space of the other, nor the potential for difference of the artistic space.

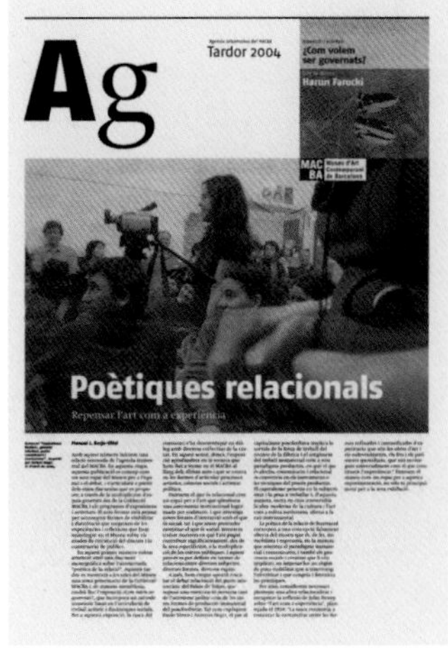

Cover of the *Ag*, Autumn 2004

Disagreements

The experience of a metropolitan institutional network that was asymmetrical in nature as a form of public intervention, the organisational method behind *How do we want to be governed?*, was translated to the state scale and an explicitly historiographic project with *Desacuerdos* (Disagreements), an institutional collaboration between 2003 and 2005.[32]

Desacuerdos emerged from the will to construct a historiographic countermodel that went beyond the academic discourse and helped to lay the basis for the reconstruction of a possible critical cultural sphere at state scale. How do we go about producing a historiographic narration of the singularity of artistic modernity in Spain, an unorthodox modernity that is inevitably linked to the political and social avatars of the last century? To what extent can cultural institutions contribute to new processes of radical democratisation of society? What meaning and utility was there in a new historiographic account produced by cultural institutions, when civil society was showing clear symptoms of revitalisation in the face of growing economic and state authoritarianism? These were some of the questions behind the desire to rethink ways of telling our history of art of the last half century, in opposition to established versions.

It was impossible to produce a critical historiographic account of given artistic policies without implementing different models of cultural management. It therefore seemed crucial to us to implement a process of research[33] with a decentralised network structure involving cultural institutions of various kinds, which activated working dynamics that reached beyond institutional limits, so that other critical areas of culture could operate without being subsumed or conditioned.

The exhibitions at the MACBA and the Centro José Guerrero de Granada granted a foremost role to the notion of archive and document as alternative elements to complement traditional artworks, necessary to a reading of history and the present, and they were presented as a visibilisation of the research process. They also reflected the work of groups, collectives and associations, which were put on a level with the individual author. An important part of *Desacuerdos* was given over to public debates, meetings and activities by the protagonists, scholars, collectives, groups and associations that carried out artistic and social practices.

This expository visibilisation did not set out to be a literal or sole translation of the research process, however. Research had produced multiple discourses and brought to light largely unknown or overlooked phenomena, aspiring to redefine what had hitherto been a subaltern history. But this was by definition a contradictory process. Not all practices can be translated to

32 *Desacuerdos. Sobre arte, políticas y esfera pública en el Estado español* (Disagreements. On art, politics and the public sphere in Spain), a research project coproduced by Arteleku-Diputación Foral de Gipuzkoa, MACBA and the Universidad Internacional de Andalucía–UNIA arteypensamiento, along with the exhibition and activities coproduced by the same institutions and the Centro José Guerrero-Diputación de Granada. **33** The results can be seen at www.desacuerdos.org and in the publications *Desacuerdos 1* and *2*.

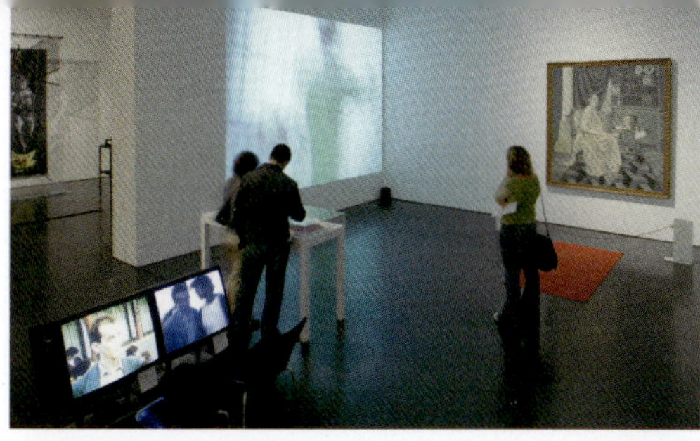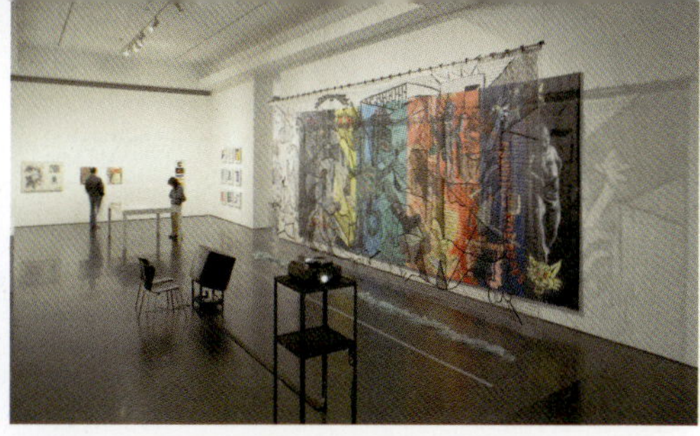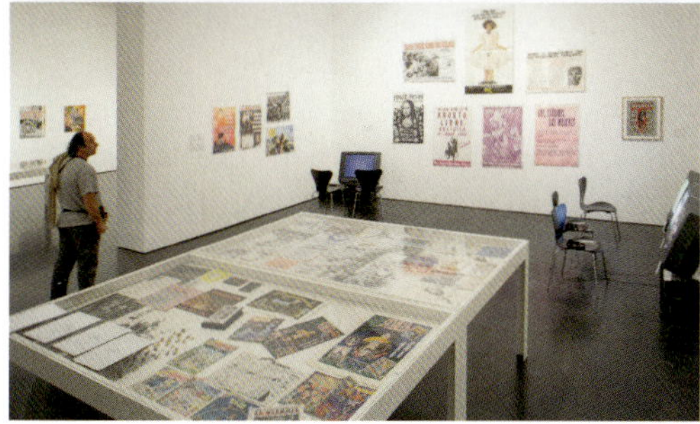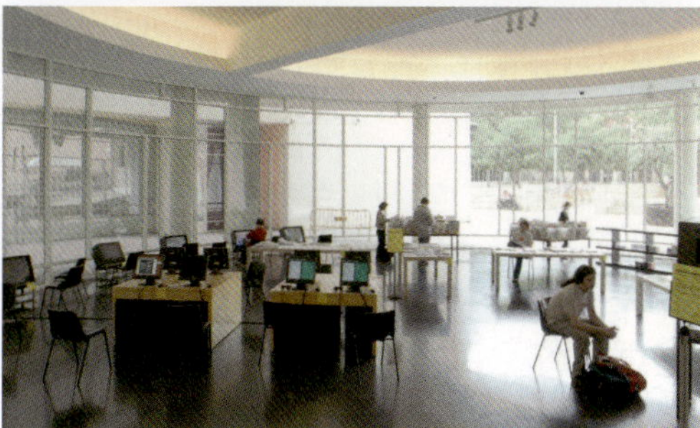

Desacuerdos exhibition, MACBA, 2005

an exhibition space, which in itself proposes a model for experimentation and knowledge that converts practices into objects. This is an important consideration in that one of the difficulties addressed by *Desacuerdos* is precisely the difficulty or impossibility of representing that which has come into being with the aim of being unrepresentable, of breaking with the given conditions. How, in an institutional exhibitionary framework, can we render visible antagonistic, process-based and experimental practices that seek to explode the established institutional frameworks and their implicit disciplinary divisions, such as for example the division between creativity and art – that is, between subjective forms of appropriation and practice of methods and artistic knowledge and the exhibitionary-institutional monumentalisation of these practices? This project embraced the paradoxes and difficulties of combining action and representation, intention and materiality, and therefore constituted historiographic investigation of a context that was close and distant, familiar and unknown. But it was also a self-critical reflection on the conditions and relations of the power of institutional knowledge and the limits of the museum.

The exhibition covered a historic period spanning the last three decades. Despite following a chronological order, however, it was presented not as a single itinerary but as a broad time framework with various possible itineraries or chronologies that were more or less continuous while also presenting discontinuities. The idea was to present a multiplicity of possible historiographic organisations of the period, thereby subverting the logic of the single hegemonic account. The objective was not to replace one account by another, but to manifest a multiplicity of potential stories.

4. Molecular museum (2006–08)

During this period, we had constant recourse to the notion of institutional critique. We saw it as a tradition of artistic practices at the museum to emerge from the transformations of the sixties, which aspired to lay bare the institution's working conditions and implicit power relations, particularly in the expository device. Here, institutional critique appears as the continuation of the modern enlightened tradition that sees the museum as a space for popular education. At the same time, it represents a self-critical break with this tradition. Institutional critique is the representation of the antagonism that constitutes the social space within the museum and corresponds to a pluralist understanding of the public sphere. Insofar as institutional critique is a translation of liberal democracy within the museum, it configures the museum as a model of the democratic public sphere.

The results of the various projects undertaken by the Museum in this process of experimentation are uneven, but they do serve to show the true limits of institutional critique, the limits of the museum itself. These limits are, firstly, the notion of representation and, secondly, the administrative and organisational forms to which the museum is subject as a part within a larger state structure.

Experimentation with the shift from a representational to a relational paradigm was one of the Museum's central tasks in this process of self-critical exploration. At this point, however, we could say that the vocation of institutional critique involved its socialisation beyond the limits of the museum. If institutional critique remains limited to the museum and the exhibition, it could easily become a new formalism. The vocation of institutional critique is to go beyond its own limits and contribute to the construction of new institutions, new practices and new rules. We at the Museum were able to contribute to this process, which is why we sought to bring down the institutional borders that exist between different fields.

We realised that the radicalisation of institutional critique involves its de-institutionalisation – it has to be removed from the museum to contribute to a new global institutional framework that takes into account demands for democratic radicalisation. We need to reinvent institutions. The big question these

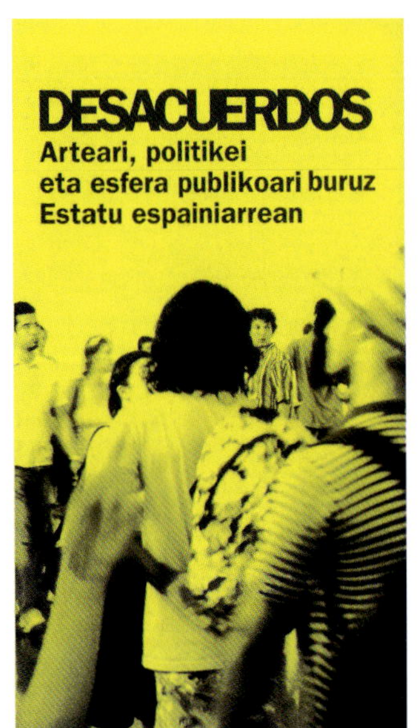

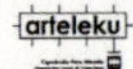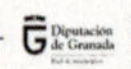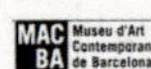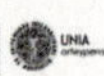

Leaflet of *Desacuerdos* at Arteleku, 2005

days is how to effect a transition from a culture of resistance to a culture of management, how to translate the radical artistic and social experiences of recent years into an effective form of management that does not lose the potential to transform.

Photographic survey

In 2006, in the framework of the PEI, we undertook another project that aspired to intervene in the space of the city beyond the walls of the Museum and bring up to date previous forms of intervention in the new specific conditions of the moment. This was a time marked by a cooling off of the social movement, the breakdown of the social democratic urban planning project and the noticeable absence of a project on a metropolitan scale for the new century. Our aim, then, was to contribute to the city-wide debate about the state of the city, post Forum 2004, this time with a project to photograph the emerging city and help to shape the city of the twenty-first century.

The project took the form of a photographic survey. It set out to address the debate about the city and its image in the misnamed post-photographic age. We thought that in a context that discredits photographic realism, due to new technologies such as Photoshop and digital photography, it was more necessary than ever to defend the photographic document and stand up to acceptance of the discourse on the death of photography, which is actually an attack on its indexical, realistic and documentary dimension. As we see it, in a situation that is tending to naturalise the end of photographic realism by means of discourses about the 'post-photographic age' or the 'death of photography', the decisive question is whether photography without realism is possible and relevant. We know that the history of photography is the history of a hybrid, contradictory but inherently realistic medium, which is inseparable from its documentary dimension, the representation of historical reality. A photograph without realism is an irrelevant, dead photograph that has lost its historic mission and its capacity to create opinion and induce social transformations. We did not consider this a desirable condition for photography. The challenge facing us was therefore to explore how photography can retain social relevance at a time of crisis for photographic realism. This gave rise to the need to invent methods to re-establish the link between the image and historic reality in a way that incorporated self-criticism. The challenge consisted in producing practices in which realism was restored and reinvented in a complex process of negotiation. The impetus for this project was not nostalgia but the pure need to recover the field of representation of self-referential debates and, therefore, to recover the possibilities of

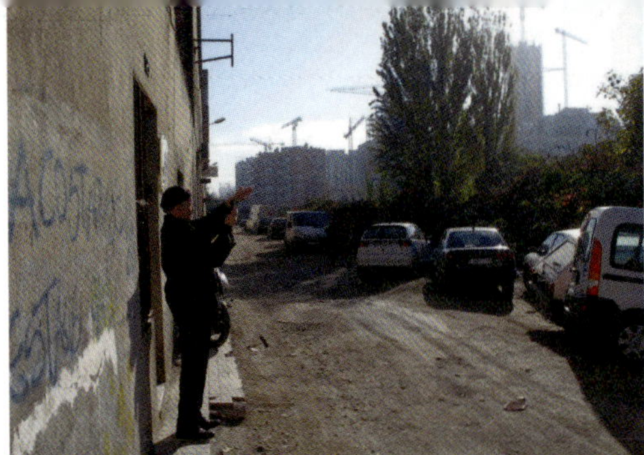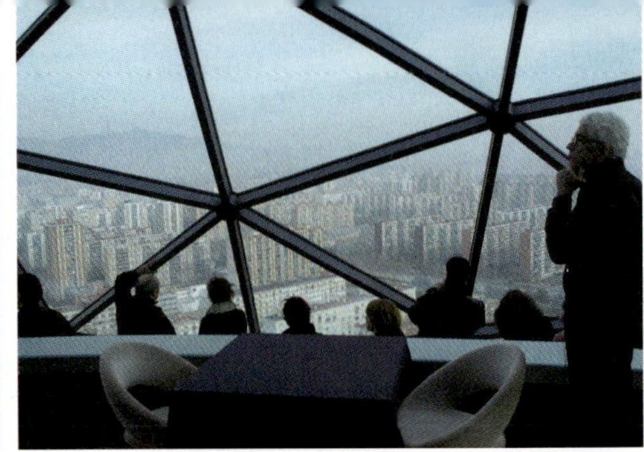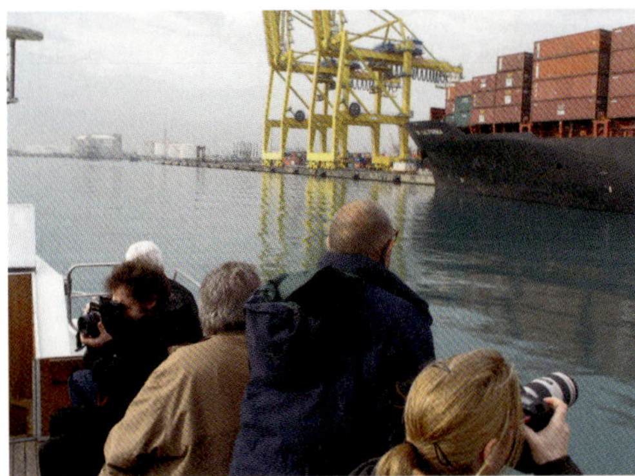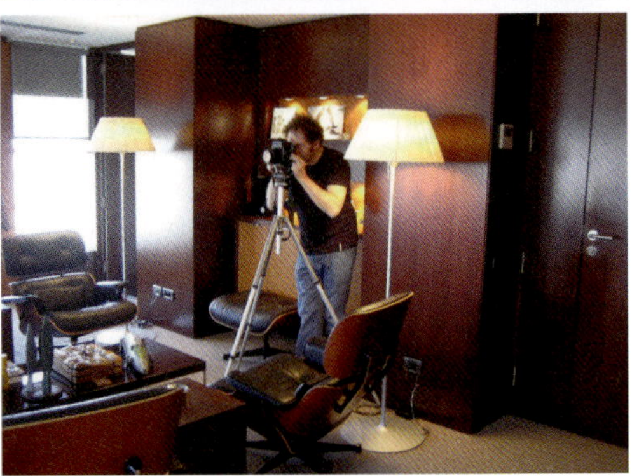

Images of the photographic survey, 2007

significant intervention of the field of art in the social world. And to do so, evidently, by accepting the conflicts and contradictions that such a task supposes today.[34]

Aware of the controversial nature of debates about realism in modern art since Courbet, from the viewpoint of defending the project of realism as an art form that turns on issues of public interest, our aim was to adopt the format of the photographic surveys of the nineteenth and twentieth centuries in a critical, deliberately controversial way (based on the premises of institutional critique). These surveys constitute a great modern tradition running through the history of photography since its origins, from the Mission Héliographique of 1851 to the DATAR mission in the eighties, via the geographical explorations from 1850 to 1870, projects such as the FSA and other big, more or less canonical projects of documentation such as those undertaken by Charles Marville, Eugène Atget, Lewis Hine, August Sander, Berenice Abbott and others, in approximately the last three decades of the nineteenth century and the first three of the twentieth. We considered that photographic missions or studies were the best embodiment of the modern photographic campaigns, of the production of great photography archives to be seen publicly with the purpose of visualising historic moments and their relation to models of government.

34 I refer more extensively to present-day conditions for the reinvention of the photographic document in 'Molecular Documents: Photography in the Post-Photographic Era, or How Not to Be Trapped into False Dilemmas', in Robin Kelsey and Blake Stimson (ed.), *The Meaning of Photography*. New Haven and London: Sterling and Francine Clark Institute and Yale University Press, 2008. See also the materials in the exhibition *Universal Archive,* MACBA, 22 October 2008– 6 January 2009, particularly the guide to the exhibition.

Our project about Barcelona began with a series of commissions to local and international photographers to find an image for an emergent metropolis that lacks representations and is, partly for this reason, difficult to imagine and understand.[35] Studying Barcelona also meant studying the global urban condition in the early twenty-first century. There seemed to us to be a shortage of eloquent images of the present-day city. It was therefore necessary to begin with a defamiliarisation of received ideas and images of the city, which even today seem to be firmly anchored in the persistent icons of the mid-twentieth century, of the golden age of the humanist paradigm. This defamiliarisation is the first step towards awareness of the real city that is being shaped, of the future city. The role played by images in this process is to allow us to visualise and sense complex and often highly abstract urban processes. This visualisation may be the basis for citizen debate and political intervention. If our photographic project sought to construct the image of the future city, it was precisely in order to contribute to the debate about that city's future.

This project was promoted as a form of public interpellation by appropriating the model of the photographic survey, historically sponsored by governmental bodies. It was a gesture of appropriation that raised questions about the prevailing model of city government. The survey came into being with the aim of constructing the image of the emergent city at a time of great transformations that were difficult to visualise. As in former key moments, the survey was the means of formalising the emergence of new historic subjects at moments of change. Unlike the fifties and sixties that saw a peak in the process of industrialisation and urban expansion, today Barcelona lacks a strong image to make the processes underway visible and provide new urban majorities with instruments for grasping the scope of the transformations, opportunities and dilemmas being presented, and understanding what is new and singular in the process. In this sense in particular, we do not yet have images and, therefore, are unable to understand the overflowing of the metropolitan framework established in the twentieth century and the need for a new model and urban project.

The working method began with a selection of specific urban polarities, which were the confluence of territories, historic processes and emerging trends-subjects, and the idea was to study them by means of various commissioned works. The aim was not to take a merely topographic approach, but to produce eloquent images of the temporary nature of historic processes. While recording the emergent processes, it situated them in the course of the twentieth century.

35 Invited to take part in the project were Xavier Basiana, Lothar Baumgarten, Sandra Balsells, Patrick Faigenbaum, Hans-Peter Feldmann, David Goldblatt, William Klein, Manolo Laguillo, Ana Muller, Marc Pataut, Xavier Ribas, Andrea Robbins and Max Becher, Gilles Saussier, Jean-Louis Schoellkopf, Allan Sekula and Ahlam Shibli.

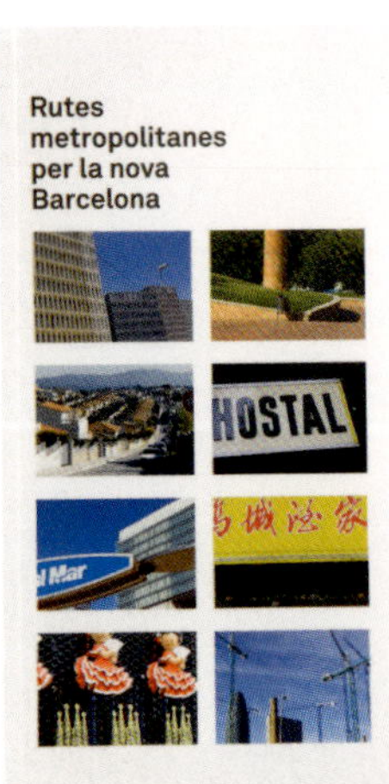

Rutes metropolitanes per la nova Barcelona guide, MACBA, 2008

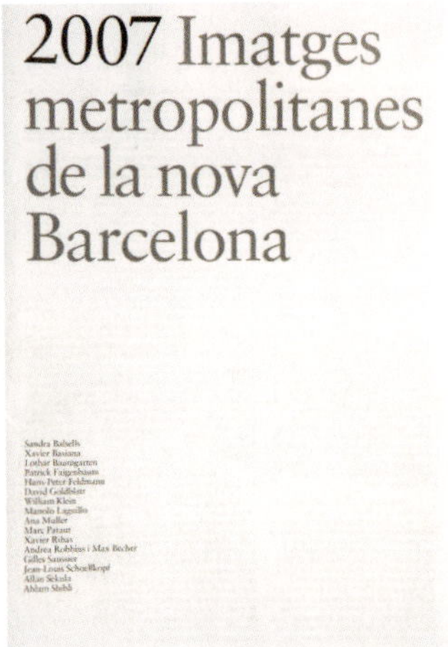

2007. Imatges metropolitanes de la nova Barcelona magazine, MACBA, 2008

36 *Universal Archive. The Condition of the Document and the Modern Photographic Utopia*, MACBA, 22 October 2008–6 January 2009.

Universal Archive

The exhibition *Universal Archive. The Condition of the Document and the Modern Photographic Utopia*[36] arose from the need to give the Barcelona survey a historic framework, seeking to contribute to an understanding of the complexity of the notion of the document in the history of photography by studying and tabling certain specific debates about the genre at various different historic moments in the twentieth century. The aim was not so much to produce a history of the genre or a comprehensive list of possible definitions, but to study the way in which the photographic document has always been ambivalent and controversial with regard to specific historic conditions, seeking in each case to outline the historic subject of the documentary genre and how it is constructed.

By studying specific cases, the aim of the exhibition was to put forward hypotheses as to the changing meanings and mechanisms of the documentary in a historic cycle that began with the rise to hegemony of the photograph in the illustrated press, in the first three decades of the twentieth century, and continued until the supposed crisis of photographic realism in the digital age, at the century's end. The exhibition was organised in non-chronological fashion around specific debates situated in time, proposing a pluralist historiographic method that explained the inherent tensions in the historical account. There were two main parts, subdivided into three and two areas, respectively. The first was a historic look at some of the principal question marks overhanging the photographic document in the modern age (approximately 1850 to 1980). The second situated the debate in Barcelona's history, as a specific case study.

The first part was organised around three main areas that looked at the subject of the documentary, the relation between the document and propaganda, and the epistemic and archival dimension of the document. The exhibition began with the official emergence of the documentary genre in photography and film at the change from the twenties to the thirties, associated with the representation of the popular classes and the underprivileged. It explored how the figure of the victim became the subject of reformist documentaries, establishing a dialectic with the models of self-representation of the international worker photography movement that aspired to supersede the paternalist-victim model of the documentary.

The second section, 'Public Photographic Spaces', presented the historic evolution of the paradigm of photography exhibition with an expanded conception of space introduced by El Lissitzky in the late twenties, its dissemination throughout

Europe after 1930 by the designers and architects of the Bauhaus, its totalitarian reinterpretation in the thirties in Italy and Germany, its introduction to the United States by Herbert Bayer and its reworking in various exhibitions at the MoMA, culminating in *The Family of Man* in 1955. It traced the path of the utopian architectural-photographic space, which involved a new type of spectator, from revolutionary Russia to the America of the Cold War.

The third area explored the notion of photography as an instrument for social science and the creation of archives in historically important projects, from the Mission Héliographique of 1851 to the DATAR mission in the eighties. This section was the largest, including some of the classic photographic explorations of the nineteenth century. Some examples were the 40th Parallel survey in the American West, Frith, Du Camp and Salzmann's journeys to the Middle East; Marville and Atget's works on Paris; August Sander's 'People of the Twentieth Century' project; various ethnographic and photographic projects about cities in the twentieth century, and the New Topographics of the seventies and early postmodern debates about the document.

The second part of the exhibition centred on photographic representations of Barcelona from the time of the 1888 Universal Exhibition to the Forum of Cultures in 2004. This section presented some hypotheses for a photographic historiography associated with a historiography of urban development. It studied the correspondence between various dominant photographic paradigms throughout the century and their correspondence with the urban model of each time. It set out to present the photographic representation of the metropolis as a space of conflict that is inseparable from the struggles for the city, at the same time examining the tension between the construction of official images and counter-images.

This part of the exhibition opened with the first images and albums of the city, from the 1850s to the 1870s, with particular emphasis on the sudden increase in photographs of the city on the occasion of the 1888 Universal Exposition. It continued with the guidebooks about the city produced for the 1929 International Exposition and the emergence of a modern official photographic construction with the transition to the Republic; the humanist paradigm from the new photographic avant-garde of the fifties and sixties to the democratic transition, showing the grey city under Franco's dictatorship; the new topographic documentary of the late seventies and eighties in association with the urban recovery of the city and democratic institutions, and the emergence of a new role for image in the urban promotion policies of the Olympic transformation in the late eighties.

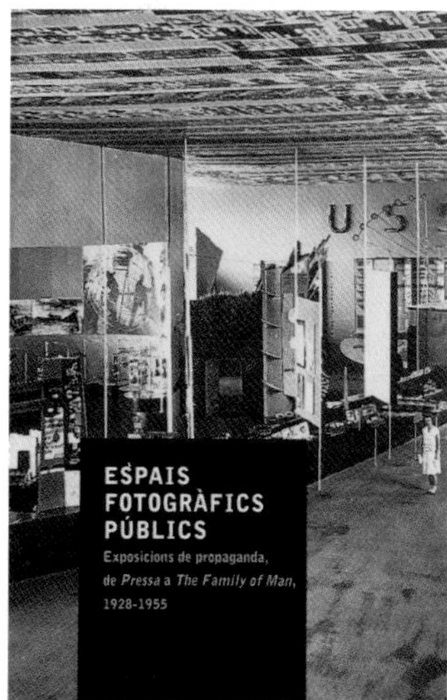

Public Photographic Spaces.
Exhibitions of Propaganda from 'Pressa'
to 'The Family of Man', 1928–55 book.
Barcelona: MACBA, 2009

It concluded with the image struggles in the nineties and the early years of the twenty-first century, between the 1992 Olympic Games and Forum 2004, in the context of a shift to an extrovert, post-industrial urban model, in which the image has acquired a new centrality both in municipal government and social conflict.[37]

The exhibition closed with the survey of the photographic work that had been commissioned in the course of the previous year, as the germ of the debate and the exhibition project, which

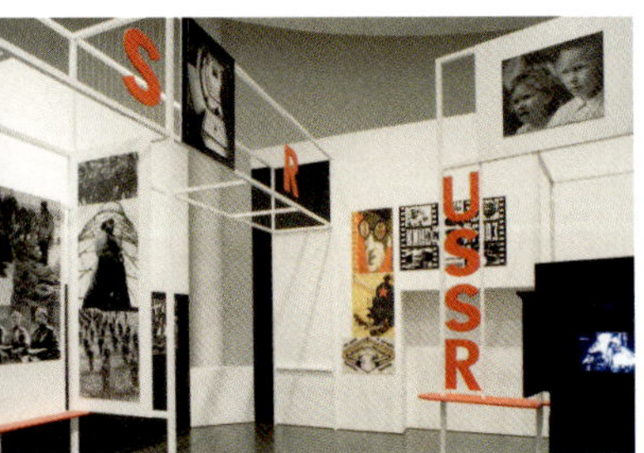

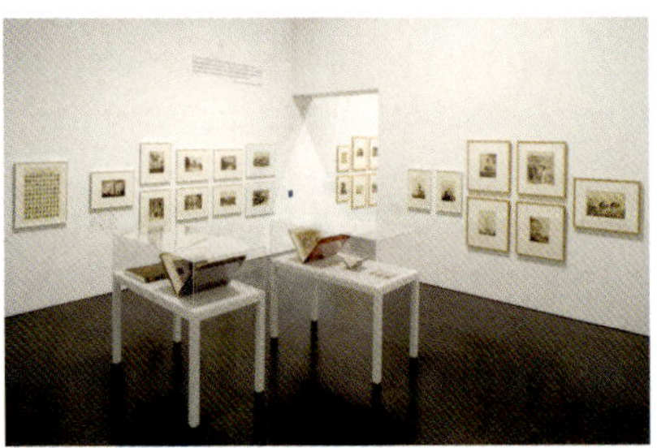

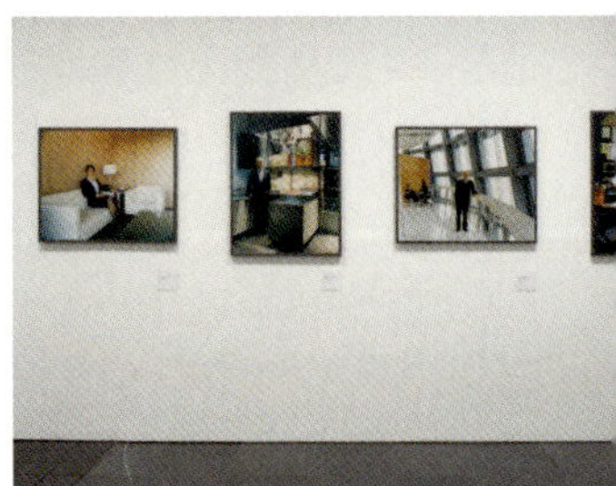

Universal Archive. The Condition of the Document and the Modern Photographic Utopia exhibition, MACBA, 2008

offered a diagnosis of the present-day city and its focuses of innovation for the twenty-first century.[38]

Molecular museum

How should we interpret in political vein the photographic project of Barcelona and the *Universal Archive* exhibition? Did this project help to expand the limits of institutional critique and radicalise previous experiments, or did it contradict them? What is the place of critique in large-scale projects? Does the shift to large-scale projects involve a reduction or even an annulment of critical potential? Does hegemony have a margin for critique?

The central political issue of this project was the question mark hanging over the possible bringing together of the macro- and micro-political scales (or, according to Deleuze and Guattari, the molar and the molecular). While the previous interventions in the city described here took the form of micro-political/molecular experiments and collaborations with social movements, in this case it is evident that the aim was to intervene in Barcelona on the molar scale, or to explore the issue of the need to address this scale to produce a politically significant, transforming project. A political reading has to take into account the pertinence of this tension between the molecular and the molar, and address both the concrete effects and the experiences of the various agents involved, and the macro-

37 On the history of photographic representations of Barcelona, see Jorge Ribalta, 'Paradigmas fotográficos en Barcelona, 1860–2004', *Quaderns del Seminari d'Història de Barcelona*, no. 22, Institut de Cultura, Ajuntament de Barcelona, 2009.
38 See the materials in the exhibition *Universal Archive. The Condition of the Document and the Modern Photographic Utopia*, particularly the guide to the exhibition. For a political interpretation of *Universal Archive*, see the interview by Miguel López, 'Ver la modernidad desde la fotografía en como entrar en la history por la puerta de servicio', in *Ramona* magazine, issue 88, March 2009; *Papel Alpha*, no. 7, 2009, and Blake Stimson, 'I Am Nothing and I Should Be Everything', in *Artforum*, XLVII, no. 6, February 2009, pp. 77–80.

institutional context of the museums and their capacity for intervention in city debates. Overall, it seems obvious that the change in scale inevitably introduces a new complexity or ambivalence into the political dimension of institutional critique, in that it suggests a new limit for the museum.

In her intervention in the *Another Relationality* seminar, Suely Rolnik explored the ways in which capitalism's penetration of subjectivity represents the 'procurement' of creativity: capitalism has turned pimp on us. At the end of this itinerary, we are inevitably brought face to face with this question. What are we being pimped for? In other words, are we breaking with the logic of neoliberal capitalism and the culture industries, or are we reproducing and extending it? Is micro-political criticism of the molecular museum a way of interiorising the demands of cognitive capitalism or a form of resistance? I stress that the obvious initial response is that it is necessary to attend to the participants in the projects, to their effects, to the singularity of the experiments – in short, an empirical, non-ideological bottom-up reading is required. This reading must also take into account the dominant logics of the institutional framework of existing museums of modern and contemporary art, and, in this context, analyse the way in which the forms of institutional work described here take their place in the macro-institutional context.

In June 2008, we organised a seminar-workshop in the framework of the PEI on the hypothesis of the molecular museum, seeking to reflect the new institutional demands being made by social movements.[39] In recent years, we have been stressing the need on the part of the new social movements to establish a type of structure that will give protest continuity. How to define a new institutional agenda on the basis of the experiences of the latest wave of institutional critique and the anti-institutional experiments that have emerged from the expansive process of the various movements in the last decade? The idea, then, is to create a space for debate about the potential of the discourses and practices of open code, copyleft, creative commons and so on, in order to implement a new institutional practice in models of management and cultural policy in the public sphere. Is this possible? And, if so, how?

Faced with the weighty institutional models that reproduce the philosophy of state bureaucracy, how could we begin to conceive of fragile, temporary, deterritorialised institutional models that have interiorised the demands of institutional critique and are capable of supporting the mobility of micro-political practices and avoiding the deadlock and bureaucracy inherent in the institutional framework, at the same time guaranteeing a framework for experiment with a degree of continuity? How can we

39 *Molecular Museum. Can Cultural Heritage be Managed by Deterritorialised Networks?*, 14 June 2008.

construct molecular spaces in molar conditions? And, conversely, how can we make the molecular more molar? The aim was to sound out some departure points for a new form of institutionality, a kind of postcolonial museum or institution that supersedes the dominant model that came to the fore in the nineteenth century as the product of a cultural and geopolitical order determined by the emergence of the culture of industrial and colonial capitalism. What is the museum of the post-industrial, postcolonial age?

Deleuze and Guattari suggest a possible direction for this new molecular institutionality: 'The real difference is, then, between on the one hand the molar machine – whether social, technical or organic – and on the other the desiring machine, which is of a molecular order. Desiring machines are the following: formative machines, whose very misfirings are functional, and whose functioning is indiscernible from their formation; chronogeneous machines engaged in their own assembly, operating by non-localizable intercommunications and dispersed localisations, bringing into play processes of temporalisation, fragmented formations, and detached parts...'[40]

Again, does this operate in accordance with the logic of capitalism, or is it a form of resistance and creation? Is the will to extend the field of institutional critique and the freedom of the artistic sphere beyond the museum a way of reproducing what is being criticised? The answers of detractors and supporters alike will be as predictable as they are insufficient. The floor is open to anyone wishing to address the question.

At the end of the nineties, we saw the birth of many new social movements. Though they had a relatively short moment of intensity, perhaps between 1999 and 2001, they brought lasting consequences. The present moment, aggravated by the worldwide financial crisis, is manifesting itself not as experimentation or social innovation, but as a time of ebbing and uncertainty. In this context, it will be necessary to rethink the spaces of institutional experimentation in a different way to the last decade, since in this respect the museum cannot work alone, and innovation can only take place when there are active social subjects with which the institution can establish alliances. My purpose here is to present experiences and actions in the form of some of the experiments undertaken by the Museum during this period. These memories of a possible future offer prototypes, cases and experiences of models or fragile, temporary, deterritorialised institutional modulations that have interiorised the demands of various waves of institutional critique. Their aim is to suggest some starting points for a new type of radically democratic institutionality.

40 Gilles Deleuze and Félix Guattari, *Anti-Oedipus: Capitalism and Schizophrenia*. New York: Viking Press, 1977.

To imagine the future of this molecular museum and a possible new critical and deterritorialised institutionality, it seems pertinent to recall Raymond Williams and his thesis about the 'long revolution', or the revolution seen not as a logic of instant transformation but as a long haul: 'It is characteristic of the history of what I see as the long revolution that such aims, once achieved, are quite quickly absorbed, and either new expectations are commonly defined or, in their absence there is a mood of both stagnation and restlessness.'[41]

41 Raymond Williams, *The Long Revolution*, Broadview Press, 2001 (1961).

LIST OF WORKS REPRODUCED

Francesc Abad
Recorregut diari, 1974
Daily Journey
Photographs, maps, tickets
and sound recording
Various dimensions
MACBA Collection. Fundació Museu
d'Art Contemporani de Barcelona
pp. 136–37

Vito Acconci
Corrections, 1970
8 mm film transferred to video, b/w,
sound, 12 min
MACBA Collection. Fundació Museu
d'Art Contemporani de Barcelona
p. 114

Openings, 1970
8 mm film transferred to video, b/w,
silent, 14 min
MACBA Collection. Fundació Museu
d'Art Contemporani de Barcelona
p. 114

Three Relationship Studies, 1970
8 mm film transferred to video, b/w
and colour, silent, 12 min 30 s
MACBA Collection. Fundació Museu
d'Art Contemporani de Barcelona
p. 115

Trappings, 1971
Single-channel video, colour, sound,
8 min
MACBA Collection. Museu d'Art
Contemporani de Barcelona
Consortium
p. 115

Claim Excerpts, 1971
Single-channel video, b/w, sound,
62 min 11 s
MACBA Collection. Fundació Museu
d'Art Contemporani de Barcelona
p. 114

Conversions, 1971
8 mm film transferred to video, b/w,
silent, 65 min
1. Light, Reflection, Self-Control,
44 min 15 s
*2. Insistence, Adaptation,
Groundwork, Display*, 13 min 45 s
*3. Association, Assistance,
Dependence*, 7 min
MACBA Collection. Fundació Museu
d'Art Contemporani de Barcelona
pp. 114–15

Pryings, 1971
Single-channel video, b/w, sound,
17 min 10 s
MACBA Collection. Fundació Museu
d'Art Contemporani de Barcelona
p. 114

Theme Song, 1973
Single-channel video, b/w, sound,
33 min 15 s
MACBA Collection. Fundació Museu
d'Art Contemporani de Barcelona
p. 114

My Word, 1974
8 mm film transferred to video,
colour, silent, 91 min 30 s
MACBA Collection. Fundació Museu
d'Art Contemporani de Barcelona
p. 115

Open Book, 1974
Single-channel video, colour, sound,
10 min 5 s
MACBA Collection. Fundació Museu
d'Art Contemporani de Barcelona
p. 115

Agustín Parejo School
Por fabor estamos parado, 1987
Please, We're Stopped
16 postcards and 1 calendar, ink
print on paper
Various dimensions
MACBA Collection. Fundació Museu
d'Art Contemporani de Barcelona
p. 194

El sur a la fuerza, 1990
The South Forced
6 posters, 8 colour photographs
and 3 slides
Various dimensions
MACBA Collection. Fundació Museu
d'Art Contemporani de Barcelona
p. 194

Apostata, 1991
Renegade
7 postcards, 2 stickers and folder
with 3 typed documents and
3 collages on paper
Various dimensions
MACBA Collection. Fundació Museu
d'Art Contemporani de Barcelona
p. 194

Sin Larios, 1992
Without Larios
Poster, map, postcards, sheets,
lighter, ballpoint pen, t-shirt,
single-channel video, colour, sound,
5 min 23 s
Various dimensions
MACBA Collection. Fundació Museu
d'Art Contemporani de Barcelona
p. 195

Chantal Akerman
Une voix dans le désert, 2002
A Voice in the Desert
Single-channel video, colour, sound,
52 min
Ed. 1 of 3 + a.p.
MACBA Collection. Fundació Museu
d'Art Contemporani de Barcelona.
Gift of El Corte Inglés
p. 201

Ibon Aranberri
(Ir. T. nº 513) zuloa, 2003
Single-channel video, colour, sound,
8 min
Ed. 4 of 6 + a.p.
MACBA Collection. Fundació Museu
d'Art Contemporani de Barcelona.
Gift of Lady Jinty Latymer
p. 182

Aspen
*Aspen. The Multimedia Magazine
in a Box, no. 5 + 6, The Minimalism
Issue*, 1967
Publication, diverse elements
Edition and design: Brian
O'Doherty. Published by: Phyllis
Johnson, Roaring Fork Press, NYC
MACBA Collection. Fundació Museu
d'Art Contemporani de Barcelona
pp. 100–01

Fikret Atay
Lalo's Story, 2004
Single-channel video, colour, sound,
4 min 55 s
Ed. 3 of 6
MACBA Collection. Museu d'Art
Contemporani de Barcelona
Consortium. Gift of Amics dels
Museus de Catalunya
p. 218

Maja Bajevic
Double Bubble, 2001
Single-channel video, colour, sound,
3 min 40 s
Ed. 3 of 5 + 2 a.p.
MACBA Collection. Fundació Museu
d'Art Contemporani de Barcelona.
Gift of María Entrecanales
p. 216

Maja Bajevic, **Emanuel Licha**
Green Green Grass of Home, 2002
Single-channel video, colour, sound,
17 min 53 s and sound recording
Ed. 4 of 5 + 2 a.p.
MACBA Collection. Fundació Museu
d'Art Contemporani de Barcelona.
Gift of María Entrecanales
p. 216

Eugènia Balcells
Presenta, 1977
Presents
16 mm film transferred to video,
colour, sound, 9 min 34 s
MACBA Collection. Fundació Museu
d'Art Contemporani de Barcelona
p. 138

The End, 1977
16 mm film transferred to video,
colour, sound, 9 min 34 s
MACBA Collection. Fundació Museu
d'Art Contemporani de Barcelona
p. 138

Fin, 1977
Book. Typographic print on paper
31.2 × 21.7 cm
MACBA Collection. Fundació Museu
d'Art Contemporani de Barcelona
p. 139

Néstor Basterretxea
Operación H, 1963
H Operation
35 mm film transferred to video,
colour, sound, 11 min 49 s
MACBA Collection. Fundació Museu
d'Art Contemporani de Barcelona
p. 63

Samuel Beckett
Film, 1965
16 mm film transferred to video,
b/w, silent, 20 min
Produced and distributed by Barnet
Rosset
MACBA Collection. Fundació Museu
d'Art Contemporani de Barcelona
pp. 76–77

Ursula Biemann
Performing the Border, 1999
Single-channel video, b/w and
colour, sound, 42 min
MACBA Collection. Fundació Museu
d'Art Contemporani de Barcelona.
Gift of El Taller de la Fundació
p. 200

Dara Birnbaum
Attack Piece, 1975
Two-channel video, b/w, sound,
7 min 45 s
Ed. 2 of 3 + a.p.
MACBA Collection. Fundació Museu
d'Art Contemporani de Barcelona
pp. 112–13

Brassaï
Untitled. Graffiti
Series VIII 'La Magie'
'Magic'
Ca. 1930. Print run ca. 1950
Silver-salt photograph
39 × 29.5 cm
MACBA Collection. Fundació Museu
d'Art Contemporani de Barcelona
p. 52

La femme (Passage Prévot). Graffiti
Series VI 'L'amour'
The Woman (Passage Prévot).
Graffiti
'Love'
Ca. 1930. Print run ca. 1950
Silver-salt photograph
50 × 40 cm
MACBA Collection. Fundació Museu
d'Art Contemporani de Barcelona
p. 53

Untitled. Graffiti
Series III 'Naissance du visage'
'Birth of the Face'
Ca. 1930. Print run ca. 1950
Silver-salt photograph
50 × 39.5 cm
MACBA Collection. Fundació Museu
d'Art Contemporani de Barcelona
p. 53

Untitled (rue Médéah). Graffiti
Series IV 'Masques et visages'
'Masks and Faces'
Ca. 1930. Print run ca. 1950
Silver-salt photograph
40 × 29.5 cm
MACBA Collection. Fundació Museu
d'Art Contemporani de Barcelona
p. 52

Untitled. Graffiti
Series VII 'La mort'
'Death'
Ca. 1930. Print run ca. 1950
Silver-salt photograph
50 × 40 cm
MACBA Collection. Fundació Museu
d'Art Contemporani de Barcelona
p. 53

*Petit lutin à la jupe triangulaire.
Graffiti*
Series IX 'Images primitives'
Little Goblin in the Triangular Skirt
'Primitive Images'
Ca. 1930. Print run ca. 1950
Silver-salt photograph
50 × 40 cm
MACBA Collection. Fundació Museu
d'Art Contemporani de Barcelona
p. 53

Marcel Broodthaers
L'art et les mots, 1973
Art and Words
Typographic print with acrylic
on canvas
9 pieces at 79.4 × 99.7 cm each
MACBA Collection. Fundació Museu
d'Art Contemporani de Barcelona
pp. 104–05

stanley brouwn
ten steps, 1975
book
10 blocks of text at 100 × 1 mm
(1000 mm) on each page;
the distance from each step is
marked in red
MACBA Collection. Fundació Museu
d'Art Contemporani de Barcelona.
Gift of Fundación Abertis
p. 103

Francesc Català-Roca
Barcelona
Book
29 × 23 cm
Barcelona: Barna, 1954
With text by Luis Romero
MACBA Collection. Study Center
p. 73

James Coleman
Slide Piece, 1972–73
Projected images and synchronised
audio narration
MACBA Collection. Fundació Museu
d'Art Contemporani de Barcelona.
Gift of Fundació Obra Social
"la Caixa"
p. 169

So Different... and Yet, 1980
Videoinstallation. Single-channel
video, colour, sound, 54 min
Performance by Olwen Fouéré
and Roger Doyle
MACBA Collection. Fundació Museu
d'Art Contemporani de Barcelona
pp. 170–71

Joan Colom
El carrer, 1960
The Street
Single-channel video, b/w, silent,
30 min
MACBA Collection. Fundació Museu
d'Art Contemporani de Barcelona.
Gift of El Taller de la Fundació
p. 70

*Izas, rabizas y colipoterras: drama
con acompañamiento de cachondeo
y dolor de corazón*
Book
23 × 22 cm
Barcelona: Lumen, Palabra e
Imagen, 1964. With text by Camilo
José Cela
MACBA Collection. Study Center
p. 71

Jordi Colomer
*Anarchitekton (Barcelona, Bucarest,
Brasilia, Osaka)*, 2002–04
Video, colour, silent, looped
projection; 4 screens; chairs and
fitted carpet
Performed by Idroj Sanicne
Photography: Marc Viaplana / Jordi
Colomer
Production: Maravills, Spanish
Embassy in Brasilia, Generalitat
de Catalunya (Departament de
Cultura) and Fundación Marcelino
Botín
Ed. 2 of 5
MACBA Collection. Fundació Museu
d'Art Contemporani de Barcelona
p. 180

Alice Creischer
*L'atelier de la peintrice. Allégorie
réelle déterminant une phase de
sept années de ma vie artistique
dans la République de Berlin*, 2000
The Woman Painter's Studio: Real
Allegory which Determines a
Seven-Year Period in My Artistic
Life in the Berlin Republic
Acrylic and collage on polyethylene,
painter's easel, touch-up table and
flashlight
232.5 × 367 cm
MACBA Collection. Fundació Museu
d'Art Contemporani de Barcelona.
Gift of María Entrecanales
pp. 204–05

Danica Dakic
Tauber Tanz / Deaf Dance, 2003
Single-channel video, colour, sound,
3 min 40 s and Cibachrome slide
in an aluminium box and fluorescent
light
Lightbox, 30 × 50 × 10 cm
Ed. 2 of 6 + a.p.
MACBA Collection. Fundació Museu
d'Art Contemporani de Barcelona.
Gift of Cementos Molins
p. 217

Guy Debord
Hurlements en faveur de Sade,
1952
Howls for Sade
Single-channel video, b/w, sound,
64 min
MACBA Collection. Museu d'Art
Contemporani de Barcelona
Consortium
pp. 74–75

Dias & Riedweg
Voracidad Máxima, 2003
Maximum Voracity
Two-channel video installation,
colour, sound, 71 min 14 s,
4 mirrors, seats and control
Ed. 1 of 3
MACBA Collection. Museu d'Art
Contemporani de Barcelona
Consortium
p. 215

Jean Dubuffet
Le chien jappeur, 1953
The Barking Dog
Oil on canvas
72.6 × 92 cm
MACBA Collection. Fundació Museu
d'Art Contemporani de Barcelona
p. 58

***ENTRE/ACTE, Imágenes
de frontera I***
Maquettes-sans-qualité archives
of 1997 updated in 2004
by Alejandra Riera and Fulvia
Carnevale
Text and partial views inspired
by 8 minutes filmed in Super 8
in November 1997 on the border
between La Quiaca, Argentina
and Villazon, Bolivia
8 mm film transferred to video,
colour, sound, 8 min, 13 sheets
of DIN A3 paper with ink print
and photocopies
Dimensions variable
MACBA Collection. Fundació Museu
d'Art Contemporani de Barcelona
p. 213

Jon Mikel Euba
Fiesta 4 puertas, 2001
4-Door Party
5 simultaneous slide projections
MACBA Collection. Fundació Museu
d'Art Contemporani de Barcelona
p. 178

Gatika doble final, 2001
Single-channel video, colour, sound,
11 min
Ed. 2 of 6 + 2 a.p.
MACBA Collection. Fundació Museu
d'Art Contemporani de Barcelona
p. 179

VALIE EXPORT
Cutting, 1967
Single-channel video, b/w, sound,
1 min 41 s
MACBA Collection. Fundació Museu
d'Art Contemporani de Barcelona
p. 102

**Marcelo Expósito, Joseantonio
Hergueta**
La tierra de la madre, 1994
The Land of the Mother
Single-channel video, b/w and
colour, sound, 21 min
MACBA Collection. Fundació Museu
d'Art Contemporani de Barcelona.
Gift of El Taller de la Fundació
p. 198

Marcelo Expósito
*Octubre en el norte: temporal
del noroeste*, 1995
October in the North: Storm
from the Northwest
Single-channel video, b/w and
colour, sound, 92 min
MACBA Collection. Fundació Museu
d'Art Contemporani de Barcelona.
Gift of El Taller de la Fundació
p. 199

**Marcelo Expósito, Arturo-Fito
Rodríguez** and **Gabriel Villota**
No haber olvidado nada, 1996–97
Not Having Forgotten Anything
Single-channel video, b/w and
colour, sound, 54 min
MACBA Collection. Fundació Museu
d'Art Contemporani de Barcelona.
Gift of El Taller de la Fundació
p. 199

Öyvind Fahlström
Andra kalaset på 'Edlund', 1956
Second Feast on 'Edlund'
Marker, felt-tip pen and coloured
ink on paper
121 × 147.5 cm
MACBA Collection. Fundació Museu
d'Art Contemporani de Barcelona.
Gift of Daniel Cordier
p. 92

*Restaurangblandning I (Himlar
och Klyftor)*, created in March-April
1961 / *Restaurangblandning II
(Soluppgång - Solnedgång)*,
created in April-May 1961
Restaurangblandning I (Heavens and
Abysses) / Restaurangblandning II
(Sunrise - Sunset)
Enamelled metal panels
Diptych, 4 pieces at 100 × 100 cm
each
MACBA Collection. Fundació Museu
d'Art Contemporani de Barcelona.
Gift of Aigües de Barcelona
pp. 90–91

Mao-Hope March, 1966
16 mm film, b/w, sound, 4 min 50 s
Director, producer and sound editor:
Öyvind Fahlström
Camera and montage: Alfons
Schilling
Interviewer: Bob Fass
MACBA Collection. Museu d'Art
Contemporani de Barcelona
Consortium
p. 93

Harun Farocki
Eye/Machine, I, II, III, 2001–03
3 two-channel videos, colour,
sound, 25 min each
Ed. 2 of 2
MACBA Collection. Fundació Museu
d'Art Contemporani de Barcelona
pp. 206–07

Hans-Peter Feldmann
100 Jahre, 2001
100 Years
Silver-salt photograph
101 photographs at 30.5 × 24.3 cm
each
MACBA Collection. Fundació Museu
d'Art Contemporani de Barcelona
pp. 152–53

Peter Fischli/David Weiss
Büsi (Kitty), 2001
Single-channel video, colour, silent,
6 min 30 s
Ed. 150 of 150
MACBA Collection. Museu d'Art
Contemporani de Barcelona
Consortium.
Gift of Peter Fischli/David Weiss
p. 187

Lucio Fontana
Concetto spaziale, 1957
Spatial Concept
Acrylic and marble dust on canvas
74.2 × 61 cm
MACBA Collection. Fundació Museu
d'Art Contemporani de Barcelona
p. 59

Robert Frank
NYC Sagamore Cafeteria, 1948
Silver-salt photograph
50.4 × 40.4 cm
MACBA Collection. Museu d'Art
Contemporani de Barcelona
Consortium. Gift of the artist
p. 68

*14th of July 1948. Day Becomes
Night...*, 1948
Silver-salt photograph
35.5 × 48 cm
MACBA Collection. Museu d'Art
Contemporani de Barcelona
Consortium. Gift of the artist
p. 69

Mallorca, 1951
Silver-salt photograph
27.7 × 25.4 cm
MACBA Collection. Museu d'Art
Contemporani de Barcelona
Consortium. Gift of the artist
p. 69

Peter Friedl
Playgrounds, 1995–2004
5 simultaneous slide projections
transferred to digital archives
and vinyl
Dimensions variable
Ed. 1 + a.p.
MACBA Collection. Fundació Museu
d'Art Contemporani de Barcelona
pp. 222–23

Pedro G. Romero/Archivo F.X.
Tesauro Anarquitectura
Antagonismos, casos de estudio,
2001
Anarchitecture Thesaurus:
Antagonisms, Case Studies
Double simultaneous slide
projection
Dimensions variable
MACBA Collection. Fundació Museu
d'Art Contemporani de Barcelona
p. 196

Pedro G. Romero
Routing slips and various
publications, 1989/2007
Series include: *La sección áurea*
(1989); *r.a.r.o.* (1991); *El tiempo
de la bomba* (1993–97);
¿Llegaremos pronto a Sevilla?
(1997–99); and the project Archivo
F.X. (1999–2007)
Various dimensions
MACBA Collection. Fundació Museu
d'Art Contemporani de Barcelona
p. 197

David Goldblatt
*Dainfern Valley, an extension
to Dainfern Golf Estate and Country
Club: the security wall and
gatehouse are in place, roadmaking
is in progress, and the velds has
been stripped to allow for special
grassing. 26 September 2001.*
'Dainfern' Series, 2001
Ink jet print on card
83 × 60 cm
MACBA Collection. Museu d'Art
Contemporani de Barcelona
Consortium. Gift of David Goldblatt
p. 210

*'Tuscan' House and Diepsloot
Outfall Sewer, Dainfern Golf Estate
and Country Club. 20 January
2002. 'Dainfern' Series*, 2002
Ink jet print on card
83 × 60 cm
MACBA Collection. Museu d'Art
Contemporani de Barcelona
Consortium. Gift of David Goldblatt
p. 211

Dan Graham
Alteration of a Suburban House,
1978–87
Plywood, fitted carpet, lightweight
cardboard, balsa wood, mirror, card,
methacrylate
184 × 267 × 120 cm
Ed. 3 of 3 + a.p.
MACBA Collection. Fundació Museu
d'Art Contemporani de Barcelona.
Private long term loan
p. 164

Rock my Religion, 1984
Single-channel video, b/w and
colour, sound, 55 min 27 s
MACBA Collection. Fundació Museu
d'Art Contemporani de Barcelona.
Gift of the Rumeu Family
pp. 166–67

Eulàlia Grau
Discriminació de la dona
Discrimination against Women
Booklet. Print on paper
24.7 × 15.5 cm
Ed. 6 of 100
Barcelona: Proyecto Arte, 1977
MACBA Collection. Fundació Museu
d'Art Contemporani de Barcelona.
Gift of the artist
p. 141

Per què?, 1979
Why?
Leaflet. Print on paper
42 × 15.2 cm
MACBA Collection. Fundació Museu
d'Art Contemporani de Barcelona.
Gift of the artist
p. 140

Grup de Treball
*Encuesta a 24 galerías de arte
de Madrid*, 1974
Survey of 24 Art Galleries in Madrid
Map of the city of Madrid, sticky
labels, typewritten pages,
handwritten pages and photocopies
Various dimensions
MACBA Collection. Museu d'Art
Contemporani de Barcelona
Consortium. Gift of Grup de Treball
p. 128

Homenatge a l'arquitectura, 1975
Homage to Architecture
Ink on paper
Various dimensions
MACBA Collection. Museu d'Art
Contemporani de Barcelona
Consortium. Gift of Grup de Treball
p. 129

Grupo de artistas de vanguardia
Tucumán Arde Archive.
Documentation related to different
actions and works carried out
by this group, 1966–68
Documents, photographs and press
cuttings
Various dimensions
MACBA Collection. Fundació Museu
d'Art Contemporani de Barcelona
pp. 124, 127

Philip Guston
Horizon, 1967
Ink on paper
44.5 × 58 cm
MACBA Collection. Fundació Museu
d'Art Contemporani de Barcelona
p. 94

Mark, 1967
Ink on paper
33 × 41.5 cm
MACBA Collection. Fundació Museu
d'Art Contemporani de Barcelona
p. 95

Edge, 1967
Ink on paper
34.5 × 40.5 cm
MACBA Collection. Fundació Museu
d'Art Contemporani de Barcelona
p. 95

Hans Haacke
*Shapolsky et al. Manhattan Real
Estate Holdings, a Real-Time Social
System, as of May 1, 1971*, 1971
Maps, graphs, typewritten pages,
silver-salt photographs, and
explanation panel
Various dimensions
Ed. of 2
MACBA Collection. Fundació Museu
d'Art Contemporani de Barcelona.
Acquired jointly by the Fundació
Museu d'Art Contemporani de
Barcelona and the Whitney Museum
of American Art, New York,
with funding from the Director's
Discretionary Fund and the
Painting and Sculpture Committee
pp. 106–07

Frank Hesse
*Florence: From St. Croce to the
Institute of Art History*, 2006
Single-channel video, colour, sound,
11 min 50 s
Ed. 1 of 5 + a.p.
MACBA Collection. Fundació Museu
d'Art Contemporani de Barcelona.
Gift of LOOP Barcelona
p. 219

Cristina Iglesias
Políptico VII, 2002
Polyptych 7
Screen print on copper mounted
on iron pannels
6 parts, 250 × 100 × 0.15 cm each
MACBA Collection. Fundació Museu
d'Art Contemporani de Barcelona
pp. 184–85

Joan Jonas
Wind, 1968
16 mm film transferred to video,
b/w, silent, 5 min 37 s
MACBA Collection. Museu d'Art
Contemporani de Barcelona
Consortium
p. 116

Organic Honey's Visual Telepathy,
1972
Single-channel video, b/w, sound,
15 min
MACBA Collection. Fundació Museu
d'Art Contemporani de Barcelona
p. 117

Joaquim Jordà
Numax Presenta..., 1980
Numax Presents
Single-channel video, b/w and
colour, sound, 105 min
MACBA Collection. Fundació Museu
d'Art Contemporani de Barcelona
pp. 144–45

Mike Kelley, Paul Mc Carthy
Fresh Acconci, 1995
Single-channel video, colour, sound,
45 min
MACBA Collection. Fundació Museu
d'Art Contemporani de Barcelona.
Gift of the Rumeu Family
p. 175

Manolo Laguillo
Nacimiento de la Diagonal, 1979
Birth of Diagonal
Platinum palladium photograph
35.5 × 61.5 cm
MACBA Collection. Fundació Museu
d'Art Contemporani de Barcelona
p. 162

*La trasera de la Plaça de Francesc
Macià*, 1980
Back Part of Plaça de Francesc Macià
Platinum palladium photograph
24.5 × 33 cm
MACBA Collection. Fundació Museu
d'Art Contemporani de Barcelona.
Gift of Manolo Laguillo
p. 162

Frente a la Sagrada Familia, 1981
Facing the Sagrada Familia
Platinum palladium photograph
51.3 × 61.3 cm
MACBA Collection. Fundació Museu
d'Art Contemporani de Barcelona
p. 163

Vall d'Hebron, 1992
Silver-salt photograph
50.5 × 75.5 cm
MACBA Collection. Fundació Museu
d'Art Contemporani de Barcelona.
Gift of Manolo Laguillo
p. 163

David Lamelas
*Film Script (La manipulación
del mensaje)*, 1972
Film Script (Manipulation
of the Message)
8 mm film transferred to 16 mm
film, colour, silent, 10 min, looped
projection and triple slide projection
Ed. 3 of 3
MACBA Collection. Fundació Museu
d'Art Contemporani de Barcelona
p. 121

Malcom Le Grice
Berlin Horse, 1970
Double projection, 16 mm film
transferred to video, b/w and colour,
sound, 7 min each
Ed. 1 of 5
MACBA Collection. Fundació Museu
d'Art Contemporani de Barcelona
pp. 118–19

Helen Levitt
In the Street, 1945–46 (1952)
16 mm film transferred to video,
b/w, silent, 15 min, and sound
recording
Co-creators: James Agee and Janice
Loeb. Piano: Arthur Kleiner
MACBA Collection. Fundació Museu
d'Art Contemporani de Barcelona.
Gift of Grupo Planeta
pp. 66–67

Ramón Masats
Neutral Corner
Book
23 × 22 cm
Barcelona: Lumen, Palabra e Imagen,
1962. With text by Ignacio Aldecoa
MACBA Collection. Study Center
p. 73

Oriol Maspons and **Julio Oubiña**
*Toreo de salón: farsa con
acompañamiento de clamor y murga*
Book
23 × 22 cm
Barcelona: Lumen, Palabra e
Imagen, 1963. With text by Camilo
José Cela
MACBA Collection. Study Center
p. 72

Gordon Matta-Clark
Fire Child, 1971
Single-channel video, colour, silent,
9 min 47 s
MACBA Collection. Museu d'Art
Contemporani de Barcelona
Consortium
p. 110

Fresh Kill, 1972
Single-channel video, colour, sound,
12 min 56 s
MACBA Collection. Museu d'Art
Contemporani de Barcelona
Consortium
p. 111

Day's End, 1975
Single-channel video, colour, silent,
23 min 10 s
MACBA Collection. Museu d'Art
Contemporani de Barcelona
Consortium
p. 111

Anthony McCall
Line Describing a Cone, 1973
16 mm film, b/w, silent, 25 min,
smoke
Dimensions variable
MACBA Collection. Fundació Museu
d'Art Contemporani de Barcelona
p. 120

Henri Michaux
Untitled, 1948
Ink on paper
32.5 × 24.5 cm
MACBA Collection. Fundació Museu
d'Art Contemporani de Barcelona
p. 54

Untitled, 1948
Watercolour on paper
39.5 × 28.2 cm
MACBA Collection. Fundació Museu
d'Art Contemporani de Barcelona
p. 55

Untitled, 1950
India ink on paper
31.5 × 23.5 cm
MACBA Collection. Fundació Museu
d'Art Contemporani de Barcelona.
Gift of Fundación Catalana
Occidente
p. 56

Untitled, 1950
India ink on paper
34.5 × 24 cm
MACBA Collection. Fundació Museu
d'Art Contemporani de Barcelona.
Gift of Fundación Catalana
Occidente
p. 56

Untitled, 1950
India ink on paper
31.5 × 24 cm
MACBA Collection. Fundació Museu
d'Art Contemporani de Barcelona.
Gift of Fundación Catalana
Occidente
p. 56

Untitled, 1950
India ink on paper
31.5 × 24 cm
MACBA Collection. Fundació Museu
d'Art Contemporani de Barcelona.
Gift of Fundación Catalana
Occidente
p. 56

Untitled, ca. 1955
Oil on wood
54.5 × 45.5 cm
MACBA Collection. Fundació Museu
d'Art Contemporani de Barcelona.
Gift of Freixenet
p. 57

Untitled, ca. 1979
Watercolour on Japanese paper
51 × 31 cm
MACBA Collection. Fundació Museu
d'Art Contemporani de Barcelona
p. 55

Xavier Miserachs
Barcelona blanc i negre
Book
33.3 × 31.2 cm
Barcelona: Aymà, 1964. With
a prologue by Joan Oliver and texts
by Josep Maria Espinàs
MACBA Collection. Study Center
p. 72

Muntadas
*Punt d'informació. Cadaqués Canal
Local*, 1974
Information Point: Cadaqués Canal
Local
Compilation of video recordings,
texts, documents and photographs,
photocopied and blown up
Various dimensions
MACBA Collection. Fundació Museu
d'Art Contemporani de Barcelona
p. 132

*Punto de información. Barcelona
Distrito Uno*, 1976
Information Point: Barcelona
District One
Documentary video, b/w, sound,
154 min 39 s; photographic panel,
glass table, photocopied documents
and photographs
Various dimensions
MACBA Collection. Fundació Museu
d'Art Contemporani de Barcelona
p. 133

TVE: primer intento, 1989
TVE: First Try
Single-channel video, b/w and
colour, 38 min 20 s
MACBA Collection. Museu d'Art
Contemporani de Barcelona
Consortium
p. 133

*On Translation: The Audience
(Barcelona)*, 1998 (2002)
Digital print on PVC
2 parts at 230 × 388 cm and
230 × 390.2 cm
MACBA Collection. Museu d'Art
Contemporani de Barcelona
Consortium. Artist's collection
p. 133

Juan Muñoz
The Nature of Visual Illusion, 1994
Acrylic on canvas and 4 figurines
in polyester resin
Dimensions variable
MACBA Collection. Fundació Museu
d'Art Contemporani de Barcelona.
Private long term loan
pp. 176–77

Deimantas Narkevicius
Scena, 2003
Scene
Super 8 mm film transferred to
video, colour, sound, 9 min 30 s
Ed. 1 of 5 + 2 a.p.
MACBA Collection. Fundació Museu
d'Art Contemporani de Barcelona
p. 220

Rosalind Nashashibi
Bachelor Machines Part I, 2007
16 mm film, colour, sound, 31 min
Ed. 3 + 2 a.p.
MACBA Collection. Fundació Museu
d'Art Contemporani de Barcelona
p. 221

Bruce Nauman
Art Make-Up, 1967–68
16 mm film transferred to video,
colour, silent, 40 min
MACBA Collection. Fundació Museu
d'Art Contemporani de Barcelona
p. 98

*Bouncing Two Balls Between
the Floor and Ceiling with Changing
Rhythms*, 1968
16 mm film transferred to video,
b/w, sound, 10 min
MACBA Collection. Fundació Museu
d'Art Contemporani de Barcelona
p. 98

Bouncing on the Corner no. 1,
1968
Single-channel video, b/w, sound,
60 min
MACBA Collection. Fundació Museu
d'Art Contemporani de Barcelona
p. 99

*Dance or Exercise on the Perimeter
of a Square (Square Dance)*, 1968
16 mm film transferred to video,
b/w, sound, 10 min
MACBA Collection. Fundació Museu
d'Art Contemporani de Barcelona
p. 99

Pinchneck, 1968
16 mm film transferred to video,
colour, silent, 1 min 54 s
MACBA Collection. Fundació Museu
d'Art Contemporani de Barcelona
p. 98

Slow Angle Walk (Beckett Walk),
1968
Single-channel video, b/w, sound,
60 min
MACBA Collection. Fundació Museu
d'Art Contemporani de Barcelona
p. 98

Wall/Floor Positions, 1968
Single-channel video, b/w, silent,
58 min 31 s
MACBA Collection. Museu d'Art
Contemporani de Barcelona
Consortium
p. 99

Revolving Upside Down, 1969
Single-channel video, b/w, sound,
61 min
MACBA Collection. Fundació Museu
d'Art Contemporani de Barcelona
p. 99

Walk with Contrapposto, 1969
Single-channel video, b/w, sound,
60 min
MACBA Collection. Museu d'Art
Contemporani de Barcelona
Consortium
p. 98

Pulling Mouth, 1969
Single-channel video, b/w, silent,
8 min
MACBA Collection. Museu d'Art
Contemporani de Barcelona
Consortium
p. 98

Violin Tuned D.E.A.D, 1969
Single-channel video, b/w, sound,
60 min
MACBA Collection. Fundació Museu
d'Art Contemporani de Barcelona
p. 99

Manipulating a Fluorescent Tube,
1969
Single-channel video, b/w, sound,
62 min
MACBA Collection. Fundació Museu
d'Art Contemporani de Barcelona
p. 99

Hélio Oiticica, Neville d'Almeida
*CC3-Maileryn. Quasi Cinema
(Block-Experiment in Cosmococa-
Program in Progress)*, 1973
5 slide projections, sound, sand,
plastic and balloons
Dimensions variable
Ed. of 1 + 2 a.p.
MACBA Collection. Fundació Museu
d'Art Contemporani de Barcelona
pp. 122–23

Jorge Oteiza
Desocupación no cúbica del espacio, 1959
Non-Cubic Freeing of Space
Steel
40 × 43.8 × 38 cm
MACBA Collection. Fundació Museu d'Art Contemporani de Barcelona. Gift of Fundación Bertrán
p. 62

Ulrike Ottinger
Freak Orlando, 1981
35 mm film transferred to video, colour, sound, 126 min
Ed. 2 of 10
MACBA Collection. Fundació Museu d'Art Contemporani de Barcelona
pp. 172–73

Mabel Palacín
La distancia correcta, 2002–03
The Right Distance
Two-channel video, colour, sound, 8 min 30 s
Ed. 2 of 6 + a.p.
MACBA Collection. Fundació Museu d'Art Contemporani de Barcelona. Gift of Agrolimen
p. 186

Pablo Palazuelo
Estudio para 'Alborada', 1950
Study for 'Alborada'
Pencil on paper
50 × 65.5 cm
MACBA Collection. Fundació Museu d'Art Contemporani de Barcelona. Fundación Pablo Palazuelo Collection
p. 64

Estudio para 'Alborada' (2), 1950
Study for 'Alborada' (2)
Graphite on paper
29.5 × 41 cm
MACBA Collection. Fundació Museu d'Art Contemporani de Barcelona. Fundación Pablo Palazuelo Collection
p. 64

Horizontal I, 1952
Gouache on paper
9 × 36.5 cm
MACBA Collection. Fundació Museu d'Art Contemporani de Barcelona. Fundación Pablo Palazuelo Collection
p. 65

Horizontal II, 1952
Gouache on paper
9.2 × 37 cm
MACBA Collection. Fundació Museu d'Art Contemporani de Barcelona. Fundación Pablo Palazuelo Collection
p. 65

Horizontal III, 1952
Gouache on paper
9 × 37 cm
MACBA Collection. Fundació Museu d'Art Contemporani de Barcelona. Fundación Pablo Palazuelo Collection
p. 65

Horizontal IV, 1952
Gouache on paper
4.1 × 35.7 cm
MACBA Collection. Fundació Museu d'Art Contemporani de Barcelona. Fundación Pablo Palazuelo Collection
p. 65

Carlos Pazos
The Floor of Fame, 1978
Single-channel video, b/w and colour, silent, 3 min 31 s. Editing made from black and white documentary photos and colour slides of the action carried out at the Centre Pompidou, Paris
MACBA Collection. Museu d'Art Contemporani de Barcelona Consortium. Artist's collection
pp. 146–47

Raymond Pettibon
The Beatles Did a Revolution Song, 1981
Ink on paper
29.2 × 22.9 cm
MACBA Collection. Fundació Museu d'Art Contemporani de Barcelona
p. 174

Female Anatomy Hasn't…, 1985
Ink on paper
36 × 26.3 cm
MACBA Collection. Fundació Museu d'Art Contemporani de Barcelona
p. 174

One of My Balls Is Gemini…, 1985
Ink on paper
26.8 × 21.2 cm
MACBA Collection. Fundació Museu d'Art Contemporani de Barcelona
p. 174

12 O'clock and All Is Well, 1986
Ink on paper
35.5 × 28 cm
MACBA Collection. Fundació Museu d'Art Contemporani de Barcelona
p. 174

Pere Portabella
Miró, l'altre, 1969
Miró, the Other
16 mm film, b/w and colour, sound, 15 min
Production: Pere Portabella, Films 59
MACBA Collection. Fundació Museu d'Art Contemporani de Barcelona. Gift of Pere Portabella
p. 130

Informe general, 1976
General Report
16 mm film, colour, sound, 173 min
Production: Pere Portabella, Films 59
MACBA Collection. Fundació Museu d'Art Contemporani de Barcelona. Gift of Pere Portabella
p. 131

Sergio Prego
Tetsuo, Bound to Fail, 1998
Single-channel video, colour, sound, 17 min 30 s
Ed. 7 of 10
MACBA Collection. Fundació Museu d'Art Contemporani de Barcelona. Gift of El Taller de la Fundació
p. 181

Joan Rabascall
68 mai 1968, 1968
68 May 1968
Offset litography on paper
56 × 47 cm
MACBA Collection. Museu d'Art Contemporani de Barcelona Consortium. Artist's collection
p. 134

Gol. Serie: 'Spain Is Different', 1975
Gol. Series: 'Spain Is Different'
Photographic emulsion on canvas
100 × 100 cm
MACBA Collection. Fundació Museu d'Art Contemporani de Barcelona
p. 135

Horario de misas. Serie: 'Spain Is Different', 1975
Mass Hour. Series: 'Spain Is Different'
Photographic emulsion on canvas
50 × 20.5 cm
MACBA Collection. Fundació Museu d'Art Contemporani de Barcelona
p. 135

Martha Rosler
*Secrets from the Street:
No Disclosure*, 1980
Single-channel video, colour, sound, 12 min 20 s
MACBA Collection. Museu d'Art Contemporani de Barcelona Consortium
p. 150

Born to Be Sold: Martha Rosler Reads the Strange Case of Baby S.M., 1988
Single-channel video, colour, sound, 35 min 20 s
MACBA Collection. Museu d'Art Contemporani de Barcelona Consortium
p. 151

Roberto Rossellini
Germania anno zero, 1947
Germany Year Zero
35 mm film transferred to video, b/w, sound, 75 min
Motion Pictures, S.A.
pp. 50–51

Dieter Roth
Reykjavik Slides, 1973–75, 1990–93
7 slide projections, large glass cases with carousel slide projectors, photomechanical reproductions on paper and city map of Reykjavik
Dimensions variable
Ed. 2 of 3 + a.p.
MACBA Collection. Fundació Museu d'Art Contemporani de Barcelona
pp. 108–09

Allan Sekula
Waiting for Tear Gas, 1999–2000
Slide projection and vinyl
Dimensions variable
MACBA Collection. Fundació Museu d'Art Contemporani de Barcelona
p. 208

Andreas Siekmann
Aus: Gesellschaft mit beschränkter Haftung, 1996–2002
From: Limited Liability Company
Tables, chairs, stickers, watercolour and marker on paper, Plasticine and expanded polyurethane
Dimensions variable
MACBA Collection. Fundació Museu d'Art Contemporani de Barcelona
pp. 202–03

Jo Spence
With the collaboration of Photography Workshop
Beyond the Family Album, 1978–79
Silver-salt photographs, chromogenic photographs and laminated press cuttings on plastic support
21 pieces at 74 × 50 cm each; 1 piece at 104 × 83 cm
MACBA Collection. Fundació Museu d'Art Contemporani de Barcelona. Gift of Terry Dennett
p. 148

With the collaboration of Rosy Martin, Maggie Murray and Terry Dennett
The Picture of Health, 1982
Silver-salt photographs, chromogenic photographs and laminated press cuttings on plastic support
52 elements in various dimensions
MACBA Collection. Fundació Museu d'Art Contemporani de Barcelona. Gift of Fundació Banc Sabadell
p. 149

Jo Spence and **Terry Dennett**
Remodelling Photo History, 1982
Laminated silver-salt photographs on plastic support
7 pieces at 66.5 × 46.5 cm each
MACBA Collection. Fundació Museu d'Art Contemporani de Barcelona. Gift of Fundació Banc Sabadell
p. 148

Nancy Spero
Artaud Painting – From this pain..., 1969
Gouache, ink and collage on paper
63.5 × 52.7 cm
MACBA Collection. Fundació Museu d'Art Contemporani de Barcelona
p. 96

Artaud Painting – That thick hemp in the neck of the priest about to be hung, 1969
Gouache, ink and collage on paper
62.9 × 50.8 cm
MACBA Collection. Fundació Museu d'Art Contemporani de Barcelona
p. 96

Artaud Painting – Un nœud d'asphyxie centrale, 1970
Artaud Painting – A Central Suffocation Knot
Gouache, ink and collage on paper
62.2 × 49.5 cm
MACBA Collection. Fundació Museu d'Art Contemporani de Barcelona
p. 97

Artaud Painting – Une fatigue de commencement du monde, 1970
Artaud Painting – A Beginning-of-the-World Fatigue
Gouache, ink and collage on paper
61.6 × 49.5 cm
MACBA Collection. Fundació Museu d'Art Contemporani de Barcelona
p. 97

Antoni Tàpies
Forma blanca, 1959
White Form
Mixed media on canvas
81 × 116 cm
MACBA Collection. Fundació Museu d'Art Contemporani de Barcelona. Ceded gratuitously by the Telefónica Art Collection
p. 60

Negre amb dos entallaments, 1962
Black with Two Carvings
Mixed media on canvas mounted on wood
202 × 177 cm
MACBA Collection. Fundació Museu d'Art Contemporani de Barcelona. Ceded gratuitously by the Telefónica Art Collection
p. 61

Isidoro Valcárcel Medina
This wall was painted by Valcárcel Medina with a no. 8 brush between 10 and 15 September 2006
MACBA Collection. Fundació Museu d'Art Contemporani de Barcelona
p. 155

Vídeo-Nou
*Jornades Llibertàries Internacionals.
Debats al Saló Diana*, 1977
International Libertarian Days:
Debates in the Diana Room
Single-channel video, b/w, sound,
120 min 56 s
MACBA Collection. Museu d'Art
Contemporani de Barcelona
Consortium. Vídeo-Nou Group long
term loan
p. 142

*Jornades Llibertàries Internacionals.
Parc Güell*, 1977
International Libertarian Days.
Parc Güell
Single-channel video, b/w, sound,
28 min
MACBA Collection. Museu d'Art
Contemporani de Barcelona
Consortium. Vídeo-Nou Group long
term loan
p. 142

*Contracultures: Manifestació
de bicicletes*, 1977
Countercultures: Bicycle
Demonstration
Single-channel video, b/w, sound,
12 min 20 s
MACBA Collection. Museu d'Art
Contemporani de Barcelona
Consortium. Vídeo-Nou Group long
term loan
p. 142

Vídeo-Nou 1977-78
Book
25 × 14 cm
[s. l.: s. n.], 1979
MACBA Collection. Study Center.
Vídeo-Nou Group long term loan
p. 143

Jeff Wall
*Dan Graham's Kammerspiel.
Interview (Chris Dercon). Recorded
at the house of Herman Daled
in Brussels. Herman Daled's version
of Suburban House*, 1987
Single-channel video, colour, sound,
55 min
MACBA Collection. Fundació Museu
d'Art Contemporani de Barcelona.
Private long term loan
p. 165

Krzysztof Wodiczko
Alien Staff, 1992–93
Crozier with video, colour, sound,
15 min 20 s and single-channel
video, colour, sound, 33 min 25 s
Dimensions variable
MACBA Collection. Fundació Museu
d'Art Contemporani de Barcelona
p. 214

Concept
Manuel J. Borja-Villel
Bartomeu Marí

Edition
Clara Plasencia

Coordination and editing
Clàudia Faus

Collection Department
Antònia M. Perelló
Ainhoa González
Núria Montclús
Anne Stenne

Registrar Department
Marta Badia

Conservation and Restoration Department
Sílvia Noguer
Lluís Roqué

Photo research
Dolores Acebal
Lorena Martín
Maite Muñoz
Gemma Planell (Coord.)

Graphic Design
Edicions de l'Eixample

Translation
e-verba translations
Elaine Fradley

Proof-reading
Keith Patrick

Pre-printing
Colornet

Printing
Igol

Publisher
Museu d'Art Contemporani
de Barcelona
Plaça dels Àngels, 1
08001 Barcelona (Spain)
publicacions@macba.cat
t:+ 34 93 412 08 10
f:+ 34 93 412 46 02
www.macba.cat

Distribution
ACTAR - D
Roca i Batlle, 2-4
08023 Barcelona (Spain)
office@actar-d.com
t:+ 34 93 418 77 59
f:+ 34 93 418 67 07
www.actar-d.com

The MACBA would like to express its most sincere thanks to all those people at the Museum and elsewhere who have made this project possible.

Image of the cover: Alice Creischer, *L'atelier de la peintrice. Allégorie réelle déterminant une phase de sept années de ma vie artistique dans la République de Berlin*, 2000 (detail)

Image of the back cover: Tutti Bianchi's demonstration against the World Bank, Barcelona, 24 June 2001 (detail)